Data-Driven 3D Facial Animation

Zhigang Deng · Ulrich Neumann
Editors

Data-Driven 3D Facial Animation

 Springer

Editors

Zhigang Deng, PhD
University of Houston
Houston, TX, USA

Ulrich Neumann, PhD
University of Southern California
Los Angeles, CA, USA

British Library Cataloguing in Publication Data
A catalogue record for this book is available from the British Library

Library of Congress Control Number: 2007928311

ISBN: 978-1-84628-906-4   e-ISBN: 978-1-84628-907-1

Printed on acid-free paper

9 8 7 6 5 4 3 2 1

Springer Science+Business Media
Springer.com

Contents

List of Contributors

Jeremy B. Badler
Smith-Kettlewell Eye Research
Institute,
2318 Fillmore Street,
San Francisco,
CA 94115

Norman I. Badler
Computer & Information Science,
University of Pennsylvania,
Philadelphia,
PA 19104-6389

Carlos Busso Viterbi School of
Engineering, University of
Southern California, Los Angeles,
CA 90089, USA
busso@usc.edu

Yong Cao
Department of Computer Science,
Virginia Polytechnic
Institute and State University
yongcao@cs.vt.edu

Edwin Chang
Pixar Animation Studios,
Emeryville, California 94608

Brian Curless
University of Washington ,Seattle,
WA 98195, USA

Zhigang Deng
Department of Computer Science,
University of Houston, Houston, TX
77204, USA zdeng@cs.uh.edu
WWW Webpage: http://zhigang.org

Mathieu Desbrun
California Institute of Technology
(mathieu@cs.caltech.edu)

Petros Faloutsos
Department of Computer Science,
University of California at Los Angeles
pfal@cs.ucla.edu

Stephane Garchery
MIRALab, University of Geneva,
Battelle Build. A, Route de
Drize 7, 1227 Carouge GE,
SWITZERLAND
garchery@miralab.unige.ch
WWW Webpage:
http://www.miralab.ch/

Thomas Di Giacomo
MIRALab, University of Geneva,
Battelle Build. A, Route de
Drize 7, 1227 Carouge GE,
SWITZERLAND
giacomo@miralab.unige.ch

Erdan Gu
Computer & Information Science,
University of Pennsylvania,
Philadelphia,
PA 19104-6389

Odest Chadwicke Jenkins
Department of Computer Science,
Brown University

Pushkar Joshi
University of California, Berkeley
(ppj@eecs.berkeley.edu)

Sooha Park Lee
Computer & Information Science,
University of Pennsylvania,
Philadelphia,
PA 19104-6389

J.P. Lewis
Computer Graphics Lab,
Stanford Graphics Lab,
Stanford University,
Stanford, CA 94305 USA
zilla@computer.org

Nadia Magnenat-Thalmann
MIRALab, University of Geneva,
Battelle Build. A, Route de
Drize 7, 1227 Carouge GE,
SWITZERLAND
thalmann@miralab.unige.ch
WWW Webpage:
http://www.miralab.ch/

Jonathan Mooser
Department of Computer Science,
University of Southern California,
Los Angeles, CA 90089
mooser@graphics.usc.edu

Shrikanth Narayanan
Viterbi School of Engineering,
University of Southern California,
Los Angeles, CA 90089, USA
shri@sipi.usc.edu

Ulrich Neumann
Viterbi School of Engineering,
Department of Computer Science,
University of Southern California,
Los Angeles, CA 90089, USA
uneumann@graphics.usc.edu

Junyong Noh
Graduate School of Culture Technology
(GSCT),
Korea Advanced Institute of Science
and Technology (KAIST), Daejon,
Korea junyongnoh@kaist.ac.kr

Frédéric Pighin
Industrial Light and Magic
(fpigin@ilm.com)

Steven M. Seitz
University of Washington, Seattle,
WA 98195, USA

Noah Snavely
University of Washington, Seattle,
WA 98195, USA

Wen Tien
Sony Computer Entertainment of
America

Thomas W. Tolles
Vicon House of Moves,
5419 McConnell Avenue,
Los Angeles, CA 90066

Li Zhang
University of Washington, Seattle,
WA 98195, USA

Chapter 1
Computer Facial Animation: A Survey

Zhigang Deng and Junyong Noh

1.1 Introduction

Since the pioneering work of Frederic I. Parke [1] in 1972, significant research efforts have been attempted to generate realistic facial modeling and animation. The most ambitious attempts perform the face modeling and rendering in real time. Because of the complexity of human facial anatomy and our inherent sensitivity to facial appearance, there is no real-time system that generates subtle facial expressions and emotions realistically on an avatar. Although some recent work has produced realistic results with a relatively fast performance, the process for generating facial animation entails extensive human intervention or tedious tuning. The ultimate goal for research in facial modeling and animation is a system that (1) creates realistic animation, (2) operates in real time, (3) is automated as much as possible, and (4) adapts easily to individual faces.

Recent interest in facial modeling and animation has been spurred by the increasing appearance of virtual characters in film and video, inexpensive desktop processing power, and the potential for a new 3D immersive communication metaphor for human-computer interaction. Much of the facial modeling and animation research is published in specific venues that are relatively unknown to the general graphics community. There are few surveys or detailed historical treatments of the subject [2]. This survey is intended as an accessible reference to the range of reported facial modeling and animation techniques.

Strictly classifying facial modeling and animation techniques is a difficult task, because exact classifications are complicated by the lack of exact boundaries between methods and the fact that recent approaches often integrate several methods to produce better results. In this survey, we roughly classify facial modeling and animation techniques into the following categories: blend shape or shape interpolation (Section 1.2), parameterizations (Section 1.3), facial action coding system-based approaches (Section 1.4), deformation-based approaches (Section 1.5), physics-based muscle modeling (Section 1.6), 3D face modeling (Section 1.7), performance-driven facial animation (Section 1.8), MPEG-4 facial animation (Section 1.9), visual speech animation (Section 1.10), facial animation editing (Section 1.11), facial animation transferring (Section 1.12), and facial gesture generation (Section 1.13). It should be noted that because the facial animation field

Z. Deng and U. Neumann, *Data-Driven 3D Facial Animation.*

has grown into a complicated and broad subject, this survey chapter does not cover every aspect of virtual human faces, such as hair modeling and animation, tongue and neck modeling and animation, skin rendering, wrinkle modeling, etc.

1.2 Blend Shapes or Shape Interpolation

Shape interpolation (blend shapes, morph targets, and shape interpolation) is the most intuitive and commonly used technique in facial animation practice. A blend-shape model is simply the linear weighted sum of a number of topologically conforming shape primitives (Eq. 1.1):

$$v_j = \sum w_k b_{kj}. \tag{1.1}$$

In Eq. 1.1, v_j is the jth vertex of the resulting animated model, w_k is blending weight, and b_{kj} is the jth vertex of the kth blendshape. The weighted sum can be applied to the vertices of polygonal models or to the control vertices of spline models. The weights w_k are manipulated by the animator in the form of sliders (with one slider for each weight) or automatically determined by algorithms [3]. It continues to be used in projects such as *Stuart Little*, *Star Wars*, and *Lord of the Rings* and was adopted in many commercial animation software packages such as Maya and 3D Studio Max. The simplest case is an interpolation between two key frames at extreme positions over a time interval (Fig. 1.1).

Linear interpolation is often employed for simplicity [4, 5], but a cosine interpolation function [6] or other variations such as spline can provide acceleration and deceleration effects at the beginning and end of an animation. When four key frames are involved, rather than two, bilinear interpolation generates a greater variety of facial expressions than linear interpolation [7]. Bilinear interpolation, when combined with simultaneous image morphing, creates a wide range of facial expression changes [8].

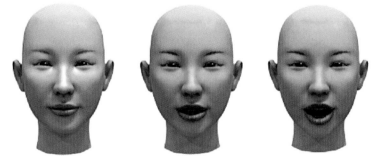

Fig. 1.1 Linear interpolation is performed on blend shapes. Left: neutral pose; right: "A" mouth shape; middle: interpolated shape.

Interpolated images are generated by varying the parameters of the interpolation functions. Geometric interpolation directly updates the 2D or 3D positions of the face mesh vertices, while parameter interpolation controls functions that indirectly move the vertices. For example, Sera et al. [9] perform a linear interpolation of the spring muscle force parameters, rather than the positions of the vertices, to achieve mouth animation.

Some recent efforts have attempted to improve the efficiency of producing muscle actuation-based blendshape animations [10, 11]. The pose space deformation (PSD) method presented by Lewis et al. [12] provides a general framework for example-based interpolation that can be used for blendshape facial animations. In their work, the deformation of a surface (face) is treated as a function of some set of abstract parameters, such as {*smile, raise-eyebrow,...*}, and a new surface is generated by scattered data interpolations.

Although interpolations are fast and they easily generate primitive facial animations, their ability to create a wide range of realistic facial configurations is restricted. Combinations of independent face motions are difficult to produce and non-orthogonal blend shapes often interfere each other, which cause animators to have to go back and forth to readjust the weights of blend shapes. Lewis et al. [13] present a user interface technique to automatically reduce blendshape interferences. Deng et al. [3] present an automatic technique for mapping sparse facial motion capture data to pre-designed 3D blendshape face models by learning a radial basis function-based regression.

1.3 Parameterizations

Parameterization techniques for facial animation [7, 14–16] overcome some of the limitations and restrictions of simple interpolations. Ideal parameterizations specify any possible face and expression by a combination of independent parameter values [2]. Unlike interpolation techniques, parameterizations allow explicit control of specific facial configurations. Combinations of parameters provide a large range of facial expressions with relatively low computational costs.

As indicated in [17], there is no systematic way to arbitrate between two conflicting parameters to blend expressions that affect the same vertices. Thus, parameterization produces unnatural human expressions or configurations when a conflict between parameters occurs. For this reason, parameterizations are designed to only affect specific facial regions. However, it often introduces noticeable motion boundaries. Another limitation of parameterization is that the choice of the parameter set depends on the facial mesh topology and, therefore, a complete generic parameterization is not possible. Furthermore, tedious manual tuning is required to set parameter values. The limitations of parameterization led to the development of diverse techniques such as morphing between images and geometry, physically faithful/pseudo muscle-based animation, and performance-driven animation.

Table 1.1 Sample single facial action units.

AU	FACS Name	AU	FACS Name	AU	FACS Name
1	Inner Brow Raiser	12	Lid Corner Puller	2	Outer Brow Raiser
14	Dimpler	4	Brow Lower	15	Lip Corner Depressor
5	Upper Lid Raiser	16	Lower Lip Depressor	6	Check Raiser
17	Chin Raiser	9	Nose Wrinkler	20	Lip Stretcher
23	Lip Tightener	10	Upper Lid Raiser	26	Jaw Drop

Table 1.2 Example sets of action units for basic expressions.

Basic Expressions	Involved Action Units
Surprise	AU1, 2, 5, 15, 16, 20, 26
Fear	AU1, 2, 4, 5, 15, 20, 26
Anger	AU2, 4, 7, 9, 10, 20, 26
Happiness	AU1, 6, 12, 14
Sadness	AU1, 4, 15, 23

1.4 Facial Action Coding System

The Facial Action Coding System (FACS) is a description of the movements of the facial muscles and jaw/tongue derived from an analysis of facial anatomy [18]. FACS includes 44 basic action units (AUs). Combinations of independent action units generate facial expressions. For example, combining the AU1 (Inner Brow Raiser), AU4 (Brow Raiser), AU15 (Lip Corner Depressor), and AU23 (Lip Tightener) creates a sad expression. A table of the sample action units and the basic expressions generated by the actions units are presented in Tables 1.1 and 1.2.

Due to its simplicity, the FACS is widely utilized with muscle or simulated (pseudo) muscle-based approaches. Animation methods using muscle models overcome the limitation of interpolation and provide a wide variety of facial expressions. Physical muscle modeling mathematically describes the properties and the behavior of human skin, bone, and muscle systems. In contrast, pseudo muscle models mimic the dynamics of human tissue with heuristic geometric deformations. Despite its popularity, there are some drawbacks of using the FACS [19]. First, AUs are purely local patterns while actual facial motion is rarely completely localized. Second, the FACS offers spatial motion descriptions but not temporal components. In the temporal domain, co-articulation effects are lost in the FACS system.

1.5 Deformation-based Approaches

Direct deformation defined on the facial mesh surface often produces quality animation. It ignores underlying facial anatomy or true muscle structures. Instead, the focus is on creating various facial expressions by the manipulation of the thin shell mesh. This category includes morphing between different models and simulated pseudo muscles in the form of splines [20–22], wires [23], or free-form deformations [24, 25].

1.5.1 2D and 3D Morphing

Morphing effects a metamorphosis between two target images or models. A 2D image morph consists of a warp between corresponding points in the target images and a simultaneous cross dissolve.[1] Typically, the correspondences are manually selected to suit the needs of the application. Morphs between carefully acquired and corresponded images produce very realistic facial animations. Beier and Neely [26] demonstrate 2D morphing between two images with manually specified correspond-ing features (line segments). The warp function is based upon a field of influence surrounding the corresponding features. Realism, with this approach, requires exten-sive manual interaction for color balancing, correspondence selection, and tuning of the warp and dissolve parameters. Variations in the target image viewpoints or features complicate the selection of correspondences. Realistic head motions are difficult to synthesize since target features become occluded or revealed during the animation.

To overcome the limitations of 2D morphs, Pighin et al. [27] combine 2D morph-ing with 3D transformations of a geometric model. They animate key facial expres-sions with 3D geometric interpolation while image morphing is performed between corresponding texture maps. This approach achieves viewpoint independent real-ism; however, animations are still limited to interpolations between predefined key facial expressions.

The 2D and 3D morphing methods can produce quality facial expressions, but they share similar limitations with the interpolation approaches. Selecting corre-sponding points in target images is manually intensive, dependent on viewpoint, and not generalizable to different faces. Also, the animation viewpoint is constrained to approximately that of the target images.

1.5.2 Free-Form Deformation

Free-form deformation (FFD) deforms volumetric objects by manipulating control points arranged in a three-dimensional cubic lattice [28]. Conceptually, a flexible object is embedded in an imaginary, clear, and flexible control box containing a 3D grid of control points. As the control box is squashed, bent, or twisted into arbitrary shapes, the embedded object deforms accordingly (Fig. 1.2). The basis for the control points is a trivariate tensor product Bernstein polynomial. FFDs can deform many types of surface primitives, including polygons; quadric, parametric, and implicit surfaces; and solid models.

Extended free-form deformation (EFFD) [24] allows the extension of the con-trol point lattice into a cylindrical structure. A cylindrical lattice provides additional flexibility for shape deformation compared to regular cubic lattices. Rational free-form deformation (RFFD) incorporates weight factors for each control point, adding

---

[1] In cross dissolving, one image is faded out while another is simultaneously faded in.

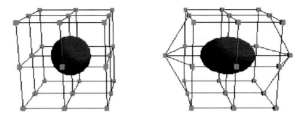

Fig. 1.2 Free-form deformation. The controlling box and embedded object are shown. When the controlling box is deformed by manipulating control points, so is the embedded object.

another degree of freedom in specifying deformations. Hence, deformations are possible by changing the weight factors instead of changing the control point positions. When all weights are equal to one, then the RFFD becomes an FFD. A main advantage of using the FFD (EFFD, RFFD) to abstract deformation control from that of the actual surface description is that the transition of form is no longer dependent on the specifics of the surface itself [29].

Displacing a control point is analogous to actuating a physically modeled muscle. Compared to Waters' physically based model [30], manipulating the positions or the weights of the control points is more intuitive and simpler than manipulating muscle vectors with a delineated zone of influence. However, the FFD (EFFD, RFFD) does not provide a precise simulation of the actual muscle and skin behavior. Furthermore, since the FFD (EFFD, RFFD) is based upon surface deformation, volumetric changes occurring in the physical muscle are not accounted for.

1.5.3 Spline Pseudo-Muscles

Although polygonal models of the face are widely used, they often fail to adequately approximate the smoothness or flexibility of the human face. Fixed polygonal models do not deform smoothly in arbitrary regions, and planar vertices cannot be twisted into curved surfaces without subdivision.

An ideal facial model has a surface representation that supports smooth and flexible deformations. Spline muscle models offer a plausible solution. Splines are usually up to C^2 continuous; hence, a surface patch is guaranteed to be smooth, and they allow localized deformation on the surface. Furthermore, affine transformations are defined by the transformation of a small set of control points instead of all the vertices of the mesh reducing the computational complexity.

Some spline-based animation can be found in [20, 21]. Pixar used bicubic Catmull–Rom spline[2] patches to model Billy, the baby in animation *Tin Toy*, and used a variant of Catmull–Clark [31] subdivision surfaces to model *Geri*, a human

---

[2] A distinguishing property of Catmull–Rom splines is that the piecewise cubic polynomial segments pass through all the control points except the first and last when used for interpolation. Another is that the convex hull property is not observed in Catmull–Rom splines.

character in the short film Geri's game. This technique is mainly adapted to model sharp creases on a surface or discontinuities between surfaces [32]. For a detailed description of Catmull–Rom splines and Catmull–Clark subdivision surfaces, refer to [31,33]. Eisert and Girod [34] use triangular B-splines to overcome the drawback that conventional B-splines do not refine curved areas locally since they are defined on a rectangular topology.

A hierarchical spline model reduces the number of unnecessary control points. Wang et al. [22] showed a system that integrated hierarchical spline models with simulated muscles based on local surface deformations. Bicubic B-splines offer both smoothness and flexibility, which are hard to achieve with conventional polygonal models. The drawback of using naive B-splines for complex surfaces becomes clear, however, when a deformation is required to be finer than the patch resolution. To produce finer patch resolution, an entire row or column of the surface is subdivided. Thus, more detail (and control points) is added where none are needed. In contrast, hierarchical splines provide the local refinements of B-spline surfaces, and new patches are only added within a specified region. Hierarchical B-splines are an economical and compact way to represent a spline surface and achieve a high rendering speed. Muscles coupled with hierarchical spline surfaces are capable of creating bulging skin surfaces and a variety of facial expressions.

1.6 Physics-based Muscle Modeling

Physics-based muscle models fall into three categories: mass-spring systems, vector representations, and layered spring meshes. Mass-spring methods propagate muscle forces in an elastic spring mesh that models skin deformation. The vector approach deforms a facial mesh using motion fields in delineated regions of influence. A layered spring mesh extends a mass-spring structure into three connected mesh layers to model anatomical facial behavior more faithfully.

1.6.1 Spring Mesh Muscle

The work by Platt and Badler [35] is a forerunner of the research focused on muscle modeling and the structure of the human face. Forces applied to elastic meshes through muscle arcs generate various facial expressions. Platt's later work [36] presents a facial model with muscles represented as collections of functional blocks in defined regions of the facial structure. Platt's model consists of 38 regional muscle blocks interconnected by a spring network. Action units are created by applying muscle forces to deform the spring network. There are some recent developments using mass-spring muscles for facial animation [37, 38]. For example, Kahler et al. [38] proposed a convenient editing tool to interactively specify mass-spring muscles into 3D face geometry.

1.6.2 Vector Muscle

A very successful muscle model was proposed by Waters [30]. A delineated deformation field models the action of muscles upon skin. A muscle definition includes the vector field direction, an origin, and an insertion point (the left panel of Fig. 1.3). The field extent is defined by cosine functions and falls off factors that produce a cone shape when visualized as a height field. Waters also models the mouth sphincter muscles as a simplified parametric ellipsoid. The sphincter muscle contracts around the center of the ellipsoid and is primarily responsible for the deformation of the mouth region. Waters animates human emotions such as anger, fear, surprise, disgust, joy, and happiness using vector-based linear and orbicularis oris muscles utilizing the FACS. The right panel of Figure 1.3 shows the Waters' muscles embedded in a facial mesh.

The positioning of vector muscles into anatomically correct positions can be a daunting task. The process involves manual trial and error with no guarantee of efficient or optimal placement. Incorrect placement results in unnatural or undesirable animation of the mesh. Nevertheless, the vector muscle model is widely used because of its compact representation and independence of the facial mesh structure. An example of vector muscles is seen in Billy, the baby in the movie *Tin Toy*, who has 47 Waters' muscles on his face.

1.6.3 Layered Spring Mesh Muscles

Terzopoulos and Waters [39] proposed a facial model that models detailed anatomical structure and dynamics of the human face. Their three layers of deformable mesh correspond to skin, fatty tissue, and muscle tied to bone. Elastic spring elements

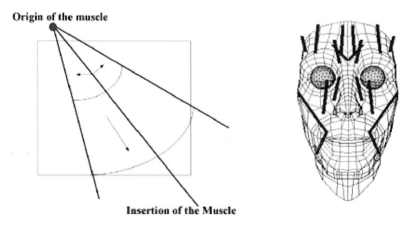

Fig. 1.3 The left panel shows the zone of influence of Waters' linear muscle model. The right panel shows muscle placement in Waters's work [30].

connect each mesh node and each layer. Muscle forces propagate through the mesh systems to create animation. This model is faithful to facial anatomy. Simulating volumetric deformations with three-dimensional lattices, however, requires extensive computation. A simplified mesh system reduces the computation time while still maintaining similar quality [40].

Lee et al. [41, 42] present face models composed of physics-based synthetic skin and muscle layers based on earlier work [39]. The face model consists of three components: a biological tissue layer with nonlinear deformation properties, a muscle layer knit together under the skin, and an impenetrable skull structure beneath the muscle layer. The synthetic tissue is modeled as triangular prism elements that are divided into the epidermal surface, the fascia surface, and the skull surface. Spring elements connecting the epidermal and fascia layers simulate skin elasticity. Spring elements that affect muscle forces connect the fascia and skull layers. The model achieves better fidelity. Tremendous computation is required, however, and extensive tuning is needed to model a specific face or characteristic.

1.7 3D Face Modeling

An important problem in facial animation is to model a specific person, i.e., modeling the 3D geometry of an individual face. A range scanner, digitizer probe, or stereo disparity can measure three-dimensional coordinates. The models obtained by those processes are often poorly suited for facial animation. Information about the facial structures is missing; measurement noise produces distracting artifacts; and model vertices are poorly distributed. Also, many measurement methods produce incomplete models, lacking hair, ears, eyes, etc. Therefore, post-processing on the measured data is often necessary.

1.7.1 Person-Specific Model Creation

An approach to person-specific modeling is to painstakingly prepare a generic animation mesh with all the necessary structure and animation information. This generic model is fitted or deformed to a measured geometric mesh of a specific person to create a personalized animation model. The geometric fit also facilitates the transfer of texture if it is captured with the measured mesh. If the generic model has fewer polygons than the measured mesh, deformation is implicit in the fitting process.

Person-specific modeling and fitting processes use various approaches such as scattered data interpolations [5, 43, 44] and projections onto the cylindrical coordinates incorporated with a positive Laplacian field function [42]. Some methods attempt an automated fitting process, but most require manual interventions.

Radial basis functions are capable of closely approximated or interpolated smooth hypersurfaces [45] such as human facial shapes. Some approaches morph a generic mesh into specific shapes with scattered data interpolation techniques based on radial basis functions. The advantages of this approach are as follows. First, the morph does not require equal numbers of nodes in the involved meshes since missing points are interpolated [43]. Second, mathematical support ensures that a morphed mesh approaches the target mesh if appropriate correspondences are selected [45, 46].

A typical process of 3D volume morphing is as follows. First, biologically meaningful landmark points are manually selected around the eyes, nose, lips, and perimeters of both face models. Second, the landmark points define the coefficients of the kernel of the radial basis function used to morph the volume. Finally, points in the generic mesh are interpolated using the coefficients computed from the landmark points. The success of the morphing depends strongly on the selection of the landmark points [27, 43].

Instead of morphing a face model, a morphable model exploits a pre-constructed set of face databases to create a person-specific model [47]. First, a scanning process collects a large number of faces to compile a database. This example 3D face models spans the space of any possible human faces in terms of geometry and texture. New faces and expressions can be represented as a linear combination of the examples. Typically, an image of a new person is provided to the system; then the system outputs a 3D model of the person that closely matches the image.

1.7.2 Anthropometry

The generation of individual models using anthropometry[3] attempts to produce facial variations where absolute appearance is not important. Kuo et al. [48] proposes a method to synthesize a lateral face from one 2D gray-level image of a frontal face. A database is first constructed, containing facial parameters measured according to anthropomorphic definitions. This database serves as priori knowledge. The lateral facial parameters are estimated from frontal facial parameters by using minimum mean square error (MMSE) estimation rules applied to the database. Specifically, the depth of one lateral facial parameter is determined by the linear combination of several frontal facial parameters. The 3D generic facial model is then adapted according to both the frontal plane coordinates extracted from the image and their estimated depths. Finally, the lateral face is synthesized from the feature data and texture-mapped.

DeCarlo et al. [49] construct various facial models purely based on anthropometry without assistance from images. This system constructs a new face model in two steps. The first step generates a random set of measurements that characterize the face. The form and values of these measurements are computed according to face anthropometry (Fig. 1.4). The second step constructs the best surface

---

[3] The science dedicated to the measurements of the human face.

Fig. 1.4 Some of the anthropometric landmarks on the face. The selected landmarks are widely used as measurements for describing the human face.

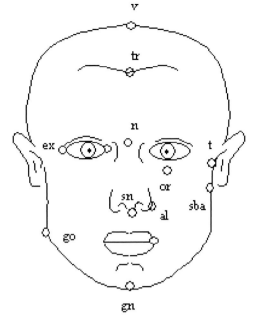

that satisfies the geometric constraints using a variational constrained optimization technique [50, 51]. In this technique, one imposes a variety of constraints on the surface and then tries to create a smooth and fair surface while minimizing the deviation from a specified rest shape, subject to the constrains. For a face modeling, anthropometric measurements are the constraints, and the remainder of the face is determined by minimizing the deviation from the given surface objective function. Variational modeling enables the system to capture the shape similarities of faces, while allowing anthropometric differences. Although anthropometry has potential for rapidly generating plausible facial geometric variations, the approach does not model realistic variations in color, wrinkling, expressions, or hair.

1.8 Performance-Driven Facial Animation

The difficulties in controlling facial animations led to the performance-driven approach where tracked human actors/actress drive the animation. Real-time video processing allows interactive animations where the actors observe the animations they create with their motions and expressions. Accurate tracking of feature points or edges is important to maintain a consistent and high-quality animation. Often the tracked 2D or 3D feature motions are filtered or transformed to generate the motion data needed for driving a specific animation system. Motion data can be used to directly generate facial animation [19] or to infer AUs of the FACS in generating facial expressions. Figure 1.5 shows animation driven from a real-time feature tracking system.

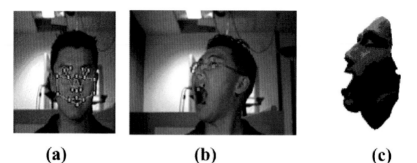

(a)   **(b)**   **(c)**

Fig. 1.5 Real-time tracking is performed without markups on the face using Eyematic Inc.'s face tracking system. Real-time animation of the synthesized avatar is achieved based on the 11 tracked features. Here (a) shows the initial tracking of the face features, (b) shows features are tracked in real time while the subject is moving, and (c) shows an avatar that mimics the behavior of the subject.

1.8.1 Snakes and Markings

Snakes, or deformable minimum-energy curves, are used to track intentionally marked facial features [52]. The recognition of facial features with snakes is primarily based on color samples and edge detection. Many systems couple tracked snakes to underlying muscles mechanisms to drive facial animation [39, 53–56]. Muscle contraction parameters are estimated from the tracked facial displacements in video sequences.

Tracking errors accumulate over long image sequences. Consequently, a snake may lose the contour it is attempting to track. In [57], tracking from frame to frame is done for the features that are relatively easy to track. A reliability test enables a reinitialization of a snake when error accumulations occur.

1.8.2 Optical Flow Tracking

Colored markers painted on the face or lips [9, 58–64] are extensively used to aid in tracking facial expressions or recognizing speech from video sequences. However, markings on the face are intrusive. Also, reliance on markings restricts the scope of acquired geometric information to the marked features. Optical flow [65] and spatio-temporal normalized correlation measurements [66] perform natural feature tracking and therefore obviate the need for intentional markings on the face [19,67]. Chai et al. [68] propose a data-driven technique to translate noisy, low-quality 2D tracking signals from video to high-quality 3D facial animations based on a preprocessed facial motion database. One limitation of this approach is that a preprocessed facial motion database is required, and its performance may depend on the match between prerecorded persons in the database and target face models. Zhang et al. [69] propose a space-time stereo tracking algorithm to build 3D face models from video sequences that maintain point correspondences across the entire sequence without using any marker.

1.8.3 Facial Motion Capture Data

A more recent trend to produce quality animation is to use 3D motion capture data. Motion capture data have successfully been used in recent movies such as *Polar Express* and *Monster House*. Typically, motion data are captured and filtered prior to the animation. An array of high-performance cameras is utilized to reconstruct the 3D maker locations on the face. Although this optical system is difficult to set up and is expensive, the reconstructed data provide accurate timing and motion information. Once the data are available, facial animation can be created by employing underlying muscle structure [70] or blend shapes [3, 71, 72].

1.9 MPEG-4 Facial Animation

Due to its increased applications, facial animation was adopted into the MPEG-4 standard, an object-based multimedia compression standard [73]. MPEG-4 specifies and animates 3D face models by defining face definition parameters (FDP) and facial animation parameters (FAP). FDPs enclose information for constructing specific 3D face geometry, and FAPs encode motion parameters of key feature points on the face over time. Face Animation Parameter Units (FAPU) that scale FAPs for fitting any face model are defined as the fractions of key facial features, such as the distance between the two eyes.

In MPEG-4 facial animation standard, 84 feature points (FPs) are specified. Figure 1.6 approximately illustrates part of the MPEG-4 feature points in a front face. After excluding the feature points that are not affected by FAPs, 68 FAPs are categorized into groups (Table 1.3). Most of the FAP groups are low-level parameters since they specify how much a given FP is moved. One FAP group (visemes and expressions) is considered as a high-level parameter group, because these parameters are not precisely specified. For example, textual descriptions are used to describe expressions. As such, reconstructed facial animation depends on the implementation of individual MPEG-4 facial animation decoder.

Previous research efforts on MPEG-4 facial animation were focused on deforming 3D face models based on MPEG-4 feature points [75, 76] and building MPEG-4 facial animation decoder systems [77–80]. For example, Escher et al. [75] deform a generic face model using a free-form deformation-based approach to generate MPEG-4 facial animations. Kshirsagar et al. [76] propose an efficient feature point based face deformation technique given MPEG-4 feature point inputs. In their approach, the motion of each MPEG-4 feature point is propagated to neighboring vertices of the face model, and the motion of each vertex (non-feature point) is the summation of these motion propagations. Various MPEG-4 facial animation

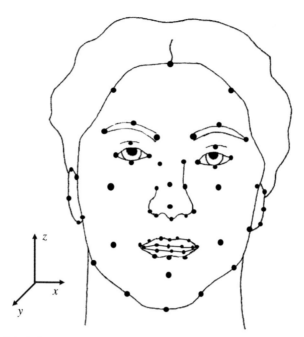

Fig. 1.6 Part of the facial feature points defined in the MPEG-4 standard. A complete description of the MPEG-4 feature points can be found in [74].

Table 1.3 FAP groups in MPEG-4.

Group	Number of FAPs
Viseme and expressions	2
Lip, chin, and jaw	26
Eyes (including pupils and eyelids)	12
Eyebrow	8
Cheeks	4
Tongue	5
Head movement	3
Nose	4
Ears	4

decoder systems [77,78] and frameworks that are targeted for Web and mobile applications [79, 80] are also proposed. For more details of MPEG-4 facial animation standard, implementations, and applications, please refer to the MPEG-4 facial animation book [81].

1.10 Visual Speech Animation

Visual speech animation can be regarded as visual motions of the face (especially the mouth part) when humans are speaking. Synthesizing realistic visual speech animations corresponding to novel text or prerecorded acoustic speech input has been a difficult task for decades, because human languages, such as English, generally have not only a large vocabulary and a large number of phonemes (the theoretical representation of an utterance/sound), but also the phenomena of *speech co-articulation* that complicates the mappings between acoustic speech signals (or phonemes) and visual speech motions. In linguistics literature, speech co-articulation is defined as follows: phonemes are not pronounced as an independent sequence of sounds, but rather that the sound of a particular phoneme is affected by adjacent phonemes. Visual speech co-articulation is analogous.

Previous research efforts in visual speech animation generation can be roughly classified into two different categories: viseme-driven approaches and data-driven approaches. Viseme-driven approaches require animators to design key mouth shapes for phonemes (termed *visemes*) in order to generate novel speech animations. On the contrary, data-driven approaches do not need predesigned key shapes, but generally require a prerecorded facial motion database for synthesis purposes.

1.10.1 Viseme-Driven Approaches

A *viseme* is defined as a basic visual unit that corresponds to a phoneme in speech. Viseme-driven approaches typically require animators to design visemes (key mouth shapes), and then empirical smooth functions [14, 82–86] or co-articulation rules [87–89] are used to synthesize novel speech animations.

Given a novel sound track and a small number of visemes, J.P. Lewis [83] proposes an efficient lip-sync technique based on a linear prediction model. Cohen and Massaro [14] propose the Cohen–Massaro co-articulation model for generating speech animations. In their approach, a viseme shape is defined via dominance functions that are defined in terms of each facial measurement, such as the lips, tongue tip, etc., and the weighted sum of dominance values determines the final mouth shapes. Figure 1.7 schematically illustrates the essential idea of the Cohen–Massaro model. Its recent extensions [84–86, 89] further improved the

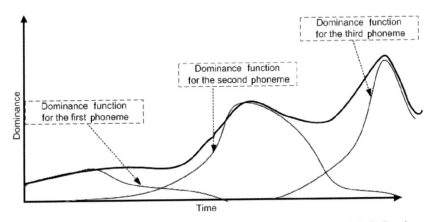

Fig. 1.7 Schematic illustration of the Cohen–Massaro co-articulation model [14]. Dominance functions of three consecutive phonemes are plotted, and the weighted sum of dominance curves is plotted as a blue curve.

Cohen–Massaro co-articulation model. For example, Cosi et al. [85] add a temporal resistance function and a shape function for more general cases, such as fast/slow speaking rates. The approach proposed by Goff and Benoît [84] calculates the model parameter values of the Cohen–Massaro model by analyzing parameter trajectories measured from a French speaker. The approach proposed by King and Parent [86] extends the Cohen–Massaro model by using viseme curves to replace a single viseme target. Bevacqua and Pelachaud [89] propose an expressive qualifier modeled from recorded speech motion data to make expressive speech animations.

Rule-based co-articulation models [87, 88] leave some visemes undefined based on their co-articulation importance and phoneme contexts. These approaches are based on the important observation that phonemes have different sensitivity to their phoneme context: some phonemes (and their visemes) are strongly affected by neighboring phonemes (and visemes), while some others are less affected. Deng et al. [90–92] propose a motion capture mining technique that "learns" speech co-articulation models for diphones (a phoneme pair) and triphones from the prerecorded facial motion data, and then generates novel speech animations by blending pre-designed visemes (key mouth shapes) using the learned co-articulation models.

Animation realism generated by the above viseme-driven approaches largely depends on the hand-crafted smoothing (co-articulation) functions and a hidden assumption that a viseme can be represented by one or several pre-designed key shapes. However, in practice, constructing accurate co-articulation functions and phoneme-viseme mappings requires challenging and painstaking manual efforts. As a new trend for speech animation generation, data-driven approaches were proposed to alleviate the painstaking manual efforts.

1.10.2 Data-Driven Approaches

Data-driven approaches synthesize new speech animations by concatenating pre-recorded facial motion data or sampling from statistical models learned from the data. Their general pipeline is as follows. First, facial motion data (2D facial images or 3D facial motion capture data) are pre-recorded. Second, there are two different ways to deal with the constructed facial motion database: either statistical models for facial motion control are trained from the data (learning-based approaches), or the facial motion database is further organized and processed (sample-based approaches). Finally, given a novel sound track or text input, corresponding visual speech animations are generated by sampling from the trained statistical models, or recombining motion frames optimally chosen from the facial motion database. Figure 1.8 shows a schematic view of the data-driven speech animation approaches.

Data-driven approaches typically generate realistic speech animation results, but it is hard to predict how much motion data are enough to train statistical models or construct a balanced facial motion database. In other words, the connection from the amount of pre-recorded facial motion data to the visual realism of synthesized

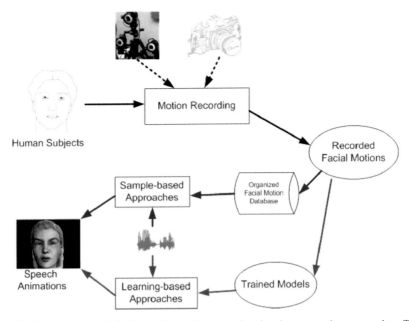

Fig. 1.8 Sketched general pipeline of data-driven speech animation generation approaches. The sample-based approaches go with the blue path, and the learning-based approaches go with the red path.

speech animations is not clear. Furthermore, these approaches often do not provide intuitive process controls for animators.

1.10.2.1 Sample-based Approaches

Bregler et al. [93] present the "video rewrite" method for synthesizing 2D talking faces given novel speech input, based on the collected "triphone video segments." Instead of using ad hoc co-articulation models and ignoring dynamics factors in speech, this approach models the co-articulation effect with "triphone video segments," but it is not generative (i.e., the co-articulation cannot be applied to other faces without retraining). The work of [94,95] further extends "the triphone combination idea" [93] to longer phoneme segments. For example, Cao et al. [95, 96] propose a greedy search algorithm to look for longer pre-recorded facial motion sequences ($\geq$ 3 phonemes) in the database. The work of [97–100] searches for the optimal combination of pre-recorded motion frame sequences by introducing various cost functions, based on dynamic programming-based search algorithms. In the work of [100], a phoneme-Isomap interface is introduced to provide high-level controls for animators, and phoneme-level emotion specifiers are enforced as search constraints.

Instead of constructing a phoneme segment database [93–95, 97–101], Kshirsagar and Thalmann [102] propose a syllable motion-based approach to synthesize novel speech animations. In their approach, captured facial motions are segmented into syllable motions, and then new speech animations are achieved by concatenating syllable motion segments optimally chosen from the syllable motion database. Sifakis et al. [103] propose a physics-based approach to generate novel speech animations by first computing muscle activation signals for each phoneme (termed *physemes*) enclosed in the pre-recorded facial motion data and then concatenating corresponding physemes given novel speech input.

1.10.2.2 Learning-based Approaches

Learning-based approaches model speech co-articulations as implicit functions in statistical models. Brand [104] learns an HMM-based facial control model by an entropy minimization learning algorithm from voice and video training data and then effectively synthesizes full facial motions for a novel audio track. This approach models co-articulations using the Viterbi algorithm through vocal HMMs to search for the most likely facial state sequence that is used for predicting facial configuration sequences. Ezzat et al. [105] learn a multidimensional morphable model from a recorded face video database that requires a limited set of mouth image prototypes and use the magnitude of diagonal covariance matrices of phoneme clusters to represent co-articulation effects: the larger covariance of a phoneme cluster means this phoneme has a smaller co-articulation, and vice versa.

Blanz et al. [106] reanimate 2D faces in images and video by reconstructing a 3D face model using the morphable face model framework [47] and learning an expression and viseme space from scanned 3D faces. This addresses both speech and expressions. Deng et al. [91, 92] propose an expressive speech animation system that learn speech co-articulation models and expression eigenspaces from recorded facial motion capture data. Some other approaches [107, 108] were also proposed for generating expressive speech animations.

Generally, these approaches construct economical and compact representations for human facial motions and synthesize human-like facial motions. However, how much data are minimally required to guarantee satisfied synthesis results is an unresolved issue in these approaches, and creating explicit correlations between training data and the visual realism of final animations would be a critical need. Furthermore, model and feature selections residing in many machine learning algorithms are still far away from being resolved.

1.11 Facial Animation Editing

Editing facial animations by posing key faces is a widely-used practice. Instead of moving individual vertices of 3D face geometry, various deformation approaches (Section 1.1.5) and the blendshape methods (Section 1.1.2) can be regarded to simultaneously move and edit a group of relevant vertices, which greatly improve the efficiency of facial animation editing. However, different facial regions are essentially correlated each other, and the above deformation approaches typically operate a local facial region at one time. The animators need to switch editing operations on different facial regions in order to sculpt 3D realistic faces with fine details, which creates a large amount of additional work for the animators. In addition, even for skilled animators, it is difficult to judge which facial pose (configuration) is closer to a real human face. Some recent work in facial animation editing [13, 72, 109–112] has been proposed to address this issue.

The ICA-based facial motion editing technique [109] applies independent component analysis (ICA) onto pre-recorded expressive facial motion capture data and interprets certain ICA components as expression and speech-related components. Further editing operations, e.g., scaling, are performed on these ICA components in their approach. Chang and Jenkins [112] propose a 2D sketch interface for posing 3D faces. In their work, users can intuitively draw 2D strokes in 2D face spaces that are used to search for the optimal pose of the face.

Editing a local facial region while preserving the naturalness of the whole face is another intriguing idea. The geometry-driven editing technique [110] generates expression details on 2D face images by constructing a PCA-based hierarchical face representation from a selected number of training 2D face images. When users move one or several points on the 2D face image, the movements of other facial control points are automatically computed by a motion propagation algorithm. Based on a blendshape representation for 3D face models, Joshi et al. [72] propose an interactive tool to edit 3D face geometry by learning controls through a physicall motivated face segmentation. A rendering algorithm for preserving visual realism in this editing was also proposed in their approach.

Besides the above approaches, the morphable face model framework [47] and the multilinear face model [111] can be used for facial animation editing: once these statistical models are constructed from training face data, users can manipulate high-level attributes of the face, such as gender and expression, to achieve the purpose of facial animation editing.

1.12 Facial Animation Transferring

Automatically transferring facial motions from an existing (source) model to a new (target) model can significantly save painstaking and model-specific animation tuning for the new face model. The source facial motions can have various formats, including 2D video faces, 3D facial motion capture data, and animated face meshes, while the target models typically are a static 3D face mesh or a blendshape face model. In this regard, the performance-driven facial animation described in Section 1.8 can be conceptually regarded as one specific way of transferring facial motions from 2D video faces to 3D face models. In this section, we will review other facial animation transferring techniques.

Transferring facial motions between two 3D face meshes can be performed through geometric deformations. Noh and Neumann [113] propose an "expression cloning" technique to transfer vertex displacements from a source 3D face model to target 3D face models that may have different geometric proportions and mesh structure. Its basic idea is to construct vertex motion mappings between models through the radial basis functions (RBF) morphing. Sumner and Popović [114] propose a general framework that automatically transfers geometric deformations between two triangle meshes, which can be directly applied to retarget facial motions from one source face mesh to a target face mesh. Both approaches need a number of initial face landmark correspondences either through heuristic rules [113] or by manually specifying.

A number of approaches were proposed to transfer source facial motions to blendshape face models [3, 11, 70, 98, 115] due to the popularized use of blendshape methods in industry practice. Choe and Ko [70] transfer tracked facial motions to target blendshape face models composed of hand-generated muscle actuation base, by iteratively adjusting muscle actuation base and analyzed weights through an optimization procedure. The work of [98, 115] transfers facial animations using example-based approaches. Essentially these approaches require animators to sculpt proper blendshape face models based on a set of key facial poses, delicately chosen from source facial animation sequences. Hence, it is difficult to apply these techniques to pre-designed blendshape models without considerable efforts. Sifakis et al. [11] first create an anatomically accurate face model composed of facial musculature, passive tissue, and underlying skeleton structure, and then use nonlinear finite element methods to determine accurate muscle actuations from the motions of sparse facial markers. Anatomically accurate 3D face models are needed for this approach, which is another challenging task itself in computer animation. Deng et al. [3] propose an automatic technique to directly map 3D facial motion capture data to pre-designed blendshape face models. In their approach, Radial Basis Function (RBF) networks are trained to map a new motion capture frame to its corresponding blendshape weights, based on chosen training pairs between mocap frames and blendshape weights.

The above approaches faithfully "copy" facial motions between models, but they provide little transformation function, for example, change affective mode during transferring. Bilinear models and multilinear models were proposed to transform facial motions [111, 116, 117]. Chuang and Bregler [116, 117] learn a facial expression mapping/transformation function from training video footage using the bilinear models [118], and then this learned mapping is used to transform input video of neutral talking to expressive talking. Vlasic et al. [111] propose a framework to transfer facial motion in video to other 2D or 3D faces by learning statistical multilinear models from scanned 3D face meshes. In their work, the learned multilinear models are controlled via intuitive attribute parameters, such as identity and expression. Varying one attribute parameter (e.g., identity) while keeping other attributes intact can transfer the facial motions from one model to another. Both approaches interpret expressions as dynamic processes, but the expressive face frames retain the same timing as the original neutral speech, which does not seem plausible in all cases.

1.13 Facial Gesture Generation

A facial gesture is typically interpreted as a gesture executed with the facial muscles and facial movement, enclosing various visual components, such as facial expressions, head movement, etc. In this section, we focus on reviewing previous research efforts in eye motion synthesis and head movement generation. As for generating facial expressions on virtual characters, refer to the state-of-the-art report written by Vinayagamoorthy et al. [119].

As "windows to the soul," the eyes are particularly scrutinized and subtle, since eye gaze is one of the strongest cues to the mental state of human beings; when someone is talking, he/she looks into our eyes to judge our interest and attentiveness, and we look into his/her eyes to signal our intent to talk. Chopra-Khullar et al. [120] propose a framework for computing gestures including eye gaze and head motions of virtual agents in dynamic environments, given high-level scripts. Vertegaal et al. [121, 122] studied whether eye-gaze direction clues can be used as a reliable signal for determining who is talking to whom in multiparty conversations. Lee et al. [123] treat "textural" aspects of gaze movement using statistical approaches and demonstrate the necessity of the gaze details for achieving realism and conveying an appropriate mental state. In their approach, signals from an eye tracker are analyzed to produce a statistical model of eye saccades. However, only first-order statistics are used, and gaze-eyelid coupling and vergence are not considered in their work. Deng et al. [124,125] propose a texture synthesis-based technique to simultaneously synthesize realistic eye gaze and blink motion, accounting for any possible correlation between the two.

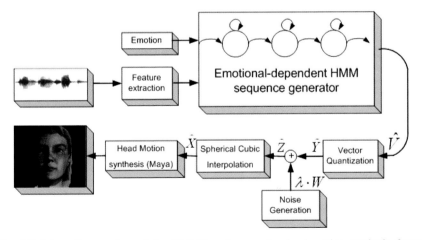

Fig. 1.9 Schematic overview of the HMM-based expressive head motion synthesis framework [126,127].

Natural head motion is an indispensable part of realistic facial animation and engaging human-computer interface. A number of approaches were proposed to generate head motions for talking avatars [126–133]. Rule-based approaches [128, 129] generate head motions from labeled text by pre-defined rules, but their focus was only the "nodding." Graf et al. [130] estimate the conditional probability distribution of major head movements (e.g., nodding) given the occurrences of pitch accents, based on their collected head motion data. Chuang and Bregler [132] generate head motions corresponding to novel acoustic speech input, by combining best-matched recorded head motion segments in the constructed pitch-indexed database. Deng et al. [133] synthesize appropriate head motions with key-framing controls, where a constrained dynamic programming algorithm was used to generate an optimal head motion sequence that maximally satisfies both acoustic speech and key-frame constraints (e.g., specified key head poses). Busso et al. [126] presented a hidden Markov models (HMMs)-based framework to generate natural head motions directly from acoustic prosodic features. This framework was further extended to generate expressive head motions [127]. Figure 1.9 shows a schematic overview of the HMM-based head motion synthesis framework [127].

1.14 Summary

We surveyed various computer facial animation techniques and classified them into the following categories: blendshape method (shape interpolation), parameterizations, Facial Action Coding Systems-based approaches, deformation-based approaches, physics-based muscle modeling, 3D face modeling, performance-driven facial animation, MPEG-4 facial animation, visual speech animation, facial animation editing, facial animation transferring, and facial gesture generation. Within each category, we described the main ideas of its approaches and compared their strength and weakness.

References

1. F. Parke. Computer generated animation of faces. In *Proc. ACM Natl. Conf.*, volume 1, pages 451–457, 1972.
2. F.I. Parke and K. Waters. *Computer Facial Animation*. A.K. Peters, Ltd. Natick, MA, USA, 1996.
3. Z. Deng, P.Y. Chiang, P. Fox, and U. Neumann. Animating blendshape faces by cross mapping motion capture data. In *Proc. ACM SIGGRAPH Symposium on Interactive 3D Graphics and Games*, 2006.
4. P. Bergeron and P. Lachapelle. Controlling facial expression and body movements in the computer generated short "tony de peltrie," tutorial, SIGGRAPH, 1985.
5. F. Pighin, J. Hecker, D. Lischinski, R. Szeliski, and D.H. Salesin. Synthesizing realistic facial expressions from photographs. In *SIGGRAPH Proceedings*, pages 75–84, 1998.
6. K. Waters and T.M. Levergood. Decface: An automatic lip-synchronization algorithm for synthetic faces, 1993.

7. F.I. Parke. A parametric model for human faces. Ph.D. Thesis, University of Utah, UTEC-CSc-75-047, 1974.

8. K. Arai, T. Kurihara, and K. Anjyo. Bilinear interpolation for facial expression and meta-morphosis in real-time animation. *The Visual Computer*, 12:105–116, 1996.

9. H. Sera, S. Morishma, and D. Terzopoulos. Physics-based muscle model for moth shape control. In *IEEE International Workshop on Robot and Human Communication*, pages 207–212, 1996.

10. B. W. Choe and H. S. Ko. Analysis and synthesis of facial expressions with hand-generated muscle actuation basis. In *IEEE Computer Animation Conference*, pages 12–19, 2001.

11. E. Sifakis, I. Neverov, and R. Fedkiw. Automatic determination of facial muscle activations from sparse motion capture marker data. *ACM Trans. Graph.*, 24(3):417–425, 2005.

12. J.P. Lewis, M. Cordner, and N. Fong. Pose space deformation: A unified approach to shape interpolation and skeleton-driven deformation. In *SIGGRAPH Proc.*, pages 165–172, 2000.

13. J.P. Lewis, J. Mooser, Z. Deng, and U. Neumann. Reducing blendshape interference by selected motion attenuation. In *Proc. ACM SIGGRAPH Symposium on Interactive 3D Graphics and Games (I3DG)*, pages 25–29, 2005.

14. M. Cohen and D. Massaro. Modeling co-articulation in synthetic visual speech. *Model and Technique in Computer Animation*, pages 139–156, 1993.

15. F.I. Parke. Parameterized models for facial animation. *IEEE Computer Graphics and Applications*, 2(9):61–68, 1982.

16. F.I. Parke. Parameterized models for facial animation revisited, In ACM Siggraph Facial Animation Tutorial Notes, 1989, 53–56.

17. K. Waters and J. Frisbie. A coordinated muscle model for speech animation. In *Graphics Interface'95*, pages 163–170, 1995.

18. P. Ekman and W.V. Friesen. *Facial Action Coding System*. Consulting Psychologists Press, 1978.

19. I.A. Essa, S. Basu, T. Darrell, and A. Pentland. Modeling, tracking and interactive animation of faces and heads using input from video. In *Proceedings of Computer Animation*, Palo Alto, California pages 85–94, 1996.

20. M. Nahas, H. Hutric, M. Rioux, and J. Domey. Facial image synthesis using skin texture recording. *Visual Computer*, 6(6):337–343, 1990.

21. M.L. Viad and H. Yahia. Facial animation with wrinkles. In *Proceedings of the Third Eurographics Workshop on Animation and Simulation*, 1992.

22. CLY Wang and D.R. Forsey. Langwidere: A new facial animation system. In *Proceedings of Computer Animation*, pages 59–68, 1994.

23. K. Singh K and E. Fiume. Wires: A geometric deformation technique. In *SIGGRAPH Proceedings*, pages 405–414, 1998.

24. S. Coquillart. Extended free-form deformation: A sculpting tool for 3D geometric modeling. *Computer Graphics*, 24:187–193, 1990.

25. P. Kalra, A. Mangili, N.M. Thalmann, and D. Thalmann. Simulation of facial muscle actions based on rational free from deformations. In *Eurographics*, volume 11, pages 59–69, 1992.

26. T. Beier and S. Neely. Feature-based image metamorphosis. In *SIGGRAPH Proceedings*, pages 35–42. ACM Press, 1992.

27. F. Pighin, J. Auslander, D. Lischinski, D.H. Salesin, and R. Szeliski. Realistic facial animation using image-based 3D morphing, Technical report UW-CSE-97-01-03, 1997.

28. T.W. Sederberg and S.R. Parry. Free-form deformation of solid geometry models. In *Computer Graphics, SIGGRAPH*, volume 20, pages 151–160, 1996.

29. N. M. Thalmann and D. Thalmann. *Interactive Computer Animation*. Prentice Hall, Englewood Cliffs; NJ, 1996.

30. K. Waters. A muscle model for animating three-dimensional facial expression. In *SIGGRAPH Proceedings*, volume 21, pages 17–24, 1987.

31. E. Catmull and J. Clark. Recursively generated B-spline surfaces on arbitrary topological meshes. *Computer Aided Design*, 10(6):350–355, 1978.

32. T. Derose, M. Kass, and T. Truong. Subdivision surfaces in character animation. In *SIG-GRAPH Proceedings*, pages 85–94, 1998.
33. E. Catmull. Subdivision algorithm for the display of curved surfaces. Ph.D. Thesis, University of Utah, 1974.
34. P. Eisert and B. Girod. Analyzing facial expressions for virtual conferencing. *IEEE Computer Graphics and Applications*, 18(5):70–78, 1998.
35. S. Platt and N. Badler. Animating facial expression. Computer graphics. *Computer Graphics*, 15(3):245–252, 1981.
36. S.M. Platt. A structural model of the human face. Ph.D. Thesis, University of Pennsylvania, 1985.
37. Y. Zhang, E. C. Parkash, and E. Sung. A physically-based model with adaptive refinement for facial animation. In *Proc. of IEEE Computer Animation'2001*, pages 28–39, 2001.
38. K. Kähler, J. Haber, and H.P. Seidel. Geometry-based muscle modeling for facial animation. In *Proc. of Graphics Interface'2001*, 2001.
39. D. Terzopoulos and K. Waters. Physically-based facial modeling, analysis, and animation. *Journal of Visualization and Computer Animation*, 1(4):73–80, 1990.
40. Y. Wu, N.M. Thalmann, and D. Thalmann. A plastic-visco-elastic model for wrinkles in facial animation and skin aging. In *Proc. 2nd Pacific Conference on Computer Graphics and Applications, Pacific Graphics*, 1994.
41. Y. Lee, D. Terzopoulos, and K. Waters. Constructing physics-based facial models of individuals. In *Proc. of Graphics Interface'93*, 1993.
42. Y.C. Lee, D. Terzopoulos, and K. Waters. Realistic face modeling for animation. In *SIG-GRAPH Proceedings*, pages 55–62, 1995.
43. F. Ulgen. A step toward universal facial animation via volume morphing. In *6th IEEE International Workshop on Robot and Human Communication*, pages 358–363, 1997.
44. B. Guenter, C. Grimm, D. Wood, H. Malvar, and F. Pighin. Making faces. *Proc. of ACM SIGGRAPH'98*, pages 55–66, 1998.
45. MJD Powell. Radial basis functions for multivariate interpolation: A review. *Algorithms for Approximation*, 1987.
46. T. Poggio and F. Girosi. A theory of networks for approximation and learning, Technical Report 1140, MIT AI Lab, 1989.
47. V. Blanz and T. Vetter. A morphable model for the synthesis of 3d faces. In *SIGGRAPH Proceedings*. ACM Press, 1999.
48. C.J. Kuo, R.S. Huang, and T.G. Lin. Synthesizing lateral face from frontal facial image using anthropometric estimation. In *Proceedings of International Conference on Image Processing*, volume 1, pages 133–136, 1997.
49. D. DeCarlo, D. Metaxas, and M. Stone. An anthropometric face model using variational technique. In *SIGGRAPH Proceedings*, 1998.
50. S. Gortler and M. Cohen. Hierarchical and variational geometric modeling with wavelets. In *Symposium on Interactive 3D Graphics*, pages 35–42, 1995.
51. W. Welch and A. Witkin. Variational surface modeling. In *SIGGRAPH Proceedings*, pages 157–166, 1992.
52. M. Kass, A. Witkin, and D. Terzopoulos. Snakes: Active contour models. *International Journal of Computer Vision*, 1(4):321–331, 1987.
53. N.M. Thalmann, A. Cazedevals, and D. Thalmann. Modeling facial communication between an animator and a synthetic actor in real time. In *Proc. Modeling in Computer Graphics*, pages 387–396, 1993.
54. D. Terzopouos and R. Szeliski. Tracking with kalman snakes. *Active Vision*, pages 3–20, 1993.
55. K. Waters and D. Terzopoulos. Modeling and animating faces using scanned data. *Journal of Visualization and Computer Animation*, 2(4):123–128, 1990.
56. D. Terzopoulos and K. Waters. Techniques for realistic facial modeling and animation. In *Proc. of IEEE Computer Animation*, pages 59–74. Springer-Verlag, 1991.

57. I.S. Pandzic, P. Kalra, and N. M. Thalmann. Real time facial interaction. *Displays* (Butterworth-Heinemann), 15(3), 1994.

58. E.M. Caldognetto, K. Vagges, N.A. Borghese, and G. Ferrigno. Automatic analysis of lips and jaw kinematics in vcv sequences. In *Proceedings of Eurospeech Conference*, volume 2, pages 453–456, 1989.

59. L. Williams. Performance-driven facial animation. In *Proc. of ACM SIGGRAPH '90*, pages 235–242. ACM Press, 1990.

60. E.C. Patterson, P.C. Litwinowicz, and N. Greene. Facial animation by spatial mapping. In *Proc. Computer Animation*, pages 31–44, 1991.

61. F. Kishino. Virtual space teleconferencing system—real time detection and reproduction of human images. In *Proc. Imagina*, pages 109–118, 1994.

62. P. Litwinowicz and L. Williams. Animating images with drawings. In *ACM SIGGRAPH Conference Proceedings*, pages 409–412, 1994.

63. L. Moubaraki, J. Ohya, and F. Kishino. Realistic 3D facial animation in virtual space tele-conferencing. In *4th IEEE International Workshop on Robot and Human Communication*, pages 253–258, 1995.

64. J. Ohya, Y. Kitamura, H. Takemura, H. Ishi, F. Kishino, and N. Teraima. Virtual space teleconferencing: Real-time reproduction of 3D human images. *Journal of Visual Communications and Image Representation*, 6(1): 1–25, 1995.

65. BKP Horn and BG Schunck. Determining optical flow. *Artificial Intelligence*, pages 185–203, 1981.

66. T. Darrell and A. Pentland. Space-time gestures. In *Computer Vision and Pattern Recognition*, 1993.

67. I.A. Essa, T. Darrell, and A. Pentland. Tracking facial motion, In Proceedings of the workshop on motion of nonrigid and articulated objects, pages 36–42. IEEE Computer Society, 1994.

68. J. Chai, J. Xiao, and J. Hodgins. Vision-based control of 3D facial animation. In *Proc. of Symposium on Computer Animation*, pages 193–206. ACM Press, 2003.

69. L. Zhang, N. Snavely, B. Curless, and S. M. Seitz. Spacetime faces: High resolution capture for modeling and animation. *ACM Trans. Graph.*, 23(3): 548–558, 2004.

70. B. Choe B, H. Lee, and H.S. Ko. Performance driven muscle based facial animation. *Journal of Visualization and Computer Animation*, 12(2):67–79, 2001.

71. J. Noh, D. Fidaleo, and U. Neumann. Gesture driven facial animation, USC Technical Report 02–761, 2002.

72. P. Joshi, W.C. Tien, M. Desbrun, and F. Pighin. Learning controls for blend shape based realistic facial animation. In *Eurographics/SIGGRAPH Symposium on Computer Animation*, pages 35–42, 2003.

73. Iso/iec 14496—MPEG-4 international standard, moving picture experts group, www.cselt.it/mpeg.

74. J. Ostermann. Animation of synthetic faces in MPEG-4. In *Proc. of IEEE Computer Animation*, 1998.

75. M. Escher, I. S. Pandzic, and N.M. Thalmann. Facial deformations for MPEG-4. In *Proc. of Computer Animation'98*, pages 138–145, Philadelphia, 1998.

76. S. Kshirsagar, S. Garchery, and N.M. Thalmann. Feature point based mesh deformation applied to MPEG-4 facial animation. In *Proc. Deform'2000, Workshop on Virtual Humans by IFIP Working Group 5.10*, pages 23–34, November 2000.

77. G.A. Abrantes and F. Pereira. MPEG-4 facial animation technology: Survey, implementation, and results. *IEEE Transaction on Circuits and Systems for Video Technology*, 9(2): 290–305, 1999.

78. F. Lavagetto and R. Pockaj. The facial animation engine: Toward a high-level interface for the design of MPEG-4 compliant animated faces. *IEEE Transaction on Circuits and Systems for Video Technology*, 9(2):277–289, 1999.

79. S. Garchery and N.M. Thalmann. Designing MPEG-4 facial animation tables for web applications. In *Proc. of Multimedia Modeling*, pages 39–59, 2001.

80. I.S. Pandzic. Facial animation framework for the web and mobile platforms. In *Proc. of the 7th Int'l Conf. on 3D Web Technology*, 2002.
81. I.S. Pandzic and R. Forchheimer. *MPEG-4 Facial Animation: The Standard, Implementation, and Applications*. John Wiley & Sons, New york, 2002.
82. A. Pearce, B. Wyvill, G. Wyvill, and D. Hill. Speech and expression: A computer solution to face animation. In *Proc. of Graphics Interface'86*, pages 136–140, 1986.
83. J.P. Lewis. Automated lip-sync: Background and techniques. *Journal of Visualization and Computer Animation*, pages 118–122, 1991.
84. B.L. Goff and C. Benoit. A text-to-audovisual-speech synthesizer for French. In *Proc. of the Int'l. Conf. on Spoken Language Processing (ICSLP)*, pages 2163–2166, 1996.
85. P. Cosi, C.E. Magno, G. Perlin, and C. Zmarich. Labial coarticulation modeling for realistic facial animation. In *Proc. of Int'l Conf. on Multimodal Interfaces 02*, pages 505–510, Pittsburgh, PA, 2002.
86. S.A. King and R.E. Parent. Creating speech-synchronized animation. *IEEE Trans. Vis. Graph.*, 11(3):341–352, 2005.
87. C. Pelachaud. Communication and coarticulation in facial animation. Ph.D. Thesis, Univ. of Pennsylvania, 1991.
88. J. Beskow. Rule-based visual speech synthesis. In *Proc. of Eurospeech 95*, Madrid, 1995.
89. E. Bevacqua and C. Pelachaud. Expressive audio-visual speech. *Journal of Visualization and Computer Animation*, 15(3-4):297–304, 2004.
90. Z. Deng, M. Bulut, U. Neumann, and S.S. Narayanan. Automatic dynamic expression synthesis for speech animation. In *Proc. of IEEE Computer Animation and Social Agents (CASA) 2004*, pages 267–274, Geneva, Switzerland, July 2004.
91. Z. Deng, J.P. Lewis, and U. Neumann. Synthesizing speech animation by learning compact speech co-articulation models. In *Proc. of Computer Graphics International*, pages 19–25, 2005.
92. Z. Deng, U. Neumann, J.P. Lewis, T.Y. Kim, M. Bulut, and S. Narayanan. Expressive facial animation synthesis by learning speech co-articulations and expression spaces. *IEEE Trans. Vis. Graph.*, 12(6):1523–1534, 2006.
93. C. Bregler, M. Covell, and M. Slaney. Video rewrite: Driving visual speech with audio. *Proc. of ACM SIGGRAPH'97*, pages 353–360, 1997.
94. E. Cosatto. Sample-based talking-head synthesis. Ph.D. Thesis, Swiss Federal Institute of Technology, 2002.
95. Y. Cao, P. Faloutsos, E. Kohler, and F. Pighin. Real-time speech motion synthesis from recorded motions. In *Proc. of Symposium on Computer Animation*, pages 345–353, 2004.
96. Y. Cao, P. Faloutsos, and F. Pighin. Expressive speech-driven facial animation. *ACM Trans. on Graph.*, 24(4), 2005.
97. E. Cosatto and H.P. Graf. Audio-visual unit selection for the synthesis of photo-realistic talking-heads. In *Proc. of ICME*, pages 619–622, 2000.
98. J. Ma, R. Cole, B. Pellom, W. Ward, and B. Wise. Accurate automatic visible speech synthesis of arbitrary 3d model based on concatenation of diviseme motion capture data. *Computer Animation and Virtual Worlds*, 15:1–17, 2004.
99. J. Ma, R. Cole, B. Pellom, W. Ward, and B. Wise. Accurate visible speech synthesis based on concatenating variable length motion capture data. *IEEE Transaction on Visualization and Computer Graphics*, 12(2):266–276, 2006.
100. Z. Deng and U. Neumann. efase: Expressive facial animation synthesis and editing with phoneme-level controls. In *Proc. of ACM SIGGGRAPH/Eurographics Symposium on Computer Animation*, pages 251–259, Vienna, Austria, 2006.
101. Z. Deng. Data-driven facial animation synthesis by learning from facial motion capture data. Ph.D. Thesis, University of Southern California, 2006.
102. S. Kshirsagar and N.M. Thalmann. Visyllable based speech animation. *Computer Graphics Forum*, 22(3), 2003.
103. E. Sifakis, A. Selle, A.R. Mosher, and R. Fedkiw. Simulating speech with a physics-based facial muscle model. In *Proc. of Symposium on Computer Animation (SCA)*, 2006.
104. M. Brand. Voice puppetry. *Proc. of ACM SIGGRAPH'99*, pages 21–28, 1999.

105. T. Ezzat, G. Geiger, and T. Poggio. Trainable videorealistic speech animation. *ACM Trans. Graph.*, pages 388–398, 2002.

106. V. Blanz, C. Basso, T. Poggio, and T. Vetter. Reanimating faces in images and video. *Computer Graphics Forum*, 22(3), 2003.

107. S. Kshirsagar, T. Molet, and N.M. Thalmann. Principal components of expressive speech animation. In *Proc. of Computer Graphics International*, 2001.

108. A.S. Meyer, S. Garchery, G. Sannier, and N.M. Thalmann. Synthetic faces: Analysis and applications. *International Journal of Imaging Systems and Technology*, 13(1):65–73, 2003.

109. Y. Cao, P. Faloutsos, and F. Pighin. Unsupervised learning for speech motion editing. In *Proc. of ACM SIGGRAPH/Eurographics Symposium on Computer Animation*, 2003.

110. Q. Zhang, Z. Liu, B. Guo, and H. Shum. Geometry-driven photorealistic facial expression synthesis. In *Proc. of Symposium on Computer Animation*, pages 177–186, 2003.

111. D. Vlasic, M. Brand, H. Pfister, and J. Popović. Face transfer with multilinear models. *ACM Trans. Graph.*, 24(3):426–433, 2005.

112. E. Chang and O.C. Jenkins. Sketching articulation and pose for facial animation. In *Proc. of Symposium on Computer Animation (SCA)*, 2006.

113. J. Y. Noh and U. Neumann. Expression cloning. *Proc. of ACM SIGGRAPH'01*, pages 277–288, 2001.

114. R.W. Sumner and J. Popović. Deformation transfer for triangle meshes. *ACM Trans. Graph.*, 23(3):399–405, 2004.

115. H. Pyun, Y. Kim, W. Chae, H.W. Kang, and S.Y. Shin. An example-based approach for facial expression cloning. In *Proc. of Symposium on Computer Animation*, pages 167–176, 2003.

116. E.S. Chuang, H. Deshpande, and C. Bregler. Facial expression space learning. In *Proc. of Pacific Graphics'2002*, pages 68–76, 2002.

117. E. Chuang and C. Bregler. Moodswings: Expressive speech animation. *ACM Trans. on Graph.*, 24(2), 2005.

118. J.B. Tenenbaum and W.T. Freeman. Separating style and content with bilinear models. *Neural Computation*, 12(6):1247–1283, 2000.

119. V. Vinayagamoorthy, M. Gillies, A. Steed, E. Tanguy, X. Pan, C. Loscos, and M. Slater. Building expression into virtual characters. In *STAR Report, Proc. of Eurographics 2006*, 2006.

120. S.C. Khullar and N. Badler. Where to look? Automating visual attending behaviors of virtual human characters. In *Proc. of Third ACM Conf. on Autonomous Agents*, pages 16–23, 1999.

121. R. Vertegaal, G.V. Derveer, and H. Vons. Effects of gaze on multiparty mediated communication. In *Proc. of Graphics Interface'00*, pages 95–102, Montreal, 2000.

122. R. Vertegaal, R. Slagter, G.V. Derveer, and A. Nijholt. Eye gaze patterns in conversations: There is more to conversational agents than meets the eyes. In *Proc. of ACM CHI 2001 Conference on Human Factors in Computing Systems*, pages 301–308, 2001.

123. S.P. Lee, J.B. Badler, and N. Badler. Eyes alive. *ACM Trans. Graph. (Proc. of ACM SIGGRAPH'02)*, 21(3):637–644, 2002.

124. Z. Deng, J.P. Lewis, and U. Neumann. Practical eye movement model using texture synthesis. In *Proc. of ACM SIGGRAPH 2003 Sketches and Applications*, San Diego, 2003.

125. Z. Deng, J.P. Lewis, and U. Neumann. Automated eye motion synthesis using texture synthesis. *IEEE Computer Graphics and Applications*, pages 24–30, March/April 2005.

126. C. Busso, Z. Deng, U. Neumann, and S. Narayanan. Natural head motion synthesis driven by acoustic prosody features. *Computer Animation and Virtual Worlds*, 16(3-4):283–290, July 2005.

127. C. Busso, Z. Deng, M. Grimm, U. Neumann, and S. Narayanan. Rigid head motion in expressive speech animation: Analysis and synthesis. *IEEE Transaction on Audio, Speech and Language Processing*, March 2007.

128. C. Pelachaud, N. Badler, and M. Steedman. Generating facial expressions for speech. *Cognitive Science*, 20(1):1–46, 1994.

129. J. Cassell, C. Pelachaud, N. Badler, M. Steedman, B. Achorn, T. Becket, B. Douville, S. Prevost, and M. Stone. Animated conversation: Rule-based generation of facial expression, gesture and spoken intonation for multiple conversational agents. In *Proc. of ACM SIGGRAPH'94*, pages 413–420, 1994.

130. H.P. Graf, E. Cosatto, V. Strom, and F.J. Huang. Visual prosody: Facial movements accompanying speech. In *Proc. of IEEE Int'l Conf. on Automatic Face and Gesture Recognition(FG'02)*, Washington, DC., May 2002.

131. M. Costa, T. Chen, and F. Lavagetto. Visual prosody analysis for realistic motion synthesis of 3d head models. In *Proc. of Int'l. Conf. on Augmented, Virtual Environments and Three-Dimensional Imaging*, Ornos, Mykonos, Greece, 2001.

132. E. Chuang and C. Bregler. Performance driven facial animation using blendshape interpolation. *CS-TR-2002-02, Department of Computer Science, Stanford University*, 2002.

133. Z. Deng, C. Busso, S.S. Narayanan, and U. Neumann. Audio-based head motion synthesis for avatar-based telepresence systems. In *Proc. of ACM SIGMM 2004 Workshop on Effective Telepresence (ETP 2004)*, pages 24–30, New York, Oct. 2004.

Chapter 2
Expressive Visual Speech Generation

Thomas Di Giacomo, Stephane Garchery, and Nadia Magnenat-Thalmann

2.1 Introduction

With the emergence of 3D graphics, we are now able to create very realistic 3D characters that can move and talk. Multimodal interaction with such characters is also possible, as various technologies have matured for speech and video analysis, natural language dialogues, and animation. However, the behavior expressed by these characters is far from believable in most systems. We feel that this problem arises due to their lack of individuality on various levels: perception, dialogue, and expression. In this chapter, we describe results of research that tries to realistically connect personality and 3D characters, not only on an expressive level (for example, generating individualized expressions on a 3D face), but also with real-time video tracking, on a dialogue level (generating responses that actually correspond to what a certain personality in a certain emotional state would say) and on a perceptive level (having a virtual character that uses expression user data to create corresponding behavior). The idea of linking personality with agent behavior has been discussed by Marsella et al. [33], with the influence of emotion on behavior in general, and Johns et al. [21] with how personality and emotion can affect decision making.

Traditionally, any text or voice-driven speech animation system uses the phonemes as the basic units of speech, and visemes as the basic units of animation. Though text-to-speech synthesizers and phoneme recognizers often use biphone-based techniques, the end user seldom has access to this information, except for dedicated systems. Most commercially and freely available software applications allow access to only time-stamped phoneme streams along with audio. Thus, in order to generate animation from this information, an extra level of processing, namely co-articulation, is required. This process takes care of the influence of the neighboring visemes for fluent speech production. This processing stage can be eliminated by using the syllable as a basic unit of speech rather than the phoneme.

Overall, we do not intend to give a complete survey of ongoing research in behavior, emotion, and personality. Our main goal is to create believable conversational agents that can interact with many modalities. We thus concentrate on emotion extraction of a real user (Section 2.3), visyllable-based speech animation (Section 2.4), dialogue systems and emotions (Section 2.5).

2.2 State-of-the-Art

2.2.1 Real-Time Video Tracking

In the last few years, the number of applications that require a multimodal interface with the virtual environment has steadily increased. Within this field of research, recognition of facial expressions is a very complex and interesting subject where there have been numerous research efforts. For instance, DeCarlo et al. [7] have applied optical flow and a generic face model-based algorithm. This method is robust, but it takes a lot of time to recognize the face, and it is not in real time. Cosatto et al. [6] use a sample-based method that needs to make a sample for each person. Kouadi et al. [25] use a database and some face markers to process it effectively in real time. However, the use of markers is not always practical, and it is more attractive to recognize features without them. Pandzic et al. [36] use an algorithm based on edge extraction in real time, without markers. The method presented in Section 2.3.1 is inspired from this method.

2.2.2 Speech Animation

Co-articulation is a phenomenon observed during fluent speech, in which facial movements corresponding to one phonetic or visemic segment are influenced by those corresponding to the neighboring segments. In the process of articulating a word or a sentence, our brain and mouth do some on-the-fly *preprocessing* in order to generate fluent and continuous speech. Among these complex processings is the mixing of lip/jaw movements to compose basic sounds or phonemes and their transitions. There are several models to explain the co-articulation effect based on empirical as well as experimental results supported by linguistic and phonetic rules. A very good analysis of these models can be found in [5]. It is interesting that none of these models can explain the effects of co-articulation in different languages or even effects observed in English by speakers of different native languages. Furthermore, it has also been suggested that in fact there may not be a single most general model for co-articulation, since it is a highly context-dependent phenomenon.

For simulating co-articulation for speech animation on a synthetic face, two main approaches were taken by Pelachaud et al. [38] and Cohen et al. [5]. Both approaches are based on the classification of phoneme groups and their observed interaction during speech pronunciation. Pelachaud arranged the phoneme groups according to the deformability and context dependence in order to decide the influence of the visemes on each other. Forward and backward co-articulation rules are applied such that a phoneme takes the lip shape of a less deformable phoneme forward or backwards. Muscle contraction and relaxation times were also considered, and the facial animation parameters were controlled accordingly. Cohen defined nonlinear dominance functions for each phoneme segment or viseme. These dominance functions have to be defined for the facial control parameters for each viseme.

Subsequently, a weighted sum of the active parameters is obtained for co-articulated speech animation. The algorithm proposed by Cohen is the one most widely used as it is rather simple to implement and gives fairly good results. However, for better results, several parameters need to be defined precisely. In most cases, these parameters are defined approximately and have to be fine-tuned by experimentation and visual perception tests. Alternatively, they can be *learned* from the large corpus of phoneme-aligned facial motion capture data.

Considering these limitations, we find a need to explore a radical shift in handling the problem of co-articulation. The most logical way is to draw inspiration from how we speak in reality. We thus turn our attention to the syllable. Each syllable contains at least one vowel and one or more consonants. A syllable is the next bigger unit of speech after a phoneme. More importantly, it is the smallest unit of speech that we naturally break our words into for the purpose of easy pronunciation. Concatenating syllables seems the most natural way of producing meaningful speech. This principle is the basis of many concatenative Text-To-Speech systems, using either diphones or syllables from the prerecorded database to concatenate and synthesize speech. Even speech recognition systems using syllable-based models rather than biphone-based models have been reported to result in more accurate recognitions [18, 20].

Some speech animation systems, especially the video-based systems, have used triphone-based approaches for speech animation [4, 19]. This approach is not commonly followed in model-based talking head systems, mainly due to the huge number of possible biphones and triphones. Furthermore, in the model-based system it is much easier to operate on the parameters to achieve co-articulation effects. Syllable as the basic unit allows the use of a biphone, a triphone, or even a quadraphone. However, not all biphones or triphones form valid syllables. Moreover, each syllable can be divided into clusters or demi-syllables, reducing the number of required units considerably. With the help of phonetic rules, the visyllable database can be designed in a much neater way and handled with efficiency.

In Section 2.4, we also address the problem associated with visyllable-based speech animation, which is syllabification. Syllabification means the segmentation of the phoneme stream into syllables. It is a well-known problem addressed in phonology. Previously reported syllabification algorithms range from simple phonetic rule-based systems [22] to more sophisticated multilingual syllabification [24]. Given a word or phoneme sequence, there could be several possible segmentations resulting in a group of syllables.

2.2.3 Personality

Research in virtual humans has moved ahead from sculpting and animating human figures toward imparting them autonomous behavior. Personification means attribution of personal qualities and representation of the qualities or ideas in the human form. The personification of a virtual human contributes greatly to its believability. We examine the problem of personification of virtual humans from a physical, expressional, logical, and emotional point of view, as illustrated by Fig. 2.1. It is evident that each of these aspects is a complete research area in itself:

- **Physical personification**: This refers to the appearance of the virtual human. The facial and body features can be carefully designed to make a virtual human look like a real-life person and even impart a unique appearance.
- **Expressional personification**: The tough challenge of simulating a realistic virtual human comes up while animating it. It is necessary to "design" how the virtual humans express themselves with facial expressions and gestures. Expressional personification means designing how the virtual human smiles, what is a typical way in which it expresses its anger, or even how it blinks and nods, etc.
- **Logical personification**: This includes the way a virtual human actually analyzes input, thinks, finds answers, and chooses the natural language responses. This is probably the most tedious phenomenon to model. It requires a combination of expertise from linguistics, natural language studies, artificial intelligence, and cognitive science. This can be looked upon as the brain of the virtual human.
- **Emotional personification**: The mind controls the way the emotions of the virtual human evolve over time and during a dialogue. We call this process emotional personification. The ability to evolve emotions makes a virtual human really different from an expert system using a knowledge database and able to answer text queries. The emotional and logical aspects of personification are closely linked.

Andre et al. [2] have given a detailed description of the work done for three projects focused on personality and emotion modeling for computer-generated

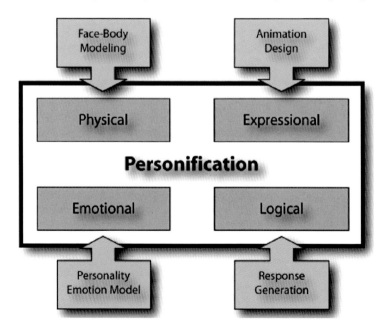

Fig. 2.1 Aspects of personification of virtual humans [28].

lifelike characters. They emphasize the use of such characters for applications such as a virtual receptionist (or user guide), an inhabited marketplace, and a virtual puppet theater. They use the Cognitive Structure of Emotions model [35] and the Five Factor Model (FFM) of personality [34]. Ball et al. [3] use the Bayesian Belief network to model emotion and personality. They discuss two dimensions of the personality; dominance and friendliness. El-Nasr et al. [12] use a fuzzy logic model for simulating emotions in agents. Velasquez [41] proposes a model of emotions, mood, and temperament that provides a flexible way of controlling the behavior of the autonomous entities. There have been various other systems developed to simulate emotions for different applications. A good overview can be found in [39].

2.3 Real-Time Video Tracking of Facial Features

In order to evaluate a user's emotional state and provide the right answer, we should be able to track user features to analyze them. The next section presents a real-time tracking system based on video input.

2.3.1 Face Motion Tracking

To obtain real-time tracking, many problems have to be solved. One important problem lies in the variety of the appearances of individuals, such as skin color, eye color, beard, moustache, glasses, and so on. The second problem comes from the camera environment. The main idea to track in real time is to get as much information at the initialization phase as possible, and reduce the computation overhead in the tracking phase. Thus, after the automatic face detection, the whole related information of the actor's face is automatically extracted. The tracking is robust for a normal condition, but weak at a changing of lighting condition [16, 17].

2.3.1.1 Initialization

The face features and its associated information are set during the initialization phase that will solve the main problem in facial feature differences between people. Figure 2.2(a) shows this initialization step. In this phase, the program automatically recognizes salient regions to decide the initial feature positions. Therefore, no manual manipulation is required and the information around the features, the edge information, and the face color information are extracted automatically. Color pixel, neighbor relation, and edge parameters used during feature tracking are then generated automatically. Those parameters contain all the relevant information for tracking the face position and its corresponding facial features without any marker.

The tracking process is then separated into two parts: mouth tracking and eye tracking. The edge and the gray-level information around the mouth and the eyes

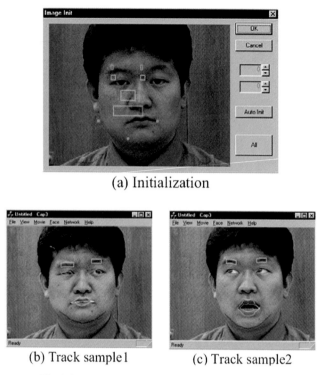

(a) Initialization

(b) Track sample1   (c) Track sample2

Fig. 2.2 Initialization and sample tracking results [17].

are the main information used during tracking. Figures 2.2(b) and (c) display two examples of the tracked features superimposed on the face images.

2.3.1.2 Mouth Tracking

The mouth is one of the most difficult face features to analyse and to track. Indeed, the mouth has a very versatile shape, and almost every muscle of the lower face drive its motion. Furthermore, the beard, moustache, tongue, or the teeth might appear sometimes and further increase the difficulty in tracking. Thus, many researchers are working on lip tracking or lip reading based on image processing. The system presented takes into account some intrinsic properties of the mouth:

- Upper teeth are attached to the head bone and therefore their position remains constant.
- Conversely, lower teeth move down from their initial position according to the rotation of the jaw joints.
- The basic mouth shape (open or closed) depends upon bone movement.

From these properties it follows that detection of the positions of hidden or apparent teeth from an image is the best way to make a robust tracking algorithm of the mouth's shape and its associated motion. The system proceeds first with the

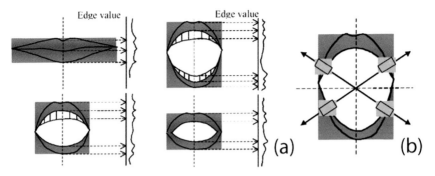

Fig. 2.3 Edge configuration for the mouth shapes [17].

extraction of all edges crossing a vertical line going from the nose to the jaw. In the second phase, the energy that shows the probability of a mouth's shape, which is based on the edge and pixel value matching combination, is calculated. Among all possible mouth shapes, the best candidate is chosen according to a "highest energy" criterion from the database, which contains rules of a combination between the basic mouth shape and the edge appearance. Figure 2.3(a) presents the simple rule contained in the database. The edge level value along the vertical line from the nose to the jaw, for different possible shape of the mouth and the corresponding detected edges, reveals

- *Closed mouth*: In this case, the center edge appears strong, the other two edges normally appear weak, and teeth are hidden inside; thus, the edge is not detected.
- *Opened mouth*: As shown in the figure, when teeth are present, the edges are stronger than the edge on the outside lips, or between a lip and the teeth or between the lip and the inside of the mouth. If the teeth were hidden inside the lips (upper or lower), the edge of the teeth would not be detected.

Once this edge detection process is done, the extracted edge information is compared with the data from a generic shape database and a first selection of possible corresponding mouth shapes is done.

A few top candidates are passed to the second phase. At the second phase, a mouth shape for each candidate is extracted. Figure 2.3(b) shows how the mouth shape is calculated. The edges are searched from the center, and the edges make an approximate mouth shape. It will not make a proper shape when the candidate is not a proper mouth shape. Thus, the shape probability for each mouth candidate is calculated from the edge connection. The best shape is chosen as the current mouth position. We can then extract and guess the approximate mouth shape in real time, not only from the image but using the mouth model information from a database.

2.3.1.3 Eye Tracking

Eye tracking is considered as a combination of pupil position tracking and recognition of eyelid position. An extraction of an eyebrow position will also help to recognize the eye tracking. Thus, the eye tracking system includes the following subsystem: pupil tracking, eyelid position recognition, and eyebrow tracking. These three subsystems are deeply dependent on one another. For example, if the eyelid is closed, the pupil position is hidden, and it is obviously impossible to detect its position. We discuss a method based on a knowledge database, where

- Both pupil positions are calculated.
- Eyebrow positions are calculated.
- Eyelid positions are extracted with respect to their possible position.
- Every data is checked for the presence of movement. After this stage, inconsistencies are checked again and a new best position is chosen if necessary.

For tracking a pupil in real time, there are some problems to be solved. One is that sometimes a pupil is hidden behind an eyelid. In such a case, the object to track (a pupil) is hidden immediately. Also, the motion speed of a human eyeball is very fast compared with the image capturing speed, 60 frames per second. Thus, if the pupil tracking is lost, there are two possible reasons: one is due to the fast motion, and the other to the eyelid action. At the first stage of pupil tracking, a kind of energy is used. This value is calculated from the maximum matching probability, edge value, color similarity calculated from the image self-correlation, and position movement. A problem occurs if there is no probability of pupil position, when it is completely hidden, or if there is much less probability, when it is almost hidden. For example, with the eyelid half-closed or when the person looks up, some part of the pupil is hidden. The method will have to take into account such cases, and the energy is weighted to the appeared pupil area. This method helps to recognize the position even if the eyelid is half-closed. When the eyelid is completely closed, the position of the pupil is obviously undefined.

We use an easy algorithm to track the eyebrows. An eyebrow is defined as a small region during the initialization, and the position is roughly the center of an eyebrow. It is sometimes difficult to indicate the region of the eyebrow correctly, because some people have very thin eyebrows at both sides. Hence, we use a small region to track the position. To detect the eyebrow's shape, first a vertical line goes down from the forehead until the eyebrow is detected. The eyebrow position is given by the maximum self-correlation value of the extracted edge image. After the center of the eyebrow is found, the edge of the brow is followed to the left and right to recognize the shape. As soon as the pupil and eyebrow locations are detected using the methods described previously, it is possible to guess an eyelid location. When the probability of pupil is large or almost the same as its initial value, this means that the eye is opened. When it is small, the eye may be closed or the person is looking up. The eyebrow position narrows the possible eyelid position. This method helps detecti the true eyelid position as opposed to a possible wrong detection that may occur with a wrinkle. Thus, the method finds the strongest edge in the considered area and sets it as the eyelid. After data around the eyes are taken, they are checked again to see if they are in a normal movement compared with templates in the database. For example, if the eyes moved to the opposite direction, the next possible position of the eyes has to be calculated again. This process improves the robustness and reliability of the whole approach.

All movement data of facial feature points are converted into normalized MPEG-4 FAP (see [14]) by using the FAPUs that correspond to the region of the face that the facial feature point is in. Eventually, we obtain a complete set of FAPs that represents a facial expression.

2.3.2 Emotion and Personality Detection

In the previous section, we presented a system to track feature points on the face. We now introduce an approach to recognize facial expression.

2.3.2.1 System Description

The tracking system presented here can recognize facial expressions that the users define. Facial expressions can be defined using several basic facial action units. This greatly enhances the flexibility of a facial expression recognition system in comparison to a system that only recognizes a few template expressions [31]. The user can define his/her individual facial expressions with a GUI by combining facial action units before recognition. The layout of this GUI is shown in Fig. 2.4.

The system consists of three parts. First, an automatic initialization of the position of the facial features is performed. Then, we can obtain MPEG-4 FAP data from these features in real time with our tracking system. From the FAP data, we recognize the facial action units for the upper and the lower face. Finally, a user-specific classifier determines the facial expression that is displayed. Figure 2.5 shows an overview of the complete real-time perceptive system.

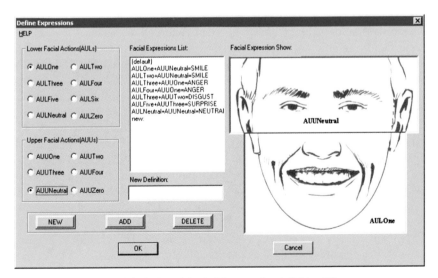

Fig. 2.4 GUI used for facial expression definition [9].

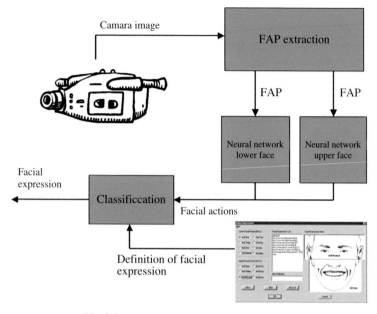

Fig. 2.5 Overview of the perceptive system [9].

2.3.2.2 Recognition of Facial Expression

One important observation of human facial expressions is that they are never exactly the same for everyone. Building a facial expression recognition system that only recognizes template facial expressions will therefore not give very satisfactory results in most cases. A second problem with these kinds of systems is that they are not easily extended to recognize additional facial expressions. Recognizing someone's facial expression needs to be done by a system tailored to this particular user. Of course, building a different facial expression recognition system for everyone is not a solution to the problem. Our system can be tailored to any user, by letting him/her define his/her facial expressions.

According to the Facial Action Coding System (FACS) [10], facial expressions consist of several facial action units. These basic building blocks are the same for everyone. Facial action units can be either upper facial action units or lower facial action units (the categories are almost independent). So if we can recognize the upper facial actions and the lower facial actions [40], we will be able to recognize the facial expressions that they consist of. Different users can indicate the upper and lower facial actions that their expressions are constructed of, using the GUI shown in Fig. 2.4. Based on this idea, we have designed our facial expression recognition system. The FAP data obtained by the facial feature tracking system are classified into four upper facial actions and six lower facial actions. This classification is done by two neural networks: one for the upper facial actions, and one for the lower facial actions. After a user has indicated which combinations of facial actions correspond to his expressions, we can easily determine the tailored facial expressions of this user from the facial actions obtained by the classified facial feature tracking data. In this method, the only information that the dialogue system gets is the conceptual information: what is the user's current expression? This data can be easily passed by a condition that can be described in XML as follows:

```
<condition type="user_expression">
joy
</condition>
```

2.4 Visyllable-based Speech Animation

In this section, we address the problem associated with visyllable-based speech animation. This approach is different than the *classical co-articulation* method used to animate lips according to a speech. This technique has great potential for application to various languages.

The system consists of two parts, an offline analysis part and a real-time synthesis part. As offline preprocessing (shown schematically in Fig. 2.6), we have motion-captured a set of English syllables. The syllables are derived from well-known phonetic literature and represent all the possible syllables in spoken English. The speaker speaks these syllable units with markers attached to her face, and an optical motion capture system outputs the 3D positions of these markers (see [30] and section 2.4.2.1 for more detail about the motion capture process).

The resulting visyllables are processed and labeled semiautomatically and stored using a compact representation of the facial movement parameters (FMPs). The FMPs are derived from the statistical analysis of the entire visyllable data. FMPs are, in fact, the basis vectors computed as a result of the principal component analysis (PCA) of the facial motion capture data. The PCA results in a reduced-dimensional

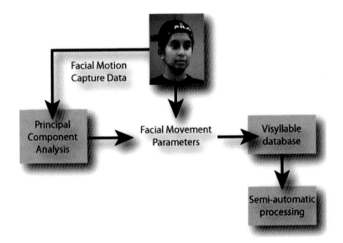

Fig. 2.6 The visyllable database using FMPs [30].

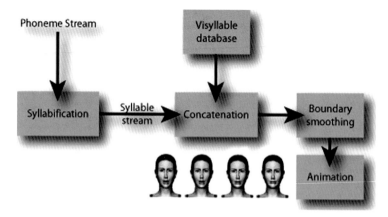

Fig. 2.7 Real-time visyllable-based speech animation.

representation of the original data by extracting the principal directions of variation. We have concluded that only eight parameters are sufficient to represent a speech posture, considerably reducing the amount of data required for the database. A visyllable is simply a time-varying trajectory of an eight-dimensional vector. However, the use of FMPs has one more significance. Each FMP represents a particular facial movement and can be assigned to be the key parameter for a class of phonemes. This feature is used in the real-time processing of the concatenated visyllables in the synthesis system (shown schematically in Fig. 2.7). The real-time synthesis system takes audio and time stamped phoneme stream as input. We automatically segment the phoneme stream into a set of syllables, a process known as syllabification. The corresponding timing information is calculated, and time-scaled visyllables are concatenated followed by boundary smoothing to generate the final animation.

2.4.1 Syllabification

Syllabification is a process of segmenting a phoneme stream into a set of syllables and clusters based on the phonological rules. We explain a syllabification algorithm based on the set of valid syllables and show how these syllables are further mapped onto the visyllables.

2.4.1.1 Valid Clusters

There are over 10,000 syllables in English, thus, it is practically impossible to use the syllable definition as it is. We use the set of valid clusters to define syllable boundaries as explained here. Given a stream of phonemes, it is a nontrivial task to extract the syllables. A meaningful syllabification should allow the breaking of a word into syllables in the most natural way, as we pronounce it. For example, the word *x-ray* can be divided into two syllables in the following ways:

1. *e-ksre*
2. *ek-sre*
3. *eks-re*
4. *eksr-e*

It is easy to see that during the pronunciation of the word, options 1 and 4 are clearly not natural. Even among options 2 and 3, though both appear equally valid, the syllable charts tell us that option 3 is the correct candidate.

Each syllable is a group of phonemes containing exactly one vowel and one or more consonants. Thus, a syllable has a maximum of three clusters or demi-syllables: an onset (group before the vowel also known as initial), a nucleus (the vowel itself), and a coda (group after the vowel also known as a final). For example, in the syllable *stim*, *st* is the onset, *i* is the nucleus, and *m* is the coda. Syllables may or may not have both an onset and a coda. We take a closer look at the clusters. They are represented by a series of letters V (referring to vowel) and C (referring to consonant). Thus, a VC cluster means a vowel followed by a consonant. Thus, seven clusters are possible in English, namely, V, VC, VCC, VCCC, CV, CCV, and CCCV. A cluster can be a monophone, a biphone, a triphone, or even a quadrphone. Of course, not any combination of Vs and Cs is possible.

There are standard charts to define valid clusters [15]. For example, a cluster *kji* is not possible in English. We believe that because there exists a most natural (if not unique) way of pronouncing a word as a sequence of syllables, this is also the best way to generate speech animation from the basic visyllable units. Our syllabification algorithm uses the basic definition of syllable and the set of valid clusters. Each word in an utterance consists of one or more syllables of the structure C^*VC^*, i.e., of a syllable nucleus (V) optionally preceded or followed, or both, by any number of consonants (C). We first locate the vowel positions. For each vowel, we search in the list of valid clusters to see which onsets and codas are possible and match the accompanying consonants in our phoneme stream. It is possible that more than one cluster is valid. For example, a stream VCCCV can be broken into VCCCV or VCC-CV. In this case, the decision is based on which group the boundary consonant lies in (explained ahead). Normally, the dissimilar consonants are grouped together, as they will have stronger co-articulation effects than similar consonants that can be smoothed in the post-processing. We note here that we apply this syllabification not only to words but also to a complete phoneme stream of a sentence, since we have no information about the word's boundaries. However, in fluent speech, co-articulation effects are observed even across the word boundaries, and hence such a syllabification is justified.

2.4.1.2 From Syllables to Visyllables

We noted previously that the number of syllables in English is too large to form a database for animation. This number is reasonably high, even after defining demi-syllables. There are about 800 initials and 1200 finals in English. However, it is easy to notice that demi-visyllables can be far less in number than demi-syllables. This is the same principle as used for the definition of visemes, and we briefly present our classification here.

In spoken English, 20 vowels are defined, as well as 24 consonants. The 20 vowels include short and long vowels (*I* in fish and *i* in tree) as well as diphthongs (*au* in owl, *aI* in bye, etc.). Doing so requires a larger number of units in the database, but ensures better results for time stretching and concatenation of visyllable units. We classify these phonemes so that subsequently the syllables can be grouped into visyllables based on which consonant forms the onset and the coda. For speech animation, it is more natural to group the phonemes according to how they appear visually when pronounced. The main classification is applied to consonants, and each vowel in fact represents its own class. This classification is based on the place and manner of articulation for the particular consonant. We have defined six different groups for consonants:

1. Glottals: articulation is at the glottis; *k*, *g*;
2. Palatals: articulation is at the palate; *ch*, *dz*, *z*, and aspirants *s*, *sh*;
3. Retroflex and dentals: articulation at the palate or back of teeth; *t*, *th*, *d*, *dh*;
4. Plosives or bilabials: articulation at the lips; *p*, *b*, and nasal *m*;
5. Labio-dental: articulation between lip and teeth, *f*, *v*;
6. Glides: *l*, *y*, *r*, *w* and nasal *n*.

As a result of such a classification, we have concluded that the total number of demi-visyllables required for our system is 900. At first glance, it still appears to be a huge number. However, with the use of FMP, the overall size of the database is quite small. Furthermore, the preparation of the database is an offline task, and with appropriate indexing and labeling tools, the formation of the database is facilitated.

2.4.2 Facial Movement Parameters

So far the two popular facial parameter sets used in computer facial animation include the FACS [13] and the MPEG-4 FAPs [14]. The FACS are inspired from the facial muscle structures. The FAPs are defined in terms of the movements of the facial feature points. However, in order to design speech animation and especially to model co-articulation effects, we believe that it is necessary to have a parameter set that clearly reflects the basic facial movements observed in fluent speech. Such a parameter set can be obtained by statistical analysis of the facial motion data. Principal component analysis (PCA) is a powerful tool for achieving this goal. Recently, Kalberer et al. [23] used the principal components (PCs) as parameters to define visemes. They used spline interpolation for key frame-based speech animation using the visemes defined by the PCs. We have previously reported the results of our analysis using the PCA that have formed the basis for this work [29]. We only briefly explain this approach and elaborate on the results that are most relevant to the visyllable-based approach.

2.4.2.1 Data Acquisition and Analysis

We used a motion capture system to acquire the analysis data. Markers are attached to the speaker's face at the locations defined by MPEG-4 feature points. The MPEG-4 feature points are optimum for defining the animation; furthermore, they also facilitate obtaining the MPEG-4 FAP animation to help directly visualize the results on a synthetic MPEG-4 compliant face [27]. We use 17 markers in total; 8 along the lip contour, 4 on the cheeks, 2 on the chin, and 3 on the nose. The speaker speaks all the possible demi-syllables in spoken English, and global head movements are compensated to obtain the 3D positions of the markers. In fact, the same data used to build the visyllable database are used for analysis. A subsequent PCA on this 3D marker position data results a new space referred to as the expression and viseme space [29]. The basis vectors of this space are the PCs, which represent the principal variation in the data—the speech-related facial movement data in our case.

2.4.2.2 Principal Components as FMPs

In general, principal components do not represent any real-life parameters. We notice, however, that, for the facial capture data, they are closely related to facial movements. As we change one PC at a time, keeping all others at a neutral position, we can easily establish the role of each parameter. The lower-order components do not contribute much to the deliberate facial movements. Since each PC can be attributed to a specific facial movement, hereafter we use the more specific FMP for the PCs. Indeed, each PC can be visualized as a parameter to define a particular facial movement. Figure 2.8 shows the influence of the first six FMPs. We also note the consonant group for which each of the FMP is a key parameter. This was observed by computing the percentage variation of the individual FMPs across all the captured demi-syllables of types VC and CV. The parameter having the maximum variation for a particular group was assigned as the key parameter for that group.

- **FMP1 Open Mouth**: This parameter results in the global movement of the opening of the jaw; a slight rotation of the jaw forcing the lips to part. This is by far the most common facial movement necessary for many phoneme pronunciations. For the consonant group 1, this is the most important parameter.

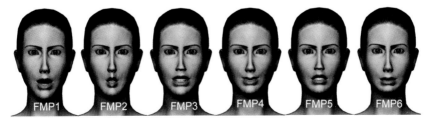

Fig. 2.8 PCs as Facial Movement Parameters (FMPs).

- **FMP2 Pucker Lips**: This movement causes the lips to form a rounded shape, necessary for pronunciation of vowels such as /o/ and /u/. It is a key parameter for consonant groups 2 and 3. This also causes the protrusion of the lips.

- **FMP3 Part Lips**: It causes separation between the lips, without opening the jaw. In the other direction, this causes pressing of lips against each other. The movement is local to the lips and does not affect the cheek region much. FMP3 is a key parameter for consonant groups 4 and 5.

- **FMP4 Raise Cornerlips**: This movement causes the vertical movement of the corner of the lips, resulting in a smiling action that slightly parts the lips. In the other direction, it causes depressing of the corner lips. It is important for consonant group 6.

- **FMP5 Raise Upperlip**: This movement causes movement of the upper lip and, combined with FMP3, can be used to control the lower lip movement, which does not have a separate parameter associated with it. Notice the change in the nose shape because of the change in the upper lip (exaggerated here) that is also observed in real life.

- **FMP6 Protrude Lowerlip**: This is a peculiar movement, causing the curling of the lower lip and slight raising of the chin. Though FMP 5 and 6 are not particularly important for any specific vowel or consonant group, they add realism to the appearance of all the visemes.

We observed that nearly 99% of the variation has been accommodated in only the first eight principal components. The FMP7 and FMP8 are combinations of the first six FMPs and do not have any particular significance. However, they are important for complete definition of any speech posture. Thus, each frame of a visyllable unit is represented as an 8-dimensional vector, reducing the amount of data in the visyllable database. Furthermore, each FMP is significant for a group of consonants. The importance of this classification for concatenating visyllables especially at consonant boundaries is explained in Section 2.4.4.

2.4.3 The Visyllable Database

We now explain the actual data capture and post-processing so that the resulting visyllable database can be used in the automatic concatenation of the visyllable units in the real-time speech animation system. Once we define a list of valid demisyllables, it is rather straightforward to capture them using a facial motion capture system. The optical motion capture system directly results in the 3D position of the feature points attached to the speaker's face. The important step in the system is the processing of the captured data. We perform this semiautomatically. With the help of interactive tools, the user segments the demi-visyllables manually. This is done by picking the points on the timeline to define the demi-syllable boundaries. Individual demi-visyllables are then segmented and stored in separate files after labeling. On average, this process takes about 5 minutes for each demi-visyllable.

We follow the labeling by boundary matching. It is ensured that the trajectories of all the FMPs match the the end of the onset (CV) and at the beginning of the coda (VC) constituting the same vowel. Initially, all the demi-visyllables ending with the same vowel are analyzed and normalized to have the same boundary values for all the FMPs. Then, this same boundary value is used for all the demi-visyllables beginning with that vowel. For example, the demi-visyllables *pa, ka, ra*, etc. are matched at the end. This is done by performing a stretch operation. The segment is stretched or compressed in amplitude, keeping the beginning or the endpoint unchanged. This preserves the overall shape of the demi-visyllable, but changes the span. Then the demi-visyllables *ap, ak, ar*, etc. are analyzed to match their beginning to the previously adjusted demi-visyllables. This is also done interactively and the user is presented the results for visual inspection of the concatenated elements CV-VC. As a result, all the vowel boundaries in all the demi-visyllables are matched for continuity and smoothness. In rare cases, certain adjustments have to be done manually. This is done interactively by adjusting the FMP trajectories. This process reduces the real-time processing of demi-visyllables to a great extent and also improves the smoothness of the resulting animation during the synthesis phase. Furthermore, the vowel boundaries of the demi-visyllables in fact represent the nucleus of the visyllables; it is important that they are continuous by definition. It is possible to perform the boundary matching for consonants as well. However, in a syllable, the consonants are affected by the nucleus of the syllable differently in each case.

2.4.4 Stitching Together

Once we have done the boundary matching for the vowels in the database, we analyzed the effects of concatenation with various examples. The input phoneme stream is divided into a demi-syllable stream and subsequently a syllable stream. The individual demi-visyllables from the database are time-warped to match the required length from the input phoneme stream. The time-warped demi-visyllables are concatenated, and the resulting animation is analyzed. The analysis is done by visual inspection of the resulting animation as well as analysis of the FMP trajectories. We found that even though much work has been done in the processing of the database, post-concatenation processing is required for smoothness. However, there is no general filtering or smoothing method that could suit well for different boundary problems. We thus treated each problem separately and formulated certain rules and procedures for post-processing and boundary smoothing of the concatenated FMP trajectories.

There are mainly two types of problems at the concatenation boundary. One is the absolute value continuity, or C0 continuity. Second is the C1 continuity or matching rate of change of parameters at the boundaries. We first ensure the C0 continuity by computing all the gaps and automatically performing shift and stretch operations on individual visyllable segments to nullify the gaps. We observed two types of gaps across the demi-visyllable boundaries. In the first case, the entire segment needs a shift in order to be continuous with the previous and the subsequent segments.

This is when the boundary gap on either side of the segment is more or less of the same magnitude and no significant amplitude stretching is required after the shift. This shift operation is performed in the first pass of our algorithm. As a result, all the segments that need such a shift are adjusted for each FMP. The shift operation preserves the overall shape and hence the characteristic of the visyllable unit, which is important for realism. However, in the second case, on one boundary the trajectory is continuous, while on the other boundary it is not. Thus, a stretch operation needs to be performed for boundary matching. We can perform the stretch operation of the segment so that one end of the segment is unaffected, whereas the other end of the segment is stretched to a new target position and the stretch required is distributed equally across the segment. However, it becomes necessary to decide which segment (segment on the left side of the boundary or on the right side) is stretched. Here we use the FMP knowledge. The segment for which the FMP under consideration is the key parameter remains unaffected, whereas the other demi-visyllable is stretched. If both consonants at the boundary belong to the same group (which is quite rare), the gap is equally distributed to both segments and both segments are stretched. This criterion improved the realism of the resulting animation.

There is an additional constraint for such a stretch operation. The most important factors are to preserve the shape of the visyllable segment and not let the amount of stretch cause any distortion. This is ensured by restricting the stretch to less than the total span of the syllable unit. For example, if the maximum and minimum values of a visyllable unit are x, then the maximum stretch is restricted to $0.75x$. This value was decided experimentally. Finally, after all the boundary smoothing operations, about 5–10% of boundaries still require additional smoothing. These are the cases where the FMP value continuity is obtained by the shift and stretch operation, but there is a sudden change in the rate of change of the FMP, causing a sharp peak or cusp. In this case, we perform a smoothing operation similar to the traditional co-articulation method. Both the segments are stretched by 10% of the length to overlap, and an exponentially decaying envelop is applied to each across the boundary. A simple average is carried out to get the final smooth trajectory. This approach, we found, works quite well in the final stages of the concatenation algorithm.

Considering different possibilities of the boundary mismatch, we have compiled all the sets of rules for smoothing of the FMP trajectories. This processing forms an important part of the synthesis system. The observed boundary mismatch can be minimized by careful design and processing of the visyllable database. However, even when the visyllable units in the database are not perfectly matched, the smoothing operations result in satisfactory animation.

2.5 Real-Time Dialogue Systems

We have previously developed an autonomous virtual human dialogue system in which the personality of the virtual human was modeled by transition probability matrices [32]. Emotional tags embedded in the dialogue database were used to generate facial expressions. In this section, we present a more general multiplayer framework for modeling personality. We do not focus on a specific application, but this model could be adapted to several applications in games, entertainment, and communication in virtual environments. We implement the Five Factor Model using a Bayesian Belief network. We also discuss a layered approach to personality modeling (Personality-Moods-Emotions). This approach not only makes the system implementation modular but enables the easy and quick design of virtual humans. We enable a complete design of personality, focusing on emotional personification.

2.5.1 Definition of Multilayered Personality

Personality is a characteristic of a virtual human that distinguishes it from others. Emotion is analogous to a state of mind that is only momentary. Mood is a prolonged state of mind, resulting from a cumulative effect of emotions. We now give a brief overview of the models used to realize these concepts. The discussion is based on well-known literature in psychology, cognitive science, and artificial intelligence. It is included here not only for the sake of completeness, but also to indicate how we incorporate these aspects in the discussed system. In order to model the personality of autonomous virtual humans, we must study the personality modeling from the viewpoint of psychology as well as computation. There are various obvious and not so obvious aspects directly linked to personality. They include the choice of language, style of talking, gestures, and thinking process. We focus here on the emotional behavior of the virtual human as a function of personality.

2.5.1.1 Personality

In psychology, the Five Factor Model (FFM) [34, 8] of personality is one of the most recent models proposed. The model was proposed not only for a general understanding of human behavior but also for psychologists to treat personality disorders. The five factors are considered to be the basis or dimensions of the personality space (see Table 2.1).

Table 2.1 Five personality dimensions.

Factor	Description	Adjectives used to describe
Extraversion	Preference for and behavior in social situations	Talkative, energetic, social
Agreeableness	Interactions with others	Trusting, friendly, cooperative
Conscientiousness	Organized, persistent in achieving goals	Methodical, wellorganized, dutiful
Neuroticism	Tendency to experience negative thoughts	Insecure, emotionally distressed
Openness	Open-mindedness, interest in culture	Imaginative, creative, explorative

All these dimensions of personality are closely related to the expressional, logical, and emotional personification to varying degrees. For example, extraversion affects the logical behavior (choice of linguistic expressions), whereas neuroticism affects the emotional behavior more closely. Nevertheless, we prefer using all the dimensions in the model, even though the focus is on emotional personality. Since the model states that these five factors form the basis of the personality space, one should be able to represent any personality as a combination of these factors.

Emotions and Expressions

By emotion, we understand a particular state of mind that is reflected visually by way of facial expression. Hence, though we use emotion and expression as two different words, conceptually, we refer to the same thing by either of them. We use the emotion categories proposed by the model of Ortony, Clore, and Collins [35], commonly known as the OCC model. The model categorizes various emotion types based on the positive or negative reactions to events, actions, and objects. The OCC model defines 22 such emotions. Table 2.2 shows these emotions with high-level categorization (positive and negative). The OCC model also describes how the intensities of the emotions are governed by internal as well as external factors. We do not currently use the cognitive processing specified by the OCC model. However, the use of the emotions specified by the OCC model facilitates the integration of a dialogue module that can generate emotions depending upon the semantics and context.

Ekman [11] defined six basic facial expressions that are recognized as universal by many facial expression and emotion researchers. These basic expressions are joy, sadness, anger, surprise, fear, and disgust. They are very useful for facial animation and can be combined to obtain other expressions. There is a partial overlap between the expressions proposed by Ekman and the ones stated by the OCC model. Only four expressions (joy, sadness, fear, and anger) are defined in the OCC model. Surprise and disgust do not find place in the OCC model, mainly because they do not involve much cognitive processing and do not correspond to valenced reactions. However, we find them important for the expressiveness of the virtual human in a conversation system. The emotions defined by the OCC model are too many in

Table 2.2 Basic emotions

Positive Emotions	Negative Emotions
Happy-for	Resentment
Gloating	Pity
Joy	Distress
Pride	Shame
Admiration	Reproach
Love	Hate
Hope	Fear
Satisfaction	Fear-confirmed
Relief	Disappointment
Gratification	Remorse
Gratitude	Anger

Table 2.3 Basic emotions grouped

Joy	Happy-for, Gloating, Joy, Pride, Admiration, Love, Hope, Satisfaction, Relief, Gratification, Gratitude
Sadness	Resentment, Pity, Distress, Shame, Remorse
Anger	Anger, Reproach, Hate
Surprise	Surprise
Fear	Fear, Fear-confirmed
Disgust	Disgust

number to directly use in the computation of emotional states. At the same time, they are important and necessary for making the dialogue rich with expressions.

We attach 24 emotions (22 defined by the OCC model, with surprise and disgust as additional emotions) to the dialogue sentences in the form of tags. To reduce the computational complexity, we use only six basic expressions to represent the emotional states. These basic expressions are used as a layer between visible facial expressions and invisible mood, described ahead. In order to facilitate the link between these two levels, we recategorize the 24 emotions into 6 expression groups (see Table 2.3). This modification in the emotion structure enables us to handle a relatively lower number of emotional states while still retaining the completeness necessary for expressive conversation.

Mood

The FFM describes the personality, but it is still a high-level description. We need to link the personality with displayed emotions that are visible on the virtual face. This is difficult to do unless we introduce a layer between the personality and the expressions. This layer, we observe, is nothing but mood. We clearly distinguish between mood and personality. Personality causes deliberative reactions, which in turn cause the mood to change. According to Velasquez [41], moods and emotions are only differentiated in terms of levels of arousal. However, we define mood as a conscious and prolonged state of mind that directly controls the emotions and hence the facial expressions. Mood is also affected by momentary emotions as a cumulative effect. Thus, mood is affected from the level above it (personality) as well as the level below it (emotional state). The expressions can exist for a few seconds or even shorter, whereas mood persists for a larger timeframe. The personality, on the highest level, exists and influences expressions as well as moods, on a much broader time scale. This relation is shown graphically in Fig. 2.9.

To summarize, the following relations are made between the layers:

1. Personality practically does not change over time. It causes deliberative reaction and affects how moods change in a dialogue over time.
2. Mood, from a higher level, is affected by the personality, and it is also affected from the lower level by emotional states.
3. On the lowest level, the instantaneous emotional state, which is directly linked with the displayed expressions, is influenced by mood as well as the current dialogue state.

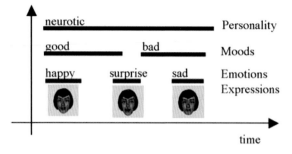

Fig. 2.9 Layered approach to personality modeling [28].

The emotion layer is further subdivided into two layers as explained previously. However, this is more of computational convenience than semantic distinction.

Considering the FFM, we observe that agreeableness, neuroticism, and extraversion are the most important dimensions of the personality, as far as emotions are concerned. A neurotic person will change moods often, and tend to go into a negative mood easily. On the other hand, an extraverted person will tend to shift to a positive mood quickly in a conversation. An agreeable person will tend to go into positive mood more often, but frequent mood changes may not be shown.

Having emphasized the importance of mood in personality modeling, we find that it is difficult to clearly distinguish all the possible various moods. We did not find sufficient literature in psychology for analysis and classification of moods and mood changes in a systematic manner. Hence, we propose to categorize mood simply into two basic categories, namely, good and bad. So the emotions categorized by the OCC model under the negative group (anger, hate, shame, etc.) are more likely to be expressed when in a bad mood. However, it may be possible that our mood forbids us from being expressive. We call this a neutral mood. In this mood, the virtual human will tend not to change its displayed expression easily and will tend to express itself with less intensity.

Bayesian Belief Network

Knowing the emotional personality definitions and emotion classifications, it could be possible to write rules mapping personality to emotional states. However, such rule-based systems are unlikely to succeed in simulating believable behaviors, mainly because uncertainty is an important aspect of human behavior. Thus, we need a computational model that can handle uncertainty while retaining the underlying principles. The Bayesian Belief Network (BBN) is the natural choice as it is used to model domains containing uncertainty [37]. Syntactically, it is a directed acyclic graph, where each node represents a state variable with mutually exclusive and independent states. The directed links represent the influence of the parent node on the child node. For each child node, a conditional probability table defines how its states are affected for each combination of possible states of the parent node. Thus, the effects (children) of the causes (parents) are encoded probabilistically into the definition of the BBN. How to initialize the transition probability values, to clearly represent the causes-and-effect relationship for a particular application, is altogether a different topic of research. For our application, we set the conditional probability values by intuition. The BBN is particularly suitable for modeling complex phenomena such as personality because of the following reasons:

1. It handles uncertainty powerfully, which is evident in its evolution of emotions.
2. It gives a structured probabilistic framework to represent and calculate otherwise very complex and rather abstract concepts related to emotions, moods, and personality.

Ball et al. [3] previously reported the use of the BBN for personality and emotion modeling. The main difference in their approach and the presented one is that we try to use the FFM of personality to devise a way of combining personalities and also to introduce an additional layer of "mood" in the model.

2.5.1.2 System Overview

In this section, we present an overview of the emotional virtual human system that we have developed. Figure 2.10 shows the various components of the system and their interactions. For the expressional personification, we use MPEG-4 Facial Animation Parameters and the real-time facial animation system using FAPs [27].

A text processing and response generation module processes the input text; in our case it is the chat-robot ALICE [1]. ALICE uses Artificial Intelligence Markup Language (AIML), which is an XML-based language, to define the dialogue database. We define the AIML database such that the emotional tags are embedded

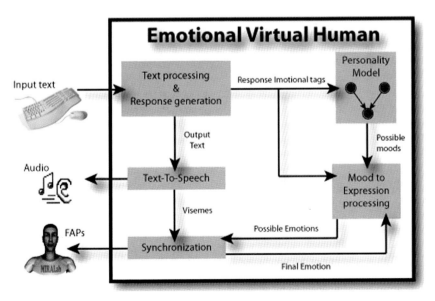

Fig. 2.10 A system overview [28].

in the responses. The emotional tags have probability values associated with them. These emotional tags are passed on to the personality model, which is a BBN. The personality model, depending upon the current mood and the input emotional tags, updates the mood. As mood is relatively stable over time, mood switching is thus not a frequent task. Depending upon the output of the personality model, mood processing is done to determine the next emotional state. This processing determines the probabilities of the possible emotional states. Though the system uses emotion tags in dialogues for evolving emotions based on mood and personality, it is possible to link the model with an affective reasoner, which can provide similar tags for emotion appraisal. The personality and mood model can process emotional tags irrespective of the process that derived them. The synchronization module analyzes previous facial expression displayed and outputs probabilities of the mood processing. It determines the expression to be rendered with appropriate time envelopes. It also generates lip movements from the visemes generated by the Text-To-Speech engine. Finally, it applies blending functions to output the facial animation parameters depicting "expressive speech." We use the technique described in [29] for this. A separate facial animation module renders the FAPs in synchrony with the speech sound.

Text Processing and Reponse Generation

All the AIML categories are not such strict matches. AIML uses various tags to introduce randomness in answers, to remember limited dialogue history, and to allow symbolic reduction. Though ALICE does not use any syntactic or semantic language analysis techniques, the features embedded in AIML and ALICE make the chat robot much more than a mere pattern matching program operating on a set of possible inputs and answers. It can engage the user in believable conversation to a considerable degree. Though originally designed for merely a chat application, AIML can be generated to tackle a particular domain queries from the user, e.g., a sales assistant or a virtual receptionist. For a complete description of AIML, interested readers are referred to [1].

   We notice that the current state of natural language processing does not allow us to relate dialogue with emotions easily and generally. Hence, we extend AIML to incorporate emotional tags in the responses. Each response may be associated with one or more emotional tags. These tags essentially represent the possible emotional state of the virtual human while rendering the particular response. Currently, we use the 24 emotional tags as explained previously. However, it is easily possible to extend this list. It could be useful to introduce bored, thinking, and frustration as new tags belonging to sad, neutral, and anger expression categories respectively. Consider a particular response: "I am very busy nowadays." This response can be associated with pride or distress. Subsequently, we can associate probability values to these possible emotions. For this particular response sentence, the probability of pride is set to 30% and that of distress is 70%. The corresponding AIML category looks like the following:

```
<category>
<pattern>What are you doing?</pattern>
<template><emo name="pride" prob="30"><emo name="distress"
    prob="70">
I am very busy nowadays.</template>
</category>
```

The introduction of emotional tags is not a trivial task. It is necessary to imagine various situations that may give rise to various emotions according to the meaning of the response sentence. A response like "I am happy to hear that" can mostly be associated with emotional tag joy with 100% probability. This ensures higher probability of joy being expressed finally as a result of the emotion-processing pipeline. We subsequently explain how these tags and corresponding probabilities are processed by the personality and mood model to generate the final emotional state. In order to facilitate introducing a variety of emotional tags with each and every possible response, we have developed an interactive tool enabling easy and quick design of "emotional" AIML. For improving the naturalness of the dialogue, we propose further modification in AIML. Instead of attaching different emotions to a single response, while creating the AIML database, we input different responses corresponding to different emotions. For example, a typical modified AIML category will look like the following:

```
<category>
  <pattern>How are you?</pattern>
  <template>
   <emo name="joy" prob="50" res="I am fine, thank you.">
   <emo name="sadness" prob="50" res="Not so good today!">
  </template>
</category>
```

The emotional tags are processed by the personality and mood processing modules. Subsequently, the processing will result into not only appropriate emotion, but also a selection of the speech response analogous to the emotion. In the future, it is possible to replace ALICE with a more sophisticated language analysis module. Such a module should create the emotional tags depending upon the semantics, context, and dialogue history of the conversation, in a more coherent way.

2.5.2 Dialogue Manager

A number of modules are available that provide for extra flexibility of the system.

Input Module. This module compares an input string to a predefined pattern. It is related to a condition that evolves to *true* or *false* defining whether or not a string follows the pattern.

Output Module. This module consists of an action that produces text output. The text can be formatted in different way and includes support for XML tags.

Emotion Module. The emotion module handles the relation between the emotional state and the running dialogue. From the dialogue, the emotional state can be updated. Also, conditions are defined that indicate if a certain emotion is above or below a given threshold, thus allowing for different behavior according to different emotional states.

User Profile Module. The goal of this module is to maintain information about the user, such as name, age, and so on. Also, it can serve as an interface between automatic facial expression and emotion tracker.

The dialogue manager generates responses that are tagged using XML. These tags indicate where a gesture should stard and end. There are many different representation languages for multimodal content, for example, Rich Representation Language (RRL) [26] or Virtual Human Markup Language (VHML) [42]. We will now give an example of how such a representation language can be used to control gesture sequences in the presented system. For testing purposes, we have defined a simple tag structure that allows for the synchronized playback of speech and nonverbal behavior. An example of a tagged sentence looks like this:

```
<begin_gesture id="g1" anim="shake_head"/>Unfortunately, I
have <begin_gesture id="g2" anim="raise_shoulders"/> no idea
<end_gesture id="g2"/> what you are talking about. <end_
gesture id="g1"/>
```

Within each gesture tag, an animation ID is provided. When the gesture animation is created, these animations are loaded from the database of gesture— also called a Gesticon [26]—and are blended using a blending engine. The timing information is obtained from the Text-To-Speech system. The animation system only activates actions at given times with specified animation lengths and blending parameters.

2.5.2.1 From Dialogue to Facial Animation

In this section, we present the techniques used to create the facial animation from the output text and speech. The output text is first converted into speech signal by the Text-To-Speech engine. At the basic level, speech consists of different phonemes. These phonemes can be used to generate the accompanying facial motions, since every phoneme corresponds to a different lip position. The lip positions related to the phonemes are called *visemes*. There are not as many visemes as phonemes, because some phonemes revert to the same mouth position. For example, the Microsoft Speech SDK defines 49 phonemes but only 21 different visemes. For each viseme, the mouth position is designed using the MPEG-4 FAPs. Constructing the facial motion is achieved by sequencing the different mouth position, taking into account the speech timing obtained from the TTS engine. An important issue to take into consideration when creating facial speech is co-articulation, or the overlapping of phonemes/visemes. Generally, co-articulation is handled by defining a dominance function for each viseme. For example, Cohen and Massaro [5] use this technique and define an exponential dominance function. Similarly, we use the following base function to construct the co-articulation curve:

$$f(x) = e^{-ax} - x.e^{-\alpha}, \tag{2.1}$$

where $0 < \alpha < \infty$. The parameter α governs the shape of the curve. Because of the generic structure of the animation engine , it is a simple task to create the facial animation from the viseme timing information. We define a blending action for each viseme, where the dominance function acts as the weight curve. The blending schedule containing the different blending actions will then automatically perform the viseme blending.

Next to facial speech animation, also any facial gestures need to be added, defined as tags in the text. An example of an eyebrow-raising facial gesture could be defined as follows:

```
Are you <begin_gesture id="g1" anim="raise_eyebrows"/>
really sure about that ? <end_gesture id="g1"/>
```

In addition to the facial gesture derived from the tagged text, the emotional state is also shown on the face by mapping the expression onto one of the six facial expressions defined by Ekman [11]. The intensity of the emotion is included by applying a corresponding scaling factor in the blending parameters. Finally, a face blinking generator is added for increased realism. Each face animation track has different weights for the FAPs. The speech animation has a higher weight on the mouth area, whereas the face expression weights are higher on the eye and eyebrow area. By blending the different facial animation tracks, the final animation is obtained.

2.6 Conclusion

2.6.1 Real-Time Video Tracking

Section 2.3.1 discussed a method to track facial features in real time. This recognition method for facial expressions does not use any special markers or makeup. It does not need training but a simple initialization of the system allowing the new user to adapt immediately. Extracted data are transformed into MPEG-4 FAPs that can be used easily for any compatible facial animation system.

2.6.2 Visyllable-based Speech Animation

One may ask what is the difference between a triphone-based approach and a demi-syllable-based approach. First, a demi-syllable can be a biphone, a triphone, or even a quadraphone. Second, as all the vowel boundaries of the demi-visyllables are normalized during the processing of the database, concatenating along the vowel boundaries is ensured to impart smooth results. Third, the co-articulation effect along the syllable boundaries is known to be weak. Thus, demi-syllable-based interpolation is justified.

We would like to highlight the strengths of the visyllable-based speech animation system:

- It is a more general and powerful approach as compared to the context-independent co-articulation algorithms. Through a complete visyllable database, all the known co-articulation effects are accounted for.
- With the help of compact representation using the Facial Movement Parameters, we observe that the data required for a complete English speech animation system are reasonably small.
- Furthermore, this method can be used for real-time as well as non-real-time high-end productions of facial animation.

The technique has great potential for application to various languages, especially Asian languages such as Indian and Japanese, which have a built-in phonetic script and pronunciation structure. In the future, we would like to continue to investigate this methodology with more perceptive tests and applicability to various languages. We would like to devise a more generalized and robust boundary smoothing algorithm. We intend to draw inspiration from concatenative speech synthesis systems in which such boundary smoothing and trajectory matching algorithms are employed for increased quality of speech. We feel that the fields of phonetics and phonology have a lot more to offer to the speech animation research.

2.6.3 Real-Time Dialogue Systems

We have prepared a dialogue scenario that best shows the strength of the model. We simulate a conversation between a manager and his virtual assistant. Since our focus is to demonstrate change in emotions governed by dialogue content as well as personality, we have designed the dialogue with many possibilities for emotions. For each possible input, we encode various possible responses attributed to different emotional states. From these possibilities, the personality and mood processing modules select the final response. Indeed, designing such a general AIML is a painstaking task. With the availability of an intelligent dialogue system capable of generating various possibilities depending upon the context, the need for creating such an AIML would be eliminated.

We have designed two contrasting personalities, agreeable and neurotic. We have chosen to model these traits because they are clearly distinguishable mainly from emotional behavior and facial expressions. In the beginning of the conversation, the moods of both personalities are set to neutral. The inputs appear on the screen as typed text. The mood change is also seen on the left corner of the frame. The agreeable personality tends to be pleasant. The neurotic personality, on the other hand, tends to change to a bad mood more easily. However, note that a good mood does not always mean a smiling face. Since both the mood and emotion computations are probabilistic, the final expressions may not be exactly the same each time we run the dialogue. However, the overall trend of the mood changes is similar. Figure 2.11 shows the snapshots from the animation depicting various facial expressions during the conversation.

Apart from the lack of an intelligent dialogue system, we are aware of several aspects for further improvement. Integration of a real-time speech recognizer will considerably add to the usability. Furthermore, controlling voice intonation and talking speed according to emotions would bring out the real expressiveness of the character. Development of such modules or the integration of such already available modules remains an important future task for the completion of the system. Within these limitations, the effectiveness of the multilayer personality model is evident. It is also a challenging but interesting task to fine-tune the conditional probabilities of the personality Bayesian Belief Networks and mood transition probability matrices. We have identified the need for thorough experimentation by users and researchers from various backgrounds. The system has great potential to be used by the emotion researchers and psychologists to study and validate the model and make improvements.

To conclude, we have presented a system incorporating a personality model for an emotional autonomous virtual human that covers the following important aspects:

- Many concepts are brought together from psychology, artificial intelligence, and cognitive science to create a layered model of human personality directly affecting the emotional and expressional behavior.
- A user is able to design personalities for virtual humans as a combination of five basic factors. Furthermore, the user can define moods for a virtual human and dictated how these moods affect the emotional state and displayed expressions.

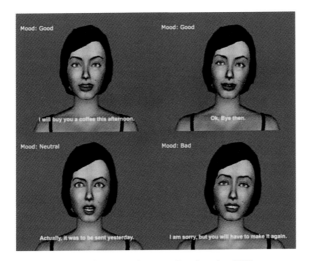

Fig. 2.11 Expressive speech animation [28].

- The model has been integrated with a chat system, demonstrating the potential use of such a model in a real-life system enabling believable communication with a virtual human in a natural language.

References

1. ALICE A.I. Foundation: http://www.alicebot.org/.
2. Andre, E., Klesen, M., Gebhard, P., Allen, S., Rist, T.: Integrating models of personality and emotions into lifelike characters. In *Workshop on Affect in Interactions* (1999) 136–149.
3. Ball, G., Breese, J.: Emotion and personality in a conversational character. In *Workshop on Embodied Conversational Characters* (1998) 83–84.
4. Bregler, C., Covell, M., Slaney, M.: Video rewrite: Driving visual speech with audio. In *SIG-GRAPH 97 Annual Conference Series 31* (1997) 353–360.
5. Cohen, M.M., Massaro, D. W.: Modeling coarticulation in synthetic visual speech. In *Models and Techniques in Computer Animation* (1993) 139–156.
6. Cosatto, E., Graf, H.P.: Sample-based synthesis of photo-realistic talking heads. In *Computer Animation* (1998) 103–110.
7. DeCarlo, D., Metaxas, D.: Optical flow constraints on deformable models with applications to face tracking. In CIS Technical Report MS-CIS-97-23.
8. Digman, J. M.: Personality structure: Emergence of the five factor model. In *Annual Review of Psychology* (1990) 417–440.
9. Egges A., Zhang X., Kshirsagar S., Magnenat-Thalmann, N.: Emotional communication with virtual humans; In *Multimedia Modelling, Taiwan* (2003).
10. Ekman, P., Friesen, W.V.: Facial action coding system: Investigators guide. *Consulting Psychologists Press*, Palo Alto, CA (1978).
11. Ekman, P.: Emotion in the human face, In Cambridge University Press, (1982).
12. El-Nasr, M.S., Ioerger, T.R., Yen, J.: PETEEI: A PET with evolving emotional intelligence. In *Autonomous Agents'99* (1999), 9–15.
13. Friesen, E.: Facial action coding system: A technique for the measurement of facial movement. In *Consulting Psychologists Press* Palo Alto, CA (1978).
14. Garchery, S., Boulic, R., Capin, T., Kalra, P.: Standards for virtual humans. In N. Magnenat-Thalmann and D. Thalmann, editors, *Handbook of Virtual Humans*, Chapter 16, pages 373–391. John Wiley and Sons, Hoboken, NJ, (2004).
15. Gimson, A.C.: An introduction to the pronunciation of english. Edward Arnold Ltd (1983).
16. Goto, T., Escher, M., Zanardi, C., Magnenat-Thalmann, N.: MPEG-4 based animation with face feature tracking. In *Eurographics Workshop on Computer Animation and Simulation* (1999) 89–98.
17. Goto, T., Kshirsagar, S., Magnenat-Thalmann, N.: Real-time facial feature tracking and speech acquisition for cloned head. In *IEEE Signal Processing Magazine* (2001) Vol. 18, No. 3, 17–25.
18. Hamaker, J., Ganapathiraju, A., Picone, J., Godfrey, J.: Advances in alphadigit recognition using syllables. In *IEEE International Conference on Acoustics, Speech and Signal Processing*, (1998) 421–424.
19. Huang, F.S., Cosatto, E., Graf, H.P.: Triphone based unit selection for concatenative visual speech synthesis. In *IEEE International Conference on Acoustics, Speech and Signal Processing(2)*, (2002) 2037–2040.
20. Jones, R.J., Downey, S., Mason, J.S.: Continuous speech recognition using syllables. In *Eurospeech97*, (1997) 1171–1174.
21. Johns, M., Silverman, B.G.: How emotions and personality effect the utility of alternative decisions: a terrorist target selection case study In *Tenth Conference on Computer Generated Forces and Behavioral Representation* (2001).

22. Kahn, D.: Syllable-based generalizations in English phonology. In Masters Thesis, Indiana University (1976).
23. Kalberer, G., Van Gool, L.: Face animation based on observed 3D speech dynamics. In *IComputer Animation*, IEEE Computer Society (2001) 20–27.
24. Kiraz, G., Mobius, B.: Multilingual syllabification using weighted finite-state transducers. In *Third ESCA Workshop on Speech Synthesis* (1998).
25. Kouadio, C., Poulin, P., Lachapelle, P.: Real-time facial animation based upon a bank of 3D facial expressions. In *Computer Animation* (1999) 128–136.
26. Krenn, B., Pirker, H.: Defining the gesticon: Language and gesture coordination for interacting embodied agents. In *Proceedings of the AISB-2004 Symposium on Language, Speech and Gesture for Expressive Characters* (2004) 107–115.
27. Kshirsagar, S., Garchery, S., Magnenat-Thalmann, N.: Feature point based mesh deformation applied to MPEG-4 facial animation. In *Deformable Avatars*, Kluwer Academic Press (2001) 24–34.
28. Kshirsagar, S., Magnenat-Thalmann, N.: A multilayer personality model. In *International Symposium on Smart Graphics* (2002) 107–115.
29. Kshirsagar, S., Molet, M., Magnenat-Thalmann, N.: Principal components of expressive speech animation. In *Computer Graphics International* (2001) 38–44.
30. Kshirsagar, S., Magnenat-Thalmann, N.: Visyllable based speech animation. In *Proceedings Eurographics*, Granada, Spain (2003).
31. Lien, J.J., Kanade T., Cohn J.F., Li, C.C.: Automated facial expression recognition based on FACS action units. In *Proceedings International Conference Automatic Face and Gesture Recognition* (1998).
32. Magnenat-Thalmann, N., Kshirsagar, S.: Communicating with autonomous virtual humans. In *Workshop on Language Technology* (2000) 1–8.
33. Marsella, S., Gratch, J.: A step towards irrationality: Using emotion to change belief. In *Proceedings of the 1st International Joint Conference on Autonomous Agents and Multi-Agent Systems*, Bologna, Italy (2002).
34. McCrae, R.R., John, O.P.: An introduction to the fivefactor model and its applications. In *Special Issue: The Fivefactor Model: Issues and Applications. Journal of Personality 60* (1992) 175–215.
35. Ortony, A., Gerald, L. Clore, G.L., Collins, A.: The cognitive structure of emotions. In Cambridge University Press (1988).
36. Pandzic, I., Capin, T., Magnenat-Thalmann, N., Thalmann, D.: Towards natural communication in networked collaborative virtual environments. In *FIVE* (1996).
37. Pearl, J.: Probabilistic reasoning in intelligent systems: Networks of plausible inference. In Morgan Kauffman Publishers Inc., San Fransisco, CA (1988).
38. Pelachaud, C., Badler, N., Steedman, M.: Generating facial expressions for speech. In *Cognitive Science, 20(1)*, (1996) 1–46.
39. Picard R.: Affective Computing. The MIT Press, Cambridge, MA (1998).
40. Tian, Y.L., Kanade, T., Cohn, J.F.: Recognizing action units for facial expression analysis. In *IEEE Trans. on Pattern Analysis and Machine Intelligence* (2001) 23(2).
41. Velasquez, J.D.: Modeling emotions and other motivations in synthetic agents. In *Proceedings AAAI-97* (1997) 10–15.
42. Virtual human markup language (vhml) http://www.vhml.org.

Chapter 3
Data-Driven Expressive Speech Animation Synthesis and Editing

Zhigang Deng and Ulrich Neumann

3.1 Introduction

The synthesis of compelling facial animations remains one of the most challenging topics in the computer graphics community, because humans are super sensitive to the subtleties of moving human faces. In the entertainment industry, animators often manually create key-frame faces every two or three frames, which is a painstaking and tedious task even for skilled animators.

In this chapter, we present a novel data-driven *e*xpressive *F*acial *A*nimation *S*ynthesis and *E*diting system (termed eFASE) [1]. Its algorithm generates expressive speech animations by searching for best-matched motion capture subsequences in the motion database given new utterance. This eFASE system is automatic, while it provides optional controls for users, and the users can specify constrained expressions for phonemes and emotion modifiers over arbitrary time intervals. It should be noted that user input is optional, only to impart them with a desired expressiveness. Figure 3.1 illustrates high-level components of the eFASE system.

This system offers intuitive and convenient tools for managing a large facial motion capture database. Since facial motion capture is often not perfect, contaminated marker motions can occasionally occur in a motion capture sequence. Eliminating these contaminated motions is important to motion synthesis, but it is often a difficult task. Our phoneme-Isomap based visualization tool displays the facial motion database in an intuitive way, which can help users to remove the contaminated motion sequences conveniently.

The contributions of this work include:

- Its expressive speech animation synthesis algorithm is an improvement over previous data-driven search algorithms, introducing more general cost functions that incorporate emotion controls and velocity/acceleration components.
- The phoneme-Isomap based visualization interface provides intuitive controls for facial animation synthesis and a convenient tool for managing a large facial motion database.

The remainder of this chapter is organized as follows: Section 3.2 reviews previous and related work on motion capture and facial animation. Section 3.3 describes the capture and processing of expressive facial motion data. Section 3.4 describes

Z. Deng and U. Neumann, *Data-Driven 3D Facial Animation.*

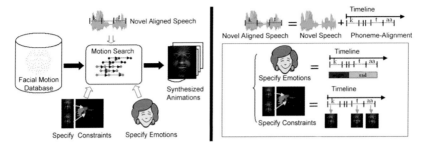

Fig. 3.1 Schematic illustration of the eFASE system. At the left, given novel phoneme-aligned speech and specified constraints, this system searches for best-matched motion nodes in the facial motion database and synthesizes expressive facial animation. The right panel illustrates how users specify motion-node constraints and emotions with respect to the speech timeline. Reproduced by kind permission of the Eurographics Association; © Eurographics Association 2006.

the construction of 2D expressive phoneme-Isomaps that allow users to interactively specify phoneme expression constraints and edit the motion database. Section 3.5 details how to perform motion editing operations and specify constraints for facial animation synthesis. Section 3.6 describes how to search for best-matched motion frames from the processed motion database to create complete animations while satisfying user-specified constraints. Finally, results (Section 3.7) and discussion and conclusions (Section 3.8) are presented.

3.2 Previous and Related Work

Since Parke's pioneering work in facial animation [2], various facial modeling and animation techniques have been proposed [3]. In this section, we only briefly review some recent related work. Data-driven speech animation approaches learn statistical models from data for facial animation synthesis and editing [4–7]. Ezzat et al. [5] proposed a multidimensional morphable model from a prerecorded video database that requires a limited set of mouth image prototypes. Chuang et al. [6] described facial expression mapping/transformation from training footage using bilinear models, and then this learned mapping is used to transform novel video of neutral talking to expressive talking.

Another way of exploiting data for facial animation synthesis is to concatenate prerecorded phoneme or syllable motion segments [8–12]. "Video rewrite" [8] generates 2D talking faces for novel speech input by recombining collected "triphone video segments." Instead of constructing a phoneme segment database, Kshirsagar and Thalmann [11] present a syllable-motion-based approach to synthesize novel speech animations. In their approach, captured facial motion are chopped and categorized into syllable motions, and then novel speech animations are generated by concatenating proper syllable motions optimally chosen from the syllable motion database. Rather than restricting the search within triphones or syllables, longer

(≥ 3) phoneme sequences can be combined in an optimal way using various search methods, including greedy search [10] or the Viterbi search algorithm [9, 12].

The eFASE system introduced in this chapter employs a constrained dynamic programming algorithm to search for the best-matched motion capture frames in a prerecorded database, similar to [9, 12]. But the distinctions of our search algorithm include (1) it introduces a new position velocity cost for favoring smooth paths, (2) by introducing a novel emotion mismatch penalty function, our algorithm can seamlessly generate expressive facial animations, and (3) it introduces motion-node constraints and emotion modifiers into the search process, which make the control of data-driven speech animation synthesis intuitive and convenient.

3.3 Facial Motion Data Capture and Processing

In order to capture subtle facial motion, a VICON optical motion capture system was deployed to capture expressive facial motions. The motion capture system can work at a high sampling rate, such as 120 Hz. In the motion capture setup stage, 102 markers were put on the face of a selected actress, and a corpus composed of 225 phoneme-balanced sentences was delicately designed. In motion capture sessions, the actress was directed to speak the corpus four times as naturally as possible. Each repetition was spoken with a different expression (four expressions are considered in this work: neutral, happiness, anger, and sadness). During data capture, simultaneous facial motion and audio were recorded by the system.

It should be noted that sentences for each expression repetition are slightly different, because some sentences are not proper for recording certain expressions. We collected more than 105,000 frames of motion data. Due to tracking errors caused by occusions and the removal of unnecessary markers, only 90 of 102 markers were used for this work. Figure 3.2 shows the 102 captured markers and the 90 used markers. The motion frames for each corpus repetition are associated with the intended expression. Except for 36 sentences that are used for cross-validation and

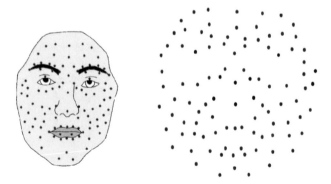

Fig. 3.2 The left is a snapshot of the captured actress. Blue and red points in the right panel represent the 102 captured markers, where the red points are the 90 markers used for this work.

test comparisons, the other captured facial motion data are used for constructing a training facial motion database.

After facial motion capture, the facial motion data are normalized as follows: (1) a facial motion frame (neutral, m-viseme) is chosen to be the reference frame; (2) all the markers were translated so that a specific marker is at the local coordinate center of each frame; and (3) a statistical shape analysis method [13] is used to calculate head motion. This head motion removal method can be summarized as follows: first, the reference frame and other motion capture frames were packed into a 90 × 3 matrix. Here y is used to represent the reference frame, and x_i for one motion capture frame. After this step, the *singular-value decomposition* (SVD), UDV^T, of matrix $y^T x_i$ was calculated. Finally, the product of VU^T gave the rotation matrix, R:

$$y^T x_i = UDV^T, \tag{3.1}$$

$$R = VU^T. \tag{3.2}$$

The *Festival* speech system [14] was used to perform automatic phoneme alignment on the captured audio. Accurate phoneme alignment is important to the success of this work, and automatic phoneme alignment is imperfect, so two linguistic experts manually checked and corrected all the phoneme alignments by examining corresponding spectrograms.

After motion data normalization, 3D positions (xyz) of all 90 markers in one motion capture frame are transformed to a 270-dimensional motion vector. We then apply principal component analysis (PCA) to these motion vectors, primarily for the purpose of dimensionality reduction. In this work, the reduced dimensionality is experimentally set to 25, which covers 98.53% of the variations of motion data. As such, each 270-dimensional motion vector was transformed to a reduced vector that concatenates the retained 25-dimensional PCA coefficients.

To make the terms used in this chapter consistent, we use *motion frames* to refer to the above PCA coefficient vectors or their corresponding facial marker configurations. Based on the phoneme timing boundaries from the phoneme-alignment results, the recorded motion capture sequences were further chopped into small subsequences, and each subsequence corresponds to the duration of a specific phoneme. These motion subsequences span several to tens of motion frames. These subsequences are referred to as *motion nodes* in this chapter. The triphone context for each motion node that includes its previous phoneme and the next phoneme is also retained in this process.

Each phoneme often occurs a number of times in the spoken corpus, with varied co-articulations. A *phoneme cluster* is defined as a cluster of motion frames that is constructed by collecting all motion nodes of a specific phoneme. A phoneme cluster typically consists of thousands of motion frames representing facial configurations that occur for a specific phoneme. Because each motion capture sequence was recorded with certain expressions, each motion frame in a phoneme cluster has an emotion/expression label and a *relative time* property (relative to the duration of the motion node that it belongs to). The specific phoneme that a motion node

Fig. 3.3 To construct a specific /w/ phoneme cluster, all expressive motion capture frames corresponding to /w/ phonemes are collected, and the Isomap embedding generates a 2D expressive Phoneme-Isomap. Colored blocks in the figure are motion nodes. Reproduced by kind permission of the Eurographics Association; © Eurographics Association 2006.

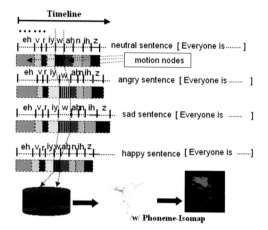

represents is called the *phoneme of this motion node*. Figure 3.3 illustrates the process of constructing phoneme clusters and motion nodes.

A facial motion-node database is accordingly constructed based on the above phoneme clusters. The constructed motion-node database can be viewed as a 3D conceptual space spanned by *sentence*, *emotion*, and *motion-node order*. Sentence is the atomic captured unit in the above motion capture sessions; as such, each motion node o_i has a predecessor motion node $pre(o_i)$ and a successor motion node $suc(o_i)$ in its sentence recording, with the exception of the first/last motion node of a sentence recording. It should be noted that in this step, motion nodes for the silence phoneme /pau/ are discarded, and if the /pau/ phoneme happens to appear in the middle of the phoneme transcript of a sentence, it will break the recorded motion sequence of this sentence into two sub-sentences when constructing the motion-node database. Figure 3.4 shows this 3D conceptual view. In this figure, these predecessor/successor relationships are illustrated as solid directional lines. As illustrated in the right panel of this figure, a synthesized facial motion sequence (yellow line) is a concatenated motion-node trajectory in this conceptual view.

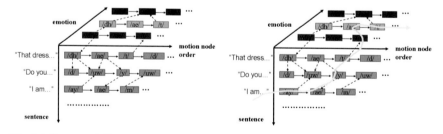

Fig. 3.4 Conceptual illustration of the constructed motion-node database. Here solid directional lines indicate predecessor/successor relations between motion nodes, and dashed directional lines indicate possible transitions from one motion node to the other. The colors of motion nodes represent different emotion categories of the motion nodes. The yellow line in the right panel illustrates a motion-node trajectory of synthesized facial motions. Reproduced by kind permission of the Eurographics Association; © Eurographics Association 2006.

3.4 2D Expressive Phoneme Isomaps

In this section, we describe how the phoneme clusters are transformed into 2D expressive phoneme-Isomaps. These 2D phoneme-Isomaps introduced in this work provide a mechanism for users to interactively browse and select motion nodes. The idea of constructing phoneme-Isomaps for control is motivated by the work of [15], where PCA is applied to a specific type of human body motion (e.g., *jumping*) to generate a low-dimensional manifold representation. In this work, the Isomap framework [16] is applied to the phoneme clusters in order to embed all motion frames in the clusters into two-dimensional manifolds.

Constructed 2D phoneme-Isomaps are compared with corresponding 2D phoneme-PCA maps that are expanded with two largest eigenvectors, by visualizing these two representations in color schemes. We found that points (motion frames) of one specific expression, visualized as the same color, are distributed throughout the 2D phoneme-PCA maps, and motion frames of various expressions are better distributed and have a better projection in the 2D phoneme-Isomaps. As such, the 2D PCA displays are not as effective as the 2D phoneme-Isomaps as a mean for frame selection. We also found that certain directions in the 2D phoneme-Isomaps, e.g., a vertical axis, roughly corresponded to certain perceptual variations of facial configurations, such as an increasingly open mouth. Figure 3.5 compares 2D PCA projections and 2D Isomap projections on the same phoneme clusters.

The point rendering in Fig. 3.5 of 2D expressive phoneme-Isomaps is not suitable for interactively browsing and selecting facial motion frames without considerable effort, because these discrete points are difficult to pick, and it is not a continuous space. In this work, an efficient Gaussian kernel-based point-rendering method is used to visualize the phoneme-Isomaps. The pixels of the rendered phoneme-Isomaps accumulate weights of Gaussian distributions centered at each embedded 2D location, and the pixel brightness is proportional to the probability of representing the phoneme. In this way, a phoneme-Isomap image is produced for each phoneme-Isomap (Fig. 3.6).

Now we describe how to construct a continuous facial configuration space from a 2D phoneme-Isomap. The 2D Delaunay triangulation algorithm is applied to embedded 2D Isomap coordinates of each phoneme-Isomap to produce a 2D triangulation network, where each vertex of these 2D triangles corresponds to an embedded phoneme-Isomap point—a motion frame in the phoneme cluster. It should be noted that these 2D triangles cover most of the space in the phoneme-Isomap image without overlap, but some points around the phoneme-Isomap image boundaries are not covered by the triangulation network due to the fact that this triangulation network is useful for interpolation, but not extrapolation.

When a point in the 2D phoneme-Isomap is picked, first its 2D position is mapped back to the 2D embedded Isomap coordinate system, and then the unique covering triangle for this picked point can be identified based on the mapped position. Finally, barycentric coordinates of the picked point are used to interpolate three vertices (motion frames) of the covering triangle to generate a new motion frame, which corresponds to the picked point. Based on the interpolated motion frame

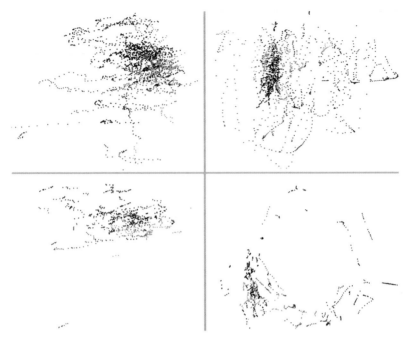

Fig. 3.5 Comparisons between 2D phoneme-PCA maps and 2D phoneme-Isomaps. The left panels are 2D phoneme-PCA maps for /aa/ (top) and /y/ (bottom), and the right panels are 2D phoneme-Isomaps for /aa/ (top) and /y/ (bottom). In all four panels, black is for neutral, red for angry, green for sad, and blue for happy. Note that some points may overlap in these plots. Reproduced by kind permission of the Eurographics Association; © Eurographics Association 2006.

for the picked point, a 3D face model is deformed correspondingly. An extension of the feature point-based mesh deformation approach [17] is used for this rapid deformation. At this point, a phoneme-Isomap image is converted to a visualized representation of a continuous space of recorded facial configurations for one specific phoneme. Figure 3.6 shows the phoneme-Isomap image of the /ay/ phoneme. It should be noted that these phoneme-Isomap images and their mapping/triangulation information were precomputed and stored for later use, so this computation was needed once.

3.5 Motion Editing

Managing and editing a large high-dimensional motion database is a challenging problem. As mentioned in Section 3.3, the constructed facial motion-node database consists of hundreds of thousands of motion capture frames. The phoneme-Isomaps provide a novel mechanism for managing motion nodes in the database conveniently and efficiently. In this work, each motion node—a sequence of motion capture frames (of one specific phoneme) in their recorded order—is visualized as a

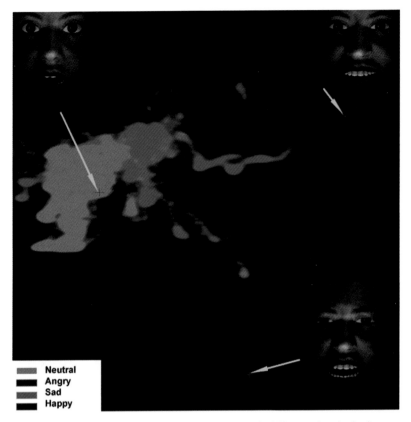

Fig. 3.6 The 2D expressive phoneme-Isomap for phoneme /ay/. Here each point in the map corresponds to a specific 3D facial configuration. Note that gray is for neutral, red for angry, green for sad, and blue for happy. Reproduced by kind permission of the Eurographics Association; © Eurographics Association 2006.

directed 2D trajectory (curve) in a phoneme-Isomap image, where the pixel color behind a motion-node trajectory represents the emotion category of its represented motion node.

Via motion-frame preview, users can conveniently check and inspect any frame of a motion node (a point on the trajectory) as follows: if any point on the motion-node trajectory is picked, its corresponding deformed 3D face will be interactively displayed in a preview window. Directly showing animations of a selected motion node is another solution: if a motion node as a whole in a 2D phoneme-Isomap is picked, a video-clip preview window will show the "expressive facial motion clips" of this motion node. This mechanism can be used for removing contaminated motion nodes in the following way: if contaminated motion nodes/frames are found at this stage, users can choose to select and delete these motion nodes from the database, so that the motion synthesis algorithm (Section 3.6) can avoid the risk of being trapped into these contaminated motion nodes. Figure 3.7 shows snapshots of motion editing in this system.

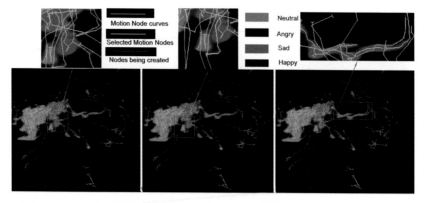

Fig. 3.7 Snapshots of motion editing for the phoneme /ay/. Here each trajectory (curve) represents one motion node, and the image color represents the emotion category. Reproduced by kind permission of the Eurographics Association; © Eurographics Association 2006.

3.6 Novel Expressive Speech Motion Synthesis

In this section, we describe how our motion synthesis algorithm generates corresponding expressive speech animations given a novel utterance. The basic idea is to search for a best-matched motion-node sequence from the constructed motion database, given a novel phoneme sequence and its emotion specifications as input. The search algorithm treats the optional motion-node constraints as "hard constraints" and emotion modifiers as "soft constraints" and then searches for a best-matched sequence (path) of motion nodes from the database by minimizing a cost function using a constrained dynamic programming algorithm.

3.6.1 Specify Motion-Node Constraints

This system is fully automatic given new utterance and emotion specifications. Furthermore, it provides controls to users. Users can optionally specify a motion-node constraint and tie it to a specific phoneme utterance's expression by interacting with its corresponding phoneme-Isomap. They first need to specify a constrained time when they want to create a constraint. The corresponding phoneme at the constrained time is called *a constrained phoneme* in this work. Since phoneme timing is enclosed in the input phrase (phoneme) transcript, once a constrained phoneme is picked, its corresponding phoneme-Isomap will be automatically loaded. Figure 3.8 illustrates this process.

During this interaction process, this system automatically highlights recommended motion nodes and their picking points using a triphone-based heuristic rule. The purpose of this highlighting is to guide users in identifying and selecting proper motion nodes effectively. Assuming a motion-node path $o_1, o_2, \ldots, o_k$ is obtained by our automatic motion-path search algorithm (the followup Section 3.6.2 details

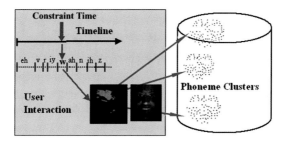

Fig. 3.8 Illustration of how to specify a motion-node constraint via the phoneme-Isomap interface. When users want to specify a specific motion node for expressing a particular phoneme utterance, its corresponding phoneme-Isomap is automatically loaded. Then, users can interact with the system to specify a motion-node constraint for this constrained phoneme. Reproduced by kind permission of the Eurographics Association; © Eurographics Association 2006.

this algorithm), users want to specify a motion-node constraint for a constrained time T_c (its corresponding constrained phoneme is P_c and its motion frame at T_c is F_c, called *current selected frame*). A normalized time, $t_c (0 \leq t_c \leq 1)$, relative to the duration of the constrained phoneme P_c, is calculated for the constrained time T_c. Then, for each motion node in the phoneme-Isomap, the system highlights one of its motion frames (*a time-correct motion frame*) whose relative time property is the closest to the current relative time t_c.

When the motion-node database was constructed (Section 3.3), the specific triphone context of each motion node was also retained. By triphone context matching, this system identifies and highlights the motion nodes in the phoneme-Isomap that have the same triphone context as the constrained phoneme, P_c. In this chapter, these motion nodes are termed *context-correct motion nodes*. Here is an example: in Fig. 3.8, the current constrained phoneme is /w/, and its triphone context is [/iy/, /w/, /ah/]; as such, this system will identify the motion nodes in the /w/ phoneme cluster that have the triphone context [/iy/, /w/, /ah/] as the context-correct motion nodes. In this way, users can choose one of these context-correct motion nodes as a motion-node constraint for P_c. This motion-node constraint is imposed per phoneme utterance, i.e., if one specific phoneme appears multiple times in a phoneme transcript input, users can specify a motion-node constraint for each occurrence of this phoneme. Figure 3.9 shows a snapshot of phoneme-Isomap highlights for specifying motion-node constraints. It should be noted that the background phoneme-Isomap image is always the same for a specific phoneme, but these highlighting symbols (Fig. 3.9) are associated with the current relative time t_c and the current triphone context.

3.6.2 Search for Best-Matched Motion Nodes

This motion-node path search problem can be formalized as follows: given a novel phomeme sequence input $\Psi = (P_1, P_2, \ldots, P_T)$ and its emotion modifiers $\Theta = (E_1, E_2, \ldots, E_T)$ (E_i can only be one of four possible values:

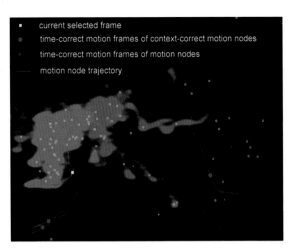

Fig. 3.9 A snapshot of phoneme-Isomap highlights for specifying motion-node constraints. Reproduced by kind permission of the Eurographics Association; © Eurographics Association 2006.

neutral, anger, sadness, and happiness), and optional motion-node constraints $\Phi = (C_{t_1} = o_{i_1}, C_{t_2} = o_{i_2}, \ldots, C_{t_k} = o_{i_k}, t_i \neq t_j)$, we want to search for a best-matched motion-node path $\Gamma^* = (o_{\rho_1}^*, o_{\rho_2}^*, \ldots, o_{\rho_T}^*)$ that minimizes a cost function $COST(\Psi, \Theta, \Phi, \Gamma^*)$. Here o_i represents a motion node with index i. The cost function $COST(\Psi, \Theta, \Gamma)$ is the accumulated summation of transition cost, $TC(o_{\rho_i}, o_{\rho_{i+1}})$, observation cost $OC(P_i, o_{\rho_i})$, emotion mismatch penalty $EMP(E_i, o_{\rho_i})$, and blocking penalty $B(t, o_{\rho_i})$, as described in Eq. 3.3.

Now we describe how the specified motion-node constraints $\Phi = (C_{t_1} = o_{i_1}, C_{t_2} = o_{i_2}, \ldots, C_{t_k} = o_{i_k}, t_i \neq t_j)$ affect the above search algorithm to guarantee that the searched motion-node path passes through the specified motion nodes at specified times. The constraints affect the search process by blocking the chances of other motion nodes (except the specified ones) at a certain recursion time. An additional cost term $B(t, o_j)$ is introduced for this purpose (see Eq. 3.4). For the details of the definition of these cost functions, please refer to the appendix to this chapter.

$$COST(\Psi, \Theta, \Gamma) = \sum_{i=1}^{T-1} TC(o_{\rho_i}, o_{\rho_{i+1}})$$

$$+ \sum_{i=1}^{T} (OC(P_i, o_{\rho_i}) + EMP(E_i, o_{\rho_i}) + B(t, o_{\rho_i})), \quad (3.3)$$

$$B(t, o_j) = \begin{cases} 0 & \text{if } \exists m, t_m = t \text{ and } j = i_m, \\ \text{HugePenalty} & \text{otherwise.} \end{cases} \quad (3.4)$$

Based on the cost definitions, we use the dynamic programming algorithm to search for the best-matched motion-node sequence. Assume there is a total of N motion nodes in the processed motion-node database and the length of a new phoneme transcript input is T. This expressive speech animation synthesis algorithm can be described as follows.

Algorithm 1 ExpressiveSpeechMotionSynthesis

Input: OC[1...T, 1...N], observation cost function
Input: EMP[1...T, 1...N], emotion mismatch penalty function
Input: TC[1...N, 1...N], transition cost function
Input: B[1...T, 1...N], blocking penalty
Input: N, size of the motion-node database; T, length of input phoneme sequence
Output: *Motion*, synthesized motion sequence

1: **for** $i = 1$ to N **do**
2:     $\varphi_1(i) = OC(P_1, o_i) + EMP(E_1, o_i)$
3: **end for**
4: **for** $j = 1$ to N **do**
5:     **for** $t = 2$ to T **do**
6:         $\varphi_t(j) = \min_i \{\varphi_{t-1}(i) + TC(o_i, o_j) + OC(P_t, o_j) + EMP(E_t, o_j) + B(t, j)\}$
7:         $\chi_t(j) = \arg\min_i \{\varphi_{t-1}(i) + TC(o_i, o_j) + OC(P_t, o_j) + EMP(E_t, o_j) + B(t, j)\}$
8:     **end for**
9: **end for**
10: $COST^* = \min_i \{\varphi_T(i)\}$
11: $\rho_T^* = \arg\min_i \{\varphi_T(i)\}$
12: **for** $t = T - 1$ to 1 **do**
13:     $\rho_t^* = \chi_{t+1}(\rho_{t+1}^*)$
14: **end for**
15: PcaSeq = ConcatenateAndSmooth($o_{\rho_1}^*, o_{\rho_2}^*, \cdots, o_{\rho_T}^*$)
16: Motion = PcaTransformBack(PcaSeq)

The time complexity of the above search algorithm is $\Theta(N^2 * T)$, N is the number of motion nodes in the database, and T is the length of the input phoneme sequence. Note that in the cost function definition (see the appendix), the parameters $\langle \alpha, \beta, \eta, \gamma, \delta, \varphi \rangle$ are used to balance the weights of different costs. In this work, the cross-validation approach [18] was used to experimentally determine these parameter values.

Given the optimal motion-node path $\Gamma^* = o_{\rho_1}^*, o_{\rho_2}^*, \ldots, o_{\rho_T}^*$, we concatenate its motion nodes by smoothing their neighboring boundaries and transforming facial motions of the motion nodes from their retained PCA space to markers' 3D space (Eq. 3.5). Finally, we transfer the synthesized marker motion sequence onto specific 3D face models:

$$MrkMotion = MeanMotion + EigMx * PcaCoef. \tag{3.5}$$

As mentioned in Section 3.3, motion nodes for the silence time (the /pau/ phoneme in the *Festival* system) were discarded when constructing the processed motion-node database. Therefore, when computing the observation cost for the /pau/ phoneme time (Eq. 3.9), as long as $P_i = /pau/$, the observation cost is simply set to zero. In other words, any motion node is perfect for expressing the silence time during the motion-node search process (Section 3.6.2). After the motion nodes are concatenated and smoothed, we need to post-process these synthesized frames corresponding to the silence time: first identify these silence-time frames based on the input phoneme transcript and then regenerate these frames by performing a linear interpolation on the boundary of non-silence frames.

During the post-processing stage, it is necessary to resample motion frames. When motion nodes are concatenated, the number of frames in the motion node may not exactly match the duration of the input phoneme. So, we use the time-warping technique to resample the searched motion nodes to obtain the desired number of motion frames. This resampling is still done at 120 Hz (the same as the original motion capture rate). Although synthesized marker motion frames are 120 frames/second, the resulting animations are often at an ordinary animation rate of 30 frames/second. Thus, before we map the synthesized marker motion frames to a specific 3D face model, we down-sample these motion frames to the ordinary animation rate.

3.7 Results and Evaluations

We developed the eFASE system using VC + + that runs on the MS Windows XP system. Figure. 3.10 shows a snapshot of the running eFASE system. As shown in this figure, the left is a basic control panel, and the right panel encloses four working windows: a synthesized motion window (top-left), a video playback window (top-right), a phoneme-Isomap interaction window (bottom-left), and a face preview window (bottom-right). Both the synthesized motion and face preview windows can switch among several display modes, including marker-drawing mode and deformed 3D face mode.

This is how this eFASE system works: first, users input a novel speech (WAV format) and its aligned phoneme transcript file, and an emotion specification (modifier) file via the basic control panel (left). And then, after the synthesis process is enabled, this system automatically generates corresponding expressive facial animations. The synthesized facial marker motions are shown in the synthesized motion window. Users can browse these synthesized marker motions frame by frame using a timeline gadget in the basic control panel. They can switch the display of the synthesized motion window between point and deformed 3D face display. Additionally, the system automatically composes an AVI video (audio-synchronized), which the users can play back immediately in the video playback window (top right in Fig. 3.10) to check the final result. This provides an interactive way for the users to check on animation synthesis results.

On the user interaction side, the users can edit the facial motion database and impose motion-node constraints via the phoneme-Isomap interaction window (bottom left in Fig. 3.10) and the face preview window (bottom right in Fig. 3.10). If any point in the phoneme-Isomap interaction window is picked, the face preview window will show its deformed 3D face (or corresponding facial marker configuration) in real time. Motion editing and management are also done in the phoneme-Isomap

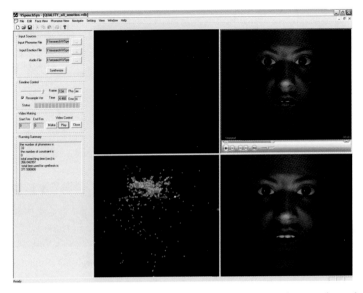

Fig. 3.10 A snapshot of the running eFASE system. The left is a basic control panel, and the right panel encloses four working windows: a synthesized motion window (top left), a video playback window (top right), a phoneme-Isomap interaction window (bottom left), and a face preview window (bottom right). Reproduced by kind permission of the Eurographics Association; © Eurographics Association 2006.

interaction window. Table 3.1 illustrates an example of a phoneme input file and an emotion specification file.

We conducted a running-time analysis on the eFASE system. The computer used was a Dell Dimension 4550 PC (Windows XP, 1 GHz Memory, Intel 2.66 GHz Processor). Table 3.2 lists the running times for some example inputs. As mentioned in Section 3.6.2, the motion node searching part (the most time-consuming part of the eFASE system) has a time complexity of $\Theta(N^2 * T)$ that is linear to the length of input phonemes (assuming N is a fixed value for a specific database). The computing times listed in Table 3.2 are approximately matched with this analysis.

We synthesized numerous expressive facial animations using novel recorded and archival speech. Figure 3.11 shows some frames of synthesized facial animations. Trajectory comparisons between synthesized expressive facial motions with corresponding ground-truth (captured) motions were also performed. Twelve additional

Table 3.1 An example of an aligned phoneme input file (left) and an emotion modifier file (right). Its phrase is "I am not happy...." Here the emotion of the starting 2.6 second is angry, and the emotion from #2.6 second to #16.6383 second is sadness. Reproduced by kind permission of the Eurographics Association; ©Eurographics Association 2006.

0.122401 pau	2.6 angry
0.24798 ay	16.6383 sad
0.328068 ae	
0.457130 m	
0.736070 n	
...	

Table 3.2 Running time for synthesis of some example phrases. Here the computer used was a Dell Dimension 4550 PC (Windows XP, 1 GHz memory, Intel 2.66 GHz Processor). Reproduced by kind permission of the Eurographics Association; ©Eurographics Association 2006.

Phrases (number of phonemes)	Time (second)
"I know you meant it" (14)	137.67
"And so you just abandoned them?" (24)	192.86
"Please go on, because Jeff's father has no idea" (33)	371.50
"It is a fact that long words are difficult to articulate unless you concentrate" (63)	518.34

Fig. 3.11 An example sequence of synthesized facial animation. Reproduced by kind permission of the Eurographics Association; © Eurographics Association 2006.

sentences were exclusively used for the test comparisons. One of these sentences was *"Please go on, because Jeff's father has no idea of how things became so horrible."* We chose a right cheek marker (#48 marker) in an expression-active area and a lower lip marker (#79 marker) in a speech-active area for the comparisons (Fig. 3.2). We plotted a part of the synthesized sequence and ground-truth motion for these marker trajectory comparisons. Figure 3.12 is for #48 marker (the right cheek marker) and Fig. 3.13 is for #79 marker (the lower lip marker). We found that the trajectories of the synthesized motions are quite close to the actual motions captured from the actress. It should be noted that the the synthesized motions for these comparisons (e.g., Figs. 3.12 and 3.13) were automatically generated without any manual intervention (i.e., without the use of motion-node constraints).

3.8 Discussion and Conclusions

A data-driven system (eFASE) for an expressive facial animation synthesis and editing system is presented in this chapter. This animation generation system is fully automatic given user-specified novel speech input. At the same time, it offers flexible user control over the facial motion synthesis process, by specifying emotion modifiers and expressions for certain phoneme utterances via 2D expressive phoneme-Isomaps. Objective motion trajectory comparisons between synthesized facial motions and ground-truth motions and novel animation synthesis experiments showed that this eFASE system is effective for generating realistic expressive speech/facial animations.

As this is a new approach to facial animation synthesis and editing, several issues deserve further investigation. The quality of novel motion synthesis depends on constructing a large facial motion database with accurate motion and phoneme

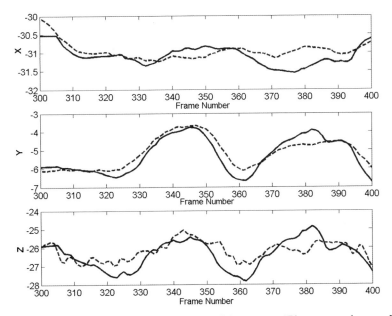

Fig. 3.12 A part of marker (#48 marker) trajectory of the sentence "Please go on, because Jeff's father has no idea of how things became so horrible." The dashed line is the ground-truth trajectory and the solid line is the synthesized trajectory. Reproduced by kind permission of the Eurographics Association; © Eurographics Association 2006.

alignment. Building this database takes care and time; integrated tools could improve this process immensely. Additionally, a significant amount of expressive facial motion data is needed to construct this system with reasonable performance, since the larger the captured facial motion database is, the better synthesis results from our systems are expected. However, it is difficult to anticipate in advance how much data are needed to generate realistic facial animations in this system, which is one of the common issues in many data-driven systems. Further research on the trade-off between synthesis quality and the size of captured facial motion database would be an interesting topic.

The current system cannot be used for real-time applications due to the efficiency of the motion search algorithm in this system. Future work on optimizing the facial motion database could improve the overall efficiency of this system, such as reducing the size of the facial motion database through clustering methods. We are also aware that subjective evaluation would be helpful to quantify the performance of this system, and we plan to look into it as our future work. Emotion intensity control that is absent in the current system is another good direction to go for future research.

Phoneme-viseme mappings are widely used in ad hoc facial animation systems, but there are no uniform phoneme-viseme mappings, and it is difficult to evaluate any mapping scheme. The 2D expressive phoneme-Isomaps introduced in this work might provide a basis for evaluating these mapping schemes or determining new phoneme-viseme mapping schemes based on the probabilities in the phoneme-Isomaps and the variations among the phoneme-Isomaps produced by different subjects.

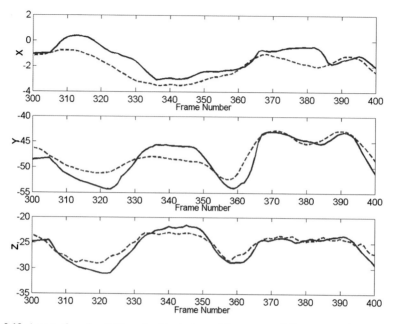

Fig. 3.13 A part of marker (#79 marker) trajectory of the sentence "Please go on, because Jeff's father has no idea of how things became so horrible." The dashed line is the ground-truth trajectory and the solid line is the synthesized trajectory. Reproduced by kind permission of the Eurographics Association; © Eurographics Association 2006.

The motions of the silence phoneme (the /pau/ phoneme in the *Festival* system) are not modeled. This phoneme and other non-speaking animations (e.g., yawning) need to be represented as motion nodes to allow more flexibility and model personalities. Lastly, there are more open questions, such as whether combining the speaking styles of different actors into one facial motion database would result in providing a greater range of motions and expressions, or if such a combination would muddle the motion-frame sequencing and expressiveness, or whether exploiting different weights for markers to guide the coherence of perceptual saliency could improve results.

Acknowledgment We would like to thank Yizhou Yu for thoughtful suggestions, Pamela Fox for face model preparation, Joy Nash, J.P. Lewis, Murtaza Bulut, and Carlos Busso for facial motion data capture and processing, and Douglas Fidaleo and the USC Computer Vision Lab for building the coarse 3D face model.

References

1. Z. Deng and U. Neumann. EFASE: Expressive facial animation synthesis and editing with phoneme-level controls. In *Proc. of ACM SIGGRAPH/Eurographics Symposium on Computer Animation*, pages 251–259, Vienna, Austria, 2006.
2. F. Parke. Computer generated animation of faces. In *Proc. ACM Natl. Conf.*, volume 1, pages 451–457, 1972.

3. F. I. Parke and K. Waters. *Computer Facial Animation*. A K Peters, Wellesley, MA, 1996.
4. M. Brand. Voice pupperty. *Proc. of ACM SIGGRAPH'99*, pages 21–28, 1999.
5. T. Ezzat, G. Geiger, and T. Poggio. Trainable videorealistic speech animation. *ACM Trans. Graph.*, pages 388–398, 2002.
6. E. Chuang and C. Bregler. Moodswings: Expressive speech animation. *ACM Trans. on Graph.*, 24(2), 2005.
7. Z. Deng, U. Neumann, J. P. Lewis, T. Y. Kim, M. Bulut, and S. Narayanan. Expressive facial animation synthesis by learning speech co-articulations and expression spaces. *IEEE Trans. Vis. Graph.*, 12(6):1523–1534, 2006.
8. C. Bregler, M. Covell, and M. Slaney. Video rewrite: Driving visual speech with audio. *Proc. of ACM SIGGRAPH'97*, pages 353–360, 1997.
9. E. Cosatto and H. P. Graf. Audio-visual unit selection for the synthesis of photo-realistic talking-heads. In *Proc. of ICME*, pages 619–622, 2000.
10. Y. Cao, P. Faloutsos, E. Kohler, and F. Pighin. Real-time speech motion synthesis from recorded motions. In *Proc. Sym. Comp. Animation*, pages 345–353, 2004.
11. S. Kshirsagar and N.M. Thalmann. Visyllable based speech animation. *Computer Graphics Forum*, 22(3), 2003.
12. J. Ma, R. Cole, B. Pellom, W. Ward, and B. Wise. Accurate visible speech synthesis based on concatenating variable length motion capture data. *IEEE Trans. Visualization Comp. Graphics*, 12(2):266–276, 2006.
13. C. Busso, Z. Deng, U. Neumann, and S. Narayanan. Natural head motion synthesis driven by acoustic prosody features. *Computer Animation and Virtual Worlds*, 16(3-4):283–290, July 2005.
14. http://www.cstr.ed.ac.uk/projects/festival/, 2004.
15. A. Safonova, J.K. Hodgins, and N.S. Pollard. Synthesizing physically realistic human motion in low-dimensional, behavior-specific spaces. *ACM Trans. Graph.*, 23(3):514–521, 2004.
16. J.B. Tenenbaum, V. de Silva, and J.C. Langford. A global geometric framework for nonlinear dimensionality reduction. *Science*, 290(5500):2319–2333, 2000.
17. S. Kshirsagar, S. Garchery, and N.M. Thalmann. Feature point based mesh deformation applied to mpeg-4 facial animation. In *Proc. Deform'2000, Workshop on Virtual Humans by IFIP Working Group 5.10*, pages 23–34, November 2000.
18. T. Hastie, R. Tibshirani, and J. Friedman. *The Elements of Statistical Learning: Data Mining, Inference, and Prediction*. Springer-Verlag, New York, 2001.

3.9 Appendix: Cost Functions for Motion-Node Path Searching

The transition cost $TC(o_{\rho_i}, o_{\rho_{i+1}})$ represents the smoothness of the transition from one motion node o_{ρ_i} to another motion node $o_{\rho_{i+1}}$:

$$TC(o_{\rho_i}, o_{\rho_{i+1}}) = \begin{cases} 0 & \text{if } pre(o_{\rho_{i+1}}) = o_{\rho_i}, \\ \beta * DSC(o_{\rho_i}, pre(o_{\rho_{i+1}})) + \\ PVC(o_{\rho_i}, o_{\rho_{i+1}}) & \text{if } viseme(o_{\rho_i}) = viseme(pre(o_{\rho_{i+1}})), \\ \beta * DSC(o_{\rho_i}, pre(o_{\rho_{i+1}})) + \\ PVC(o_{\rho_i}, o_{\rho_{i+1}}) + PNT & \text{if } viseme(o_{\rho_i}) \neq viseme(pre(o_{\rho_{i+1}})), \\ \alpha * PNT & \text{if } pre(o_{\rho_{i+1}}) = NIL. \end{cases}$$

$$(3.6)$$

The direct smoothing cost $DSC(o_{\rho_i}, pre(o_{\rho_{i+1}}))$ and the position velocity cost $PVC(o_{\rho_i}, o_{\rho_{i+1}})$ are defined in Eqs. 3.7 and 3.8:

$$DSC(o_{\rho_i}, pre(o_{\rho_{i+1}})) = \int Blending(warp(o_{\rho_i}), pre(o_{\rho_{i+1}}))'' dt, \qquad (3.7)$$

$$PVC(o_{\rho_i}, o_{\rho_{i+1}}) = \eta * PosGap(o_{\rho_i}, o_{\rho_{i+1}}) + VeloGap(o_{\rho_i}, o_{\rho_{i+1}}). \qquad (3.8)$$

The observation cost $OC(P_i, o_{\rho_i})$, which measures the goodness of a motion node o_{ρ_i} for expressing a given phoneme P_i, is computed as follows: if the phoneme of o_{ρ_i} is our expected P_i or P_i is the silence phoneme /pau/, we set the cost to zero. If they are the same in terms of viseme category, then we set it to a discounted penalty value $(0 < \gamma < 1)$; otherwise, the cost is a penalty value. Equation 3.9 defines the observation cost:

$$OC(P_i, o_{\rho_i}) = \begin{cases} 0 & \text{if } P_i = pho(o_{\rho_i}) \text{ or } P_i = /pau/, \\ \gamma * \delta * PNT & \text{if } viseme(P_i) = viseme(o_{\rho_i}), \\ \delta * PNT & \text{otherwise.} \end{cases} \qquad (3.9)$$

If the emotion label of a motion node o_{ρ_i} is the same as the specified emotion modifier E_i, we set the emotion mismatch penalty to zero; otherwise, it is set to a constant penalty value. Equation 3.10 describes this definition. The emotion mismatch penalty cost $EMP(E_i, o_{\rho_i})$ is defined as follows:

$$EMP(E_i, o_{\rho_i}) = \begin{cases} 0 & \text{if } E_i = emotion(o_{\rho_i}), \\ \varphi * PNT & \text{otherwise.} \end{cases} \qquad (3.10)$$

Chapter 4
Eye Movements, Saccades, and Multiparty Conversations

Erdan Gu, Sooha Park Lee, Jeremy B. Badler, and Norman I. Badler

4.1 Introduction

In describing for artists the role of eyes, Faigin [20] illustrates that downcast eyes, upraised eyes, eyes looking sideways, and even out-of-focus eyes are all suggestive of states of mind. Given that eyes are a window into the mind, we propose a new approach for synthesizing the kinematic characteristics of the eye: the spatiotemporal trajectories of saccadic eye movement. "*Saccadic eye movements take their name from the French 'saccade', meaning 'jerk', and connoting a discontinuous, stepwise manner of movement as opposed to a fluent, continuous one. The name very appropriately describes the phenomenological aspect of eye movement*" [4].

We present a statistical eye movement model based on both empirical studies of saccades and acquired eye movement data. There are three strong motivations for our work. First, for animations containing close-up views of the face, natural-looking eye movements are desirable. Second, traditionally it is hard for an animator to obtain accurate human eye movement data. Third, the animation community appears to have had no models for saccadic eye movement models that are easily adopted for speaking or listening faces. We apply the eye model to conversational agents in which gaze direction and role are modeled on saccades during talking, listening, and "thinking" as well as on the social aspects of interaction behaviors such as turn-taking and feedback signals. A preliminary eye saccade model is the basis for the present work [28].

As computer animation techniques mature, there has been considerable interest in the construction and animation of human facial models. Applications include such diverse areas as advertising, film production, game design, teleconferencing, social agents and avatars, and virtual reality. To build a realistic face model, many factors including modeling of face geometry, simulation of facial muscle behavior, lip synchronization, and texture synthesis have been considered. Several early researchers [25, 32, 37, 43] were among those who proposed various methods to simulate facial shape and muscle behavior. A number of investigators have recently emphasized building more realistic face models [8,21,30,36]. Others have suggested automatic methods of building varied geometric models of human faces [7, 16, 29]. Motion capture methods can be used to replay prerecorded facial skin motion or behaviors [19, 35].

Z. Deng and U. Neumann, *Data-Driven 3D Facial Animation.*   79
© Springer-Verlag London Limited 2008

Research on faces has not focused on eye movement, although the eyes play an essential role as a major channel of nonverbal communicative behavior. Eyes help to regulate the flow of conversation, signal the search for feedback during an interaction (gazing at the other person to see how she follows), look for information, express emotion (looking downward in case of sadness, embarrassment, or shame), or influence another person's behavior (staring at a person to show power) [18, 34].

Recently, eye movement has attracted attention among computer animation researchers. Directional gaze cues are frequently present to communicate the nature of the interpersonal relationship in face-to-face interactions [1]. It is estimated that 60% of conversation involves gaze and 30% involves mutual gaze [34]. Some researchers [15, 44] analyze frequencies of mutual gaze to simulate patterns of eye gaze for the participants. Social gaze serves to regulate conversation flow. Cassell and colleagues [11–13] in particular have explored eye engagement during social interactions or discourse between virtual agents. They discuss limited rules of eye engagement between animated participants in conversation. Eye movements are linked to visual attention processing: task actions generate the appropriate attentional (eye gaze or looking) behavior for virtual characters existing or performing tasks in a changing environment, such as "walk to the lamp post," "monitor the traffic light," or "reach for the box" [14].

Eye-gaze patterns for an avatar interacting with other real or virtual participants have also become important areas of study and simulation. Gaze patterns are investigated to see how observers react to whether an avatar is looking at or looking away from them [15]. Simulations for face-to-face conversation are mainly dyadic, and turn allocation using gaze signals is relatively simple. Multiparty turn-taking behavior has been less explored, and some attempts [39, 41] have been based largely on the dyadic situation. Much of this work focuses on user-perceptual issues or has involved mediated communication rather than conversational agent simulation. Intuitively, a significant difference exists in gaze behaviors between dyadic and multiparty situations: at the minimum, the latter must include mechanisms for multiple audience turn requests, acknowledgement, and attention capture.

We propose a new approach for synthesizing the trajectory kinematics and statistical distribution of saccadic eye movements. First, we present an eye movement model based on both empirical studies of saccades and statistical models of eye-tracking data. Then we address the role of gaze in multiparty conversation, giving a procedure for turn allocation, turn request, and expression of conversational feedback signals. The overview of our approach is as follows. First, we analyze a sequence of eye-tracking images in order to extract the spatiotemporal trajectory of the eye. Although the eye-tracking data can be directly replayed on a face model, its primary purpose is for deriving a statistical model of the saccades that occur. The eye-tracking video is further segmented and classified into two modes, a talking mode and a listening mode, so that we can construct a saccade model for each. The models reflect the dynamic (spatiotemporal) characteristics of natural eye movement, which include saccade magnitude, direction, duration, velocity, and inter-saccadic interval. Based on the model, we synthesize an animated face with more natural-looking and believable eye movements. Communicative aspects of eye movement are layered on top of the saccade model to give multiparty conversational signals.

This article describes our approach in detail. Section 4.2 reviews pertinent research about saccadic eye movements and the role of gaze in communication. Section 4.3 presents an overview of our system architecture. Section 4.4 introduces our statistical model based on the analysis of eye-tracking images. An eye saccade model is constructed for both talking and listening modes and adapted for "thinking" mode. Section 4.5 shows the model implemented in agents who use appropriate social signals to simulate interactive conversations. Section 4.6 describes the architecture of our eye movement synthesis system. Finally we give our conclusions and closing remarks.

4.2 Background

4.2.1 Saccades

Saccades are rapid movements of both eyes from one gaze position to another [31]. They are the only eye movement that can be readily, consciously, and voluntarily executed by human subjects. Saccades must balance the conflicting demands of speed and accuracy, in order to minimize both time spent in transit and time spent making corrective movements.

There are a few conventions used in the eye movement literature when describing saccades. The magnitude (also called the amplitude) of a saccade is the angle through which the eyeball rotates as it changes fixation from one position in the visual environment to another. Saccade direction defines the 2D axis of rotation, with $0°$ being to the (person's) right. This essentially describes the eye position in polar coordinates. For example, a saccade with magnitude $10°$ and direction $45°$ is equivalent to the eyeball rotating $10°$ in a right-upward direction. Saccade duration is the amount of time that the movement takes to execute, typically determined using a velocity threshold. The inter-saccadic interval is the amount of time that elapses between the termination of one saccade and the beginning of the next one.

The metrics (spatiotemporal characteristics) of saccades have been well studied (for a review, see [4]). A normal saccadic movement begins with an extremely high initial acceleration (as much as $30,000°/sec^2$) and terminates with almost as rapid a deceleration. Peak velocities for large saccades can be $400 - 600°/sec$. Saccades to a goal direction are accurate to within a few degrees. Saccadic reaction time is 180–220 msec on average. Minimum inter-saccadic intervals range from 50–100 msec.

The duration and velocity of a saccade are functions of its magnitude. For saccades between $5°$ and $50°$, the duration has a nearly constant rate of increase with magnitude and can be approximated by the linear function

$$D = D_0 + d*A,$$ (4.1)

where D and A are the duration and amplitude of the eye movement, respectively. The slope d represents the increment in duration per degree. It ranges from 2–2.7 msec/deg. The intercept or catch-up time D_0 typically ranges from 20–30 msec [4].

Saccadic eye movements are often accompanied by a head rotation in the same direction (gaze saccades). Large gaze shifts always include a head rotation under natural conditions; in fact, naturally occurring saccades rarely have a magnitude greater than $15°$ [3]. Head and eye movements are synchronous [6, 42].

4.2.2 Gaze in Social Interaction

According to psychological studies [1, 18, 26], there are three functions of gaze:

1. sending social signals: speakers use glances to emphasize words, phrases, or entire utterances while listeners use glances to signal continued attention or interest in a particular point of the speaker, or in the case of an averted gaze, lack of interest or disapproval;
2. open a channel to receive information: a speaker will look up at the listener during pauses in speech to judge how his words are being received and whether the listener wishes him to continue while the listener continually monitors the facial expressions and direction of gaze of the speaker;
3. regulate the flow of conversation: the speaker stops talking and looks at the listener, indicating that the speaker is finished and conversational participants can look at a listener to suggest that the listener be the next to speak.

Gaze aversion can signal that a person is thinking. For example, someone might look away when asked a question as she composes her response. Gaze is lowered during discussion of cognitively difficult topics. Gaze aversion is also more common while speaking as opposed to listening, especially at the beginning of utterances and when speech is hesitant. Kendon found additional changes in gaze direction, such as the speaker looking away from the listener at the beginning of an utterance and toward the listener at the end [26]. He also compared gaze during two kinds of speech pauses: phrase boundaries (the pause between two grammatical phrases of speech), and hesitation pauses (delays that occur when the speaker is unsure of what to say next). The level of gaze rises at the beginning of a phrase boundary pause, similarly to what occurs at the end of an utterance in order to collect feedback from the listener. Gaze level falls at a hesitation pause, which requires more thinking.

4.3 Overview of Eye Movement System Architecture

Figure 4.1 depicts the overall eye movement system architecture and animation procedure. First, the eye-tracking images are analyzed and a statistical eye movement model is generated using MATLAB® (The MathWorks, Inc.) (Block 1). For

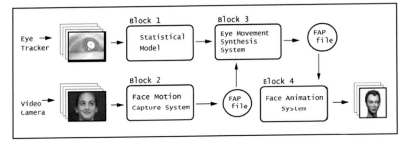

Fig. 4.1 Overall eye movement system architecture.

lip movements, eye blinks, and head rotations, we use the alterEGO face motion analysis system (Block 2), which was developed at face2face.com. The alterEGO system analyzes a series of images from a consumer digital video camera and generates a MPEG-4 Face Animation Parameter (FAP) file [24, 35]. The FAP file contains the parameter values of lip movements, eye blinks, and head rotation [35]. These components are executed offline, before the animation is created. Our principal contribution, the Eye Movement Synthesis System (EMSS) (Block 3), takes the FAP file from the alterEGO system and adds values for eye movement parameters based on the statistical model. EMSS outputs a new FAP file that contains eyeball movement as well as the lip and head movement information. We constructed the Facial Animation System (Block 4) by adding eyeball movement capability to face2face's Animator plug-in for 3D Studio Max® (Autodesk, Inc.). In other applications, such as the multiparty conversation ahead, we can output the FAP file to a different animated face model, such as the Greta head [33]. In the next section, we will explain the analysis of the eye-tracking images and the building of the statistical eye model (Block 1). More detail about the EMSS (Block 3) will be presented in Section 4.5.

4.4 Analysis of Eye-Tracking Data

4.4.1 Images from the Eye Tracker

We analyzed sequences of eye-tracking images in order to extract the spatiotemporal characteristics of the eye movements. Eye movements were recorded using a lightweight eye-tracking visor (ISCAN, Inc.). The visor is worn like a baseball cap and consists of a monocle and two miniature cameras. One camera views the visual environment from the perspective of the participant's left eye and the other views a close-up image of the left eye. Only the eye image was recorded to a digital videotape using a DSR-30 digital VCR (Sony Inc.). The ISCAN eye-tracking device measures the eye movement by comparing the corneal reflection of the light source (typically infrared) relative to the location of the pupil center. The position of the

Fig. 4.2 (**a**) Original eye image from the eye tracker (left); (**b**) output of the Canny enhancer (right) distribution.

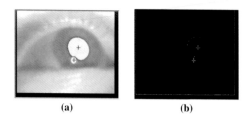

(**a**) (**b**)

pupil center changes during rotation of the eye, while the corneal reflection acts as a static reference point.

The sample video we used is 9 minutes long and contains an informal conversation between two people. The speaker had used the eye-tracking device many times prior to this sample session; hence, it was not disruptive to her behaviors. The speaker was allowed to move her head freely while the video was taken. It was recorded at the rate of 30 fps. From the video clip, each image was extracted using Adobe Premiere® (Adobe Inc.). Figure 4.2(a) is an example frame showing two crosses, one for the pupil center and one for the corneal reflection.

We obtained the image (x, y) coordinates of the pupil center by using a pattern matching method. First, the features of each image are extracted by using the Canny operator [10] with the default threshold gray level. Figure 4.2(b) is a strength image output by the Canny enhancer. Second, to determine a pupil center, the position histograms along the x- and y-axes are calculated. Then the coordinates of the two center points with maximum correlation values are chosen. Finally, the sequences of (x, y) coordinates are smoothed by a median filter.

4.4.2 Saccade Statistics

Figure 4.3(a) shows the distributions of the eye position in image coordinates. The red circle is the primary position (PP), where the speaker's eye is fixated upon the listener. Figure 4.3(b) is the same distribution plotted in 3D, with the z-axis representing the frequency of occurrence at that position. The peak in the 3D plot corresponds to the primary position.

The saccade magnitude is the rotation angle between its starting position $S = (x_s, y_s)$ and ending position $E = (x_e, y_e)$, computed by

$$\theta \approx \arctan(d/r) = \arctan\left(\frac{\sqrt{(x_e - x_s)^2 + (y_e - y_s)^2}}{r}\right), \tag{4.2}$$

where d is the Euclidean distance traversed by the pupil center and r is the radius of the eyeball. The radius r is assumed to be one half of x_{max}, the width of the eye-tracker image (640 pixels).

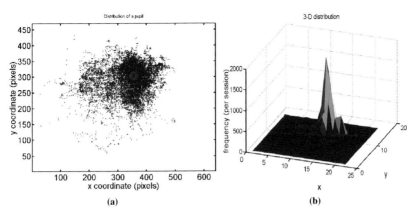

Fig. 4.3 (a) Distribution of pupil centers; (b) 3D view of same distribution.

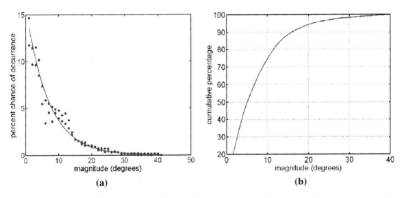

Fig. 4.4 (a) Frequency of occurrence of saccade magnitudes; (b) cumulative percentage of magnitudes

The frequency of occurrence of a given saccade magnitude during the entire recording session is shown in Fig. 4.4(a). Using a least-mean-squares criterion, the distribution was fitted to the exponential function

$$P = 15.7e^{-\frac{A}{6.9}}, \tag{4.3}$$

where P is the percent chance to occur and A is the saccade magnitude in degrees. The fitted function is used for choosing a saccade magnitude during synthesis. Figure 4.4(b) shows the cumulative percentage of saccade magnitudes: the probability that a given saccade will be smaller than magnitude x. Note that 90% of the time the saccade angles are less than 15°, which is consistent with a previous study [3].

Saccade directions are also obtained from the video. For simplicity, the directions are quantized into 8 evenly spaced bins with centers 45° apart. The distribution of saccade directions is shown in Table 4.1. One interesting observation is that up-down and left-right movements occurred more than twice as often as diagonal movements. Also, up-down movements happened equally as often as left-right movements.

Table 4.1 Distribution of saccade directions.

Direction	0°	45°	90°	135°	180°	225°	270°	315°
%	15.54	6.46	17.69	7.44	16.80	7.89	20.38	7.79

Fig. 4.5 Instantaneous velocity functions of saccades.

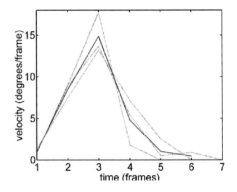

Saccade duration was measured using a velocity threshold of 40°/sec (1.33°/frame). The durations were then used to derive an instantaneous velocity curve for every saccade in the eye-track record. Sample curves are shown in Fig. 4.5 (black dotted lines). The duration of each eye movement is normalized to six frames. The normalized curves are used to fit a 6-dimensional polynomial (red solid line):

$$Y = 0.1251X^6 - 3.1619X^5 + 31.5032X^4 - 155.8713X^3 \qquad (4.4)$$
$$+ 394.0271X^2 - 465.9513X + 200.3621,$$

where x is frame 1 to 6 and y is instantaneous velocity (°/frame).

The inter-saccadic interval is incorporated by defining two classes of gaze, *mutual* and *away*. In mutual gaze, the subject's eye is in the primary position, while in gaze away it is not. The duration that the subject remains in one of these two gaze states is analogous to the inter-saccadic interval. Figures 4.6(a) and (b) plot

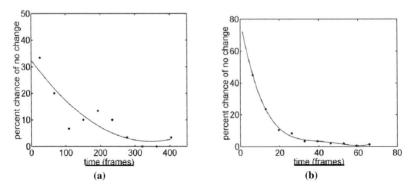

Fig. 4.6 (a) Frequency of mutual gaze duration while talking; (b) frequency of gaze away duration while talking.

duration distributions for the two types of gaze while the subject was talking. They show the percent chance of remaining in a particular gaze mode (i.e., not making a saccade) as a function of elapsed time. The polynomial fitting function for mutual gaze duration is

$$Y = 2.5524e - 4X^2 - 0.1763X + 32.2815 \qquad (4.5)$$

and for gaze away duration is

$$Y = 1.8798e - 5X^4 + 0.0034X^3 + 0.2262X^2 + 6.7021X + 78.831. \qquad (4.6)$$

Note that the inter-saccadic interval tends to be much shorter when the eyes are not in the primary position.

4.4.3 Talking Mode vs. Listening Mode

Characteristics of gaze differ depending on whether a subject is talking, listening, or thinking [1]. We manually segmented the video eye movement data to obtain the statistical properties of saccades in these modes. Figures 4.7(a) and (b) show the eye position distributions for talking and listening, respectively. While talking, 92% of the time the saccade magnitude is 25° or less. While listening, over 98% of the time the magnitude is less than 25°. The average magnitude is $15.64° \pm 11.86°$ (mean±stdev) for talking and $13.83°\pm8.88°$ for listening. In general, the magnitude distribution of listening is much narrower than that of talking: when the subject is speaking, eye movements are more dynamic and active. This is also apparent while watching the eye-tracking video.

Inter-saccadic intervals also differ between talking and listening modes. While talking, the average mutual gaze and gaze away durations are 93.9 ± 94.9 frames and 27.8 ± 24.0 frames, respectively. The complete distributions are shown in Figs. 4.7(a) and (b). While listening, the average durations are 237.5 ± 47.1 frames

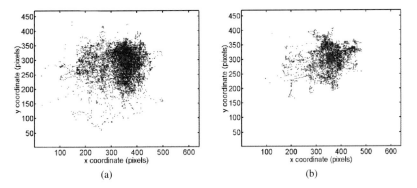

(a)   (b)

Fig. 4.7 Distribution of saccades **(a)** in talking mode; **(b)** in listening mode.

Table 4.2 Neurolinguistic information processing and corresponding eye movement patterns.

Eye Movement	Information Processing
Eye up and to the right	Trying to envision an event that has never been seen
Eye up and to the left	Recalling an event that has been seen
Unfocused eyes looking fixedly into space	Visualizing an event, real or imagined
Eye down and to the right	Sorting out sensations of the body
Eye down and to the left	Carrying on an internal conversation

for mutual gaze and 13.0 ± 7.1 frames for gaze away. These distributions were far more symmetric and could be suitably described with Gaussians. The longer mutual gaze times for listening are consistent with earlier empirical results [1] in which the speaker was looking at the listener 41% of the time, while the listener was looking at the speaker 75% of the time.

While watching a different video of a subject performing a monologue ("tell us about yourself"), we observed eye movements during periods where the subject was not speaking (and she clearly wasn't "listening" to someone else). During such subjective "thinking" modes, we found that people tend to make more eye movements upward or downward in order to avoid outside information and concentrate on their inner thoughts and emotional state. In fact, neurolinguistic programming theory postulates that the direction of eye movement is a reflection of cognitive activity [27]. This theory associates eye positions with different types of information processing (Table 4.2). Although neurolinguistic ideas often fail to survive rigorous experimental testing, the patterns for eye movement have received independent validation [9]. Remembering a has-been-seen event is significantly suggestive of a state of mind so that turning eyes up and to the left most frequently occurs when people are thinking. At that time, we observe the eyeball will have a long hold when it reaches the maximum magnitude of the current saccade. When we animate a character using the talking, listening, and thinking modes, we monitor long pauses in a speech signal as a trigger for the thinking mode and adjust the upward and downward direction distribution from the preliminary study.

4.5 Gaze Role in Multiparty Turn-Taking

Directional gaze behaviors and visual contact signal and monitor the initiation, maintenance, and termination of communicative messages [13]. Two participants use mutual gaze to look at each other, usually in the face region. Gaze contact means they look in each other's eyes. In gaze aversion, one participant looks away when others are looking toward her. Short mutual gaze ($\sim$1 sec) is a powerful mechanism that induces arousal in the other participants [27]. Gaze diminishes when disavowing social contact. By avoiding eye gaze in an apparently natural way, an audience expresses an unwillingness to speak.

Table 4.3 Turn-taking and associated gaze behaviors.

State	Signals	Gaze Behavior
Speaker	Turn yielding	Look toward listener
	Turn claiming suppression signal	Avert gaze contact from audience
	Within turn signal	Look toward audience
	No turn signal	Look away
Audiences	Back channel signal	Look toward speaker
	Turn claiming signal	Seek gaze contact from speaker
	Turn suppression signal	Avert gaze contact from speaker
	Turn claiming suppression signal	Look toward other aspiring audiences to prevent their speaking
	No response	Random

Conversation proceeds in turns. Two mutually exclusive states are posited for each participant: the speaker who claims the speaking turn and the audience who does not. Gaze provides turn-taking signals to regulate the flow of communication. Table 4.3 shows how gaze behaviors act to maintain and regulate multiparty conversations. Figure 4.8 shows sample images of the face2face.com animated face with eye movements.

In dyadic conversation, at the completion of an utterance or thought unit, the speaker gives a lengthy glance to the audience to yield a speaking turn. This gaze cue persists until the audience assumes the speaking role (Fig. 4.9(a)). The multiparty case requires a turn-allocation strategy. Inspired by Sacks [38], we address

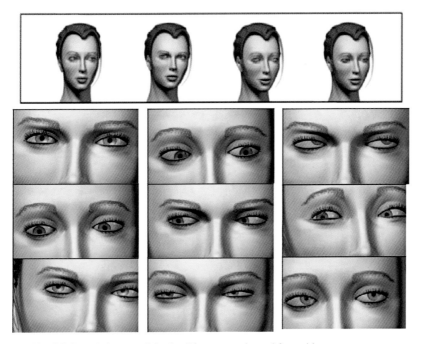

Fig. 4.8 Sample images of the face2face.com animated face with eye movements.

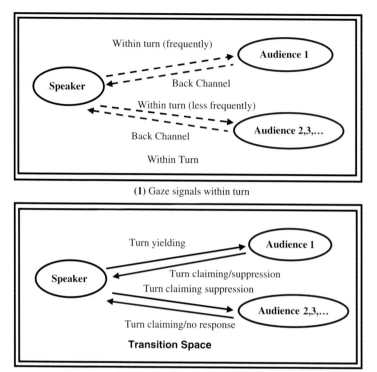

(1) Gaze signals within turn

(2) Gaze signals in Transition Space

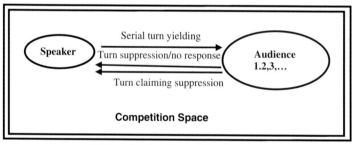

(3) Gaze signals in Competition Space

Fig. 4.9 Diagrams for turn taking allocation employed conversational gaze signal.

the multiparty issue with two mechanisms: a *transition space*, where the speaker selects the next speaker, and a *competition space*, where the next turn is allocated by self-selection.

Transition space (Fig. 4.9(b))

Speaker:

1: She gives a lengthy glance (turn yielding) to one of the audiences.

    2.i: Receiving gaze contact (turn claiming) from the audience, the speaker relinquishes the floor.

2.ii: Receiving gaze aversion (turn suppression) from the audience, the speaker decides to keep transition space to find another audience or go to competition space directly. If no one wants to speak, the speaker has the option of continuing or halting.

Audience:

1: An audience who wants a turn will look toward speaker's eyes to signal her desire to speak (turn claiming), and want to draw the attention of the speaker.
2: An audience receiving speaker gaze (turn yielding) uses quick gaze contact (turn claiming) to accept the turn or lengthy gaze aversion (turn suppression) to reject it.

Competition space (Fig. 4.9(c))
Speaker:
She scans all the audiences, serially sending a turn yielding signal (see Figs. 4.10(a) and (b)).

(a)

(b)

(c)

Fig. 4.10 Sample images from a five-party conversation demonstration. (a) A full-view image of five conversational agents sitting around a table; the main speaker is in the foreground with her back to the camera. (b) The main speaker sends a turn-yielding gaze signal to the agent sitting to her right. (c) The main speaker sends a turn gaze-yielding signal to the agent sitting on the first place to her left.

Audience:

They may have eye interactions at that time. The aspiring audience looks toward the speaker to signal a desire to speak (turn claiming). After receiving visual contact from the speaker, she looks at all the other aspiring audiences to signal her taking the floor (turn claiming suppression). Non-aspiring audiences may follow the speaker's gaze direction or use random gaze (no response).

Turns begin and end smoothly, with short lapses of time in between. Occasionally an audience's turn-claim in the absence of a speaker's turn signal results in simultaneous turns [27] between audiences, even between audience and speaker. Favorable simultaneous turns will occur that show it is a comfortable and communicative circumstance. The general rule is that the first speaker continues and the others drop out. The dropouts lower gaze or avert gaze to signal giving up.

Within a turn, audiences spend more time looking toward the speaker (back channel) to signal attention and interest. They focus on the speaker's face area around the eyes. The speaker generally looks less often at audiences except to monitor their acceptance and understanding (within turn signal). The speaker glances during grammatical breaks, at the end of a thought unit or idea, and at the end of the utterance to obtain feedback. The speaker usually assigns a longer and more frequent glance to the audience to whom she would like pass the floor.

4.6 Synthesis of Natural Eye Movement

A detailed block diagram of the eye movement synthesis model is illustrated in Fig. 4.11. The key components of the model consist of the (1) **Attention Monitor (AttMon)**, (2) **Parameter Generator (ParGen)**, and (3) **Saccade Synthesizer (SacSyn)**.

AttMon monitors the system state and other necessary information, such as whether it is in talking, listening, or thinking mode, whether the direction of the

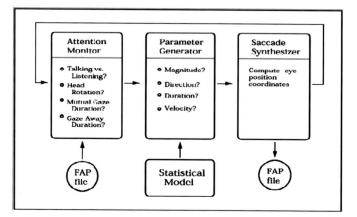

Fig. 4.11 Block diagram of the statistical eye movement model.

head rotation has changed, or whether the current frame has reached the mutual gaze duration or gaze away duration. By default, the synthesis state starts from the mutual gaze state.

If the direction of head rotation has changed and its amplitude is larger than an empirically chosen threshold, then it invokes **ParGen** to initiate eye movement. Also, if the timer for either mutual gaze or gaze away duration is expired, it invokes **ParGen**. **ParGen** determines saccade magnitude, direction, duration, and instantaneous velocity. It also decides the gaze away duration or mutual gaze duration depending on the current state. Then it invokes **SacSyn**, where appropriate saccade movement is synthesized and coded into FAP values.

Saccade magnitude is determined using the inverse of the exponential fitting function of Fig. 4.4(a). First, a random number between 0 and 15 is generated. The random number corresponds to the y-axis (percentage of frequency) in Fig. 4.4(a). The magnitude is computed from the inverse of Eq. 4.3,

$$A = -6.9*\log(P/15.7), \qquad (4.7)$$

where A is the saccade magnitude in degrees and P is the random number generated, i.e., the percentage of occurrence. This inverse mapping using a random number guarantees that the saccade magnitude has the same probability distribution as shown in Fig. 4.4(a). Based on the analysis result in Section 4.4.3, the maximum saccade magnitude is limited to $27.5°$ for talking mode and $22.7°$ for listening mode. The maximum magnitude thresholds are determined by the average magnitude plus one standard deviation for each mode.

Saccade direction is determined by two criteria. If the head rotation is larger than a threshold, the saccade direction follows the head rotation. Otherwise, the direction is determined based on the distribution shown in Table 4.1. A uniformly distributed random number between 0 and 100 is generated and 8 non-uniform intervals are assigned to the respective directions. That is, a random number between 0–15.54 is assigned to the direction $0°$ (right), a number between 15.54–22.00 to the direction $45°$ (up-right), and so on. Thus, 15.54% of the time a pure rightward saccade will occur, and 6.46% of the time an up-rightward saccade will be generated.

Given a saccade magnitude A, the duration is calculated using Eq. 4.1 with values $d = 2.4$ msec/deg and $D_0 = 25$ msec. The velocity of the saccade is then determined using the fitted instantaneous velocity curve (Eq. 4.4). Given the saccade duration D in frames, the instantaneous velocity model is resampled at D times the original sample rate (1/6). The resulting velocity follows the shape of the fitted curve with the desired duration D.

In talking mode, the mutual gaze duration and gaze away duration are determined similarly to the other parameters, using inverses of the polynomial fitting functions (Eqs. 4.5 and 4.6). Using the random numbers generated for the percentage range, corresponding durations are calculated by root-solving the fitting functions. The resulting durations have the same probability distributions. In listening mode, intersaccadic intervals are obtained using Gaussian random numbers with the duration values given in Section 4.4.3: 237.5 ± 47.1 frames for mutual gaze and 13.0 ± 7.1 frames for gaze away.

SacSyn collects all synthesis parameters obtained above and calculates the sequence of coordinates for the eye centers. The coordinate values for eye movements are then translated into FAP values for the MPEG-4 standard [24]. For facial animation, we merge the eye movement FAP values with the parameters for lip movement, head movement, and eye blinks provided by the alterEGO system. After synthesizing a saccade movement, **SacSyn** sets the synthesis state to either gaze away state or mutual gaze state. Again, **AttMon** checks the head movement, internal mode of the agent, and the timer for gaze away duration.

When a new eye movement has to be synthesized, **ParGen** is invoked to determine the next target position, e.g., another agent's face. Depending on the next target position, the state either stays at the gaze away state or returns to the mutual gaze state. In addition to applying the saccade data from the FAP file, we incorporate the vestibulo-ocular reflex (VOR). The VOR stabilizes gaze during head movements (as long as they are not gaze saccades) by causing the eyes to counter-roll in the opposite direction [31].

4.7 Conclusions

We presented eye saccade models based on the statistical analysis of an eye-tracking video. The eye-tracking video is segmented and classified into talking, listening, and thinking modes. A saccade model is constructed for each of the three modes. The models reflect the dynamic characteristics of natural eye movement, which include saccade magnitude, duration, velocity, and inter-saccadic interval. In a sample experiment with 12 observers, 10 of 12 judged the model visually and psychologically superior to two alternate methods of automatic gaze generation: no saccades and randomized saccades [28]. This model is implemented on conversational agents during face-to-face interaction. Simultaneously, the role of gaze on the turn-taking allocation strategy, appearance of awareness, and expression of the feedback signal are addressed in the simulation.

One way to generate eye movements on a face model is to replay the eye-tracking data previously recorded from a subject. Preliminary tests using this method indicated that the replayed eye movements looked natural by themselves, but were often not synchronized with speech or head movements. An additional drawback to this method is that it requires new data to be collected every time a novel eye-track record is desired. Once the distributions for the statistical model are derived, any number of unique eye movement sequences can be animated.

The eye movement video used to construct the saccade statistics was limited to a frame rate of 30 Hz, which can lead to aliasing. In practice, this is not a significant problem, best illustrated by an example. Consider a small saccade of $2°$, which will have a duration of around 30 msec (Eq. 4.1). To completely lose all information on the dynamics of this saccade, it must begin within 3 msec of the first frame capture, so that it is completely finished by the second frame capture 33 msec later. This can be expected to happen around 10% of the time (3/33). From Fig. 4.5(b), it can be seen that saccades this small comprise about 20% of all saccades in the record, so only around 2% of all saccades should be severely aliased. This small percentage has little effect on the instantaneous velocity function of Fig. 4.6. Since saccade starting and ending positions are still recoverable from the video, the magnitude and direction are much less susceptible to aliasing problems.

A more important consideration is the handling of the VOR during the eye movement recording. A change in eye position that is due to a saccade (e.g., up and to the left) must be distinguishable from a change that is due to head rotation (e.g., down and to the right). One solution is to include a sensor that monitors head position. When head position is added to eye position, the resultant gaze position is without the effects of the VOR. However, this introduces the new problem that eye and head movements are no longer independent. An alternate approach is to differentiate the eye position data, and threshold the resultant eye velocity (e.g., at $80°/\text{sec}$) to screen out non-saccadic movements. Although this can be performed post-hoc, it is not robust at low sampling rates. For example, revisiting the above example, a $2°$ position change that occurred between two frames may have taken $33\,\text{msec}$ (velocity $=$ $60°/\text{sec}$) or $3\,\text{msec}$ (velocity $=$ $670°/\text{sec}$). In this study, head movements in subjects occurred infrequently enough that they were unlikely to severely contaminate the saccade data. However, in future work they must be better controlled, using improved equipment, more elaborate analysis routines, or a combination of both.

A number of enhancements to our system could be implemented in the future. During the analysis of eye-tracking images, we noticed a high correlation between the eyes and the eyelid movement that could be incorporated; Deng's model can be applied to improve this aspect of the simulation [17]. A scan-path model could be added, using not only the tracking of close-up eye images but also the visual environment images taken from the perspective of the participant's eye. Additional subjects could be added to the pool of saccade data, reducing the likelihood of idiosyncrasies in the statistical model. Other modeling procedures themselves could be investigated, such as neural networks or Markov models. Improvements such as these will further increase the realism of a conversational agent.

Acknowledgment This article is derived and extended from the paper [28] originally published by ACM. The original document may be found at http://doi.acm.org/ 10.1145/566570.566629. Permission to use material for it for this publication is greatly appreciated. Thanks to Eric Petajan, Doug DeCarlo, Minkyu Lee, Ed Roney, Jan Allbeck, Karen Carter, and Koji Ashida for their help and comments, face2face.com for the face-tracking software, John Trueswell for the eye-tracking data, and Andrew Weidenhammer for the face model and subject data. Catherine Pelachaud kindly supplied the Greta head we attached to the UGS Jack bodies running in the Lockheed-Martin Moorestown Human Testbed software. This research was partially supported by the Office of Naval Research K-5-55043/3916-1552793 and N000140410259, NSF IIS-9900297 and IIS-0200983, and NSF-STC Cooperative Agreement number SBR-89-20230.

References

1. Argyle M, Cook M (1976) *Gaze and Mutual Gaze*. Cambridge University Press, London.
2. Argyle M, Dean J (1965) Eye-contact, distance and affiliation. *Sociometry*, 28: 289–304.
3. Bahill AT, Adler D, Stark L (1975) Most naturally occurring human saccades have magnitudes of 15 degrees or less. In: *Investigative Ophthalmol. Vis. Sci.*, 14: 468–469.

4. Becker W (1989) Metrics. In: RH Wurtz and ME Goldberg (eds). *The Neurobiology of Saccadic Eye Movements*, Elsevier Science Publishers BV (Biomedical Division), New York, NY, ch. 2 pp, 13–67.

5. Beeler GW (1965) Stochastic processes in the human eye movement control system. Ph.D. thesis, California Institute of Technology.

6. Bizzi E, Kalil RE, Morasso P, Tagliasco V (1972) Central programming and peripheral feedback during eye-head coordination in monkeys. *Bibl. Ophthal.*, 82: 220–232.

7. Blanz V, Vetter T (1999) A morphable model for the synthesis of 3D faces. In: *Computer Graphics (SIGGRAPH Proc.)*, pp 187–194.

8. Brand M (1999) Voice puppetry. In: *Computer Graphics (SIGGRAPH Proc.)*, pp 21–28.

9. Buckner W, Reese E, Reese R (1987) Eye movement as an indicator of sensory components in thought. *J. Counseling Psych*, 34(3): 283–287.

10. Canny J (1986) A computational approach to edge detection. *IEEE Trans. on Pattern Analysis and Machine Intelligence*, 8(6): 679–698.

11. Cassell J, Pelachaud C, Badler N, Steedman M, Achorn B, Becket T, Douville B, Prevost S, Stone M (1994) Animated conversation: Rule-based generation of facial expression gesture and spoken intonation for multiple conversational agents. In: *Computer Graphics (SIGGRAPH Proc.)*, pp 413–420.

12. Cassell J, Torres O, Prevost S (1999) Turn taking vs. discourse structure: How best to model multimodal conversation. In: Y Wilks (ed) *Machine Conversations*. Kluwer: The Hague, pp 143–154.

13. Cassell J, Vilhjalmsson H, Bickmore T (2001) BEAT: The Behavior Expression Animation Toolkit. In: *Computer Graphics (SIGGRAPH Proc.)*, pp 477–486.

14. Chopra-Khullar S, Badler N (2001) Where to look? Automating visual attending behaviors of virtual human characters. *Autonomous Agents and Multi-Agent Systems*, 4(1/2): 9–23.

15. Colburn A, Cohen MF, Drucker SM (2000) The role of eye gaze in avatar mediated conversational interfaces. Microsoft Tech Report 2000–81.

16. DeCarlo D, Metaxas D, Stone M (1998) An anthropometric face model using variational techniques. In: *Computer Graphics (SIGGRAPH Proc.)*, pp 67–74.

17. Deng Z, Lewis JP, Neumann U (2005) Automated eye motion using texture synthesis. In: *IEEE Computer Graphics and Applications*, 25(2): 24–30.

18. Duncan S (1974) Some signals and rules for taking speaking turns in conversations. In: Weitz (ed) *Nonverbal Communication*. Oxford University Press, New York.

19. Essa I, Pentland A (1995) Facial expression recognition using a dynamic model and motion energy. In: *Proc. ICCV*, pp 360–367.

20. Faigin G (1990) *The Artist's Complete Guide to Facial Expression*. Watson-Guptill Publications, New York.

21. Guenter B, Grimm C, Wood D (1998) Making faces. In: *Computer Graphics (SIGGRAPH Proc.)*, pp 55–66.

22. Gu E (2006) Multiple influences on gaze and attention behavior for embodied agents. Ph.D. thesis, University of Pennsylvania.

23. Gu E, Badler NI (2006) Visual attention and eye gaze during multiparty conversations with distractions. In: *Proc. Intelligent Virtual Agents*, LNAI 4133, pp 193–204.

24. ISO/IEC JTC 1/SC 29/WG11 (1999) N3055/N3056. MPEG-4 Manuals.

25. Kalra P, Mangili A, Magnenat-Thalmann N, Thalmann D (1992) Simulation of muscle actions using rational free form deformations. In: *Proc. Eurographics, Computer Graphics Forum*, 2(3): 59–69.

26. Kendon A (1967) Some functions of gaze direction in social interaction. *Acta Psychologica*, 26: 22–63.

27. Knapp ML, Hall JA (1997) The effects of eye behavior on human communication. In: *Nonverbal Communication in Human Interaction*, 4th ed. Harcourt Brace, Fort Worth, TX.

28. Lee SP, Badler J, Badler N (2002) Eyes alive. *ACM Trans. on Graphics (SIGGRAPH Proc.)*, 21(3): 637–644.

29. Lee WS, Magnenat-Thalmann N (2000) Fast head modeling for animation. In: *Image and Vision Computing*, 18(4): 355–364.

30. Lee Y, Terzopoulos D, Waters K (1995) Realistic modeling for facial animation. In: *Computer Graphics (SIGGRAPH Proc.)*, pp 55–62.
31. Leigh RJ, Zee DS (2006) *The Neurology of Eye Movements*, 4th ed. Oxford University Press, New York.
32. Parke F (1982) Parameterized models for facial animation. *IEEE Computer Graphics and Applications*, 2(9): 61–68.
33. Pasquariello S, Pelachaud C (2001) Greta: A simple facial animation engine. In: 6th Online World Conf. on Soft Computing in Industrial Applications, Session on Soft Computing for Intelligent 3D Agents.
34. Pelachaud C, Badler N, Steedman M (1996) Generating facial expressions for speech. *Cognitive Science*, 20(1): 1–46.
35. Petajan E (1999) Very low bitrate face animation coding in MPEG-4. In: *Encyclopedia of Telecommunications*, 17: 209–231.
36. Pighin F, Hecker J, Lischinski D, Szeliski R, Salesin DH (1998) Synthesizing realistic facial expressions from photographs. In: *Computer Graphics (SIGGRAPH Proc.)*, pp 75–84.
37. Platt S, Badler N (1981) Animating facial expressions. In: *Computer Graphics (SIGGRAPH Proc.)*, pp 245–252.
38. Sacks H, Schegloff EA, Jefferson, G (1974) A simplest systematics for the organization of turn-taking for conversation. *Language*, 50: 696–735.
39. Vertegaal R, Slagter R, van der Veer G, Nijholt A (2000b) Why conversational agents should catch the eye. In: Summary of ACM CHI 2000 Conference on Human Factors in Computing Systems.
40. Vertegaal R, Slagter R, van der Veer G, Nijholt A (2001) Eye gaze patterns in conversations; there is more to conversational agents than meets the eyes. In: ACM CHI Conference on Human Factors in Computing Systems, pp 301–308.
41. Vertegaal R, van der Veer G, Vons H (2000a) Effects of gaze on multiparty mediated communication. In: *Proc. Graphics Interface*, Morgan Kaufmann, San Francisco, pp 95–102.
42. Warabi T (1977) The reaction time of eye-head coordination in man. *Neuroscience Letters*, 6: 47–51.
43. Waters K (1987) A muscle model for animating three-dimensional facial expression. In: *Computer Graphics (SIGGRAPH Proc.)*, pp 17–24.
44. Garau M, Slater M, Bee S, Sasse M (2001) The impact of eye gaze on communication using humanoid avatars, In *Proc. CHI*, pp. 309–316.

Chapter 5
Realistic Eye Motion Synthesis by Texture Synthesis

Zhigang Deng, J.P. Lewis, and Ulrich Neumann

5.1 Introduction

Making realistic facial animations is generally regarded as one of the most challenging research topics in the graphics and computer animation community, partly due to the fact that producing photo-realistic and emotive virtual characters requires a demanding combination of face modeling, animation, and rendering. Of the parts of the face, the eye motions are particularly scrutinized. Furthermore, eye motion is one of the strongest cues to the mental states of a person, as reflected in the saying, "the eyes are windows to the soul." In fact, in attempts to create realistic animated virtual characters, the eyes are often the things that observers point out as looking wrong.

In this chapter, we describe an automated approach for generating eye motions using texture synthesis.[1] The goal of this work is to improve the realism of aspects of eye movements, including gaze saccades and correlated eyelid motions. We formalize the synthesis of eye motions as a one-dimensional texture synthesis problem. While applying efficient one-dimensional versions of the popular nonparametric sampling paradigm, we found that synthesized eye motions are hard to distinguish from the captured eye motions.

Explicitly characterizing and modeling eye motions is difficult, because though there may be some connection between eye gaze and eyelid motions, the connection is not strictly deterministic. For example, as suggested in Figs. 5.2–5.4, gaze changes often appear to be associated with blinks. A data-driven stochastic modeling approach is more appropriate in this case, because without explicitly determining the possible correlations, data-driven approaches are still valid for synthesizing eye motions—if the correlations are in the data, the synthesis (properly applied) will reproduce them. Further, it should be noted that the combined gaze-blink vector signal does not have obvious segmentation points. Thus, we think adapting texture synthesis approaches to the problem of realistic eye motion synthesis would be more appropriate than motion graph approaches. In this work, eye gaze and aligned eye

---

[1] Portions reprinted, with permission, from (Z Deng, JP Lewis, and U Neumann, Automated eye motion using texture synthesis, IEEE Computer Graphics & Applications, 25(2), March/April 2005, pp. 24–30). © 2005 IEEE.

Z. Deng and U. Neumann, *Data-Driven 3D Facial Animation.*

blink motion will be considered together as an *eye motion texture* sample and will be used for synthesizing novel but similar-in-character eye motions.

To justify this choice of a texture synthesis approach over a hand-crafted statistical model, consider the *order statistics* classification of statistical models: the first-order statistics *p(x)* used in [1] capture the probability of events of different magnitude but do not model any correlation between different events. Correlation *E[xy]* is a "second-order moment," or an average of the second-order statistics, *p(x,y)*. Third-order statistics would consider the joint probability of triples of events *p(x,y,z)*, etc. Increasing the order of statistics would result in more powerful models, but suffers from the accordingly increased complexity of modeling algorithms and poor performance if the model is derived from insufficient training data. On the other hand, low-order statistics models are generally incapable of modeling complex correlations and clearly do not capture some visible features (Fig. 5.1).

Hidden Markov models (HMM), a powerful probabilistic modeling framework proved in speech recognition applications, would be another possible choice for eye motion synthesis. The challenge in applying HMMs to this problem is that the required architecture and number of hidden states is not obvious; because the model must potentially capture subtle "mental states" (such as agitated, distracted, etc.) as manifested in eye movement, the mappings between the hidden states and observations also may not be easily created. As such, even though HMM-based

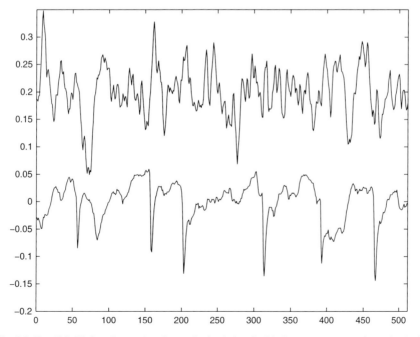

Fig. 5.1 Eye "blink" data (bottom) and a synthesized signal with the same autocovariance (top). A simple statistical model cannot reproduce the correlation and asymmetry characteristics evident in the data. Reprinted with permission from ©2005 IEEE.

approaches would probably work for this problem to some extent, the effort of designing and training suitable HMMs may not be worth the effort if the goal is simply to synthesize animated eye movements mimicking an original sample. By adopting a data-driven texture synthesis idea, we avoid this issue and let the data "speak for itself," thereby generating eye movements that are indistinguishable in character from captured eye motions.

The remaining sections are organized as follows: Section 5.2 briefly reviews related work in eye motion generation. Section 5.3 describes the eye motion data acquisition and pre-processing. Section 5.4 describes the eye motion synthesis algorithm. Section 5.5 addresses the patch-size selection issue encountered in the synthesis algorithm. The final sections of this chapter describe our results and evaluations (Section 5.6) and conclusions and future work (Section 5.7).

5.2 Related Work

There has been quite a lot research effort that model eye gaze motions in different scenarios [2, 3, 4, 5, 6, 1, 7]. For example, the rule-based approach proposed by Cassell et al. [2, 3] generates animated nonverbal behaviors based on linguistic and context analysis of input texts. Chopra-Khullar et al. [4] present a psychologically motivated framework for computing visual attending behaviors including eye and head motions of virtual agents in dynamic environments, given high-level scripts. Experiments by Vertegaal et al. [5, 6] were designed to validate whether eye gaze direction cues can be used as a reliable signal for determining who is talking to whom in multi-agent, multi-user environments. Their results indicated that gaze directions indeed have a high correlation with the person who is talking and listening. Lee et al. [1] gave a detailed summary of these and other investigations of eye movement. Most of these approaches take a goal-directed approach to gaze and focus on major gaze events such as those for effecting conversational turn-taking. These high-level directions indicate what the eyes should do and where the eyes should look, but not the details of eye motions. There is still some freedom as to how particular gaze changes should be performed—the detailed timing of eye saccades and blinks can convey various mental states such as excited or sleepy.

The "Eyes Alive" work by Lee et al. [1] presented the first in-depth treatment of these "textural" aspects of eye movements and built a first-order statistical model of eye saccades based on gaze signals from an eye tracker. Their work also demonstrated the necessity of this detail for achieving realism and conveying an appropriate mental state. However, eye movements are remarkably complex, and not all aspects of eye movements are considered in their work. Specifically, only first-order statistics are used, and gaze-eyelid coupling and vergence are not considered. In this work we will address the first two of these issues by introducing a more powerful statistical model that simultaneously captures gaze blink coupling.

5.3 Eye Motion Acquisition and Preprocessing

A Vicon motion capture system is used to capture facial motions of a human subject who spoke naturally like a newscaster, with markers on his face. The motion capture rig consists of 6 cameras and works with a 120-Hz sampling frequency. Two markers are put on the eyelids to capture eye blink motions. Besides the motion capture system, a commercial video camera was used to record his front face simultaneously. The recorded motion capture data consist of about 16,500 motion capture frames.

After motion data were acquired from the system, first we need to convert the recorded eyelid motion into an "eye blink" texture signal, which is one-dimensional. Because the motions in three directions (X, Y, and Z) are strongly correlated—and among all aspects of eyelid movement, eyelid openness is the main aspect we want to address in this work—the eye blink motion in three dimensions can be represented by a one-dimensional "blink" signal based on the dominant Y (vertical) direction. As shown in Fig. 5.2, we found that the motion of the left eyelid is approximately synchronized with that of the right eyelid. We only need the motion capture trace of one eye to create eye blink texture signals. We further normalized the extracted eye blink signals into the range [0,1]—here 0 denotes a closed eyelid, 1 denotes a fully open eyelid, and any value between 0 and 1 represents a partially open eyelid. During this process, outliers in the motion data are discarded, and the gap will be filled by interpolating neighbor points.

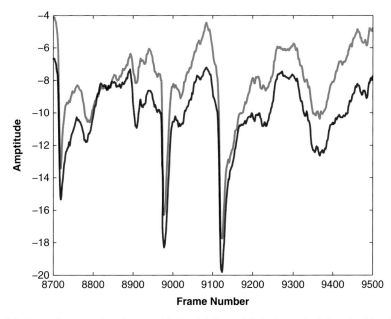

Fig. 5.2 Y-coordinate motion of captured left and right eye blinks (green for left and red for right). Reprinted with permission from ©2005 IEEE.

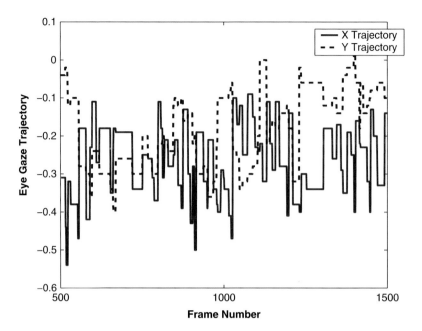

Fig. 5.3 Labeled eye gaze signals: solid red for X trajectory and dashed blue for Y trajectory. Reprinted with permission from ⓒ2005 IEEE.

Various eye-tracking algorithms have been proposed, such as velocity-threshold identification and dispersion-based algorithms. A detailed summary and comparisons of these eye-tracking algorithms can be found in the work of Sawucci and Goldberg [8]. In this work, fixation and saccade signals of the eyes were obtained by manually estimating the eye direction in recorded video clips frame by frame using an "eyeball tracking widget" in a custom GUI (Fig. 5.5). Achieving complete accuracy through the manual estimation is a very difficult task, but the estimated eye signals qualitatively capture the character and cadence of real human gaze movement, and the gaze durations are frame-accurate. The resulting gaze signals are shown in Fig. 5.3. It should be noted that the piecewise-continuous character of these signals is consistent with the fact that our eyes tend to fixate on some point for a period of time and then rapidly shift to another point (called saccades). When doing a large change in gaze direction, it appears that the eyes often execute several smaller shifts rather than a single large and smooth motion. We also observed that gaze changes frequently occur during blinks.

5.4 Eye Motion Synthesis

Data-driven approaches for human motion synthesis have been the subject of increasing attention in the computer animation community. Several approaches partition human motion data into small segments and then concatenate these

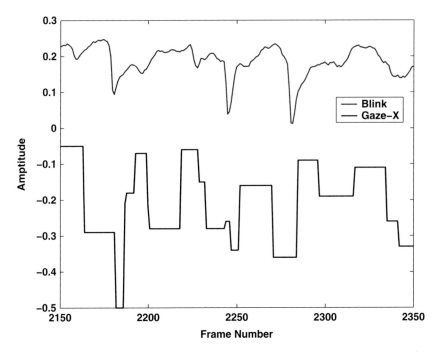

Fig. 5.4 Eye blink and gaze-x signals are plotted simultaneously. Reprinted with permission from ©2005 IEEE.

segments together based on specified constraints [9, 10]. Texture synthesis techniques are originally used to generate a large texture based on a small texture sample, and it can be considered as another kind of data-driven approaches. The basic idea of non-parametric sampling [11, 12, 13] is to grow one sample (or one patch) at a time given an initial seed, by identifying all regions of the sample texture that are sufficiently similar to the neighborhood of the sample, and randomly selecting the corresponding sample (or patch) from one of these regions (the left panel of Fig. 5.6). These texture synthesis algorithms have some resemblance to the above approaches [9, 10], though they differ in that the entire texture training data is searched for matching candidates, whereas in the motion capture case the data are divided into segments in advance and only transitions between these segments are searched—this trade-off assumes that possible matches in texture-like data are too many and too varied to be profitably identified in advance. In this work, texture synthesis algorithms are used in the one dimension case (the right panel of Fig. 5.6). The patch-based sampling algorithm [13] is chosen due to its time efficiency. For more details about this algorithm, please refer to [13].

In this work, each texture sample (analogous to a pixel in the 2D image texture case) consists of three elements: the eye blink signal, the x position of eye gaze signal, and the y position of the eye gaze signal. If $t^i = (b, g_1, g_2)$ is used to represent

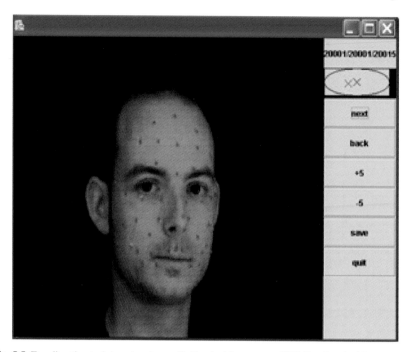

Fig. 5.5 Eye direction training signals are digitized with a custom GUI. Reprinted with permission from ©2005 IEEE.

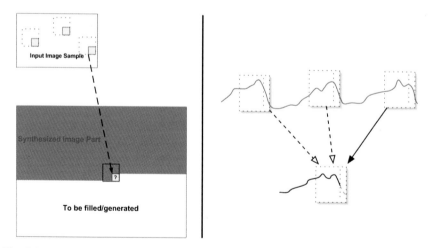

Fig. 5.6 Non-parametric sampling for texture synthesis. The left panel shows the standard 2D image case, and the right panel shows our eye motion signal case. In the right panel, regions in a sample signal (top) that are similar to the neighborhood of the signal being synthesized (bottom) are identified. One such region is randomly chosen, and new samples are copied from it to the synthesized signal.

one eye motion texture sample, we compute its elements as follows: the variance of each element is estimated in a standard way (Eq. 5.1):

$$V_\tau = \frac{1}{N-1} \sum_{i=1}^{N} (t_\tau^i - \bar{t}_\tau)^2. \qquad (5.1)$$

Here $\tau = b, g_1, g_2$.

After their variances, V_b, V_{g_1}, and V_{g_2}, are computed respectively from the above step, each element (component) is divided by its variance to give it an equal contribution to the candidate patch searching. To measure the similarity between two (eye motion) patches, we need to define a distance metric. In this work, a distance metric between two texture patches is defined as follows:

$$d(B_{\text{in}}, B_{\text{out}}) = \left(\frac{1}{W} \sum_{k=1}^{W} dtex(T\text{in}^k, T\text{out}^k)\right)^{1/2}, \qquad (5.2)$$

$$dtex(t^s, t^d) = (b^s - b^d)^2 / V_b + (g_1^s - g_1^d)^2 / V_{g_1} + (g_2^s - g_2^d)^2 / V_{g_2}. \qquad (5.3)$$

Here T[in] represents input eye motion samples, T[out] represents synthesized (output) eye motion samples, and W is the size of boundary zone that functions as a search window. The patch size essentially depends on the properties of a given texture, and a proper choice is critical to the success of the above eye motion synthesis algorithm. If the patch size is too small, it cannot capture the characteristics of eye motions (e.g., it may cause the eye gaze to change too frequently and look too active); if it is too large, there are fewer possible matching patches and more training data are required to produce variety in the synthesized motion. In this work, the patch size is experimentally set to 20 and the boundary zone size is set to 4. (Section 5.5 describes how to determine the proper patch size from the data.)

Another parameter used in this algorithm is the distance tolerance, which is defined as follows:

$$d_{\max} = \epsilon \left(\frac{1}{W} \sum_{k=1}^{W} dtex(t_{\text{out}}^k, 0_3)^2\right)^{1/2}. \qquad (5.4)$$

Here 0_3 is a three-dimensional zero vector. In this study, we experimentally set the tolerance constant to 0.2. Figures 5.7 to 5.9 illustrate synthesized eye motions. Note that the synthesized signals in these figures are synthesized at the same time, which is necessary to capture the possible correlations between them.

5.5 Patch Size Selection

As mentioned in Section 5.4, proper patch size is important to the success of this eye motion synthesis algorithm. In order to determine the proper patch size in this eye motion synthesis algorithm, we look into transition interval distributions in the recorded eye motion data.

We count all the time intervals (in terms of frame number) between two adjacent approximate eye blink actions in the recorded eye blink data. If the eye blink value (openness of eyelid) is less than a threshold value (experimentally set to 0.2), then it is counted as an "approximate eye blink." It should be noted that setting this threshold is subjective and experimental, but this threshold is used only for the purpose of choosing the texture patch size. The eye blink synthesis uses the original un-thresholded data.

For eye gaze data, we count all the time intervals between two adjacent "large saccadic movements." These are defined as places where either the x- or y-movement is larger than a threshold value (experimentally set to 0.1). Then, we collect all these time intervals and plot their distributions (Fig. 5.10). From Fig. 5.10, we found that a time interval of 20 is a good transition point: when the time interval is less than 20, the covered percentage increased rapidly, while it slows down when it is larger than 20. The accumulated coverage is about 55.68% of the "large eye motions" when the

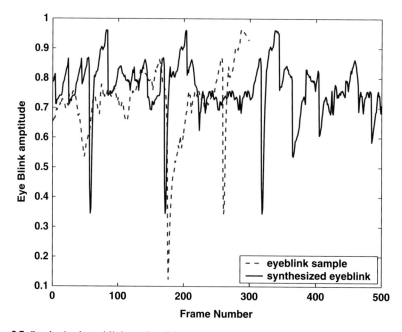

Fig. 5.7 Synthesized eye blink motion (blue) vs. eye blink sample (red dots). The X-axis represents the frame number and Y-axis represents the eyelid opening. Reprinted with permission from ⓒ2005 IEEE.

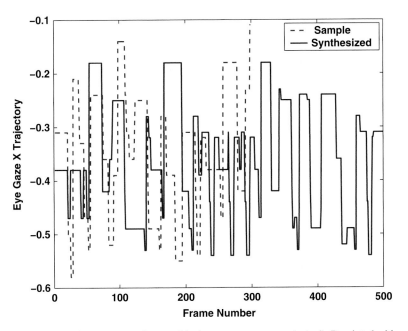

Fig. 5.8 Synthesized eye gaze *x* trajectory (blue) vs. eye gaze-*x* sample (red). Reprinted with permission from ©2005 IEEE.

time interval limit is set to 20. As such, we experimentally set 20 as the proper patch size for the eye motion synthesis algorithm.

The size of the boundary zone is another tricky parameter used in the algorithm, which is used to control the number of "texture-block candidates": if the size of boundary zone is too large, then few candidates are available and the diversity of the synthesized motion is impaired. On the other hand, if this size is too small, some of the higher-order statistics of eye motion are not captured and the resulting synthesis looks *jumpy*. We adopted a similar strategy as used in [13], where the size of the boundary zone is a fraction of the patch size, e.g., 1/6. As such, we chose 4 as the size of boundary zone; in practice, it works well.

5.6 Results and Evaluations

To evaluate this approach, we took one segment from extracted eye motion sequence as an "eye motion texture sample" and synthesized novel eye motions based on this sample; finally, we conducted subjective experiments. We found that our synthesis algorithm produces eye movement that looks alert and lively, rather than other moods (e.g., the drugged, agitated, or "schizophrenic" moods), although the realism is difficult to judge since the face model itself is not completely photo-realistic. Figure 5.11 shows some frames of synthesized eye motions.

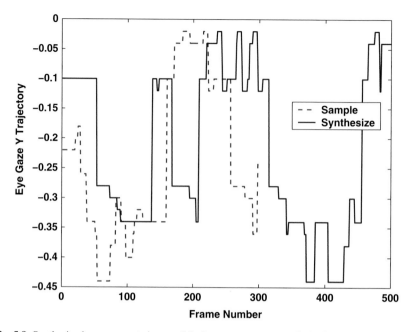

Fig. 5.9 Synthesized eye gaze *y* trajectory (blue) vs. eye gaze-*y* sample (red). Reprinted with permission from ©2005 IEEE.

To compare this method with other approaches, we synthesized eye motions using three different methods. Subjective evaluations were conducted on these eye motions that were played on the same face model. In the first result (Method I), the Eyes Alive model [1] was used to generate gaze motion, and the eye blink motion was sampled from a Poisson distribution (note that "discrete event" in this Poisson distribution means "eyelid close" event). In the second result (Method II), both random eye gaze and eye blink were sampled from Poisson distributions. In the third (Method III), this method synthesized eye blink and gaze motion simultaneously.

Three eye motion videos with the same duration time were presented in random order to 22 viewers who are undergraduate and graduate students at a university. The viewers were asked to rate each eye motion video on a scale from 1 to 10, with 10 indicating a completely natural and realistic motion. Among these 22 participants, one of them thought these two were equivalent and declined to make any choice, and he/she was considered as "an invalid viewer" in our test. We plotted average ratings and standard deviation of this evaluation (Fig. 5.12). As shown in the figure, both Method I (Eyes Alive) and Method III (this approach) received much higher scores than Method II (random), and in fact viewers slightly preferred the synthesized eye motion by this approach (Method III) over that of Method I.

A second subjective test was also conducted to see whether it is possible to distinguish the synthesized eye motions by this approach from the original captured eye motions. In this test, 15 viewers were asked to forcibly identify the original (assuming the original has better motions) after they carefully watched two eye motion

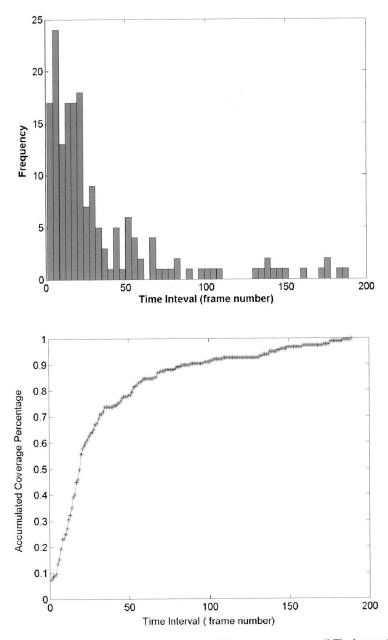

Fig. 5.10 The top is the histogram of time intervals of "large eye movements." The bottom is the accumulated covered percentage vs. time interval limit. When the time interval limit is 20, the covered percentage is 55.68%. Reprinted with permission from ©2005 IEEE.

Fig. 5.11 Some frames of synthesized eye motion. Reprinted with permission from ©2005 IEEE.

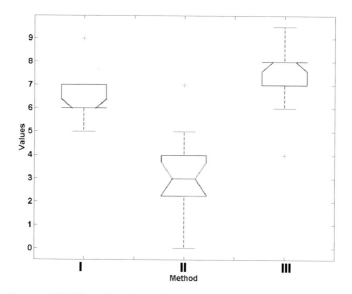

Fig. 5.12 One-way ANOVA results of our evaluations. The *p*-value is 2.3977e-10. Reprinted with permission from ©2005 IEEE.

videos (one is original captured eye motion, the other is synthesized from this captured segment) a number of times. Evaluations results are as follow: seven out of 15 made correct choices, and the other eight subjects made wrong choices. We used a normal approximation to the binomial distribution with $p = 7/15$, and found that equality ($p = 0.5$) is easily within the 95% confidence interval (See the appendix). It should be noted that because of this small number of participants in our test, more experiments and tests are still needed to fully conclude that the original and synthesized video clips are truly indistinguishable.

5.7 Conclusions and Future Work

In this chapter, instead of generating eye motions from programmer-defined rules or heuristics, or using a hand-crafted statistical model, we explore a "motion texture" strategy and successfully apply it to produce realistic eye motions. We also demonstrated that texture synthesis techniques can be applied in the animation realm, to the modeling of incidental facial motion. Our subjective evaluations validated that the quality of statistical modeling and the introduction of gaze-eyelid coupling are improvements over previous work, and the synthesized results are hard to distinguish from actual captured eye motions.

A limitation of this approach is that it is hard to know in advance how much data are needed to avoid getting stuck in the motion synthesis procedure. However, after generating some animations it is easy to evaluate the variety of synthesized movement, and more data can be obtained if necessary. Our approach works reasonably well for applications where nonspecific but natural-looking automated eye motions are required, such as for action game characters, etc. We are aware that complex eye gaze motions exist in many scenarios, especially communications among multiple agents.

In future work, we want to verify whether different *moods* (attentive, bored, nervous, etc.) can be reproduced by our approach. Head rotation (and, especially rotation-compensated gaze) and vergence will need to be addressed, for example, properly incorporating data-driven head motion generation techniques [14, 15] would enhance the overall realism of virtual avatars. It should also be noted that fully realistic eye movement involves a variety of phenomena not considered here, such as upper eyelid shape changes due to eyeball movement, skin deformation around the eyes due to muscle movement, etc.

References

1. S.P. Lee, J.B. Badler, and N. Badler. Eyes alive. *ACM Trans. Graph. (Proc. ACM SIG-GRAPH'02)*, 21(3):637–644, 2002.
2. J. Cassell, C. Pelachaud, N. Badler, M. Steedman, B. Achorn, T. Becket, B. Douville, S. Prevost, and M. Stone. Animated conversation: Rule-based generation of facial expression, gesture and spoken intonation for multiple conversational agents. In *Proc. ACM SIG-GRAPH'94*, pages 413–420, 1994.
3. J. Cassell, H. Vilhjalmsson, and T. Bickmore. Beat: The behavior expression animation toolkit. In *Computer Graphics (Proc. ACM SIGGRAPH'01)*, pages 477–486, Los Angeles, 2001.
4. S.C. Khullar and N. Badler. Where to look? Automating visual attending behaviors of virtual human characters. In *Proc. Third ACM Conf. on Autonomous Agents*, pages 16–23, 1999.
5. R. Vertegaal, G.V. Derveer, and H. Vons. Effects of gaze on multiparty mediated communication. In *Proc. Graphics Interface'00*, pages 95–102, Montreal, Canada, 2000.
6. R. Vertegaal, R. Slagter, G.V. Derveer, and A. Nijholt. Eye gaze patterns in conversations: There is more to conversational agents than meets the eyes. In *Proc. ACM CHI 2001 Conf. Human Factors in Computing Systems*, pages 301–308, 2001.
7. E. Gu and N. Badler. Visual attention and eye gaze during multiparty conversations with distractions. In *Proc. Int. Conf. Intelligent Virtual Agents 06*, pages 193–204, 2006.
8. D.D. Salvucci and J.H. Goldberg. Identifying fixations and saccades in eye-tracking protocols. In *Proc. Symp. on Eye Tracking Research and Applications (ETRA)*, pages 71–78, 2000.
9. O. Arikan and D.A. Forsyth. Interactive motion generation from examples. In *ACM Trans. Graph. (Proc. ACM SIGGRAPH'02)*, volume 21, pages 483–490. ACM Press, 2002.
10. L. Kovar, M. Gleicher, and F. Pighin. Motion graphs. *ACM Trans. Graph. (Proc. ACM SIGGRAPH'02)*, 21(3), 2002.

11. A. Efros and T.K. Leung. Texture synthesis by non-parametric sampling. In *ICCV'99*, pages 1033–1038, 1999.
12. L.Y. Wei and M. Levoy. Fast texture synthesis using tree-structured vector quantization. In *Proc. SIGGRAPH'00*, 2000.
13. L. Liang, C. Liu, Y. Q. Xu, B. Guo, and H.Y. Shum. Real-time texture synthesis by patch-based sampling. *ACM Trans. Graphics*, 20(3), 2001.
14. Z. Deng, C. Busso, S.S. Narayanan, and U. Neumann. Audio-based head motion synthesis for avatar-based telepresence systems. In *Proc. ACM SIGMM 2004 Workshop on Effective Telepresence (ETP 2004)*, pages 24–30, New York, Oct. 2004.
15. C. Busso, Z. Deng, U. Neumann, and S. Narayanan. Natural head motion synthesis driven by acoustic prosody features. *Journal of Computer Animation and Virtual Worlds*, 16(3-4): 283–290, July 2005.

Appendix

Suppose N subjects were asked to make evaluations, and n out of N made wrong choices. Now we estimate the probability distribution of making wrong choices. First, suppose X denotes the probability of making wrong choices, D denotes the observed data, I denotes prior information about X, and $P(X|I)$ is uniform in $(0,1)$.

According to Bayes's theorem, we get the following:

$$P(X = x|D, I)dx = (P(X|I)_{x->x+dx}P(D|X, I)_{X=x})/(P(D|I)),$$

$$P(X|I)_{x->x+dx} = 1.dx, P(D|X = x, I) = x^n(1 - x)^{N-n},$$

$$P(D|I) = \int_0^1 P(D|X = x, I)dx = (n(N - n))/((N + 1)).$$

Thus, $P(X|D, I) = ((N + 1))/(n(N - n)).x^n.(1 - x)^{N-n}$. Let $d(P(X|D, I))/dx = 0$; then we get estimated X' and its standard deviation σ $X' = n/N$,

$$\sigma = \sqrt{\text{var}(x)} = \sqrt{\int_0^1 (x - x')^2.(N + 1)/(n(N - n)).x^n(1 - x)^{N-n}dx},$$

$$= \sqrt{2/((N + 2)(N + 3)) + X'(1 - X')(N - 6)/((N + 2)(N + 3))}.$$

Chapter 6
Learning Expressive Human-Like Head Motion Sequences from Speech

Carlos Busso, Zhigang Deng, Ulrich Neumann, and Shrikanth Narayanan

6.1 Introduction

With the development of new trends in human-machine interfaces, animated feature films, and video games, better avatars and virtual agents are required that more accurately mimic how humans communicate and interact. Gestures and speech are jointly used to express intended messages. The tone and energy of the speech, facial expression, rigid head motion, and hand motion combine in a nontrivial manner as they unfold in natural human interaction. Given that the use of large motion capture data sets is expensive and can only be applied in planned scenarios, new automatic approaches are required to synthesize realistic animation that capture and resemble the complex relationship between these communicative channels. One useful and practical approach is the use of acoustic features to generate gestures, exploiting the link between gestures and speech.

Since the shape of the lips is determined by the underlying articulation, acoustic features have been used to generate visual *visemes* that match the spoken sentences [4, 5, 12, 17]. Likewise, acoustic features have been used to synthesize facial expressions [11, 30], exploiting the fact that the same muscles used for articulation also affect the shape of the face [44, 46]. One important gesture that has received less attention than other aspects in facial animations is rigid head motion.

Head motion is important not only to acknowledge active listening or replace verbal information (e.g., "nod"), but also for many aspect of human communication (for details, see [26]). Graf et al. suggested that rigid head motion is used to segment the linguistic units of spoken content, since the timing between the prosodic structure and head motion is consistent [23]. Head motion also improves acoustic perception, as noted by Munhall et al. [36]. They also suggested that head motion helps to distinguish between interrogative and declarative statements. Hill and Johnston show that head motion is used to recognize speaker identity [27]. Moreover, Jefferies et al. suggest that head motion influences the perception of the personality of the animated character. Similarly, our previous work indicates that head motion affects the emotional perception of facial animations [6].

Given the importance of head motion in human-human interaction, this nonverbal channel needs to be properly modeled for realistic facial animation. Kuratate et al. have estimated the correlation levels between prosodic and head motion features [32]. Based on the high correlation levels achieved ($r = 0.8$), they concluded that the production of speech and head motion are internally linked. Even though head motion patterns depend on many other factors such as the underlying semantic content and the personality of the subjects, these results suggest that speech can be used to generate head motion sequences.

In this chapter, the relationship between rigid head motion and prosodic speech is analyzed in terms of emotional categories (neutral state, sadness, happiness, and anger). The results show that head motion and prosodic speech are strongly connected. However, the relationship varies from emotion to emotion, suggesting that emotional models need to be built to generate realistic head motion sequences. Based on this study, a novel approach to synthesize head motion sequences from prosodic speech is presented. In this framework, head poses are quantized in a finite number of clusters or codebooks. For each of these codebooks, a *hidden Markov model* (HMM) is built, taking prosodic features as observations. In the synthesis step, the acoustic features of the test speech are entered in the HMMs and the most likely head motion sequences are generated. Smoothing techniques based on first-order Markov models followed by spherical cubic interpolation are used to ensure continuous head motion sequences. To include emotional patterns in the generated sequences, different sets of HMMs are built for each emotional category. Evaluations of this framework reveal that the generated sequences follow the temporal dynamics of speech well. Moreover, the generated sequences were judged by human raters at the same level of naturalness as the captured head motion sequences. Previous versions of this framework were published in [6, 7].

This chapter is organized as follows: Section 6.2 presents previous work on head motion synthesis. It also motivates the importance of modeling emotion for engaging animated characters. Section 6.3 describes the audio-visual database and the procedure used to extract the audio-visual features. In Section 6.4, the relationship between head motion and prosodic features is analyzed in terms of emotional categories. Section 6.5 describes the framework used to synthesize head motion sequences. Section 6.6 presents the objective and subjective evaluations of this approach. Finally, Section 6.7 gives the concluding remarks and our future research directions.

6.2 Related Work

6.2.1 Head Motion Synthesis

Different approaches have been used to synthesize head motion sequences, given the relationship between head motion and the verbal message. For instance, plain text enriched with manual annotations of discourse functions were used to synthesize well-known head motion gestures such as head "tilt" and "nod." De Carlo et al. present a coding-based platform for real-time facial animation that supports head motion rotation and translation [14]. The movements of the head are driven by manual annotations of specific head motion gestures co-occurring with prominent words in the text. Pelachaud et al. propose a rule-based system to synthesize head movement from text responding to discourse function (e.g., conversational signal and punctuators) [37]. If the emotion of the animation is specified, the velocity and the global pose of the head motion are modified according to predefined rules (e.g., for sadness, the global pose was set with a downward direction). Similar rule-based systems are presented in [10, 43].

Instead of using text, other approaches have been proposed to exploit the prosodic structure of the acoustic signal. The prominence in speech prosody is closely related to head motion [10, 24, 32]. Therefore, it can be used to estimate head motion sequences. Albrecht et al. propose the generation of head movements based on the pitch contour [1]. If the difference between two maxima of the pitch exceeds a threshold, the head is raised. If the difference between two minima exceeds a given threshold, the head is lowered. The amplitude of the upward and downward movements is proportional to the magnitude of the differences. Random movements in the horizontal and vertical axes are added to prevent repetitive movements.

Graf et al. analyze the relationship between head motion and the prosodic structure in the speech [23]. They define few primitives to describe head motion (e.g., "nod") that were consistently observed across speakers. The co-occurrence between these primitives and prosodic events, which were labeled using the *Tones and Break Indices* (ToBI) scheme, are used to estimate the conditional probability of major head movement given pitch accents. A similar approach is presented by Sargin et al., in which specific head motion sequences for "nod" and "tilt" are generated when pitch accent is detected [40]. Unfortunately, these approaches only generate limited head motion gestures, which do not reflect the wide range of head motion patterns displayed during human-human interaction.

Chuang and Bregler present a data-driven approach to synthesize head motion sequences [11]. In this approach, the head motion and pitch contour corresponding to segments in the training data are recorded. The prosodic structure of each new speech signal is compared with the ones in the database with similar emotional content. After selecting the top M matches for each segment in that sentence, a dynamic programming algorithm is used to find the optimum path of the head motion sequences. The cost function is designed to achieve smooth transitions between segments. Deng et al. developed a similar head motion synthesis technique [16]. In addition to searching the M best matches between the novel speech material and the ones in the database, they proposed the inclusion of optional key framing controls. With this extension, the designers were able to incorporate specific rigid head gestures in the animation, such as "head nod." Then, a dynamic programming algorithm maximizes the optimum path between the head motions segments, constrained by the specified key head poses. One advantage of these two studies is that the head motion sequences are not restricted to a few prototype rigid head gestures.

In the proposed framework, the focus is on modeling the temporal relationship between head motion and prosodic features. HMMs are used to estimate discrete representation of head poses from prosodic features. As shown in Section 6.6, the resulting head motion sequences preserve the temporal relation between head motion and speech. More importantly, in the context of facial animation, human evaluators perceived them as natural as the captured head motion sequences.

6.2.2 Emotion in Facial Animation

For engaging talking avatars, special attention needs to be given to include emotional capability in the virtual characters. Importantly, Picard has underscored that emotions play a crucial rule in rational decision making, in perception, and in human interaction [38]. In fact, Gratch and Marsella have proposed the use of emotions as a crucial component in the decision-making model of human-like characters [25]. Therefore, applications such as virtual teachers, animated films, and new human-machine interfaces can be significantly improved by designing control mechanisms to animate the character to properly convey and react according to the desired emotion. Human beings are especially good not only at inferring the affective state of other people, even when emotional clues are subtly expressed, but also in recognizing non-genuine gestures, which challenges the designs of these control systems.

The production mechanisms of gestures and speech are internally linked in the brain. Cassell et al. mention that these mechanisms are not only strongly connected, but also systematically synchronized in different scales (phonemes-words-phases-sentences) [10]. They suggest that hand gestures, facial expressions, head motion, and eye gaze occur at the same time as speech and convey information similar to that in the acoustic signal. Similar observations are mentioned by Kettebekov et al. [31]. They studied *deictic* hand gestures (e.g., pointing) and speech prosody in the context of gesture recognition. They concluded that there is a multimodal co-articulation of gestures and speech, which are loosely coupled.

From an emotional expression point of view in communication, it has been observed that human beings jointly modify gestures and speech to express emotions. Communicative channels such as facial expressions [21, 22], head motion [6, 37], pitch [13, 41], and short-time spectral envelope [47] all present specific patterns under emotional states. Therefore, a more complete human-computer interaction system should include details of the emotional modulation of gestures and speech.

In sum, all these findings suggest that the control system to animate virtual human-like characters needs to be closely related and synchronized with the information provided by the acoustic signal. In addition, these control systems need to model the emotional content that the animated character is supposed to convey. This chapter proposes the use of emotion-dependent models driven by prosodic features to synthesize realistic head motion sequences.

6.3 Audio-Visual Database

The audio-visual database was recorded from an actress who was asked to read a semantically neutral, custom-made, phoneme-balanced corpus four times, expressing different emotions: neutral state, sadness, happiness, and anger, at each reading. Facial markers were attached to her face according to the layout illustrated in Fig. 6.1. The markers were tracked with a VICON motion capture system with three cameras at a sampling rate of 120 frames per second (right of Fig. 6.1). Her

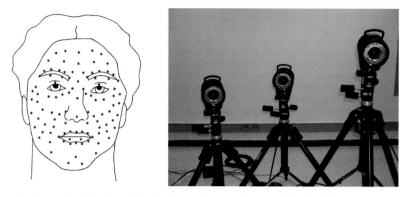

Fig. 6.1 Audio-visual database. The left figure shows the layout of the 102 facial markers, and the right figure shows the motion capture system.

speech was simultaneously recorded with a close talking SHURE microphone at 48 KHz. In total, 640 sentences were used in this work. Notice that the actress was instructed to act naturally without any specific instructions about how to move her head.

After the data were collected, the markers' positions were translated to make the lower nose marker the center of the coordinate system. After that, the three degrees of head rotation were estimated using a technique based on *singular-value decomposition* (SVD) [2]. In this technique, a reference frame was selected from a neutral pose. The 3D positions of the markers were arranged as a 102×3 matrix, referred here on as M_{ref}. Each of its rows contains the x, y, and z location of the markers. Then, for frame t, a matrix M_t is created following the same order as in M_{ref}. Then the SVD, UDV^T, of the matrix $M_t \cdot M_{\mathrm{ref}}$ is calculated. The product VU^T gave the rotation matrix for frame t:

$$M_{\mathrm{ref}}^T \cdot M_t = UDV^T, \qquad (6.1)$$
$$R_t = VU^T. \qquad (6.2)$$

Finally, head motion is modeled as the 3D Euler angles, x_t, corresponding to head rotation, which are derived from R_t (Fig. 6.2). Notice that head motion is usually parameterized with 6 *degrees of freedom* (DOF), corresponding to rotation (3 DOF) and translation (3 DOF) [16, 45]. As discussed in Section 6.5, the proposed framework requires discrete head poses, which are estimated using vector quantization. For a constant quantization error, the number of clusters significantly increases if 6 DOF are considered instead of 3 DOF. Fortunately, from a practical point of view, most applications require a close view of the face, in which translation effects are less important than rotation effects.

The acoustic features were extracted using the Praat speech processing software [3]. The analysis window was set to 25 msec, with an overlap of 8.3 msec, producing 60 frames per second. The pitch (F0) and the RMS energy were estimated. The pitch was smoothed to remove any spurious spikes and interpolated to

Fig. 6.2 Head motion parameterization.

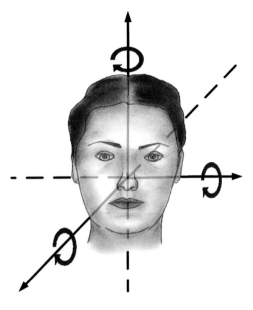

avoid zeros in the unvoiced region of the speech, using the corresponding options provided by the Praat software. The first and second derivatives of these features were also considered, since they provided useful temporal information. In sum, a 6D feature vector was used. Notice that prosodic features predominantly describe the source of the speech rather than the vocal tract. Therefore, this head motion framework is independent of the specific lexical content of the sentence, reducing the size of the database needed to train the models.

6.4 Analysis of Head Motion During Expressive Speech

In this section, a brief analysis of the relationship between head motion and prosodic features in terms of emotional categories is studied. For this purpose, the database was split into emotional categories, and different statistical measures were computed. The main goal of this study is to quantify differences in the head motion patterns displayed under expressive utterances.

To measure the relationship between head motion and prosodic features, *canonical correlation analysis* (CCA) [28] was applied to the data. CCA provides a scale-invariant optimal linear framework to measure the correlation between two streams of data with equal or different dimensionality. In this method, the feature vectors are projected into a common space in which Pearson's correlation can be measured. Table 6.1 shows the average first-order canonical correlation between head motion and speech. The results show correlation levels higher than $r = 0.69$ across emotional categories. This result agrees with the observation made in [32], about the close relation between head motion and prosodic features. Notice, however, that the correlation levels vary from emotion to emotion [8]. A one-way *analysis*

Table 6.1 Statistics of head rotation [6].

	Neu	Sad	Hap	Ang
	Canonical correlation Analysis			
	0.74	0.74	0.71	0.69
	Motion Coefficient [°]			
α	3.32	4.76	6.41	5.56
β	0.88	3.23	2.60	3.67
γ	0.81	2.20	2.32	2.69
	Range [°]			
α	9.54	13.71	17.74	16.05
β	2.31	8.29	6.14	9.06
γ	2.27	6.52	6.67	8.21
	Velocity Magnitude [°/sample]			
Mean	.08	0.11	0.15	0.18
Std	.07	0.10	0.13	0.15

of variance (ANOVA) evaluation indicates that there are significant differences between emotional categories (F[3,640], $p = 0.0013$). In fact, multiple comparison tests reveal that the average CCA of neutral head motion sequences is different from the average CCA of sadness ($p = 0.001$) and anger ($p = 0.001$).

To measure the level of head movement activity, a *motion coefficient*, Ψ, is defined as the standard deviation of the sentence-level mean-removed signal:

$$\Psi = \sqrt{\frac{1}{N \cdot T} \sum_{u=1}^{N} \sum_{t=1}^{T} (x_t^u - \overline{\mu^u})^2},$$ (6.3)

where T is the number of frames, N is the number of utterances, and $\overline{\mu^u}$ is the mean of the sentence u. The average results of this *motion coefficient* when applied to head motion features are presented in Table 6.1. The results indicate that head motion activity during emotional utterances is significantly higher than in neutral utterances. Happiness and anger present the highest levels of head motion activity. As an aside, it is interesting to notice that similar trends were also observed in the articulatory domain for tongue and jaw movement [33].

Table 6.1 also gives the average range and velocity of expressive head motion patterns. These results indicate that during emotional utterances the head moves over a wider range than in the neutral case. Likewise, for happiness and anger the head motion velocity increase more than 90%, compared to the neutral case. These results, which agree with previous work [37], indicate that the temporal dynamics of head motion during neutral speech presents important differences compared to the patterns displayed during emotional speech.

A discriminant analysis was applied to the data, to infer how distinct the head motion patterns are under different emotional categories. The mean, standard deviation, range, maximum, and minimum of the head motion features computed at the sentence level were used as features. Fisher classification was implemented

Table 6.2 Emotional discriminant analysis of head rotation [6].

	Neu	Sad	Hap	Ang
Neu	0.92	0.02	0.04	0.02
Sad	0.15	0.61	0.11	0.13
Hap	0.14	0.09	0.59	0.18
Ang	0.14	0.11	0.25	0.50

with the leave-one-out cross-validation method. Table 6.2 shows the results. On average, the recognition rate was 65.5% using only head motion features. Notice that the emotional class with the lowest performance (anger) is correctly classified with accuracy higher than 50% (chance is 25%). These results suggest that there are distinguishable emotional characteristics in rigid head motion. Also, the high recognition rate of the neutral state implies that global patterns of head motion in normal speech are completely different from the patterns displayed under an emotional state.

Previous work has shown than prosodic features are also affected by emotional modulation [13, 41]. As a result, it is not surprising that the relationship between head motion and prosodic features is emotion-dependent.

These results agree with our previous work, which indicates that head motion is one of the facial gestures that is less constrained by articulatory processes [9]. As a result, it can be used with less restriction to express other non-linguistic messages, such as emotions. Therefore, emotion-dependent head motion models are needed for human-like expressive facial animation. Further details on the analysis can be found in [6, 8, 9].

6.5 Head Motion Framework

As discussed in the previous section, head motion and prosodic features are closely related across time. The *hidden Markov model* (HMM) is a statistical time-series framework that has been used to model similar data. Accordingly, we propose to generate head motion sequences using HMMs. Instead of estimating a mapping function [23], designing rules according to specific comunicative functions [10, 37, 43], or finding similar samples in the training data [11, 16], we model the problem as classification of discrete representations of head motion using acoustic prosody as feature. That is to say, the relationship between head motion and prosodic features is directly learned from data, without specifying the high-level functions in the speech. We will discuss this point further in Section 6.7.

Since an HMM will be built for each head pose, a discrete representation of head motion is needed. This representation is obtained by using the *Linde–Buzo–Gray vector quantization* (LBG-VQ) technique [34]. The 3D space spanned by the head motion features is split in K Voronoi cells. For cell V_i with $i \in \{1, \ldots, K\}$, the mean, U_i, and covariance matrix Σ_i of the points inside the cluster are estimated

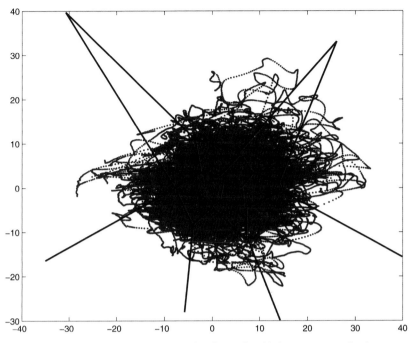

Fig. 6.3 2D projection of the Voronoi regions using 16-size vector quantization.

(Fig. 6.3). In the quantization step, the continuous Euler angles of each frame are approximated with the closest vector code in the codebook.

For each of the head pose cluster (V_i), an HMM is built to generate the most likely head motion sequence, given the observation O, which corresponds to the prosodic features. Therefore, the number of models that will be built is given by the number of clusters (K) used to represent the head poses. The HTK toolkit is used to build these HMMs [48].

To guarantee a continuous head motion sequence without breaks, two smoothing constraints are imposed. The first smoothing technique takes place in the decoding step of the HMMs. In this approach, transitions between head motion cluster are constrained according to their appearance in the training data. The second smoothing constraint is imposed as a post-processing step, by using spherical cubic interpolation. Further details of these smoothing techniques are given in Sections 6.5.1 and 6.5.2, respectively.

As discussed in Section 6.4, the relationship between head motion and prosodic features depends on the emotional content of the utterance. If human-like facial animations are required, the specific emotional patterns of the gestures, in this case head motion, need to be appropriately designed. In this proposed approach, the relationship between head motion and prosodic features is learned in terms of emotional categories. The data is split according to the emotional labels, and emotion-dependent HMMs are separately built. Therefore, the specific emotional patterns are directly included in the models.

6.5.1 Learning Head Motions

To synthesize human-like head motion, our technique searches for the sequences of discrete head poses that maximize the posterior probability of the cluster models $V = (V_{i_1}^t, V_{i_2}^{t+1}, \ldots)$, given the observations $O = (o^t, o^{t+1}, \ldots)$:

$$\arg\max_{i_1, i_2, \ldots} P(V_{i_1}^t, V_{i_2}^{t+1}, \ldots | O). \tag{6.4}$$

Instead of directly modeling this posterior probability, the problem is solved by training the prior probability, $P(O)$, and the likelihood, $P(O|V_{i_1}^t, V_{i_2}^{t+1}, \ldots)$, by making use of Bayes' rule:

$$P(V|O) = \frac{P(O|V) \cdot P(V)}{P(O)}. \tag{6.5}$$

The likelihood distribution, $P(O|V)$, models how well the head motion models fit the data. Here, it is modeled as a first-order Markov process with S states. Therefore, the probability description at time t includes only the current and the previous states, which significantly simplifies the problem. In each of the states, the distribution of the observations are modeled with a *mixture of M Gaussians*. As noted in [6, 7], the mapping between head motion and prosodic features is *many-to-many*. By using mixture of Gaussians to model the distribution of the observations, this ambiguous relationship is included in the models. Under this formulation, building the likelihood distribution of head motion sequences is reduced to learning the parameters of standard HMMs. For this training problem, well-known techniques such as forward-backward and Baum–Welch re-estimation algorithms are used. For more information about HMM, readers are referred to [39, 48].

The prior probability, $P(V)$, in Eq. 6.5 plays an important role in this framework. It models the transition probability between head motion clusters based only on prior information. Here, $P(V)$ is used as a first smoothing technique to guarantee valid transitions between the discrete head poses. Similar to bi-gram models used for language models [48], this prior probability is modeled as a first-order state machine. The transitions between clusters are learned by counting their relative frequency in the training data. In the decoding step of the HMMs, this prior information is used to reward or penalize transitions that are frequently or seldom observed in the database, respectively. According to the analysis presented in Section 6.4, head motion dynamics are also affected by the underlying emotion of the subject. Therefore, this prior probability is separately learned from each emotional category.

$P(O)$ does not depend on the head motion models and is a constant in Eq. 6.4. Therefore, it can be ignored in this framework.

Notice that in the training procedure the segmentation of the acoustic signal is obtained from the vector quantization of the head motion space. Therefore, the HMMs were initialized with this known segmentation, avoiding the use of forced alignment, as it is usually done in automatic speech recognition to align phonemes with the speech features.

6.5.2 Head Motion Synthesis

Figure 6.4 describes the proposed framework to generate human-like head motion sequences. After the HMMs are trained, the prosodic features described in Section 6.3 are extracted from the acoustic signal of the test database. This feature vector is used as an observation of the HMMs, which generates the most likely sequences of head poses codebooks, $\widehat{V} = (\widehat{V}_{i_1}^t, \widehat{V}_{i_2}^{t+1}, \ldots)$, according to Eq. 6.5. After the sequence $\widehat{V}$ is generated, the means of the clusters are used to form a 3D sequence, $\widehat{Y} = (U_{i_1}^t, U_{i_2}^{t+1}, \ldots)$, which is the first approximation of the head motion.

The next step in this approach is to blur the sequence $\widehat{Y}$ with additive colored noise (Eq. 6.6). The purpose of this step is to compensate for the quantization error yielded during vector quantization. Hence, the noise is added such that the covariance of the noise matches the covariance matrix associated with the codebooks (Σ). Therefore, the power of the noise is distributed in proportion of the quantization error. The parameter λ is included in Eq. 6.6 to attenuate, if desired, the noise level used to blur the sequence $\widehat{Y}$ (e.g., $\lambda = 0.7$). Notice that this is an optional step that can be ignored by setting λ equal to one, if no attenuation is desired, or to zero if no noise is desired. The solid blue line in Fig. 6.5 shows an example of the noisy version of the head motion sequences, $\widehat{Z}$:

$$\widehat{Z}_i^t = \widehat{Y}_i^t + \lambda \cdot W(\Sigma_i). \tag{6.6}$$

As can be observed from Fig. 6.5, the noisy version of the head motion sequence ($\widehat{Z}$) presents a break in the cluster transitions. This problem is observed even when the number of codebooks or the noise level is increased (K). To avoid these discontinuities, a second smoothing technique is applied to the sequence. If a standard cubic interpolation is separately applied to each of Euler's angles, it is well known that the resulting sequence may present jerky movements and undesired effects such as *Gimbl lock* [42]. Instead, the proposed smoothing technique is based on spherical cubic interpolation [20]. With this technique, the 3D Euler angles are

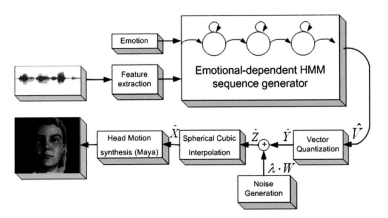

Fig. 6.4 Emotion-dependent head motion synthesis framework.

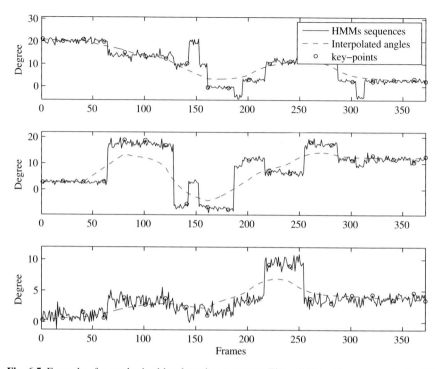

Fig. 6.5 Example of a synthesized head motion sequence. The solid blue line represents the 3D noisy signal $\widehat{Z}$ from Eq. 6.6. The circles are the key points used for spherical cubic interpolation. The dashed red line is the smoothed head motion sequences used in the animation ($\widehat{X}$).

jointly interpolated in the unit sphere by using quaternion representation, avoiding the artifact mentioned before.

   In the interpolation step, the sequence $\widehat{Z}$ is downsampled to 6 points per second to obtain equidistant frames. These frames are referred, from here on, as key points and are marked in Fig. 6.5 as a black circle. These 3D Euler angle points are then transformed into the quaternion representation [20]. Spherical cubic interpolation (squad) is then applied over these quaternion points. The squad function builds upon the spherical linear interpolation (slerp). The functions slerp and squad are defined by Eqs. 6.7 and 6.8, respectively:

$$\text{slerp}(q_1, q_2, \mu) = \frac{\sin(1 - \mu)\theta}{\sin\theta} q_1 + \frac{\sin\mu\theta}{\sin\theta} q_2, \tag{6.7}$$

$$\text{squad}(q_1, q_2, q_3, q_4, \mu) = \text{slerp}(\text{slerp}(q_1, q_4, \mu), \text{slerp}(q_2, q_3, \mu), 2\mu(1 - \mu)), \tag{6.8}$$

where q_i (with $i \in \{1, \ldots, 4\}$) are quaternions, $\cos\theta = q_1 \cdot q_2$, and μ is a parameter that ranges between 0 and 1 and determines the frame position of the interpolated quaternions. With these equations, the head motion sequence is interpolated in the unit sphere by varying the parameter μ to recover the original sample rate (120

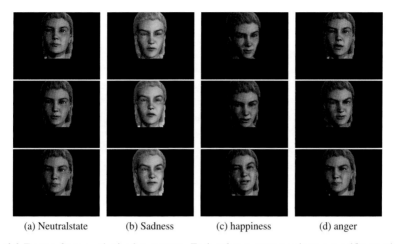

(a) Neutralstate	(b) Sadness	(c) happiness	(d) anger

Fig. 6.6 Frames from synthesized sequences. Each column corresponds to a specific emotional category.

frames per second). The last step in this smoothing technique is to transform the interpolated quaternions into an Euler angle representation.

Notice that the noise is added before the spherical cubit interpolation technique is applied. Therefore, the resulting head motion sequence, referred by $\widehat{X}$, is a continuous and smooth 3D signal without the jerky behavior of noise. An example of this sequence is illustrated in Fig. 6.5 as dashed red line.

The final step in this framework is to include the head motion sequence $\widehat{X}$ in the facial animation. Here, a blendshape face model composed of 46 blend shapes is used, which is modeled and rendered using Maya [35]. The head motion sequence $\widehat{X}$ is directly applied to the angle control parameters of the face model. For realistic human-like expressive animation, other facial components such as expressive visual speech and eye motion are also modeled and synthesized. The details of those approaches can be found in [15, 17–19].

Figure 6.6 shows frames of the synthesized sequences for each of the four emotional categories considered here.

6.5.3 Parameter Configuration of the Models

An important parameter in this framework is the HMM topology, which is defined by the number and interconnection of the states. The most common topologies are the *left-to-right topology* (LR), in which only transitions in the forward direction between adjacent states are allowed, and the ergodic topology (EG), in which the states are fully connected. In the LR topology, fewer parameters are required. Therefore, less data are needed to train its parameters. The EG topology is less restricted, so it can learn the state transitions from the database. However, more parameters are needed to learn the models, which increase the requirement on the size of training data.

In this particular problem, it is not clear which HMM topology provides the best description of the head motion dynamics. In our previous work, different generic HMM configurations were evaluated. By generic models, we mean emotion-independent HMMs that were learned without considering the emotional category of the sentences (the entire database was used for training). The left-to-right HMM, with three states (S) and two mixtures (M), achieved the best result. Notice that if the database were big enough, an ergodic topology with more states and mixtures could perhaps give better results.

When emotional models are used instead of generic models, the training data are even smaller, since the emotion-dependent models are separately trained. Therefore, the HMMs used in the experiments were implemented using a LR topology with two states ($S = 2$) and two mixtures ($M = 2$).

Another important parameter of this model is the number of clusters (K) used to create the discrete representation of head motion, which is directly related with the number of HMMs to be built. If K increases, the quantization error of the discrete representation of head poses decreases. However, the discrimination between models will significantly decrease and more training data will be needed. Therefore, there is a trade-off between the quantization error and the inter-cluster discrimination. As shown in [6, 7], a 16-word codebook was adequate to synthesize realistic facial animation. In the experiments reported here, K was also set to 16.

The audio-visual database mentioned in Section 6.3 was randomly split into training (80%) and testing data (20%).

6.6 Head Motion Evaluation

The head motion sequence framework presented here was objectively and subjectively evaluated. This section presents the main results.

6.6.1 Objective Evaluation

The first-order canonical correlation between the original and synthesized head motion sequences was computed to analyze whether this framework is able to capture the temporal relationship between head motion and prosodic features. The average results are presented, separately for each emotional category, in Table 6.3. The results show that the sequences generated with prosodic features are highly correlated with the original captured sequences. This suggests that this framework appropriately models the temporal behavior of head motion sequences. Notice that the first-order correlation between head motion and prosodic features was about $r \approx 0.72$ (Table 6.1). Interestingly, the first-order canonical correlation between the original and synthesized head motion sequences was over $r > 0.85$. Even

Table 6.3 Canonical correlation analysis between original and synthesized head motion sequences [6].

	Neutral	Sadness	Happiness	Anger
Mean	0.86	0.88	0.89	0.91
Std	0.12	0.11	0.08	0.08

though prosodic features do not provide all the information needed to synthesize head motion sequences, this result indicates that the performance of the proposed system is notably high.

6.6.2 Subjective Evaluation

For subjective assessments of this framework, 17 human subjects were asked to rate the naturalness of videos with facial animation rendered with the synthesized and original head motion sequences. Likewise, they were also asked to rate the naturalness of the animation without head motion (rigid head), to study how important head motion is for realistic facial animation. In total, one video per each emotional category was presented to the evaluators, resulting in 12 videos: 4 emotions × 3 modalities (synthesized, original, and rigid). Although the facial animations included other facial gestures such as lips and eyes, the only gesture that was modified was head motion.

The animations were presented in random order. The naturalness of the animation was rated using a five-point scale. The extremes were called *robot-like* (value 1), and *human-like* (value 5). The evaluators received instructions to rate their overall impression of the animation and not individual aspects such as head movements or voice quality. The subjects were not made aware that head motion was the component of the facial animation that was under assessment.

Table 6.4 presents the results for the subjective assessment. With the exception of sadness, the synthesized sequences were judged to be more natural than the animation with the original head motion sequences. This result indicates that the head motion synthesis approach presented here was able to generate realistic human-like head motion sequences. One aspect that significantly improves the naturalness perception of the facial animation is the synchronism between the prosodic structure of the speech and the head motion. Prominence in the speech was systematically accompanied with head motion gestures, which indicates that this framework was able to model the nontrivial relationship between head motion and speech.

Table 6.4 also shows how the listeners assessed the naturalness of the facial animation without head motion. These results show that the naturalness perception significantly decreases when head motion is not included in the facial animation. This implies that head motion is an important component for human-like facial animations that needs to be appropriately modeled for engaging animated characters.

The inter-evaluator average variance in the scores rated by human subjects was 0.97. This result indicates that the concept of naturalness of the animation is perceived slightly differently between the evaluators. However, since we are

Table 6.4 Naturalness assessment of rigid head motion sequences [1—robot-like, 5—human-like] [6].

Head Motion Data	Neutral		Sadness		Happiness		Anger	
	Mean	Std	Mean	Std	Mean	Std	Mean	Std
Original	3.76	0.90	3.76	0.83	3.71	0.99	3.00	1.00
Synthesized	4.00	0.79	3.12	1.17	3.82	1.13	3.71	1.05
Fixed head	3.00	1.06	2.76	1.25	3.35	0.93	3.29	1.45

interested in the mean differences of each group, this variability does not bias these results.

6.7 Discussion and Conclusions

Head motion is an important component in interpersonal human interactions. Therefore, this gesture needs to be properly modeled and included in realistic human-like facial animations. The subjective evaluations presented in this chapter support this observation, since the naturalness perception significantly decreases when the animations were rendered without head motion.

As analyzed in this chapter, the head motion patterns displayed under expressive utterances vary across emotional categories. For instance, the range and velocity of the head present higher values for happiness, anger, and sadness, compared with the values for neutral utterances. In fact, the results reveal that head motion can be used to discriminate between emotional categories. Since prosodic features are also affected by the affective state of the subject, the relationship between head motion and prosodic features is emotion-dependent. This observation is supported by the canonical correlation analysis, which indicates that the correlation levels between head motion and prosodic features are significantly different across emotional categories. Furthermore, our previous work indicates that head motion influences the emotional perception of facial animations [6]. As results, emotion-dependent head motion models need to be designed for human-like facial animation.

Based on previous observations, a novel data-driven framework to synthesize head motion sequences based on prosodic features was presented. In this technique, discrete representations of head poses, estimated with vector quantization, were modeled with HMMs, which took prosodic features as inputs. A set of HMMs was separately trained for each emotional category, building emotion-dependent head motion models. The subjective and objective evaluations indicate that this framework successfully modeled the temporal relationship between head motion and speech. Furthermore, the facial animations with the synthesized head motion sequences were perceived as having the same level of naturalness as the animations with the motion captured head motion sequence.

In this work, head motion is only modeled with 3 DOF corresponding to head rotation. However, the human neck allows the head not only to rotate, but also to translate, especially back and forward. An interesting question is how to include in this framework this extra 3 DOF of head translation.

Another limitation of this work is that the database was recorded from only one subject. We are collecting similar data from other subjects to validate and expand these results. As suggested by [27], head motion is speaker-dependent. By studying and learning interpersonal differences, head motion sequences can be used to provide a desired personality to the animation [29].

One interesting extension of this work is to include key frame controls to specify gestures such as head "nod" and "tilt" (similar to [16]). Therefore, the designer can add believable head motion in response to facial conversation signals, as proposed by Cassell et al. [10].

Another interesting question is how to include other facial gestures such as eyebrow and lip motion in the animation. As mentioned before, gestures and speech are related in a nontrivial manner. Furthermore, different gestures are also related with each other, since most of the time the same set of muscles jointly trigger them. Our research efforts are focused on modeling these relationships to generate facial animations that are perceived to be more natural and engaging.

Acknowledgment This research was supported in part by funds from the NSF (through the Integrated Media Systems Center, a National Science Foundation Engineering Research Center, Cooperative Agreement No. EEC-9529152 and a CAREER award), the Department of the Army, and a MURI award from the Office of Naval Research (ONR). Any opinions, findings, and conclusions or recommendations expressed in this paper are those of the authors and do not necessarily reflect the views of the funding agencies.

References

1. I. Albrecht, J. Haber, and H.P. Seidel. Automatic generation of non-verbal facial expressions from speech. In *Computer Graphics International (CGI 2002)*, pages 283–293, Bradford, U.K., July 2002.
2. K.S. Arun, T.S. Huang, and S.D. Blostein. Least-squares fitting of two 3-d point sets. *IEEE Trans. Pattern Anal. Mach. Intell.*, 9(5):698–700, 1987.
3. P. Boersma and D. Weeninck. Praat, a system for doing phonetics by computer. Technical Report 132, Institute of Phonetic Sciences of the University of Amsterdam, Amsterdam, Netherlands, 1996. http://www.praat.org.
4. M. Brand. Voice puppetry. In *Proc. 26th Ann. Conf. Computer Graph. Interactive Techniques (SIGGRAPH 1999)*, pages 21–28, New York, 1999.
5. C. Bregler, M. Covell, and M. Slaney. Video rewrite: Driving visual speech with audio. In *Proc. 24th Annual Conf. Computer Graphics Interactive Techniques (SIGGRAPH 1997)*, pages 353–360, Los Angeles, CA, August 1997.
6. C. Busso, Z. Deng, M. Grimm, U. Neumann, and S. Narayanan. Rigid head motion in expressive speech animation: Analysis and synthesis. *IEEE Transactions on Audio, Speech and Language Processing*, 15(3): 1075–1086, March 2007.
7. C. Busso, Z. Deng, U. Neumann, and S.S. Narayanan. Natural head motion synthesis driven by acoustic prosodic features. *Computer Animation and Virtual Worlds*, 16(3–4):283–290, July 2005.
8. C. Busso and S. Narayanan. Interrelation between speech and facial gestures in emotional utterances: A single subject study. Accepted to appear in IEEE Transactions on Speech, Audio and Language Processing, 2007.

9. C. Busso and S.S. Narayanan. Interplay between linguistic and affective goals in facial expression during emotional utterances. In *7th International Seminar on Speech Production (ISSP 2006)*, pages 549–556, Ubatuba-SP, Brazil, December 2006.

10. J. Cassell, C. Pelachaud, N. Badler, M. Steedman, B. Achorn, T. Bechet, B. Douville, S. Prevost, and M. Stone. Animated conversation: Rule-based generation of facial expression gesture and spoken intonation for multiple conversational agents. In *Computer Graphics (Proc. ACM SIGGRAPH'94)*, pages 413–420, Orlando, FL, 1994.

11. E. Chuang and C. Bregler. Mood swings: Expressive speech animation. *ACM Transactions on Graphics*, 24(2):331–347, April 2005.

12. M.M. Cohen and D.W. Massaro. Modeling coarticulation in synthetic visual speech. In Magnenat-Thalmann N., Thalmann D. (Eds.), *Models and Techniques in Computer Animation, Springer Verlag*, pages 139–156, Tokyo, 1993.

13. R. Cowie and R.R. Cornelius. Describing the emotional states that are expressed in speech. *Speech Communication*, 40(1–2):5–32, April 2003.

14. D. DeCarlo, C. Revilla, M. Stone, and J.J. Venditti. Making discourse visible: coding and animating conversational facial displays. In *Computer Animation (CA 2002)*, pages 11–16, Geneva, Switzerland, June 2002.

15. Z. Deng, M. Bulut, U. Neumann, and S. Narayanan. Automatic dynamic expression synthesis for speech animation. In *IEEE 17th International Conference on Computer Animation and Social Agents (CASA 2004)*, pages 267–274, Geneva, Switzerland, July 2004.

16. Z. Deng, C. Busso, S. Narayanan, and U. Neumann. Audio-based head motion synthesis for avatar-based telepresence systems. In *ACM SIGMM 2004 Workshop on Effective Telepresence (ETP 2004)*, pages 24–30, ACM Press, New York, 2004.

17. Z. Deng, J.P. Lewis, and U. Neumann. Automated eye motion using texture synthesis. *IEEE Computer Graphics and Applications*, 25(2):24–30, March/April 2005.

18. Z. Deng, J.P. Lewis, and U. Neumann. Synthesizing speech animation by learning compact speech co-articulation models. In *Computer Graphics International (CGI 2005)*, pages 19–25, Stony Brook, NY, June 2005.

19. Z. Deng, U. Neumann, J.P. Lewis, T.Y. Kim, M. Bulut, and S. Narayanan. Expressive facial animation synthesis by learning speech co-articultion and expression spaces. *IEEE Transactions on Visualization and Computer Graphics (TVCG)*, 12(6):1523–1534, November/December 2006.

20. D. Eberly. *3D Game Engine Design: A Practical Approach to Real-Time Computer Graphics*. Morgan Kaufmann Publishers, San Francisco, CA, 2000.

21. P. Ekman. Facial expression and emotion. *American Psychologist*, 48(4): 384–392, April 1993.

22. P. Ekman and E.L. Rosenberg. *What the Face Reveals: Basic and Applied Studies of Spontaneous Expression Using the Facial Action Coding System (FACS)*. Oxford University Press, New York, 1997.

23. H.P. Graf, E. Cosatto, V. Strom, and F.J. Huang. Visual prosody: Facial movements accompanying speech. In *Proc. of IEEE International Conference on Automatic Faces and Gesture Recognition*, pages 396–401, Washington, DC, May 2002.

24. B. Granström and D. House. Audiovisual representation of prosody in expressive speech communication. *Speech Communication*, 46(3–4):473–484, July 2005.

25. J. Gratch and S. Marsella. Lessons from emotion psychology for the design of lifelike characters. *Applied Artificial Intelligence*, 19(3–4):215–233, March–April 2005.

26. D. Heylen. Challenges ahead head movements and other social acts in conversation. In *Artificial Intelligence and Simulation of Behaviour (AISB 2005), Social Presence Cues for Virtual Humanoids Symposium*, page 8, Hertfordshire, U.K., April 2005.

27. H. Hill and A. Johnston. Categorizing sex and identity from the biological motion of faces. *Current Biology*, 11(11):880–885, June 2001.

28. H. Hotelling. Relations between two sets of variates. *Biometrika*, 28(3/4): 321–377, December 1936.

29. L.N. Jefferies, J.T. Enns, S. DiPaola, and A. Arya. Facial actions as visual cues for personality. *Computer Animation and Virtual Worlds*, 17(3–4):371–382, July 2006.

30. K. Kakihara, S. Nakamura, and K. Shikano. Speech-to-face movement synthesis based on HMMS. In *IEEE International Conference on Multimedia and Expo (ICME)*, volume 1, pages 427–430, New York, April 2000.
31. S. Kettebekov, M. Yeasin, and R. Sharma. Prosody based audiovisual coanalysis for coverbal gesture recognition. *IEEE Transactions on Multimedia*, 7(2): 234–242, April 2005.
32. T. Kuratate, K.G. Munhall, P.E. Rubin, E. Vatikiotis-Bateson, and H. Yehia. Audio-visual synthesis of talking faces from speech production correlates. In *Sixth European Conference on Speech Communication and Technology, Eurospeech 1999*, pages 1279–1282, Budapest, Hungary, September 1999.
33. S. Lee, S. Yildirim, A. Kazemzadeh, and S. Narayanan. An articulatory study of emotional speech production. In *9th European Conference on Speech Communication and Technology (Interspeech'2005—Eurospeech)*, pages 497–500, Lisbon, Portugal, September 2005.
34. Y. Linde, A. Buzo, and R. Gray. An algorithm for vector quantizer design. *IEEE Transactions on Communications*, 28(1):84–95, January 1980.
35. Maya software, Alias Systems division of Silicon Graphics Limited. http://www.alias.com, 2005.
36. K.G. Munhall, J.A. Jones, D.E. Callan, T. Kuratate, and E. Vatikiotis-Bateson. Visual prosody and speech intelligibility: Head movement improves auditory speech perception. *Psychological Science*, 15(2):133–137, February 2004.
37. C. Pelachaud, N. Badler, and M. Steedman. Generating facial expressions for speech. *Cognitive Science*, 20(1):1–46, January 1996.
38. R.W. Picard. Affective computing. Technical Report 321, MIT Media Laboratory Perceptual Computing Section, Cambridge, MA, November 1995.
39. L.R. Rabiner. A tutorial on hidden Markov models and selected applications in speech recognition. *Proceedings of the IEEE*, 77(2):257–286, February 1989.
40. M.E. Sargin, O. Aran, A. Karpov, F. Ofli, Y. Yasinnik, S. Wilson, E. Erzin, Y. Yemez, and A.M. Tekalp. Combined gesture-speech analysis and speech driven gesture synthesis. In *IEEE International Conference on Multimedia and Expo (ICME 2006)*, pages 893–896, Toronto, ON, Canada, July 2006.
41. K.R. Scherer. Vocal communication of emotion: A review of research paradigms. *Speech Communication*, 40(1–2):227–256, April 2003.
42. K. Shoemake. Animating rotation with quaternion curves. *Computer Graphics (Proceedings of SIGGRAPH85)*, 19(3):245–254, July 1985.
43. K. Smid, I.S. Pandzic, and V. Radman. Autonomous speaker agent. In *IEEE 17th International Conference on Computer Animation and Social Agents (CASA 2004)*, pages 259–266, Geneva, Switzerland, July 2004.
44. E. Vatikiotis-Bateson, K.G. Munhall, Y. Kasahara, F. Garcia, and H. Yehia. Characterizing audiovisual information during speech. In *Fourth International Conference on Spoken Language Processing (ICSLP 96)*, volume 3, pages 1485–1488, Philadelphia, PA, October 1996.
45. H. Yehia, T. Kuratate, and E. Vatikiotis-Bateson. Facial animation and head motion driven by speech acoustics. In *5th Seminar on Speech Production: Models and Data*, pages 265–268, Kloster Seeon, Bavaria, Germany, May 2000.
46. H. Yehia, P. Rubin, and E. Vatikiotis-Bateson. Quantitative association of vocal-tract and facial behavior. *Speech Commun.*, 26(1–2):23–43, 1998.
47. S. Yildirim, M. Bulut, C.M. Lee, A. Kazemzadeh, C. Busso, Z. Deng, S. Lee, and S.S. Narayanan. An acoustic study of emotions expressed in speech. In *8th International Conference on Spoken Language Processing (ICSLP 04)*, Jeju Island, Korea, 2004.
48. S. Young, G. Evermann, T. Hain, D. Kershaw, G. Moore, J. Odell, D. Ollason, D. Povey, V. Valtchev, and P. Woodland. *The HTK Book*. Entropic Cambridge Research Laboratory, Cambridge, UK, 2002.

Chapter 7
A User Interface Technique for Controlling Blendshape Interference

J.P. Lewis, Jonathan Mooser, Zhigang Deng, and Ulrich Neumann

7.1 Introduction

Blend shapes are a standard approach to computer facial animation.[1] The technique was popularized in the pioneering character animation of Tony de Peltrie [2], and it continues to be used in projects such as *Stuart Little, Star Wars*, and *the Lord of the Rings* movies. The technique is described by other names, including "morph targets" and "shape interpolation."

A blendshape model is simply the linear weighted sum of a number of topologically conforming shape primitives,

$$\mathbf{f}_j = \sum w_k \mathbf{b}_{kj}, \tag{7.1}$$

where $\mathbf{f}_j$ is the jth vertex of the resulting animated model, w_k are the blending weights, and $\mathbf{b}_{kj}$ is the jth vertex of the kth blendshape. The weighted sum can be applied to the vertices of polygonal models, or to the control vertices of spline models. The weights w_k are manipulated by the animator in the form of sliders, with one slider for each weight. Weight values (slider positions) are keyframed to produce animation over time.

One of the major issues in constructing and using blendshape models is that of *blendshape interference*. The problem is seen in definition (7.1): the individual blend shapes $\mathbf{b}_k$ often have overlapping (competing or reinforcing) effects. For example (see Fig. 7.1), the animator may initially adjust the eyelid by moving one slider, but by adjusting other sliders (eyebrows, forehead, etc.) the eyelid may be raised or further lowered from its desired position. The animator then has to go back and readjust the first slider.

In practice, the interference problem is often minimized by sculpting the individual blend shapes to be as local and independent in effect as possible, and by iteratively refining these shapes when interference is found. Blendshape interference cannot be entirely eliminated, however, because desirable blendshape targets naturally have overlapping effects. For example, the blend shapes to effect a smile,

---

Z. Deng and U. Neumann, *Data-Driven 3D Facial Animation.*
© Springer-Verlag London Limited 2008

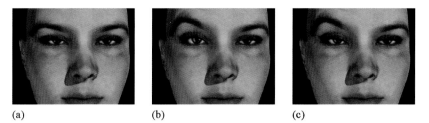

(a)   (b)   (c)

Fig. 7.1 (a) We attempt to mimic the "Jack Nicholson" expression of partially closed eyes with an arched eyebrow. First the eyelids are partially closed. (b) The model has three controls over eyebrow shape. The desired arched eyebrow is easily obtained, but the eyelid is changed as a side effect. (c) The model is capable of approximating the desired expression however, by readjusting the eyelid control (or, by using our technique).

raise the corner of the mouth, and produce the vowel "A" all affect the corner of the mouth region. Interference is thus considered by the animator as an expected cost of using the blendshape approach.

That cost is considerable, however. Blendshape models used in entertainment practice may take as long as a year or more to construct and can have more than 100 individual blend shapes [3], resulting in thousands of potential pairwise interference effects. An animator working with a poorly designed model may spend much more time readjusting previously adjusted sliders than doing "new" animation. In the "Gollum" model used on the recent *Lord of the Rings* movies, the pairwise effects of many blend shapes were explicitly corrected in the model construction. The result was a model with a total of 946 blend shapes, the majority of which were used to correct for the behavior of an original set of 64 shapes (the correction shapes were automatically invoked, with only 64 sliders being exposed to the animator). More than 10,000 blend shapes were sculpted in the process of developing the final model [4].

Figure 7.2 shows another example of an interference problem in a professionally developed model [5]. Figure 7.2(a) is the unaltered neutral pose—all slider weights are set to zero. Figure 7.2(b) shows the effect of a single slider move. Presumably, an animator making such an adjustment has positioned the brow exactly as desired. But as further moves are made [Fig. 7.2(c)], the brow continues to furrow, requiring readjustment of the first slider. It should be emphasized that

- although the geometric movement being discussed is sometimes subtle, the character animator's art requires him to produce and control such subtle movement in order to distinguish geometry similar facial expressions (such as "worried" and "angry").

In this chapter, we show that the interference problems in a given model can be greatly reduced during animation without resculpting the model. We present a technique that allows the animator to temporarily designate portions of the model that should not be altered during a set of subsequent editing operations.

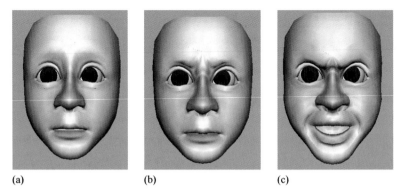

(a)   (b)   (c)

Fig. 7.2 (a) Another example, using a well-known model [5]. (b) The effect of moving the fourth slider, `Furrow`, to a value of 0.4. (c) Further slider moves, mostly affecting the mouth, are made, but the middle of the brow has continued to move downward as well, below the desired position. Neutral pose of the blendshape model.

7.2 Related Work

Despite its popularity the blendshape technique has had relatively little development since the 1980s, though it is often used as a representation in research on facial animation and tracking, e.g., [6, 7]. Prior to [2], Parke demonstrated cross-fading between whole-face models in his well-known early work [8]. In the "delta" blendshape form introduced in the late 1980s (see Section 3), the individual blend shapes are all offsets from a common "neutral" face. Delta blend shapes were implemented at Pacific Data Images [9], and the Symbolics animation system also had a sophisticated implementation [10, 11]. Kleiser [12] describes segmenting the face into separate regions (e.g., upper and lower face regions) that are blended independently, thus reducing memory usage and improving performance (though, segmenting does not by itself improve the power of the model, because a blend shape that affects a local region is no different than a blend shape with global support that is zero outside the local region).

An exception to the lack of attention to blend shapes in the research community is the recent paper by Joshi et al. [13]. In this paper, the segmentation of the face into regions is obtained automatically using a physically motivated approach. Segmenting prevents interference across segments but does not eliminate the problem, because many interference effects result from overlapping blendshapes that effect the same local region (c.f. Fig. 7.5).

Principal component (PCA) face models derived from data [14] can strictly be regarded as blend shapes, though they are outside the spirit of the term: blend shapes are understood as a representation suitable for manual animation, with the individual blend shapes having intuitive or "semantic" meanings such as `raise-left-eyebrow`. Typically, only the first few eigenvectors of a PCA model have any intuitive interpretations. The effect of the remaining PCA blend shapes is distributed and difficult to characterize, as shown in Fig. 7.3, and doing key-frame animation in a PCA representation would be very difficult. (On the other hand, converting

Fig. 7.3 Principal component targets are orthogonal, but only the first few have any interpretable role, making them difficult to use and remember. This is the nineth eigenvector (PCA face target) of a motion-captured facial performance. (Motion capture data provided by George Borshukov.)

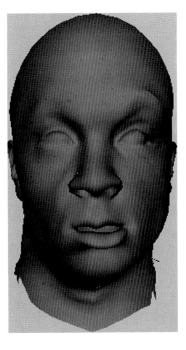

between a PCA and another representation is a simple matter of linear algebra, so an internal PCA representation would pose no issues if it were not presented to the user.)

Blend shapes are a standard component of commercial animation packages such as Maya and Softimage. Although the algorithms used in these packages are unpublished, in the case of a simple technique such as blend shapes it is easy to surmise the underlying approach from the documentation, available controls, and behavior of the controls. Maya, for example, implements the standard delta blendshape scheme, with one extension: multiple "intermediate" blendshape targets can be situated at points along a particular slider. The system cross-fades among these to produce the ultimate blend shape for that slider, which then takes part in the blendshape weighted sum.

Our solution to the interference problem resembles inverse kinematics (IK) [15, 16] in that we constrain particular points. It differs, however, in that IK *automatically* determines the pose of unconstrained parts of the character given the constraint of a *moved* part, whereas in our technique the user manually explores facial poses while the system keeps particular points stationary. On the other hand, the IK "pin-and-drag" editing presented in [15] directly anticipates the working style needed to use our technique. Blend shapes can be considered a form of skinning; pointers to the general literature on this subject include the popular SSD or linear-blend skinning technique [17] and recent improvements [18]. Recent example-based approaches [19] to skinning have produced excellent results, but have not yet been applied in facial animation.

7.3 A Linear Algebra View of Blend Shapes

To simplify notation, a model will be expressed as a vector of length $3n$ (for n vertices), by packing the individual vertices in the vector in some arbitrary but consistent order such as xyzxyzxyz...or xxxx...yyyy...zzzz.... The vectors $\mathbf{b}_k$ representing each blend shape are gathered in the columns of a blendshape basis matrix $\mathbf{B}$. The blendshape sum for the complete model is

$$\mathbf{f} = \mathbf{Bw},$$

where $\mathbf{f}$ is a $3n \times 1$ vector containing the resulting model, $\mathbf{B}$ is a $3n \times m$ matrix containing m blend shapes, and $\mathbf{w}$ is the $m \times 1$ vector of weights.

Two variants of the blendshape idea are the "whole-face" formulation and "delta" blend shapes. In the former, the vectors $\mathbf{b}_k$ represent the complete face in some pose such as a smile, or with the mouth posed to produce a particular vowel. Whole-face blend shapes were used in Disney's *Dinosaur* movie and some approaches inspired by Eckman's Facial Action Coding System (FACS) [20], for example.

In the delta form, the individual blend shapes are added to a "neutral" face model $\mathbf{f}_0$:

$$\mathbf{f} = \mathbf{f}_0 + \mathbf{Dw}, \tag{7.2}$$

where columns of the delta blendshape basis $\mathbf{D}$ are simply the corresponding columns of the original basis $\mathbf{B}$ with the neutral shape subtracted: $\mathbf{d}_k = \mathbf{b}_k - \mathbf{f}_0$, and $\mathbf{D}$ has $m - 1$ rather than m columns.

The whole-face formulation is preferable for the modeler because sculpting delta shapes is difficult, and it has been used to guarantee that particularly important expressions appear (by sculpting that exact expression and adding it to the blendshape basis) [21]. The delta form is often preferred by animators because (with appropriately sculpted blend shapes) it can reduce interference; for example, sufficiently localized blend shapes may affect only one eyebrow, raise one corner of the mouth, etc., or roughly mimic the effect of individual facial muscles [7].

Proponents of each system sometimes claim that their choice is the most powerful (an alternate claim is that theirs is the only possible system in which any combination of weights produces a reasonable or "legal" face shape). Simple algebra shows that these opinions are incorrect, at least if "powerful" is interpreted to refer to the range of achievable face shapes. Although they present different advantages to the user, the whole-face and delta formulations are identical in power because any posed blendshape model in one formulation can be represented exactly in the other form. For example, to convert a delta model to the whole-face form, set $\mathbf{b}_1 = \mathbf{f}_0$, and set $\mathbf{b}_k$ to $\mathbf{f}_0 + \mathbf{d}_{k-1}$ for $k = 2, \ldots, m$ ($\mathbf{d}_k$ is the kth column of $\mathbf{D}$). A particular pose in the delta model represented by the weight vector $\mathbf{w}_{1\ldots m-1}$ is then represented in the whole-face model by the weights $(1 - \Sigma w_k, w_1, w_2, \ldots)$. In the whole-face formulation, the weights should sum to one, a constraint that prevents scaling of the model. With one fewer weight, the delta form does not have this "barycentric" constraint.

Because the algorithm we present ahead transforms the weight vector such that its sum may change, we assume the use of the delta form throughout this chapter. This does not limit the results, because the two forms are equivalent in power and are easily exchanged.

7.4 Possible Approaches to Reducing Interference

An obvious approach to reducing the interference of new slider movements on a recently obtained facial pose might be to find all rows in the blendshape matrix **D** that correspond to vertices that have recently been moved and set those rows to zero. With this change, further adjustments made to the sliders are guaranteed not to move those vertices. Such a brute-force approach will generally produce poor results, however. There are cases where a single blend shape affects most of the vertices in the model, at least slightly. If we freeze the position of all those vertices, the model cannot be animated. More importantly, an underlying assumption of blend shapes is that the columns of **D** span the desired and allowable movement of the model. Zeroing rows of **D** allows facial poses that depart from the designed subspace in undesirable ways. For example, suppose slider 1 affects vertex 1, while slider 2 affects both vertex 1 and its neighbor vertex 2. If vertex 1 is frozen, the adjustment of slider 2 will move vertex 2 away from its neighbor vertex 1, disrupting the smoothness of the surface.

A more subtle approach is to enforce vector orthogonality between some of the blendshape vectors. This would allow an animator to select a set of one or more blend shapes to be "locked." Then, the effect of the remaining blendshape vectors would be altered by projecting them onto a space orthogonal to the locked vectors. This ensures orthogonality between previous changes and any future changes.

Although this avoids problems introduced by the first approach, in our experience the results are still not as desired. The main problem arises from the fact that orthogonality between high-dimensional vectors representing the entire face does not sufficiently constrain the movement of particular vertices. Further, even at a local level orthogonality is not always what is desired. Imagine a blend shape that moves a particular vertex up and to the right and another blend shape that moves the same vertex up and to the left. Those two movements might be orthogonal, but arguably they disrupt each other.

7.5 Coordinate Motion Attenuation

The technique we present overcomes these problems by allowing the user to select a subset of coordinates to remain as stationary as possible. Those coordinates may ultimately move as the sliders are adjusted, but their movements will be relatively attenuated.

We treat this as a minimization problem. For any weight vector $\mathbf{w}$, we want to find a new weight vector $\mathbf{w}'$ such that the resulting coordinate changes, $\mathbf{Dw}'$, are as close as possible, in Euclidean distance, to 0 for the selected coordinates and as close as possible to $\mathbf{Dw}$ for the unselected coordinates. In other words, we want to minimize

$$||\mathbf{Sw}'||^2 + ||\bar{\mathbf{S}}(\mathbf{w}' - \mathbf{w})||^2 = \mathbf{w}'^T\mathbf{S}^T\mathbf{Sw}' + (\mathbf{w}' - \mathbf{w})^T\bar{\mathbf{S}}^T\bar{\mathbf{S}}(\mathbf{w}' - \mathbf{w}),$$

where $\mathbf{S}$ is a matrix made up of the rows of $\mathbf{D}$ corresponding to the selected coordinates, and $\mathring{\mathbf{S}}$ is a matrix made up of every other row of $\mathbf{D}$.

We can simplify the notation by defining

$$\mathbf{P} = \bar{\mathbf{S}}^T\bar{\mathbf{S}},$$
$$\mathbf{Q} = \mathbf{S}^T\mathbf{S},$$

so the expression to be minimized becomes

$$\mathbf{w}'^T\mathbf{Qw}' + (\mathbf{w}' - \mathbf{w})^T\mathbf{P}(\mathbf{w}' - \mathbf{w}).$$

Minimizing this expression strikes a balance between keeping the selected coordinates motionless and letting the other coordinates move freely. One might wonder whether simultaneously achieving both of these goals is possible. In fact, it is quite possible in some, but not all, cases, as will be described in the next subsection.

A user should be able to control the relative weight of each of these goals, so we multiply $\mathbf{Q}$ by a user-controlled scaling factor, α:

$$\mathbf{w}'^T(\alpha\mathbf{Q})\mathbf{w}' + (\mathbf{w}' - \mathbf{w})^T\mathbf{P}(\mathbf{w}' - \mathbf{w}) \tag{7.3}$$

(α will be discussed further ahead).

Taking the gradient of (7.3) and setting to 0, we get the desired weight vector $\mathbf{w}'$:

$$\nabla\mathbf{w}'^T(\alpha\mathbf{Q})\mathbf{w}' + (\mathbf{w}' - \mathbf{w})^T\mathbf{P}(\mathbf{w}' - \mathbf{w}) = 0,$$
$$2\alpha\mathbf{Qw}' + 2\mathbf{Pw}' - 2\mathbf{Pw} = 0,$$

so

$$\mathbf{w}' = \mathbf{Aw}, \tag{7.4}$$

where

$$\mathbf{A} = (\mathbf{P} + \alpha\mathbf{Q})^{-1}\mathbf{P}. \tag{7.5}$$

We refer to the matrix $\mathbf{A}$ as the *attenuation matrix*, which remains constant as long as a given set of coordinates is selected. Inserting (7.4) into the original delta blendshape formulation (7.2) yields

$$\mathbf{f} = \mathbf{f}_0 + \mathbf{Dw}' = \mathbf{f}_0 + \mathbf{DAw}. \tag{7.6}$$

Now, whenever the animator sets the sliders to $\mathbf{w}$, the application will internally calculate and use the transformed weights $\mathbf{w}'$.

Note that when coordinate motion attenuation is enabled, the transformation will not only affect subsequent slider moves, but will modify the current pose as well. The change to the current pose is expected (since it results from a user action) and is generally small for reasons to be described in the next subsection. Nevertheless, a minor change in formulation can eliminate this change to the current pose, if desired.

We introduce a modified neutral pose $\mathbf{f}_0'$ such that

$$\mathbf{f}_0' + \mathbf{DAw}_1 = \mathbf{f}_0' + \mathbf{Dw}. \tag{7.7}$$

Solving for $\mathbf{f}_0'$, we get

$$\mathbf{f}_0' = \mathbf{f}_0 + \mathbf{D}(\mathbf{I} - \mathbf{A})\mathbf{w}, \tag{7.8}$$

and the overall formula for the facial pose becomes

$$\mathbf{f} = \mathbf{f}_0' + \mathbf{DAw}. \tag{7.9}$$

When the animator wishes to deactivate motion attenuation and return to normal editing, the neutral pose would be altered again. By an analogous derivation, a new neutral pose, $\mathbf{f}_0''$, becomes

$$\mathbf{f}_0'' = \mathbf{f}_0' + \mathbf{D}(\mathbf{A} - \mathbf{I})\mathbf{w}. \tag{7.10}$$

Conceptually, we present these results in terms of the attenuation matrix, $\mathbf{A}$, transforming the weight vector $\mathbf{w}$. The solution (7.9), however, offers a dual interpretation in which $\mathbf{A}$ post-transforms the blendshape matrix $\mathbf{D}$ so that

$$\mathbf{D}' = \mathbf{DA}$$

and

$$\mathbf{f} = \mathbf{f}_0' + \mathbf{D}'\mathbf{w}. \tag{7.11}$$

In practice, this formulation offers implementation advantages. The blendshape matrix $\mathbf{D}$ is constant throughout the animation process, so we only need to compute $\mathbf{D}'$ once each time motion attenuation is activated or deactivated, rather than continuously calculating the adjusted internal weight values $\mathbf{w}'$. The formulation also allows the actual weights to be exposed to the user, rather than requiring a distinction between internal weights $\mathbf{w}'$ and the user-adjusted weights $\mathbf{w}$.

7.5.1 The Balancing Factor α

The factor α controls the balance between attenuating the movement of selected coordinates and allowing the unselected coordinates to move freely. If α is very small,

$$\alpha \mathbf{Q} \approx 0,$$
$$\mathbf{w}' \approx (\mathbf{P} + 0)^{-1}\mathbf{P}\mathbf{w} = \mathbf{w},$$

so $\mathbf{w}'$ will be close to the original values $\mathbf{w}$, which is to say the algorithm favors allowing the unselected vertices to move. As α takes on increasingly large values, (7.3) will be dominated by $\mathbf{w}'^T \mathbf{Q}\mathbf{w}'$, which is minimized when $\mathbf{w}'$ is in the nullspace of $\mathbf{Q}$, and thus is in the nullspace of $\mathbf{S}$:

$$\mathbf{S}\mathbf{w}' = 0.$$

In this case, the selected vertices will not move at all.

From this observation we can see that it is possible to move coordinates in $\mathring{\mathbf{S}}$ without significantly displacing coordinates in $\mathbf{S}$ to the extent that $\mathbf{S}$ has small (even if not strictly zero) singular values. We see this in practice in Figs. 7.4 and 7.5.

The two terms in (7.3) have unequal contributions, with typically fewer selected than unselected coordinates. We compensate for this by initializing α to the ratio of the number of unselected and selected vertices.

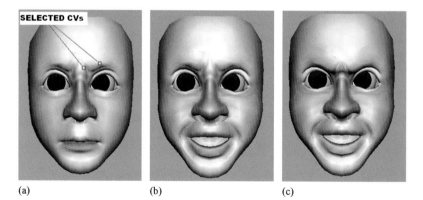

(a)   (b)   (c)

Fig. 7.4 (a) The user selects two vertices whose motion is to be attenuated. The algorithm operates at the level of coordinates rather than vertices, so in effect six coordinates are selected. (b) The results of the same slider moves shown in Fig. 7.2(c), but with coordinate movement attenuation [compare to Fig. 7.2(c)]. (c) Repeated from Fig. 7.2(c) for comparison.

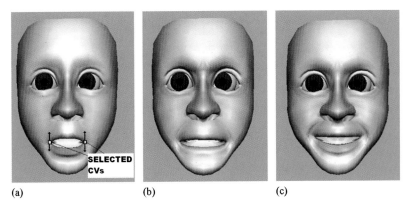

Fig. 7.5 (a) The *y*-component of two vertices are selected. (b) Sliders `SmirkLeft` and `SmirkRight` are increased to 0.7. We see their normal effects of stretching out the mouth and pushing back the cheeks, but the selected vertices maintain their vertical positions. (c) The same slider moves with no attenuation. The corners of the mouth move significantly in the *y*-direction.

7.6 Results

We implemented the weight correction (7.9) in Matlab, making use of the commercial animation package Maya to perform coordinate selection interaction and render the results. Figure 7.4 illustrates the effect of applying the correction algorithm to the case shown in Fig. 7.2. Note that the mouth is sculpted as desired, but the position of the brow is undisturbed.

The algorithm operates on coordinates, allowing the animator to independently select the *x*-, *y*-, and/or *z*-components of a particular vertex, thus attenuating its movement along particular axes. Figure 7.5(a) shows a pose with only two coordinates selected: the y-components of the corners of the mouth. After further slider moves, Figure 7.5(b) shows a new pose where the corners of the mouth have moved along the *x*-axis, but not along the *y*-axis. Figure 7.5(c) shows the effect of the same slider moves without coordinate attenuation.

Figure 7.6 shows an example of poses created using the same slider weights but different values of α. At very high values, the results are almost indistinguishable from the attenuated pose. At very low values, none of the vertices, selected or unselected, moves very much.

The computations required are simple and fast enough to be performed at interactive speeds on a modern desktop machine. As such, selected motion attenuation would be relatively easy to add to an existing blendshape animation package. In addition to the usual slider interface, there would be controls to invoke motion attenuation, select vertices, and adjust the value of α. Until motion attenuation is turned off, weights would be automatically transformed as the sliders move. Using motion attenuation in conjunction with a one-level undo is a particularly simple strategy: if any slider has undesired side effects, the animator simply undoes the slider move, applies motion attenuation to the area(s) exhibiting the interference, and releases the attenuation after adjusting the slider as desired.

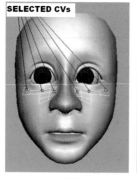
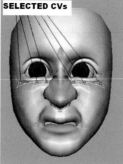
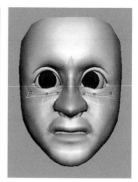

(a) 6 vertices (18 coordinates) are selected below the eye.

(b) Slider moves without attenuation: Wince, SneerLeft, and SneerRight are all set to 0.7. The selected vertices move significantly as the face is deformed

(c) The same slider moves with attenuation applied. Mouth movement is similar to Fig.6b, but the movement of the selected verticesis attenuated.α is left at its default initialization value here, $\alpha = 335$.

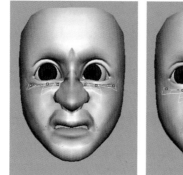
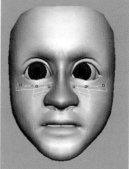

(d) The user adjusts α to 25. Now the mouth moves exactly as in Fig. 6b, but so do the selected vertices.

(e) $\alpha = 3000$. The algorithm favors keeping the selected vertices stationalry, but at the cost of not moving unselected vertices either. The animator should reduce α.

Fig. 7.6 an example of poses created using the same slider weights but different values of α.

7.7 Conclusions and Future Work

This chapter has demonstrated an interactive technique that provides animators improved control over blendshape interference. In order to take advantage of this technique, an animator needs to be aware of the new controls, understand them, and make ongoing decisions about when to use them. The need for judgment on the animator's part is ultimately not a disadvantage; animators rely on human judgment and necessarily become intimately familiar with the models they use. In fact, the use of our technique reduces the need for animators to learn and remember the interactions between blend shapes. Note that a somewhat similar "pin-and-drag" style of inter-action has also been proposed for inverse kinematics [15]. Reducing the need for repeated correction of blendshape interference has the potential to save valuable modeling and animation effort.

It is also worth investigating the possibility of incorporating these techniques into the modeling process. A modeler would apply constraints to the blendshape system, dictating that a given vertex should only be moved by certain sliders or that it should remain within specific bounds. How these controls might be defined and presented to a modeler is the subject of future work.

Acknowledgment We thank Hiroki Itokazu and Bret St. Clair for model preparation, Fred Parke, Craig Reynolds, and Lance Williams for information on the early history of blend shapes, and Fred Pighin for additional discussion of these topics.

References

1. J. P. Lewis, J. Mooser, Z. Deng, and U. Neumann. Reducing blendshape interference by selected motion attenuation. In *SI3D '05: Proceedings of the 2005 Symposium on Interactive 3D graphics and games*, pages 25–29, ACM Press, New York, 2005.
2. P. Bergeron and P. Lachapelle. Controlling facial expression and body movements in the computer generated short "Tony de Peltrie". In *SIGGRAPH Tutorial Notes*. ACM Press, New York, 1985.
3. S. Jenkins. Personal communication. Disney Feature Animation, 2004.
4. B. Raitt. The making of Gollum. Presentation at U. Southern California Institute for Creative Technologies's *Frontiers of Facial Animation* Workshop, August 2004.
5. C. Landreth. *Bingo*. Computer generated short film directed by Chris Landreth, 1998.
6. F. Pighin, J. Hecker, D. Lischinski, R. Szeliski, and D.H. Salesin. Synthesizing realistic facial expressions from photographs. In *Proceedings of ACM SIGGRAPH 1998*, pages 75–84, 1998.
7. B. Choe, H. Lee, and H.-S. Ko. Performance-driven muscle-based facial animation. *Journal of Visualization and Computer Animation*, 12(2):67–79, 2001.
8. F.I. Parke. Computer generated animation of faces. *Proceedings ACM Annual Conference.*, August 1972.
9. T. Beier. Personal communication. Hammerhead Productions, 2005.
10. Philippe Bergeron. 3-d character animation on the symbolics system. *SIGGRAPH Course Notes: 3-D Character Animation by Computer*, July 1987.
11. M. Elson. "Displacement" facial animation techniques. *SIGGRAPH Course Notes: State of the Art in Facial Animation*, 1990.
12. Jeff Kleiser. A fast, efficient, accurate way to represent the human face. In *SIGGRAPH '89 Course Notes 22: State of the Art in Facial Animation*, 1989.
13. P. Joshi, W.C. Tien, M. Desbrun, and F. Pighin. Learning controls for blend shape based realistic facial animation. *Eurographics/SIGGRAPH Symposium on Computer Animation (SCA)*, 2003.
14. T. Blanz and T. Vetter. A morphable model for the synthesis of 3d faces. In *Proceedings of ACM SIGGRAPH 1999*, pages 187–194, August 1999.
15. K. Yamane and Y. Nakamura. Natural motion animation through constraining and deconstraining at will. *IEEE Transaction on Visualization and Computer Graphics*, 9(3): 352–360, 2003.
16. K. Grochow, S.L. Martin, A. Hertzmann, and Z. Popovic. Style-based inverse kinematics. *ACM Transactions on Graphics*, 23(3):522–531, 2004.

17. N. Magnenat-Thalmann, R. Laperriere, and D. Thalmann. Joint-dependent local deformations for hand animation and object grasping. In *Proceedings of Graphics Interface*, pages 26–33, 1988.

18. A. Mohr, L. Tokheim, and M. Gleicher. Direct manipulation of interactive character skins. In *Symposium on Interactive 3D Graphics*. ACM, 2003.

19. Tsuneya Kurihara and Natsuki Miyata. Modeling deformable human hands from medical images. In *SCA '04: Proceedings of the 2004 ACM SIGGRAPH/Eurographics Symposium on Computer Animation*, pages 355–363. ACM, 2004.

20. P. Ekman and W. Friesen. *Manual for Facial Action Coding System*. Consulting Psychologists Press Inc., Palo Alto, CA, 1978.

21. X. Zhao. Personal communication. Disney Feature Animation, 2001.

Chapter 8
Sketching Articulation and Pose for Facial Animation

Edwin Chang and Odest Chadwicke Jenkins

8.1 Introduction

Articulating and posing are both tasks inherent to the animation of 3D meshes. Defining the **articulation** (or rigging) of a mesh traditionally involves specification of several deformation variables over the range of desired motion. To achieve satisfactory results, a user may need to manually specify deformation settings for hundreds of vertices. Furthermore, an infinite number of plausible deformations can exist for a given mesh that range from the realistic flexing and extending of underlying muscle to cartoon squash and stretch motion. Consequently, articulation is often a tedious and complex process requring substantial technical as well as artistic skill. This problem is compounded when defining the articulation of a facial mesh, where motion is quickly discernable as natural or unnatural to a human viewer.

Once articulation is performed, an animator creates animations by specifying **poses** of the mesh in the articulation space.

To specify a pose efficiently, an animator is often provided with a control rig comprised of widgets and sliders that provide a puppet-like control of the mesh deformation. Unfortunately, users face a considerable learning curve to understand and utilize such control rigs, often requiring as much time as creating the control rig itself.

To address the lack of accessiblity in current rigging systems, the process in this chapter aims to leverage the familiarity of 2D sketching as an interface for 3D mesh animation. While current articulation and posing interfaces provide detailed control, such interfaces lack intuition and accessiblity for novices and traditional animators trained with pencil and paper. A sketching interface, however, provides a familiar interface while still providing a high level of control to users. It can be particularly helpful to a novice who lacks a strong understanding of facial movement but is comfortable working with simple line drawings of a face. For traditional animators, sketching provides a direct correlation between hand-drawn and 3D animation.

In this chapter, we present a 2D sketching interface to facilitate procedures for articulating a single mesh and posing an articulated mesh. This method focuses on the inference of reference and target curves on the mesh from user sketch input. In the posing procedure, the user first draws a sketch to place a reference curve on the mesh. The user then draws a sketch to identify a target curve, which specifies the desired manipulation of the reference curve. The posing system then uses the

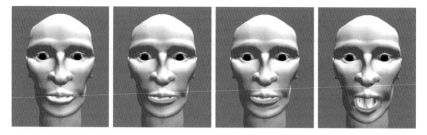

Fig. 8.1 A reference curve (green) and target curve (blue) are sketched to pose the lower lip of an articulated mesh in the sketch-based posing system. ©Eurographics Association 2006; Reproduced by kind permission of the Eurographics Association.

downhill simplex method to optimize the mesh pose in the articulation space such that the distance between these two curves is minimized. The user can additionally introduce additional constraints to pin parts of the mesh in place. In the articulation procedure, reference curves are generated from the sketching of regions of interests on the mesh that are then manipulated by sketched target curves.

Both the articulation and posing methods can work in tandem or independently such that one can be replaced by alternative mechanisms. We show results from using this posing method with a mesh articuated by blend shapes modeled in Alias Maya. While these methods are suited to facial meshes, the same procedures are applicable to other types of meshes as well.

8.1.1 Background

There exists much previous work in mesh articulation and deformation as well as in the related field of mesh editing. One typical approach for facial articulation is to create several meshes with the same topology and blend between them, i.e., a blendshape approach. While robust and granting users a high amount of control, this approach often requires users to create a large number of blend shapes. The blendshape process has also been combined with a skeletal approach to provide the flexibility of a skeletal system with the expressiveness of a blendshape system [19]. Shapes have also been used as examples for a combination of shape and transform blending [20].

Free-form deformation (FFD) [10] is one method that provides a wide range of possible deformation without requiring multiple shapes. The deformations used for articulation in this chapter parallel the use of FFDs, in particular a curve-based FFD method that warps the mesh [3, 11]. This type of FFD provides a method of smooth deformation that facilitates the use of curves sketched by users. Sketches have also been used to specify FFDs based on scalar field manipulation [9] and as input to a gesture-based FFD interface [14]. Outside their use in FFDs, sketches have also been used as skeletal strokes [8] to bend and twist two-dimensional images.

Recent work has also focused on drawing directly onto the image plane in order to specify deformation. This poses challenges when interpreting the intent of users as well as providing a coherent translation from 2D to 3D space. This problem has also been encountered in 3D modeling using 2D sketches. One modeling method interprets 2D sketches as silhouettes to infer and construct 3D polygonal shapes [16]. A similar approach uses implicit surfaces, allowing for surface modification by silhouette oversketching [26]. Another solution used for mesh editing is to treat the process as an inverse NPR process [4], where the mesh is transformed to match user-drawn contours and silhouette contours. This method of interpretation of user-drawn curves is very natural to users; while the approach here differs, it aims to replicate its functionality. Silhouette sketches additionally have been used to stylize previously animated motion by specifying the silhouette contours of the desired pose [2]. Sketches have also been used to specify curves in a free-form skeleton method [5], but the approach was limited to deformation in appendage-like parts of a mesh, e.g., tails, legs, or arms.

Often one limitation of drawing on the image plane is that deformations remain parallel to the image plane. One approach to this problem that is described in this chapter constrains vertices to follow a surface, similar to the method used in manipulating clothing [13], where cloth can be positioned by moving it across the surface of a mesh.

Posing an articulated mesh involves its own unique challenges separate from those encountered in articulation. Control widgets are often added that allow users to interact directly with the articulation parameters. Sketching has been applied to manipulate multiple control points in order to pose the mesh [7], but these control points must have been previously defined by a user. Sketches have also been used to describe the motion of a figure across time rather than through individual poses [21]. Other work has treated the posing problem as an optimization problem, attempting to determine the pose of a human figure that best matches hand-drawn sketches [6]. The approach in this chapter also views the problem as an optimization problem but focuses on posing articulated facial meshes. Posing a facial mesh has been approached previously using a blendshape method [12] but required users to build a set of key blend shapes instead of using a previously created set. Other work has applied inverse kinematics to sets of existing blend shapes [17], allowing users to interactively pose between the blend shapes.

One of the methods of evaluation used for the posing process described in this chapter involves the use of curves generated from the tracking of facial features in video. The eigenpoints approach [22] is used in order to determine these curves. This approach uses an eigenfeature-based method in order to place control points onto unmarked images, which are then used to define curves for posing. Other work has also used video with facial models, creating high-resolution models of a moving face that can be used to pose new expressions by interactively dragging surface points [25].

8.2 Sketching Articulation and Pose

While the posing and articulation methods described here are independent, they share a simple interaction scheme based on sketching reference and target curves. Reference and target curves are 3D features on the mesh inferred from a 2D sketch. These curve features are used in a slightly different manner for the articulation and

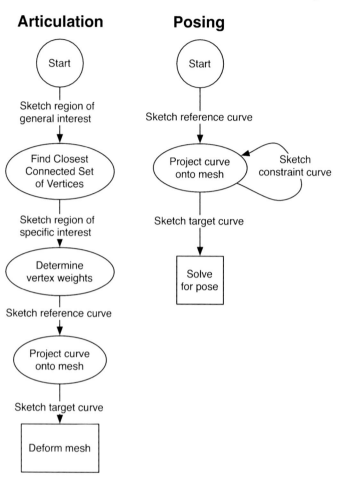

Fig. 8.2 The flow of user control for articulation and posing.

posing processes. The articulation method uses the additional selection of regions of interests to compute reference curves. The posing procedure incorporates user-selected constraints to keep parts of the mesh in place. Figure 8.2 presents the flow of user control in both these processes. In the remainder of this section, we explain further these differences in the computation of feature curves from sketching.

8.2.1 Sketch-based Mesh Posing

Given an articulated mesh, posing that mesh presents challenges in estimating the appropriate articulation parameters. The approach here casts pose parameter estimation as an optimization problem. We apply this approach to an articulated mesh based on blendshape interpolation as well as one from the sketch-based articulation method.

The user first draws a reference curve C_r, an ordered set of points $\{\mathbf{r}_1, \ldots, \mathbf{r}_n\}$ on the image plane. Each of these points is projected from the camera onto the closest visible face of the mesh (Fig. 8.3) and stored as weights of the vertices of that face. As the mesh is deformed, the system recalculates new 3D positions for these points based on the vertex weights so that the curve follows the surface of the mesh during deformation. The user then draws a target curve C_t, an ordered set of points $\{\mathbf{t}_1, \ldots, \mathbf{t}_n\}$, which is projected onto the mesh. The system reverses the order of the points of C_t if the target curve's endpoint, $\mathbf{t}_n$, is closer to the reference curve's start point, $\mathbf{r}_1$, than the target curve's own start point, $\mathbf{t}_1$ (i.e., reverse C_t if $||\mathbf{t}_n - \mathbf{r}_1|| < ||\mathbf{t}_1 - \mathbf{r}_1||$). In this case, reversing the order of the points facilitates a more coherent interpolation scheme between the two curves. The system then reparameterizes the target curve to match n, the number of points in the reference curve. The curve is reparameterized by choosing the new points by distance along the original line, where $\mathbf{r}_i'$ is the ith of n points along the reparameterized curve:

$$\mathbf{r}_i' = C_r \left(\frac{i-1}{n} \right). \tag{8.1}$$

The target curve is then projected into 3D space using the distances from the camera along the reference curve C_r. The system then searches the articulation space M^d of d deformers to find an optimal pose P given by the optimal articulation parameters $\mathbf{x}$ that minimizes the distance between the reference curve, which maintains its position on the mesh, and the target curve (Fig. 8.1). The distance term for the optimization is given by the following, where $\mathbf{r}_i$ and $\mathbf{t}_i$ are corresponding points on the reference and target curves for a given pose P in an articulation space of d dimensions:

$$E(P) = \sum_{i=1}^{n} ||\mathbf{r}_i - \mathbf{t}_i||. \tag{8.2}$$

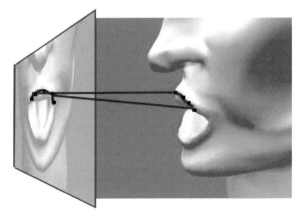

Fig. 8.3 A reference curve drawn on the image plane is projected onto the mesh. ©Eurographics Association 2006; reproduced by kind permission of the Eurographics Association.

Algorithm 1 Downhill Simplex Method

$S \Leftarrow \{P_1, P_2, ...P_d\}$ // simplex shape of poses
$S_E \Leftarrow \{E(P_1), E(P_2), ...E(P_d)\}$ // simplex pose values
loop
    $P_{high} \Leftarrow P_i$ where $E(P_i)$ is $max(S_E)$
    $P_{nexthigh} \Leftarrow P_i$ where $E(P_i)$ is $max(S_E - \{E(P_{high})\})$
    $P_{low} \Leftarrow P_i$ where $E(P_i)$ is $min(S_E)$
    $r_{tol} \Leftarrow 2.0 * |(E(P_{high}) - E(P_{low}))|/|E(P_{high}) + E(P_{low}) + \epsilon|$
    if $r_{tol} < f_{tol}$ **then**
        // found minimum under simplex tolerance
        return P_{low}
    end if
    $P_{try} \Leftarrow reflect(S, P_{high})$ // try reflecting simplex from high point
    if $compare(S, P_{try}, P_{high})$ **then**
        $P_{try} \Leftarrow extrap(S, P_{high})$ // try additional extrapolation
        $compare(S, P_{try}, P_{high})$
    else if $E(P_{try}) \geq E(P_{nexthigh})$ **then**
        $P_{try} \Leftarrow contract1D(S, P_{high})$ // try one-dimensional contraction
        if not $compare(S, P_{try}, P_{high})$ **then**
            // contract around lowest point and update S and S_E
            $contract(S, P_{low})$
        end if
    end if
end loop

define $compare(S, P_{try}, P_{high})$
    if $E(P_{try}) < E(P_{high})$
        $replace(S, P_{high}, P_{try})$ // replace P_{high} with P_{try} in S
        $replace(S_E, E(P_{high}), E(P_{try}))$ // update S_E
        return true
    else
        return false
    endif
end define

In order to solve this optimization problem, the downhill simplex method [15] is used, which provides the ability to perform optimization without the use of derivatives (Algorithm 1). Since this is the case, the optimization process does not need knowledge of the underlying articulation system and can work with any type of articulation. The downhill simplex method searches a d-dimensional space using a simplex shape of $d + 1$ points that searches the space by reflecting and contracting itself until it reaches its goal (Fig. 8.4). The optimization works best with non-hierarchical articulation (like faces, rather than arms), however, and is only efficient for a limited number of variables ($d < 20$). We propose methods to deal with this limitation in Section 8.4.

Using the downhill simplex method, the system reaches an acceptable solution when the vector distance traveled in one iteration, r_{tol}, is less than a fractional tolerance, f_{tol} of 0.05. After this solution is found, the system performs a cleanup stage. Since several of the articulation parameters may have had no effect on the region of interest, these parameters may have become unneccessarily changed through

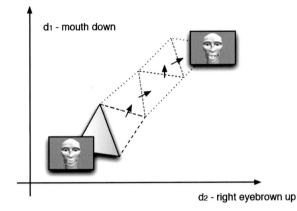

d₁ - mouth down

d₂ - right eyebrown up

Fig. 8.4 Searching in a two-dimensional articulation space using the downhill simplex method. ©Eurographics Association 2006; reproduced by kind permission of the Eurographics Association.

searching the articulation space in the optimization process. A pose P_i is evaluated for each articulation variable x_i, where x_i is set to its original value and all other variables are set to those from $\mathbf{x}_o$, the set of articulation variables derived from optimization. If the difference between $E(P_i)$ and $E(P_o)$ (where P_o is the pose set by $\mathbf{x}_o$) is minimal, x_i returns to its original value.

This system also provides a method for the user to set constraints on the mesh with additional curves in order to keep parts of the mesh in place. For each constraint curve K_j, a set of ordered points $\{k_1, \ldots, k_n\}$ is projected onto the mesh. When a pose is evaluated using Eq. 8.2, the following term is also added for each constraint, where k_i' is the position of k_i in the new pose P:

$$E_j(P) = \sum_{i=1}^{n} \|k_i' - k_i\|, \qquad (8.3)$$

Constraint curves are useful, as a deformer on a mesh may have a small effect on the region the reference curve lies on even though it mainly deforms a separate area. For example, a cheek deformer could slightly affect the vertices around the lips on a mesh. When the user attempts to pose the lips, the cheeks could then be undesirably affected. These constraints are drawn on the mesh in the same manner as the reference curve. Previously used reference curves can also be used as constraint curves in order to keep a previously specified deformation in place.

8.2.2 Sketch-based Mesh Articulation

Users specify one articulated deformation at a time in our system in a four-step process. Users first select a region of general interest and then a region of specific interest. Users can then draw reference and target curves to specify the deformation.

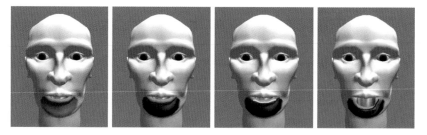

Fig. 8.5 (a) A region of general interest is selected and then (b) a region of specific interest to specify articulation weights. (c) A reference curve and (d) target curve are then drawn to specify the deformation. ©Eurographics Association 2006; reproduced by kind permission of the Eurographics Association.

Each of these deformations becomes one dimension in the articulation space. The four steps are pictured in Fig. 8.5.

8.2.3 Regions of Interest

In the first step, the user must pick a general region on the mesh where the deformation is desired, a set of vertices V_g. To do so, the user first draws a curve C_g to encircle the region on the image plane, selecting a set of vertices V_a. The desired set of vertices will be a subset of the set of all selected vertices ($V_g \subseteq V_a$), but often $V_g \neq V_a$, as some vertices in V_a may be behind the desired region or occluded by other parts of the mesh. In order to avoid selecting these vertices, V_g is chosen to be the set of connected vertices containing the vertex closest to the camera and of sufficient size ($|V_k| > 10$, where $V_k \subseteq V_a$ and V_k is connected). Each vertex in this set ($\mathbf{v}_i \in V_g$) is then projected to the image plane in order to determine its 2D distance to the drawn curve C_g, which is then stored. We will call this distance g_i for every vertex $\mathbf{v}_i$ in V_g.

The user then encircles a region of specific interest with a new curve C_s to specify a set of vertices V_s, where $V_s \subseteq V_g$. Each vertex $\mathbf{v}_i$ in V_g is then assigned articulation weights by the following equation, where w_i is the articulation weight and c_i is the distance to the curve C_s on the image plane:

$$
w_i = \begin{cases} 1.0 & \text{if } \mathbf{v}_i \in V_s, \\ \frac{g_i}{g_i + c_i} & \text{otherwise.} \end{cases} \tag{8.4}
$$

In this manner, articulation weights smoothly blend off from 1.0 to 0.0 from the region of specific interest to the borders of the region of general interest. The system displays the articulation weights to users by coloring vertices white if unselected, and blue to black from 1.0 to 0.0. The camera is restricted from movement in this step as g_i and c_i are 2D distances calculated on the image plane. Using different camera views when selecting the two regions may result in an undesirable blend of articulation weights. This camera restriction only exists at this step.

8.2.4 Estimating a Reference Curve

The system then generates a reference curve C_r, an ordered set of points $\{r_1, \ldots, r_n\}$, that estimates a skeletal curve in 3D space for the region of specific interest. The curve C_r is determined by ordering the vertices in V_s by their x-values when projected to the image plane, where x and y refer to the horizontal vertical axes on the image plane. If the difference in the minimum and maximum y-values of the vertices when projected to the image plane in V_s is larger than the minimum and maximum x-values, the y-value of each vertex is used to order C_r instead. This 3D curve is then smoothed through convolution with a triangle filter reference $f(j)$ across a kernel size v that is one third the number of vertices in the curve ($v = |C_r|/3$):

$$\mathbf{r}'_i = \sum_{j=-v/2}^{v/2} f(j)\mathbf{r}_{i+j}. \tag{8.5}$$

In some cases, this estimated curve may not be satisfactory to the user, especially when the region of interest does not have a distinct curve-based feature, like the cheek of a face. If desired, the user can redraw the curve C_r on the image plane, which is then projected onto the mesh to form the reference curve. The reference curve, either estimated or not, is then slightly smoothed to account for noise (convolved with a triangle filter reference) and reparameterized to have a regular spacing.

With the reference curve C_r smoothed and reparameterized in 3D space, the user can choose to move the camera and view the mesh at different angles. In order to facilitate this, the system does not depth-test when rendering curves, instead overlaying them over the entire image.

In the final step, the user draws a target curve C_t, an ordered set of points $\{t_1, \ldots, t_n\}$, indicating how the mesh should be deformed so that the reference curve meets the target curve. The order of the points of the curve is reversed if the target curve's endpoint, t_n, is closer to the reference curve's start point, r_1, than the target curve's own start point, t_1 (i.e., reverse C_t if $\|t_n - r_1\| < \|t_1 - r_1\|$). The target curve is then reparameterized to match the number of points in the reference curve, n. The points of the target curve are then projected into 3D space by using the distances to the camera of the corresponding points on the reference curve, d_1 to d_n.

8.2.5 Curve Interpolation

Since the target and reference curves now share the same number of points, we can determine rotations between the matching line segments on the two curves by finding the cross product of the two segments and the angle between them. We will call these rotations ϕ_j for each segment j. The system stores these rotations as relative for each segment, such that each rotation assumes all rotations previous to a line segment have been applied. By keeping rotations relative, the system can determine

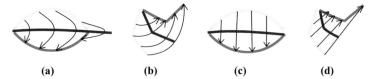

Fig. 8.6 (a), (b) Rotation-scale and (c), (d) translation methods of interpolation, where the initial curve is yellow, the in-between curve is red, and the final curve is blue. ©Eurographics Association 2006; reproduced by kind permission of the Eurographics Association.

partial rotations between points on the curves when we perform the mesh deformation. The system also calculates a scale change s_i between the two segments, as the two curves may have different lengths:

$$s_i = \frac{\|t_{i+1} - t_i\|}{\|r_{i+1} - r_i\|}. \tag{8.6}$$

With the rotations and scales for each segment of the lines, the system can then interpolate between the curves by applying a partial transformation α (where $0 \le \alpha \le 1$) of $\alpha\phi_j$ and αs_i to the line segments of the reference curve.

In certain situations, however, applying scale and rotation to interpolate is inappropriate. The curves in Figs. 8.6(a) and (b) are interpolated using the rotation-scale method. In Fig. 8.6(a) this works well, especially if these lines pose an appendage like a leg. In Fig. 8.6(b), however, the curve becomes undesirably extended, which would be inappropriate if these curves were posing a blinking eyelid. For this case, the system instead linearly interpolates between corresponding points on the two curves, translating the points without regard to scale or rotation of the line segments [Fig. 8.6(c)]. The system automatically chooses this method if the endpoints of the reference and target curves are within 10 pixels of each other, but also allows the user to specify otherwise.

8.2.6 Mesh Deformation

Once the system has an appropriate method of interpolation between the reference and target curves, it can deform the vertices of the mesh according to those curves. Each vertex v_i in V_g is projected onto the reference curve to find the closest point on that curve, which is then stored as a proportional distance along the length of the entire curve, l_i, where $0 \le l_i \le 1$. This projection is done on the image plane in 2D space so that vertices farther from the camera than other vertices still project to an appropriate reference point r_i. The system then determines the corresponding point on the target curve, which we will call the target point t_i, by the distance along the target curve according to l_i. The system then applies the translation from the reference point to the target point $(t_i - r_i)$ to the vertex. A rotation transformation must also be applied to the vertex centered around the target point. Since this point does not likely lie on the end of a line segment on the curve, the rotation must be calculated.

(a)   (b)

Fig. 8.7 Examples of desirable (a) and undesirable (b) mesh deformation with rotation. ©Eurographics Association 2006; reproduced by kind permission of the Eurographics Association.

The system first combines all the line segment rotations previous to the target point, ϕ_j from 1 to $k - 1$, where the target point lies on segment k. The system then applies a partial rotation of the last line segment's rotation, ϕ_k, according to the length where the target point lies on that segment, a value from 0 to 1 we will call u. We express this in the following equation, where the final rotation is ϕ_t. The rotations are centered about the target point.

$$\phi_t = \left(\prod_{j=1}^{k-1} \phi_j \right) (\phi_k u) \tag{8.7}$$

In order to pose between the reference and target curves, the system applies the same operations, but instead uses an interpolated curve, determined using the method described earlier, instead of the target curve. For similar reasons discussed concerning curve interpolation, rotations are not always desired in the mesh deformation. In Fig. 8.7, a mesh deformation with rotations on three vertices is depicted in two examples. Rotations are appropriate for Fig. 8.7(a), but less so for Fig. 8.7(b), especially if this were deforming an eyelid. Vertices past the endpoints of the curves can move greater distances than expected due to rotation. For this reason, when curve interpolation does not use rotations, they are not applied in mesh deformation as well.

Since deformations are specified using curves in the image plane, it can be difficult to specify deformation outside one plane of movement. To facilitate this, the user can set the deformation to follow the surface of a sphere. In Fig. 8.8,

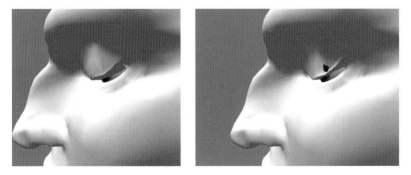

Fig. 8.8 An eyelid deformation constrained and not constrained to follow the eyeball surface. ©Eurographics Association 2006; reproduced by kind permission of the Eurographics Association.

the deformation is constrained to maintain the vertices' distance from the eyeball sphere. Otherwise, the vertices move in only one direction and the eyelid intersects the eyeball. While only a sphere is used here, other surfaces could be used by constraining the vertices to maintain their original distance from the surface by projecting outward from the normal of the closest point on that surface.

Once all the vertices have been repositioned according to the target curve, they are returned to their original positions according to the value of the articulation weights determined previously. The transformation is calculated as a linear translation for each vertex, where vertices with weight 0 return completely to their original position and vertices with weight 1 stay in their new position. In this manner, smooth deformations are ensured even when the region is enclosed by other parts of the mesh.

8.3 Applications of Posing and Articulation

We begin with the mesh of a face and articulate it using the system to specify a deformation for each eyelid, eyebrow, cheek, jaw, and various movements of the lips (Fig. 8.11), for a total of 15 deformers. Figure 8.9 depicts these deformers as separately colored regions that fade to black according to articulation weights. Figure 8.12 shows some of the poses that can be acheived using this articulation. Each of these deformations was created quickly, in under 2 minutes each. By comparison, specifying similar deformations in a blendshape approach required 10–20 minutes per shape. For eyelid deformations, deformations were set to follow the surface of a sphere centered at the eye. The system also works for nonfacial meshes, like the trunk of an elephant (Fig. 8.10).

Bringing this articulated mesh into the posing system, one can pose the face using reference and target curves. We also test this posing system with a mesh articulated

Fig. 8.9 An articulated mesh colored according to deformer and articulation weights. ©Eurographics Association 2006; reproduced by kind permission of the Eurographics Association.

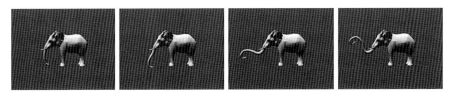

Fig. 8.10 Deformation of an elephant's trunk using the articulation system. ©Eurographics Association 2006; reproduced by kind permission of the Eurographics Association.

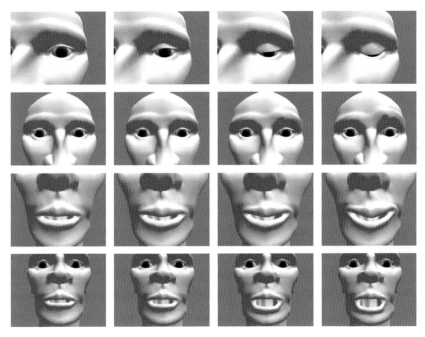

Fig. 8.11 A few of the individual deformations created in the sketch-based articulation system. ©Eurographics Association 2006; reproduced by kind permission of the Eurographics Association.

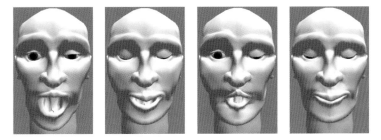

Fig. 8.12 A sampling of poses in our articulation space. ©Eurographics Association 2006; reproduced by kind permission of the Eurographics Association.

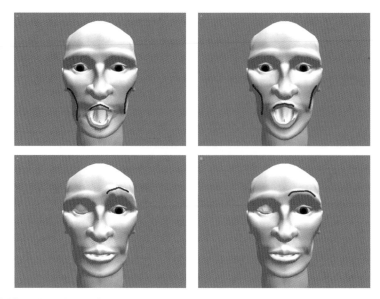

Fig. 8.13 Posing using similar curves on a sketch-based articulation (left) and a blendshape articulation (right). ©Eurographics Association 2006; reproduced by kind permission of the Eurographics Association.

by a blendshape method using shapes created in Alias Maya (Fig. 8.13) and achieve similar results in both. In the top examples, the mouth is posed in two iterations, one for the upper lip and one for the lower lip. In total, with the cheek constraints, six curves were drawn to pose the face (two constraint curves, and two pairs of reference and target curves). In the lower examples, the right eyelid and left eyebrow were posed using four curves (two pairs of reference and target curves).

8.3.1 Facial Animation from Video Features

The posing process is not only limited to sketching, but can be used with any image features about a moving mesh. We used the posing process with curves generated from tracking of facial features in video on a sketch-based articulated mesh. These curves were determined through the eigenpoints method [22] and follow the eyebrows, eyelids, and lips of the subject in the video shown in Fig. 8.14.

The eigenpoints method associates points with a model of the image that is created through principal component analysis of a set of previously labeled images. This image model is then used to find features in new, unlabeled images and estimates the positions of the points associated with those features, which are then used to create the curves we use.

These tracked curves, while slightly noisy, remain unfiltered in our testing. Since the facial features of the subject do not match those in the 3D mesh, relative changes in the tracked curves are applied to user-drawn reference curves to create new target

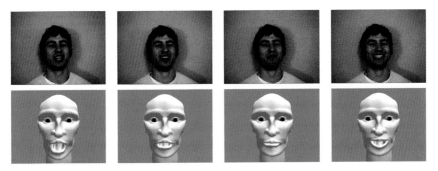

Fig. 8.14 Posing using curves from tracking of facial features in video. ©Eurographics Association 2006; reproduced by kind permission of the Eurographics Association.

curves. For one curve from video C_{vf} in frame f, relative changes, $\{c_1, \ldots, c_n\}$, from frame to frame for each point were determined. These relative changes were then applied to a user-drawn curve C_u reparameterized to have n points, $\{d_1, \ldots, d_n\}$. For each frame of video a new curve C'_u was determined by applying c_i to every point d_i. The change c_i was also scaled up in order to account for difference in length between C_{v0} and C_u:

$$d'_i = d_i + c_i \frac{|C_u|}{|C_{v0}|}. \tag{8.8}$$

When posing the face from video features, the limited articulation of the mesh does not fully match the range of expression in the human face. Even so, the posing process works well at capturing the motion of the face across frames (Fig. 8.14).

The optimization process for posing requires many iterations before convergence and results in a pause in the posing system after drawing the target curve. On an AMD XP 2000+ processor, the computation time is under 5 seconds for the blendshape method and under 10 seconds for our articulation method. The optimization takes longer for our articulation method because it takes slightly longer to pose than the blendshape method. From pose to pose, this time is small [the mesh can be posed at ($\sim$50 fps), but is still longer than the blend shape method ($\sim$90 fps)].

8.4 Discussion

The implementation described here allows users to quickly sketch a wide range of articulations for a mesh. Users also maintain a level of control with deformations comparable to blendshape approaches (Fig. 8.13). Furthermore, this method does not face the limitations blend shapes have, such as the issues linear blending between shapes can cause. For example, it is difficult to have rotational movement with blend shapes, like an eye blink or jaw movement. This method can recreate these motions and allows users to apply the strengths of free-form deformation to enclosed areas of the mesh while maintaining smooth deformation.

The posing process is likewise simple to use and requires little to no training or knowledge of the articulation system. Through sketching curves to pose the mesh, the user has intuitive control over the articulation space while unaware of the actual articulation parameters. Usability testing would be needed to further substantiate the intuitive nature of this approach.

The optimization required for posing is not instantaneous and does not work at interactive rates (> 15 Hz), though it is fast enough for user interaction (typically within 5 seconds per pose). Further limitations involve the limit of the number of variables the optimization process can deal with. The downhill simplex method is only effective to under 20 variables, and a large number of variables will further slow down the optimization. As many professional facial animation systems often have several hundred controls, this method may be impractical. The problem can be reduced, however, by limiting the articulation search space only to those articulation variables that affect the reference curve. If the search space still remains overly large, the method can be used in stages, first posing articulation variables that have a large effect and then smaller variables in greater detail. Another possible approach would be to create low-dimensional subspaces [23] or probabilistic priors [24] from previously generated poses.

In this chapter, we presented a sketch-based method of preparing a mesh for animation in two processes—articulation and posing. The system focused on inference of reference and target curves for facial animation but was adept at animating motion for meshes with different kinematic structures. This system has a simple and intuitive interface that allows for a wide span of deformation to be specified. This approach to posing is flexible for usage with typical articulation and rigging systems, including blendshape interpolation.

Acknowledgment We thank John F. Hughes for his comments and advice on our work. Special thanks also go to the Brown Graphics Group, in particular Olga Karpenko and Tomer Moscovich for initial discussions on this work.

References

1. Chang E, Jenkins O (2006) Sketching articulation and pose for facial animation. *ACM SIGGRAPH/Eurographics Symposium on Computer Animation*: 271–280.
2. Li Y, Gleicher M, Xu Y, Shum H (2003) Stylizing motion with drawings. *ACM SIGGRAPH/Eurographics Symposium on Computer Animation*:309–319.
3. Wagner T, Jensen R, Thayer C, Finkelstein A (1998) Texture mapping for cel animation. *SIGGRAPH 98 Proceedings*:435–446.
4. Nealen A, Sorkine O, Alexa M, Cohen-Or D (2005) A sketch-based interface for detail-preserving mesh editing. *SIGGRAPH 05 Proceedings*:1142–1147.
5. Kho Y, Garland M (2005) Sketching mesh deformations. *Symposium on Interactive 3D Graphics and Games Proceedings*:147–154.
6. Davis J, Agrawala M, Chuang E, Popović, Salesin D (2003) A sketching interface for articulated figure animation. *SIGGRAPH/Eurographics Symposium on Computer Animation*: 320–328.
7. Swain M, Duncan B (2004) SketchPose: Artist-friendly posing tool. SIGGRAPH 2004 sketch.

8. Hsu S, Lee I (1994) Drawing and animation using skeletal strokes. *SIGGRAPH 94 Proceedings*:109–118.
9. Hua J, Qin H (2003) Free-form deformations via sketching and manipulating scalar fields. *ACM Symposium on Solid Modeling and Applications Proceedings*:328–333.
10. Sederberg T, Parry S (1986) Free-form deformation of solid geometric models. *Conference on Computer Graphics and Interactive Techniques Proceedings*:151–160.
11. Singh K, Fiume E (1998) Wires: A geometric deformation technique. *Conference on Computer Graphics and Interactive Techniques Proceedings*:405–414.
12. Chuang E (2002) Performance driven facial animation using blendshape interpolation. Stanford University, Department off Computer Science.
13. Igarashi T, Hughes J (2002) Clothing manipulation. *ACM Symposium on User Interface Software and Technology Proceedings*:91–100.
14. Draper G, Egbert P (2003) A gestural interface to free-form deformation. *Graphics Interface 2003 Proceedings*:113–120.
15. Press W, Flannery B, Teukolsky S, Vetterling W (1992) *Numerical Recipes in C—The Art of Scientific Programming*. Cambridge University Press, New York.
16. Igarashi T, Matsuoka S, Tanaka H (1999) Teddy: A sketching interface for 3D freeform design. *Graphics Interface 2003 Proceedings*:113–120.
17. Sumner R, Zwicker M, Gotsman C, Popoviç J (2005) Mesh-based inverse kinematics. *SIGGRAPH 05 Proceedings*:488–495.
18. Capell S, Green S, Curless B, Duchamp T, Popoviç Z (2002) Interactive skeleton-driven dynamic deformations. *Conference on Computer Graphics and Interactive Techniques Proceedings*:586–593.
19. Lewis J, Cordner M, Fong N (2000) Pose space deformation: A unified approach to shape interpolation and skeleton-driven deformation. *Conference on Computer Graphics and Interactive Techniques Proceedings*:165–172.
20. Sloan P, Rose C, Cohen M (2001) Shape by example. *Symposium on Interactive 3D Graphics Proceedings*:135–143.
21. Thorne M, Burke D, Van de Panne, M (2004) Identifying and sketching the future: Motion doodles: An interface for sketching character motion. *SIGGRAPH 04 Proceedings*:424–431.
22. Covell M, Bregler C (1996) Eigen-points. *IEEE International Conference on Image Processing Proceedings*:471–474.
23. Safanova A, Hodgins J, Pollard N (2004) Synthesizing physically realistic human motion in low-dimensional, behavior-specific spaces. *SIGGRAPH 04 Proceedings*:514–521.
24. Grochow K, Martin S, Hertzmann A, Popoviç Z (2004) Style-based inverse kinematics. *SIGGRAPH 04 Proceedings*:522–531.
25. Zhang L, Snavely N, Curless B, Seitz S (2004) Spacetime faces: High resolution capture for modeling and animation. *SIGGRAPH 04 Proceedings*:548–558.
26. Karpenko O, Hughes J, Raskar R (2002) Free-form sketching with variational implicit surfaces. *Computer Graphics Forum*:585–594.

Chapter 9
Learning Controls for Blendshape-based Realistic Facial Animation

Pushkar Joshi, Wen Tien, Mathieu Desbrun, and Frédéric Pighin

9.1 Introduction

Detailed and expressive facial animation is essential for high-end character animation.[1] When the character is speaking or displaying emotions, the character's face may need to express a wide range of configurations. Since infinitely many facial expressions may be necessary, the face model should be able to deform to arbitrary configurations. Such a face model is called a *deformable* or *morphable* model of the face.

Often, a deformable face model can be constructed by mimicking the actual facial anatomy. Such a physically based model generally simulates various skin layers, muscles, fatty tissues, bones, and all the necessary components to approximate the real facial mechanics (see [15] for an example of recent work). The physically correct model provides precise control over the facial expressions. However, it is often very difficult and time-consuming to construct an accurate, anatomical model of the face that allows precise control over the facial expressions. Moreover, in character animation, simulating all the facial tissues is unnecessary; only the outermost surface layer needs to be deformed properly.

An easier method to construct a deformable face model is to use blendshapes. A blendshape model mostly disregards the facial muscle mechanics. Instead, the model directly considers every facial expression as a linear combination (i.e., a linear "blend") of a few select facial expressions: the blendshapes. By varying the weights of the linear combination, a full range of facial expressions can be generated with very little computation. During the control of the blendshape model, the user can design expressions with intuitive commands (e.g., 30% happy, 70% surprised), thereby making a blendshape model easier to use for non-experts. Blendshape interpolation can be traced back to Parke's pioneering work in facial animation [11, 12].

Sometimes in character animation tasks, parameterization and control of the blendshape model can be difficult. Spanning a complete range of highly detailed facial expressions might require a large number of blendshapes. For instance, the

---

[1] An earlier version of this paper [7] appreared in the 2003 ACM SIGGRAPH/ Eurographics Symposium on Computer Animation. All images are © Eurographics Association 2006; reproduced by kind permission of the Eurographics Association.

Z. Deng and U. Neumann, *Data-Driven 3D Facial Animation.*
© Springer-Verlag London Limited 2008

facial animations of Gollum in the feature film *The Two Towers* required 675 blendshapes [6]. To build a facial expression from such a large database of expressions, an animator needs to tweak the blend weights of each blendshape — an inconvenient and arduous task. Assigning an independent parameter value to every blendshape is not practical and often leads to a tedious trial-and-error process for the animator.

Splitting the face geometry into smaller regions slightly alleviates the problem of blendshape control. The task of specifying weights is done independently per region. By manipulating the configuration of the smaller regions separately, the animator is guaranteed that the modification will impact only a specific part of the face (e.g., the left eyebrow). For a given region, the animator needs to specify weights only for those blendshapes that are expressive over that region. Segmentation can also be used to minimize the total number of blendshapes required. Studies [5] have shown that it is possible to create complex and believable facial expressions using only a few blendshapes by combining smaller, local shapes. If the regions can be manipulated independently, the number of possible combinations (and therefore the number of possible expressions) increases significantly. Therefore, segmenting the face into regions helps in controlling a blendshape model. Kleiser [8] extended Parke's original idea of blendshape interpolation to a segmented face where the regions are blended individually, thereby allowing a wider range of expressions from a relatively small set of blendshapes.

Traditionally, face segmentation is done *manually*. A typical example is the segmentation of a face into an upper region and a lower region: the upper region is used for expressing emotions with the eyes and eyebrows, while the lower region expresses speech with the lips and lower jaw. Although this approximation is often used in practice, such an ad hoc separation does not reflect the subtle inter-region dependencies appearing in the actual face. Ideally, the face segmentation should be adaptive to the blendshapes and reflect the idiosyncrasies of the face being modeled. Additionally, the segmentation should provide control for editing at different levels of detail. We propose that a proper segmentation of the face helps us with the tasks of parameterization and control of a blendshape model.

9.1.1 Contribution and Overview

In this chapter, we describe a simple, automatic, and fast face segmentation method that addresses the problems of *parameterization* and *control* of blendshape models. We design an *automatic* technique that extracts a set of parameters (regions) from a blendshape model. Instead of deriving our control mechanism from the biomechanics of the face, we learn it directly from the available data. Our solution is thus specific to the input blendshapes and reflects the facial idiosyncrasies present in those blendshapes. We demonstrate the usefulness of our improved face segmentation in two well-known facial animation tasks: motion capture mapping and key-frame construction.

9.1.2 Related Work

As mentioned before, blendshape interpolation is almost as old as the idea of computerized facial animation [11, 12]. Blendshape models are also used in the computer vision community for analyzing face images and video. Blanz and Vetter [1] designed an algorithm that fits a blendshape model onto a single image. Their result is an estimate of the geometry and texture of the person's face. Pighin et al. [14] extend this work by fitting their model to a whole sequence of images, allowing manipulation of the video by editing the fitted model throughout the video sequence.

Pighin et al. [13] describe a key-frame construction system that uses a palette of facial expressions along with a painting interface to assign blending weights. The system gives the animator the freedom to assign the blending weights at the granularity of a vertex. Note that in many character animation tasks, this freedom is actually a drawback: it is rather difficult to create realistic expressions by tweaking blend weights. The system we propose is quite different: it respects the mechanics of the face through an analysis of the captured, real data. As a result, our system is more intuitive and helps generate plausible facial expressions.

9.2 Blendshape Face Model

We define a blendshape face model as being a convex linear combination of n basis vectors, each vector being one of the blendshapes. Each blendshape is a face model that includes geometry and texture. All the blendshape meshes for a given model share the same topology. The coordinates of a vertex $\mathbf{V}$ belonging to the blendshape model can then be written as follows:

$$\mathbf{V} = \sum_{i=1}^{n} \alpha_i \mathbf{V}_i,$$

where the scalars α_i are the blending weights, $\mathbf{V}_i$ is the location of the vertex in the blendshape i, and n is the number of blendshapes. These weights must satisfy the convex constraint:

$$\alpha_i \geq 0, \text{ for all } i$$

and must sum to one for rotational and translational invariance:

$$\sum_{i=1}^{n} \alpha_i = 1.$$

Similarly, the texture at a particular point of the blendshape model is a linear combination (i.e., alpha blending) of the blendshape textures with the same blending weights as those used for the geometry.

9.2.1 Learning Controls

In this section, we describe a segmentation process that leverages face deformation information directly from the input data to create meaningful blend regions. First, we describe our approximation of the physical model of the face skin, and then we give the method used to extract regions.

9.2.2 Physical Analogies

We assume that the face configuration corresponding to the neutral expression is the face at rest position. For all the other blendshapes, we analyze the deformation from the rest position to learn the material properties of the face skin. The deformation of every blendshape is measured by the displacement field **d** between each vertex's current position and its rest position. We model the physical properties of the face skin using *linear elasticity*. The governing equation of motion of a linear elastic model is the Lamé formulation:

$$\rho\mathbf{a} = \lambda\Delta\mathbf{d} + (\lambda + \mu)\nabla(\nabla \cdot \mathbf{d}). \tag{9.1}$$

In our current context, **d** is the displacement of the vertex from its position on the neutral face, ρ is the averaged face mass density, **a** is the vertex' acceleration, and λ and μ are the Lamé coefficients that determine the material's behavior (related to Young's modulus and the Poisson ratio). The interpretation of the previous equation is relatively simple: the Laplacian vector $\Delta\mathbf{d}$ of the displacement field represents the propagation of deformation through the blendshape, while the second term represents the area-restoring force. These two second-order operators, null for any rigid deformation, are therefore *two complementary measures of deformation* of our face model. To further simplify our model, we will assume that the area distortion is negligible on a face (our tests confirm that this assumption does not change the results significantly). Therefore, we can use only the Laplacian magnitudes to identify disjoint regions of the face that have a similar amount of deformation. Since the deformation on the face is continuous, these disjoint regions often move together coherently during face motion. Consequently, we can use these regions to segment the face.

9.2.3 Segmentation

Debunne et al. [4] have introduced a simple discrete (mesh-based) formula for the Laplacian operator present in Eq. 9.1. We compute this discrete Laplacian value at every vertex of every non-neutral (i.e., expressive) blendshape mesh and take the magnitude of the resulting vectors. This provides us with a deformation map for each expression. We gather these maps into a single deformation map M by computing for each vertex independently its maximum deformation value across all expressions. This resulting map (see Fig. 9.1(a)—expressed as an RGB colored vector map to show direction of deformation) measures the maximum amount of *local deformation* that our face model has for the blendshapes used. A fast segmentation can now be performed by simply splitting this map into regions with low deformation and regions with high deformation. The threshold for this split can be chosen as

$$threshold = \mathbf{D}n\,t,$$

where $\mathbf{D}$ is the array of sorted deformation values, n is the size of this array, and t is a scalar between 0 and 1. (That is, first sort all the deformation values, and then obtain the deformation at the position that is a function of the number of values.) The value t determines the granularity of the regions, as this single parameter can control the level of region detail. For instance, to generate the segmentations in Figs. 9.1(b) and (c), we used $t = 0.25$ and $t = 0.75$, respectively.

Depending on the threshold, disconnected regions are created all across the mesh. We automatically clean up the regions by absorbing isolated regions into larger

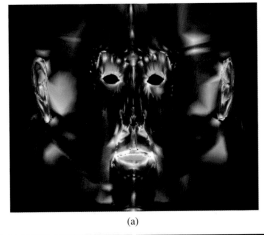

(a)

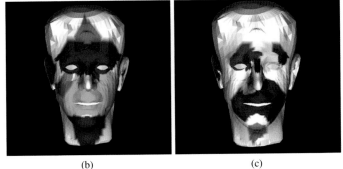

(b)   (c)

Fig. 9.1 Automatically generated regions: (a) deformation map (the deformation in x, y, and z directions is expressed as a respective RGB triplet); (b) segmentation for a low threshold and (c) for a high threshold.

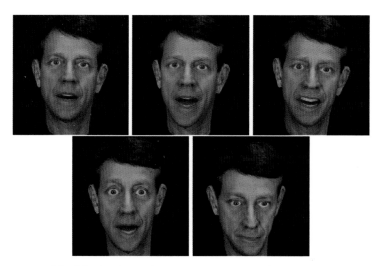

Fig. 9.2 Mapping motion capture data on a set of blendshapes.

regions and minimizing concavity of the regions. Finally, each region is extended by one vertex all around its boundary, in order to create an overlap with the neighboring regions. The result is one large, least deformed region (i.e., the background) and a number of overlapping regions where there is generally more significant deformation in the range of expressions. These latter regions [see Figs. 9.1(b) and (c)] correspond to vertices that generally undergo similar deformation: locally, each region deforms in a quasi-rigid way. Thus, linear blending in each of these regions will reconstruct realistic target face expressions. The entire region extraction routine is fast (about 1 minute for our example with 10 blendshapes) and is generally performed as a pre-process.

9.3 Animation with Motion Capture

We express the motion in the motion capture data using the blendshape model. That is, we assume that the motion (or the per-frame position) of a motion marker can be expressed as a linear combination of corresponding points in the blendshapes. Namely,

$$\mathbf{M}_j = \sum_{i=1}^{n} \alpha_i \mathbf{V}_{ij},$$

where $\mathbf{M}_j$ is a location on the face whose motion was recorded and $\mathbf{V}_{ij}$ is the corresponding location in blendshape i. m is the number of motion markers and n the number of blendshapes (as in Choe et al. [3]).

Given several such equations, we find the blending weights α_i. We use a least-squares solution, where we minimize the sum of the squared differences:

$$\sum_{j=1}^{m}\left[\mathbf{M}_j - \left(\sum_{i=1}^{n}\alpha_i\mathbf{V}_{ij}\right)\right]^2. \tag{9.2}$$

We get a linear system of equations where the unknowns α_i are the weights in the blendshape combination. We use an iterative quadratic programming solver [10] to obtain the optimal values of the blending weights α_i in the least-squares sense. Solving this system is equivalent to orthogonally projecting the motion onto the set of blendshapes.

Note that, in general, Eq. 9.2 is an overconstrained system that does not have an exact solution. If the positions of the motion markers are outside the range of motion spanned by the blendshape model, the motion mapping using only blendshape interpolation produces unsatisfactory results. To solve this problem and produce an animated mesh that follows the motion more precisely, we complement the projection on the blendshape basis by translating the vertices in the mesh by the residual $(\mathbf{M}_j - \sum_{i=1}^{n}\alpha_i \cdot \mathbf{V}_{ij})$. The residual, which is only known for a small set of points, is interpolated to the rest of the facial mesh using radial basis functions [9]. The final coordinates, $\mathbf{V}_j$, of a vertex on the face are then constructed using

$$\mathbf{V}_j = \mathbf{P}_j + RBF(\mathbf{P}_j),$$

where $\mathbf{P}_j$ is the projection on the set of blendshape:

$$\mathbf{P}_j = \sum_{i=1}^{n}\alpha_i\mathbf{V}_{ij}$$

and $RBF(\mathbf{P}_j)$ is the interpolated residual at vertex $\mathbf{P}_j$:

$$RBF(\mathbf{P}_j) = \sum_{i=1}^{m}\exp(-||\mathbf{M}_i - \mathbf{P}_j||)\mathbf{C}_i. \tag{9.3}$$

In Eq. 9.3, the vectors $\mathbf{C}_i$ are computed using the known values of the residual at $\mathbf{M}_i$. Since the system of equations is linear in the unknowns, using least squares provides an estimate of the unknowns [13]. Note that bypassing the solution of Eq. 9.2 and directly solving for the radial basis weights would have a very different effect. By first projecting on the set of blendshapes, we obtain a face geometry that reflects the idiosyncrasies unique to the character. This geometry is then brought closer to the prescribed marker motion by interpolating the residual. Choe et al. [3] use a similar approach to map motion onto a set of face muscle actuator parameters. The main difference is how the residual is handled. In their approach, the generic blendshapes are modified (as part of the muscle actuator training) to adapt to the motion of the target character. We, on the other hand, use radial basis functions to modify the geometry on a per-frame basis.

Instead of solving the above system for the entire model, we solve for each region created using our automatic segmentation process. Doing so gives us localized control over the face mesh and results in better enforcement of the spatial constraints. This also allows us to express a wide range of motion using only a limited number of blendshapes (ten, in our case).

For every frame and for every region, we construct the above minimization problem and obtain blending weights. The same weights are then used to obtain, for all vertices of the region, new positions that match the motion. Thus, for every frame of motion, we can solve a minimization problem to obtain the blending weights and consequently the face mesh that follows the motion capture data.

9.4 Key-Frame Editing

Using our blendshape model, we can interactively construct face meshes that can be used as key frames in a key framing-based facial animation tool. In order to control the face configuration at smaller granularity, we segment the blendshape model into regions using our automatic segmentation technique.

9.4.1 User Interface for Creating Key Frames

The blendshape model reads in the various regions and presents the face in the neutral expression to the user. The user interactively specifies positions of arbitrarily chosen control points by direct manipulation (clicking and dragging vertices). The system treats these control points like motion markers and uses blendshape interpolation (see Eq. 9.2) to interpolate the user-specified deformation over the region that contains the marker. The core least-squares solver is the same as the one used for mapping motion data. Often times, the system of equations is underconstrained; in this case, we solve for the blend weights that minimize the norm of the residual. The resulting system is interactive, intuitive, and easy to use.

9.4.2 Extensions for Key-Frame Editing

We describe some additional functionality for improving the key-frame construction and editing system.

9.4.2.1 Region Hierarchy

In order to allow key-frame editing at various degrees of control (global versus local), we build a hierarchy of regions. This hierarchy is created by first running the segmentation algorithm described in Section 9.2.1 with a high threshold value so as to generate small and localized regions. These regions constitute the lowest region level. We can then merge regions iteratively so that contiguous regions are merged together as we generate higher region levels.

9.4.2.2 Motion Damping

Some parts of the face do not move significantly throughout the entire set of blend-shapes (e.g., tip of the nose). If we were to select such a part and try to deform it using the interface described so far, a small deformation of the control point could trigger a dramatic change in the facial expression. To reduce the sensitivity of the system, we need to scale the displacement of the control point according to that part's ability to deform. Our scale factor is the inverse of the maximum displacement of the control point across all blendshapes in the blendshape model. This is a simple method to add stiffness to those parts of the face that typically show higher resistance to deformation.

Figure 9.3 displays a sequence of manipulations performed on a key frame. The successive key-frame editing is performed with increasing levels of detail to refine the facial expression in a localized manner.

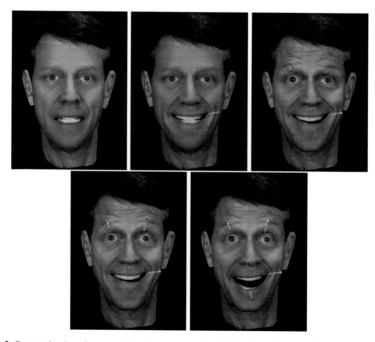

Fig. 9.3 Successive key-frame editing from coarse (top left) to fine (bottom right) level of details.

9.5 Rendering Realistic BlendShapes

9.5.1 Basic Process

Rendering the blendshape model is pretty straightforward and can be done in two steps: first the consensus geometry is evaluated, and then it is rendered as many times as there are blendshapes in the model to blend the texture maps. This latter step is done by assigning to each vertex's alpha channel the corresponding weight for a given blendshape.

9.5.2 Realistic Textures

Texture misregistration is a common problem with blendshape rendering for realistic facial animation. If the textures do not correspond at each point on the face geometry, combining them linearly will result in a blurred rendering. Thus, the frequency content of the rendered face images varies as a function of time. Figure 9.4 provides an illustration of this phenomenon. The leftmost image shows our model rendered with only one contributing blendshape. The middle image shows the rendered model with seven equally contributing blendshapes. In the middle rendering, a lot of the details of the face texture have disappeared.

To alleviate this problem, we borrow an approach from the image processing community [2] and perform a bandpass decomposition of the textures. More specifically, we build a two-level Laplacian image pyramid out of each blendshape texture map. This results in the creation of two texture maps for each blendshape: the first is a low-pass version of the original texture, and the second is a signed detail texture. We first render the lowpass texture maps for each blendshape by using alpha blending. Then we render the detailed (high-frequency) texture map of a single blendshape (usually the neutral expression) using the consensus geometry and add it to the previous rendering. The result is a rendering that both better preserves the original spectral content of the blendshape textures and maintains the high-frequency content constant throughout the animation. Figure 9.4(c) illustrates the improvement obtained by using this technique.

9.6 Results

The techniques described in this paper have been implemented and tested with a set of blendshapes modeled to capture the facial expression of an actor. We created 10 blendshapes corresponding to extreme expressions. We used an image-based modeling technique similar to the one developed by Pighin et al [13]. Three photographs of the actor were processed to model each blendshape: front facing, 30 degree right, and 30 degree left. All the animations were computed and rendered in

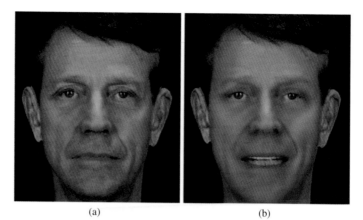

(a)   (b)

(c)

Fig. 9.4 Blendshape renderings: (a) a single contributing blendshape; (b) seven equally contributing blendshapes without detail texture; (c) seven equally contributing blendshapes with detail texture.

real time (30 Hz) on a 1 GhZ PC equipped with an NVidia GeForce 3 graphics card. To enhance realism with only little overhead, we decided to animate the tongue, the lower teeth, and the upper teeth in a simple procedural manner; they are moved rigidly and follow the motion of separate sets of manually selected points on the mesh. The eyeballs are moved rigidly according to the rigid motion of the head.

9.6.1 Motion Capture

As described in Section 9.3, we can project recorded motion onto the blendshape model. We also tried this approach for a few animated sequences. As expected, the resulting deformations of the face are very natural and reflect the actor's personality. Figure 9.2 shows some of the frames obtained. The example shown uses only 10 blendshapes. To animate speech motion, usually a much larger set of shapes needs to be used. We are able to animate the lips by using radial basis functions as described in Section 9.3.

9.6.2 Key-Frame Editing

We also experimented with the interactive tool described in Section 9.4. The tool proved to be very efficient, helping us sculpt a face quickly and in a very intuitive way. We started manipulating the face with a set of coarse regions and refined the expression by using increasingly finer segmentations.

Video sequences generated with our implementation are available on the Web at `http://www.geometry.caltech.edu/Movies/BlendShapes/`.

Acknowledgment The authors would like to thank J.P. Lewis for discussions about blendshape animation and Andrew Gardner for its initial development. This project was supported in part by the National Science Foundation (CCR-0133983, DMS-0221666, DMS-0221669, EEC-9529152) and the U.S. Army Research Institute for the Behavioral and Social Sciences under ARO contract number DAAD 19-99-D-0046. Any opinions, findings, conclusions, or recommendations expressed in this paper are those of the authors and do not necessarily reflect the views of the Department of the Army.

References

1. T. Blanz and T. Vetter. A morphable model for the synthesis of 3D faces. In *SIGGRAPH 99 Conference Proceedings*. ACM SIGGRAPH, August 1999.
2. P.J. Burt and E.H. Adelson. A multiresolution spline with application to image mosaics. *ACM Transactions on Graphics*, 2(4), October 1983.
3. B. Choe, H. Lee, and H. Ko. Performance-driven muscle-based facial animation. In *Proceedings of Computer Animation*, volume 12, pages 67–79, May 2001.
4. G. Debunne, M. Desbrun, M. Cani, and A. Barr. Adaptive simulation of soft bodies in real-time. In *Proceedings of Computer Animation 2000*, pages 15–20, May 2000.
5. P. Ekman and W.V. Friesen. *Unmasking the Face. A Guide to Recognizing Emotions fron Facial Clues*. Prentice-Hall, Inc., Englewood Cliffs, NJ, 1975.
6. J. Fordham. Middle earth strikes back. *Cinefex*, (92):71–142, 2003.
7. P. Joshi, W.C. Tien, M. Desbrun, and F. Pighin. Learning controls for blendshape based realistic facial animation. In *SCA '03: Proceedings of the 2003 ACM SIGGRAPH/Eurographics Symposium on Computer Animation*, pages 187–192, Aire-la-Ville, Switzerland, 2003.
8. J. Kleiser. A fast, efficient, accurate way to represent the human face. In *SIGGRAPH '89 Course Notes 22: State of the Art in Facial Animation*, 1989.
9. G.M. Nielson. Scattered data modeling. *IEEE Computer Graphics and Applications*, 13(1):60–70, January 1993.
10. J. Nocedal and S.J. Wright. *Numerical Optimization*. Springer, New York, 1999.
11. F.I. Parke. Computer generated animation of faces. *Proceedings ACM Annual Conference.*, August 1972.
12. F.I. Parke. A parametric model for human faces. PhD thesis, University of Utah, Salt Lake City, Utah, December 1974. UTEC-CSc-75-047.

13. F. Pighin, J. Hecker, D. Lischinski, R. Szeliski, and D.H. Salesin. Synthesizing realistic facial expressions from photographs. In *SIGGRAPH 98 Conference Proceedings*, pages 75–84. ACM SIGGRAPH, July 1998.
14. F. Pighin, R. Szeliski, and D.H. Salesin. Resynthesizing facial animation through 3d model-based tracking. In *Proceedings, International Conference on Computer Vision*, 1999.
15. E. Sifakis, I. Neverov, and R. Fedkiw. Automatic determination of facial muscle activations from sparse motion capture marker data. *ACM Trans. Graph.*, 24(3):417–425, 2005.

Chapter 10
Speech Motion Decomposition and Editing

Yong Cao, Petros Faloutsos, and Frédéric Pighin

10.1 Introduction

Complex facial expressions and speech motions are generated by hundreds of individual muscles.[1] We don't understand quite well the dynamic of these muscles nor their collaborative effects. Realistic physical simulation of these muscles can be computationally expensive or lack details. Using motion capture is an attractive alternative. Current motion capture technology can record accurately the motions of a character's face. These motions can then be mapped onto a face model to produce realistic animations. It is, however, impossible to record all the motions a face can do. Thus, the motion capture sessions should be carefully planned to meet the needs of the production. A different approach is to record a representative set of motions and use machine learning techniques to estimate a generative statistical model. The goal is then to find and fit a model that is able to re-synthesize the recorded data. Finding an appropriate model that can reproduce the subtleties of the recorded motion can be a very difficult task. In addition, the parameters of the model might not be appropriate for manipulating or editing the data. Fitting statistical models generally involves minimizing an error function regardless of the semantics of the data or what the model's parameters really represent. Interpretation of the data is generally best done by a human observer who can annotate the data and specify its semantics. A function can then be learned that expresses the correlation among the annotations, the input, and the motions, the output. We can use this function to manipulate the data. However, when the size of the data becomes large, human intervention and annotation are impractical. Our method addresses this issue.

In this chapter, we introduce an unsupervised learning technique, based on *independent component analysis* (ICA), that splits the recorded motions into linear mixtures of statistically independent sources. These sources, called *independent components*, offer a compact representation of the data with clear semantics. The lack of structure or model underlying the recorded data makes it really hard to edit. In contrast, the decomposition provides a meaningful parameterization of the original data that is suitable for editing. The technique is automatic and does not require annotating the data.

---

[1] This chapter is an improved version of the authors' previous work [1]. Reproduced by kind permission of the Eurographics Association; ©Eurographics Association 2003.

The remainder of the chapter is organized as follows. Section 10.2 reviews some related research. Section 10.3 introduces ICA and describes its application to recorded facial motion. Section 10.4 explains how to determine the semantics of the resulting decomposition. Section 10.5 describes editing operations using the ICA representation of the motion. Section 10.6 presents some experimental results. Lastly, Section 10.7 summarizes the chapter.

10.2 Related Work

Other works extract facial expressions from speech motion. In this section, we give a brief review of these works.

Chuang et al. [2] present an interesting attempt to separate visual speech into content and style (emotion). Based on factorization [3, 4], their method produces a bilinear model that extracts emotion and content from input video sequences.

The pattern recognition community has performed a significant amount of work on facial expression analysis. Expressions are typically based on tracking the motion of particular facial elements such as the eyes, the rigid body motion of the face, or transient features such as wrinkles [5–11]. These systems are quite effective for facial feature recognition.

Learning the style and content from recorded variations of a motion has been also investigated in the area of full-body animation. Pullen et al. [12] propose a technique that decomposes motion into different frequency bands. The low-frequency components represent the basic motion, while the higher-frequency ones capture the style of the motion. Combining the basic signals with different higher-frequency bands results in stylistic variations of the basic motions. Brand et al. [13] train *hidden Markov models* to capture the style variations of example dance data. The resulting style models can be applied to novel dance sequences. Unuma et al. [14] decompose example motion into high and low frequencies using Fourier analysis. Manipulating the resulting coefficients provides an intuitive way to alter the original motion.

10.3 Facial Motion Decomposition

In this section, we present an overview of *independent component analysis*. We then discuss our decomposition technique and the way we determine the semantics of the resulting independent components.

10.3.1 Independent Component Analysis

Independent component analysis is an unsupervised learning technique [15]. It assumes that a set of observed random variables can be expressed as linear combinations of independent latent variables. In a way it deconvolves the recorded

signals into a set of statistically independent random variables. It is often associated with the "blind source separation" problem. One instance of this problem can
be found in audio processing: imagine that the sound in a room comes from two
sources, the voice of a speaker and the humming of an air conditioning system.
Solving the blind source separation problem in this context would involve recording
the sound in the room (from two different locations) and processing it statistically
so that the two original sources can be separated. This audio separation problem is a
very difficult one. ICA can successfully separate the two sources by exploiting their
statistical independence.

Let us examine the mathematics of ICA. Assume that we observe n random variables $x_1, \ldots, x_n$, each of which is a linear mixture of n latent or hidden variables
$u_1, \ldots, u_n$ such that

$$x_j = \sum_{i=1}^{n} a_{ji} u_i,$$

or, in matrix notation,

$$\mathbf{x} = \mathbf{Au}. \tag{10.1}$$

Equation 10.1 represents a generative model: it describes how the recorded data $\mathbf{x}$
are generated by the sources $\mathbf{u}$. The sources u_i, which are called the independent
components, cannot be observed directly. The matrix of coefficients $\mathbf{A}$, called the
mixing matrix, is also unknown. ICA provides a framework to estimate both $\mathbf{A}$ and
$\mathbf{u}$. In practice, estimating $\mathbf{A}$ is sufficient, since if the matrix is known, its inverse, W,
can be applied to obtain the independent components:

$$u = \mathbf{Wx}.$$

To estimate the matrix $\mathbf{A}$, ICA takes advantage of the fact that the components are
statistically independent. The key to estimating the ICA model is non-Gaussianity.
According to the central limit theorem, the sum of two independent random variables usually has a distribution closer to a Gaussian distribution. The idea then is to
iteratively extract random variables from the recorded data that are as non-Gaussian
as possible. How non-Gaussianity is measured is beyond the scope of this paper.
Different metrics have been used, leading to a variety of implementations. For more
details, see [15, 16]. In our experiments, we use a publicly available implementation
called FastICA [17].

10.3.2 Pre-Processing

Before ICA is applied, the facial motion data have to go through a preprocessing
phase that consists of two steps, *centering* and *whitening*.

Centering shifts the data toward its mean so that the resulting random variables
have zero mean. *Whitening* transforms the centered set of observed variables into a

set of uncorrelated variables. *Principal component analysis* (PCA) can be used to perform this transformation. After pre-processing, the model of Eq. 10.1 takes the form

$$x = E\{x\} + \mathbf{PA}u, \qquad (10.2)$$

where $E\{x\}$ is the expectation of x and P is an n by m matrix obtained by applying PCA to the centered data. m is the number of principal components we keep. Matrix P will not be square ($m < n$) if we decide to only retain a subset of the principal components. This reduction in dimension reduces the number of independent components to the same number as well.

10.3.3 PCA vs. ICA

PCA and ICA are related statistical techniques. They both provide a linear decomposition of sampled data. The fundamental difference is that PCA assumes the latent variables are uncorrelated, whereas ICA assumes they are independent. Independent random variables are also uncorrelated, but not vice versa. The goal of PCA is to find a sequence of uncorrelated random variables (components) where each variable covers as much of the variance of the data as possible. The resulting sequence is ordered by decreasing variance coverage. For this reason, PCA is often an effective compression technique: by keeping the first few components, most of the variance in the data can be covered. The independent components produced by ICA provide a separation mechanism between sources that are assumed independent rather than a compression mechanism.

10.3.4 Application to Facial Motion

Applying ICA to recorded facial motion is straightforward. The motion is represented as a set of time series $x_i(t)$ that captures the Euclidean coordinates of the motion capture markers in time. Each of these time series can be thought of as samples of random variables x_i. Then we can directly apply ICA decomposition on this set of variables, x_i, using Eq. 10.2.

This decomposition results in a set of independent components that have intuitive interpretation. In the next section, we will describe how to determine the meaning of the independent components.

10.4 Interpretation of the Independent Components

ICA decomposes speech-related motions into a set of sources that can be clearly interpreted and manipulated for editing purposes. In particular, we apply ICA to separate the data into style and content components. In our case, we equate style with expressiveness or emotion and contents with the part of the motion responsible for the formation of speech.

10.4.1 Number of Independent Components

Before applying ICA to the data, we have to determine the number of components we need to extract. There is no clear rule here. In practice, the whitening pre-processing step (Section 10.3) reduces the dimension of the data and determines the number of independent components. We can experimentally determine how many components to keep so that we preserve the subtleties of the motion. For most of the experiments, keeping enough components to cover 95%–98% of the variance proved to be sufficient.

In what follows, we describe how to associate specific meaning to the independent components.

10.4.2 Emotion

We recorded the motion of an actor's face while he was uttering a set of sentences multiple times, each time expressing a different emotion. Let us denote as $(\mathbf{x}^i, \mathbf{y}^i)$ p pairs of motions that corresponds to the same sentence but two different emotions. Applying ICA to each pair of motions in our data set results in pairs of corresponding independent component sets, $(\mathbf{u}^i, \mathbf{v}^i)$. We would expect that the independent components related to emotion differ significantly between two speech motions that have the same content but different emotion. In contrast, if an independent component is not related to emotion, its value in time for two corresponding motions should be the same except for some timing differences. In order to verify this property, we align each pair of corresponding motions using a *dynamic time-warping* (DTW) algorithm [18]. Let us denote $(\mathbf{u}'^i, \mathbf{v}'^i)$ the independent components of two aligned motions after time warping. We compute their difference using the root mean-square (RMS) error as follows:

$$d_{\text{emotion},j} = \left(\frac{1}{\sum q_i} \left(\sum_{i=1}^{p} \sum_{k=1}^{q_i} (u'^i_j(t_k) - v'^i_j(t_k))^2 \right) \right)^{\frac{1}{2}},$$

where q_i is the number of aligned time samples for pair i. The distance $d_{\text{emotion},j}$ is designed such that it should be large if component j is related to emotion.

Figure 10.1(a) shows a plot of the $d_{\text{emotion},j}$-values of six independent components estimated from 32 pairs of sentences of *frustrated* and *happy* motions. These data total 11,883 frames or 99 seconds. A clear peak can be observed for the third component. This strongly indicates that this component is related to emotional variations. The other components participate to a lesser degree to the

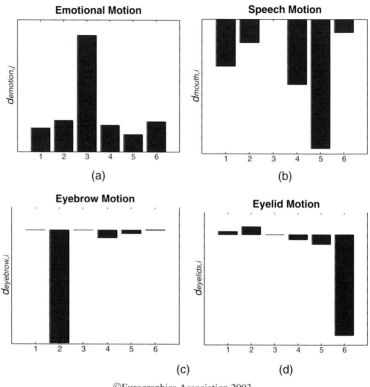

Fig. 10.1 These graphs [1] illustrate the classification of independent components. Each graph illustrates a category of motion: (a) for emotions, (b) for speech, (c) for eyebrows, and (d) for eyelids. The horizontal axis represents the index of independent components. The vertical axis shows the distance metrics that we describe in Section 10.4.

emotional content of the motions. This shows that speech motion cannot be strictly separated into statistically independent components. Our approach is albeit a successful approximation. As further proof, in Fig. 10.2 we plot the evolution of the different components over time for a set of five pairs of motions. On the timeline, we alternate *frustrated* and *happy* motions. The behavior of the third component appears very much related to changes in emotions (illustrated with different gray levels).

10.4.3 Content

We define content as the part of the motion associated with the formation of speech independent of expressiveness. For this case we only consider the motion of the markers in the mouth area (12 markers in our data set).

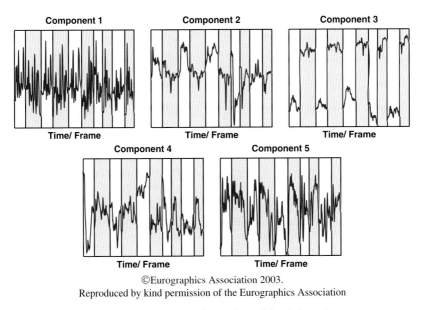

Fig. 10.2 These graphs [1] present the evolution in time of five independent components corresponding to five pairs of *frustrated* and *happy* motions. The timeline alters between frustrated (light) and happy (dark) motions. Notice how the third component oscillates between extreme values when the emotion changes.

Let us define a distance metric between two motions that have been reconstructed using two subsets of independent components, A and B:

$$d_{\text{mouth}}(\mathbf{x}_A, \mathbf{x}_B) = \left(\frac{1}{q} \sum_{k=1}^{q} \left(\frac{1}{r} \sum_{l=1}^{r} (x_A^l(t_k) - x_B^l(t_k))^2 \right) \right)^{\frac{1}{2}}, \qquad (10.3)$$

where $\mathbf{x}_A$ and $\mathbf{x}_B$ are the motions reconstructed using component subset A and B, respectively, q is the number of time samples of both motions, and r is the number of the markers considered for the mouth region (12 markers).

Reconstructing the motion of the mouth markers using all the independent components produces $\mathbf{x}_{\text{all}}$. In general, this is different from the captured motion because of the compression done in the pre-processing step (Section 10.3). In order to evaluate how much independent component i contributes to the mouth motion, we compute the following metric:

$$d_{\text{mouth},i} = d_{\text{mouth}}(\mathbf{x}_{E \cup \{i\}}, \mathbf{x}_{\text{all}}) - d_{\text{mouth}}(\mathbf{x}_E, \mathbf{x}_{\text{all}}), \qquad (10.4)$$

where E is the subset of independent components responsible for emotion and $\mathbf{x}_E$ is the marker motion reconstructed from subset E.

In Eq. 10.4, $d_{\text{mouth},i}$ quantifies the influence of independent component i on the motion of the mouth. The larger in absolute value this number is, the more influence component i has over the mouth motion. Figure 10.1(b) shows the value of $d_{\text{emotion},i}$

for six independent components. Notice how large $d_{mouth,1}$, $d_{mouth,4}$, and $d_{mouth,5}$ are compared to the rest of the components. We can visually verify that the motion $x_{\{1\}\cup\{4\}\cup\{5\}}$ reconstructed using components 1, 4, and 5 captures most of the speech motion.

10.4.4 Blinking and Non-Emotional Eyebrow Motions

Our experiments show that some independent components cannot be associated with emotion or content. We have experimentally determined that we can further classify such components into two groups: one for blinking motion and the other for non-emotional eyebrow motion. The latter refers to eyebrow motion that reflects stress and emphasis in the speech rather than in the emotional state of the speaker.

In order to identify the components related to these two types of motion, we use the same method employed for finding content-related components. We define $d_{eyebrow}$ and $d_{eyelids}$ according to Eq. 10.3 while considering only the markers on the eyebrows and the eyelids, respectively. We use these two metrics to define $d_{eyebrow,i}$ and $d_{eyelids,i}$ from Eq. 10.4 for the eyebrows and the eyelids, respectively.

Figure 10.1(c) shows the value of the distance metric $d_{eyebrow,i}$ for six independent components. Notice how much larger $d_{eyebrow,2}$ is compared to the distance metric of the rest of the components. Clearly, component 2 captures most of the eyebrow motion. Similarly, Fig. 10.1(d) shows the value of the distance metric $d_{eyelids,i}$ for each of the six components. In this case, $d_{eyelids,6}$ dominates the rest of the components. We conclude that component 6 captures most of the eyelid motion.

10.5 Editing

Based on the decomposition provided by ICA, we can build a facial motion editing tool that allows the user to interactively change the apparent emotional content of visual speech.

We are now defining multiple operations in ICA space to change the emotion expressed in a recorded motion. We use the ICA representation to resynthesize the motion after editing the parameters of the model. The ICA model can be written (see Section 10.3)

$$x = E\{x\} + PAu. \tag{10.5}$$

Three parameters can be manipulated: the mean $E\{\mathbf{x}\}$, the mixing matrix PA, and the independent components $\mathbf{u}$. The independent components contribute to the motion as an offset around the mean. Changing the mean often results in unnatural motion or violation of physical constraints such as lip intersection. However, modifying the mixing matrix and/or the independent components yields interesting editing operations.

10.5.1 Translate

In Section 10.4 and Fig. 10.1(a), it is made clear that a single independent component captures the difference between *frustrated* and *happy* motions. Moreover, this component seems to vary between two extreme values as a function of emotion. A straightforward way of modifying emotion is then to estimate these extreme values and translate the time series responsible for emotion between them. With this technique, we can change the emotion continuously between the two emotions present in the training set. Editing can be expressed as

$$x = E\{x\} + PA(u + \alpha e_E),$$

where α is a scalar that quantifies the amount of translation in the emotional component and e_E is the vector in the canonical basis of the ICA mixing matrix that corresponds to the emotional component.

10.5.2 Copy and Replace

Another editing operation is to replace the emotional component of a motion with the emotional component of a different motion without changing the content (speech-related motion) of the original motion. To do this we replace the time series that corresponds to the emotional component u_1 in ICA space by the emotional component of a second motion u_2. This manipulation can then be written as follows:

$$x = E\{x\} + PA(u_1 + ((u_2 - u_1)^T e_E)e_E).$$

10.5.3 Copy and Add

We can also add an emotional component that was not present in the original motion. Let's consider u_1 and u_2 as the emotional components of two motions. In order to add the emotional component of motion 1 to motion 2, we perform the following operation:

$$x = E\{x\} + (PA)_1 u_1 + (PA)_2((u_2^T e_E^2)e_E^2),$$

where $(PA)_1$ and $(PA)_2$ are the mixing matrices of the two motions. e_E^2 is the vector in the canonical basis of the ICA mixing matrix A_2 that corresponds to the emotional component.

Notice that all the editing operations we have described so far are applied to motions that are already in the training set used to estimate the ICA model. In order to edit a motion x that does not belong to the training set, we can project it to extract the independent components:

$$\mathbf{u} = (\boldsymbol{PA})^+(\mathbf{x} - E\{\mathbf{x}_{\text{training}}\}),$$

where $^+$ indicates the pseudo-inverse of a matrix and $\mathbf{x}_{\text{training}}$ the expectation of the motions in the training set. After projection, the motion can be edited in ICA space.

10.6 Results

To demonstrate ICA decomposition and editing operations, we show the results of several experiments we did in our previous work [1]. Please see demonstration videos at http://people.cs.vt.edu/~yongcao.

10.6.0.1 Motion Capture and Rendering

The data used in these experiments are captured by a Vicon8 optical motion capture system. We used 109 markers to sample the face geometry fairly densely. The sampling rate of the data is 120 frame/sec. To drive a 3D textured face mesh, the markers are mapped to corresponding mesh points, and the rest of the mesh is deformed using *radial basis functions* [19].

10.6.0.2 Editing

The introduced method provides an intuitive decomposition of facial motion that allows us to edit the apparent emotion of visual speech. Figure 10.3 shows three rendered frames from an editing session. The *neutral* and *sad* independent components are mixed with different percentages. Figure 10.4 shows an emotion session that changes the emotional content by translating among *neutral, sad*, and *angry*.

10.7 Summary

In this chapter, we describe a method that can extract meaningful components from facial motions. This method, based on *independent component analysis*, provides a representation of the data that has much more intuitive semantics than the original data. Each independent component can be associated with a clear meaning and can be edited separately. We can see that facial motions should lend themselves so easily to a linear decomposition, despite the complexity of the associated control system (the brain) and of the mechanisms responsible for these motions.

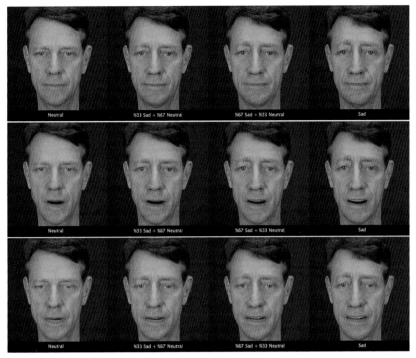

Fig. 10.3 Three snapshots of editing visual speech. Each row shows the same speech content but a different amount of *neutral* and *sad* emotions.

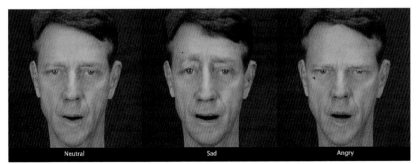

Fig. 10.4 Translating among three emotions; *neutral, sad*, and *angry*.

References

1. Y. Cao, P. Faloutsos, and F. Pighin. Unsupervised learning for speech motion editing. In *SCA '03: Proceedings of the 2003 ACM SIGGRAPH/Eurographics Symposium on Computer Animation*, pages 225–231, Aire-la-Ville, Switzerland, 2003.
2. E. Chuang, H. Deshpande, and C. Bregler. Facial expression space learning. In *Proceedings of Pacific Graphics*, 2002.
3. Z. Grahramani and M.I. Jordan. Factorial hidden markov models. *Machine Learning*, (29):245–275, 1997.
4. J.B. Tenenbaum and W.T. Freeman. Separating style and content with bilinear models. *Neural Computation*, 12(6):1247–1283, 2000.
5. I. Essa and A. Pentland. A vision system for observing and extracting facial action parameters. In *Proceedings of IEEE Computer Vision Pattern Recognition Conference*, 1994.
6. I. Essa, S. Basu, T. Darell, and A. Pentland. Modeling, tracking and and interactive animation of faces and heads using input from video. *Computer Animation Conference*, pages 68–79, June 1996.
7. I. Essa and A. Pentland. Coding, analysis, interpretation, and recognition of facial expressions. *IEEE Transactions on Pattern Analysis and Machine Intelligence*, 19(7):757–763, July 1997.
8. J. Cohn, J. Lien, A. Zlochower, and T. Kanade. Feature point tracking by optical flow discriminates subtle differences in facial expression. In *Proceedings, Third IEEE International Conference on Automatic Face and Gesture Recognition*, pages 396–401, 1998.
9. M. Black and Y. Yacoob. Tracking and recognizing rigid and non-rigid facial motions using local parametric models of image otions. In *Proceedings, International Conference on Computer Vision*, pages 374–381, 1995.
10. J. Lien, J. Cohn, T. Kanade, and C.C. Li. Automatic facial expression recognition based on FACS action units. In *Proceedings, Third IEEE International Conference on Automatic Face and Gesture Recognition*, pages 390–395, 1998.
11. J.N. Bassili. Emotion recognition: The role of facial movement and the relative importance of upper and lower areas of the face. *Journal of Personality and Social Psychology*, 39: 2049–2059, 1979.
12. K. Pullen and C. Bregler. Motion capture assisted animation: texturing and synthesis. In *Proceedings of the 29th Annual Conference on Computer Graphics and Interactive Techniques*, pages 501–508, 2002.
13. M. Brand and A. Hertzmann. Style machines. In *Proceedings of the 27th Annual Conference on Computer Graphics and Interactive Techniques*, pages 183–192, 2000.
14. M. Unuma, K. Anjyo, and R. Takeuchi. Fourier principles for emotion-based human figure animation. In *Proceedings of ACM SIGGRAPH 1995*, pages 91–96, 1995.
15. A. Hyvarinen, J. Karhunen, and E. Oja. *Independent Component Analysis*. John Wiley & Sons, New York, 2001.
16. A. Hyvärinen. Survey on independent component analysis. In *Neural Computing Surveys*, pages 94–128, 1999.
17. http://www.cis.hut.fi/projects/ica/fastica/.
18. D. Sankoff and J.B. Kruskal. *Time Warps, String Edits, and Macromolecules: The Theory and Practice of Sequence Comparison*. CSLI Publications, 1983.
19. T.H. Nelsons. *Literary Machiness*. Mindful Press, Sausalito, CA, 1993.

Chapter 11
Facial Animation by Expression Cloning

Junyong Noh and Ulrich Neumann

11.1 Introduction

Facial animation aims at producing expressive and plausible animations of a 3D face model. Some approaches model the anatomy of the face, deriving facial animation from the physical behaviors of the bone and muscle structures [21, 30, 36, 37]. Others focus only on the surface of the face, using smooth surface deformation mechanisms to create dominant facial expressions [15, 17, 29]. These approaches make little use of existing data for the animation of a new model. Each time a new model is created for animation, a method-specific tuning is inevitable or the animation is produced from scratch. Animation parameters do not simply transfer between models. If manual tuning or computational costs are high in creating animations for one model, creating similar animations for new models will take similar efforts.

A parametric approach associates the motion of a group of vertices to a specific parameter [27]. This manual association must be repeated for models with different mesh structures. Vector-based muscle models place the heuristic muscles under the surface of the face [36, 37]. This process is repeated for each new model. No automatic placement strategy has been reported except for the case where a new model has the same mesh structure. Muscle contraction values are transferable between models only when the involved models are equipped with properly positioned muscles. Even then, problems still arise when muscle structures are inherently different between two models, i.e., a human and a cat face. A three-layer mass-spring-muscle system requires extensive computation [21]. The final computed parameters are, however, only useful for one model. Free-form deformation manipulates control points to create key facial expressions [17], but there is no automatic method for mapping the control points from one model to another. Expression synthesis from photographs can capture accurate geometry as well as textures with a painstaking model fitting process for each key frame [29]. In practice, animators often sculpt key-frame facial expressions for every three to five frames to achieve

This work is based on an earlier work: Expression cloning, in *Proceedings of Siggraph* © **ACM**, 2001. http://doi.acm.org/10.1145/383259.383290

the best-quality animations [22]. Obviously, those fitting or sculpting processes must be repeated for a new model even if the desired expression sequences are similar.

Our goal is to produce facial animations by reusing motion data. Once high-quality facial animations are created for any model by any available mechanisms, expression cloning (EC) reuses the dense 3D motion vectors of the vertices of the source model to create similar animations on a new target model. Animations of completely new characters can be based on existing libraries of high-quality animations created for many different models. If the animations of the source are smooth and expressive, the animations of the target model will also have the same qualities. Another advantage of EC is the speed of the algorithm; source animations created by computationally intensive physical simulations can be quickly cloned to new target models. After some pre-processing, target model animations are produced in real time, making EC also useful for interactive control of varied target models driven from one generic model, e.g., for text-to-speech applications [26].

Similar to EC, performance-driven facial animation (PDFA) and MPEG-4 both use measured motion data [2, 10, 15, 26, 38]. In PDFA, 2D or 3D motion vectors are recovered by tracking a live actor in front of a camera to drive the facial animation. With this approach, the quality of the animation depends on the quality of feature tracking and correspondences between the observed face and target model. MPEG-4 specifies 84 feature points. Accurately identifying corresponding feature points is difficult and a daunting manual task. Degraded animation is expected if only a subset of the feature points is identified or tracked. In contrast, EC reuses animations already containing precise dense 3D motion data. A sophisticated mechanism identifies dense surface correspondences from a small set of correspondences. For models with typical human facial structure, a completely automated correspondence search is described in Section 11.6.

Expression cloning also relates to 3D metamorphosis research where establishing correspondences between two different shapes is an important issue [18]. Harmonic mapping is a popular approach for recovering dense surface correspondences [8]. Difficulty arises, however, when specific points need to be matched between models. For instance, a naïve harmonic mapping could easily flip the polygons if a user wanted to match the tip of the noses or lip corners between the source and the target models. Proposed methods to overcome this issue include partitioning models into smaller regions [18] or model simplification [20] before applying harmonic mapping. A spherical mapping followed by image warping is used in the case of star-shaped models [19]. Our approach to finding dense correspondences starts with specific feature matches, followed by a volume morphing and a cylindrical projection.

Our work is also motivated by techniques for retargeting full-body animations from one character to another [13]. While we consign the creative decisions (how does a cat smile?) to the user's choice of the source animation as in [13], our technique of cloning a facial animation is significantly different in approach from that dealing with articulated body motions.

11.2 System Overview

Expression cloning directly maps an expression of the source model onto the target model. The first step determines which surface points in the target correspond to vertices in the source model. See the arrow labeled with Deform in Fig. 11.1, where the source model is deformed to the target model's shape to find the dense surface correspondences. No assumptions are made about the number of vertices or their connectivity in either model. We compute the dense correspondences by using a small set of initial correspondences to establish an approximate relationship. Identifying initial correspondences requires manual selection of fewer than 10 (and possibly zero) vertices after an automated search is applied. Without the automated search, experiments showed that 15 to 35 manually selected vertices were required, depending on the shape and the complexity of the model. Automatic correspondence search bootstraps the whole cloning process, and detailed heuristic rules are given in Section 11.6.

The second step transfers motion vectors from source model vertices to target model vertices, labeled as motion transfer in Fig. 11.1. The magnitude and direction of transferred motion vectors are properly adjusted to account for the local shape of the model. Using the dense correspondences computed in the first step, motion transfers are well defined with linear interpolation using barycentric coordinates.

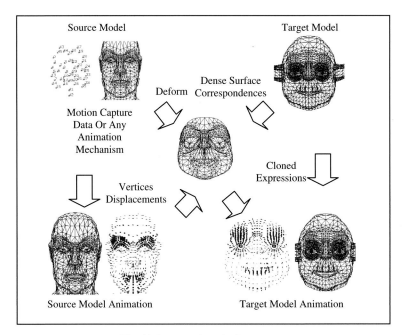

Fig. 11.1 Expression cloning system.

11.3 Dense Surface Correspondences

Assuming N sparse correspondences are available, dense surface correspondences are computed by volume morphing with radial basis functions (RBF) followed by a cylindrical projection. Volume morphing roughly aligns features of the two models such as eye sockets, nose ridge, lip corners, and chin points. As shown in Fig. 11.2(a), volume morphing with a small set of initial correspondences does not produce a perfect surface match. A cylindrical projection of the morphed source model onto the target model ensures that all the source model vertices are truly embedded in the target model surface, as shown in Fig. 11.2(b). See Fig. 11.11 for more examples.

When multi-quadrics is used for an RBF, $h(r) = \sqrt{r^2 + s^2}$,

$$x^{\varpi\,\text{target}}_i = F(x^{\varpi\,\text{source}}_i) = \sum_{j=1}^{N} w_j \sqrt{||x^{\varpi\,\text{source}}_i - x^{\varpi}_j||^2 + s_j{}^2}. \qquad (11.1)$$

This network is trained three times with the 3D coordinates of source correspondences as $x^{\varpi\,\text{source}}_i$, and the x-, y-, or z-values of target correspondences as $x^{\varpi\,\text{target}}_i (i = 1, 2, \ldots, W)$. The distance s_j is measured between c^{ϖ}_j and the nearest x^{ϖ}_i, leading to smaller deformations for widely scattered feature points and larger deformations for closely located points [7]:

$$s_j = \min_{i \neq j} ||x^{\varpi}_i - c^{\varpi}_j||. \qquad (11.2)$$

Given λ, the weight w^{ϖ} to be computed is

$$w^{\varpi} = (H^T H + \lambda I)^{-1} H^T x^{\varpi\,\text{target}}_i. \qquad (11.3)$$

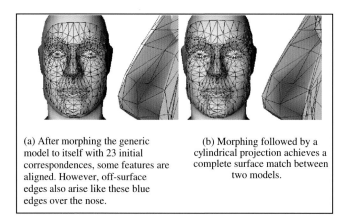

(a) After morphing the generic model to itself with 23 initial correspondences, some features are aligned. However, off-surface edges also arise like these blue edges over the nose.

(b) Morphing followed by a cylindrical projection achieves a complete surface match between two models.

Fig. 11.2 Surface correspondences by morphing and projection.

The regularization parameter λ is a smaller number and can be determined empirically. Once all the unknowns are computed, the RBF network smoothly interpolates the non-corresponding points, mapping the source model onto the target model's shape.

After the RBF deformation, each vertex in the source model is projected onto the target model's surface to ensure a complete surface match. A cylindrical projection centerline is established as a vertical line through the centroid of the head. A ray perpendicular to the projection centerline is passed through each vertex in the source model and intersected with triangles in the target model. The first intersection found is used in cases of multiple valid intersections. Although this could cause a potential problem, visual artifacts are not observed with various models in practice. A reason may be that motions are similar for any of the valid intersections due to their regional proximity.

Referring to the notations in Fig. 11.3, the line equation passing through the center of the projection x_o^ϖ and a point in the source model x_p^ϖ is

$$x^\varpi = (x_p^\varpi - x_0^\varpi)t + x_0^\varpi. \tag{11.4}$$

The plane equation that contains the triangle in the target model is

$$n^\varpi \bullet (x^\varpi - x_1^\varpi) = 0. \tag{11.5}$$

Plugging Eq. (11.4) into (11.5) and solving for t yield

$$t = \frac{n_1(x_1 - x_0) + n_2(y_1 - y_0) + n_3(z_1 - z_0)}{n_1(x_p - x_0) + n_2(y_p - y_0) + n_3(z_p - z_0)}. \tag{11.6}$$

Then the intersection x_i^ϖ is computed with equation (11.4) with t from (11.6) plugged in.

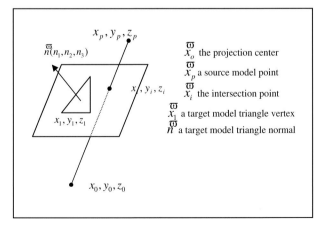

Fig. 11.3 Notations used in Eqs. 11.4, 11.5, and 11.6.

To test for intersections within a triangle, compute the barycentric coordinates of the intersection point with respect to the vertices of the target triangle. Computing barycentric coordinates is equivalent to solving a 3×3 linear system:

$$\begin{bmatrix} x_1 & x_2 & x_3 \\ y_1 & y_2 & y_3 \\ z_1 & z_2 & z_3 \end{bmatrix} \begin{bmatrix} b_1 \\ b_2 \\ b_3 \end{bmatrix} = \begin{bmatrix} x_i \\ y_i \\ z_i \end{bmatrix}. \tag{11.7}$$

By a property of barycentric coordinate systems, if $0 \leq b_1, b_2, b_3 \leq 1$, then the intersection lies inside the triangle. In reality, due to numerical precision limits, we subtract and add 0.005 from zero and one, respectively.

11.4 Animation with Motion Vectors

A cloned expression animation displaces each target vertex to match the motion of a corresponding source model surface point. Since we have dense source motion vectors, linear interpolation with barycentric coordinates is sufficient to determine the motion vectors of the target vertices from the enclosing source triangle vertices.

Note that although the source model vertices are embedded in the surface of the target model by the RBF morphing followed by the cylindrical projection, the opposite is not necessarily true (Fig. 11.4). To obtain the barycentric coordinates needed for motion interpolation, we also project the target model vertices onto the source model triangles. In other words, we do the same operation described in Section 11.3, but this time reversing the source and target models. The barycentric coordinates of each target vertex determine both the enclosing source model triangle and the motion interpolation coefficients.

Since facial geometry and proportions can vary greatly between models, source motions cannot simply be transferred without adjusting the direction and magnitude of each motion vector. As shown in Fig. 11.5, the direction of a source motion vector must be altered to maintain its angle with the local surface when applied to the target model. Similarly, the magnitude of a motion vector must be scaled by the local size variations. Examples are shown in Fig. 11.12.

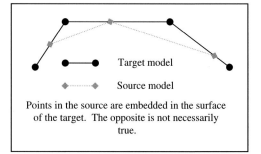

Target model

Source model

Points in the source are embedded in the surface of the target. The opposite is not necessarily true.

Fig. 11.4 Side view of two models after the projection.

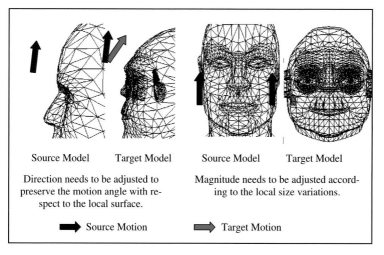

Source Model   Target Model   Source Model   Target Model

Direction needs to be adjusted to   Magnitude needs to be adjusted accord-
preserve the motion angle with re-   ing to the local size variations.
spect to the local surface.

➡ Source Motion   ⇨ Target Motion

Fig. 11.5 Direction and magnitude adjustment of the motion vector.

To facilitate motion vector transfer while preserving the relationship with the local surface, a local coordinate system is attached to each vertex in both the original and deformed source model.[1] The transformation between these local coordinate systems defines the motion vector direction adjustment (Fig. 11.6). The local coordinate system is constructed as follows. First, the x-axis is determined by the average of the surface normals of all the polygons sharing a vertex. To ensure continuous normal (x-axis) variations across the surface, a noise filter [32] is applied by averaging neighbor vertex normals. Second, the y-axis is defined by the projection of any edge connected to the vertex onto the tangent plane whose normal is the just-determined x-axis. Lastly, the z-axis is the cross product of the x-and y-axes. To obtain the deformed motion vector $m^{\omega\prime}$ for a given source vector m^{ω} (Fig. 11.6),

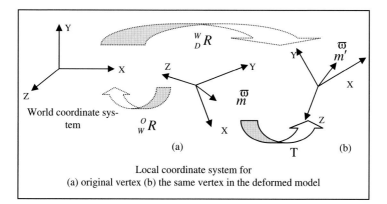

Local coordinate system for
(a) original vertex (b) the same vertex in the deformed model

Fig. 11.6 Transformation matrix as a means to adjust a motion vector direction.

---

[1] A deformed source model is the source model after the morphing and projection described in Section 11.3.

the transformation matrices are computed between the two local coordinate systems and the world coordinate system:

$$
{}^{O}_{W}R = \begin{bmatrix} x^{\varpi}_{w} \bullet x^{\varpi}_{o} & y^{\varpi}_{w} \bullet x^{\varpi}_{o} & z^{\varpi}_{w} \bullet x^{\varpi}_{o} \\ x^{\varpi}_{w} \bullet y^{\varpi}_{o} & y^{\varpi}_{w} \bullet y^{\varpi}_{o} & z^{\varpi}_{w} \bullet y^{\varpi}_{o} \\ x^{\varpi}_{w} \bullet z^{\varpi}_{o} & y^{\varpi}_{w} \bullet z^{\varpi}_{o} & z^{\varpi}_{w} \bullet z^{\varpi}_{o} \end{bmatrix}, \tag{11.8}
$$

$$
{}^{W}_{D}R = \begin{bmatrix} x^{\varpi}_{d} \bullet x^{\varpi}_{w} & y^{\varpi}_{d} \bullet x^{\varpi}_{w} & z^{\varpi}_{d} \bullet x^{\varpi}_{w} \\ x^{\varpi}_{d} \bullet y^{\varpi}_{w} & y^{\varpi}_{d} \bullet y^{\varpi}_{w} & z^{\varpi}_{d} \bullet y^{\varpi}_{w} \\ x^{\varpi}_{d} \bullet z^{\varpi}_{w} & y^{\varpi}_{d} \bullet z^{\varpi}_{w} & z^{\varpi}_{d} \bullet z^{\varpi}_{w} \end{bmatrix}. \tag{11.9}
$$

The matrix ${}^{O}_{W}R$ denotes the rotation from a local source vertex coordinates axes to the world coordinate axes, and ${}^{W}_{D}R$ is the rotation matrix from world axes to the local deformed model axes. Prior to the dot product computation in Eqs. (11.8) and (11.9), each component denoting the direction of x-, y-, and z-axes is normalized. Finally, the transformation matrix is

$$
{}^{O}_{D}R = {}^{W}_{D}R\,{}^{O}_{W}R. \tag{11.10}
$$

This mapping at each vertex determines the directions of the deformed source model motion vectors given the source model motion vectors.

If the source and target face models have similar proportions, the motion vectors may simply be scaled in proportion to the model sizes. However, to preserve the character of animations for models with large geometry differences (e.g., the unusually big ears of Yoda), the magnitude of each motion vector is adjusted by a local scale factor constrained within a global threshold. The local scale at a vertex is determined by a bounding box (BB) around the polygons sharing the vertex. In deforming a source model to fit a target model, the local geometry around a vertex is often scaled and rotated. Rotations are eliminated to facilitate a fair comparison of local scale. The source BB is transformed by the rotation matrix of Eq. (11.10). For each source model vertex in a BB, we compute its rotated position due to model deformation:

$$
v^{\varpi\prime} = {}^{O}_{D}R v^{\varpi}. \tag{11.11}
$$

The local scale change due to deformation is the ratio of the rotated source BB and the deformed BB (between b and c in Fig. 11.7):

$$
S^{\varpi}_{x,y,z} = \frac{size_{x,y,z}(Deformed\,Source\,Model\,Local\,Bouding\,Box)}{size_{x,y,z}(Source\,Model\,Local\,Bounding\,Box)}. \tag{11.12}
$$

A protrusion or noise in the local geometry (e.g., a bump on the face in either model) can exaggerate motion vector scaling, making the scaling unnecessarily large or small. One solution is to limit scale factors by a global threshold such as

Fig. 11.7 Local bounding box.

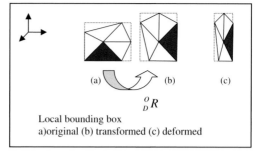

$$^{O}_{D}R$$

Local bounding box
a)original (b) transformed (c) deformed

the standard deviation of all scale factors. Scale factors greater than the standard deviation are discarded and replaced by the results of a noise filter [32] that averages neighboring values. The filter is then applied over the whole face to ensure smooth, continuous scale factors.

The transformation matrix that accounts both for the direction and magnitude adjustments of a motion vector is given by

$$T = S^{O}_{D} R, \tag{11.13}$$

where $S = \begin{bmatrix} S_x & 0 & 0 \\ 0 & S_y & 0 \\ 0 & 0 & S_z \end{bmatrix}$ from Eq. (11.12). During animation, the motion vector for each deformed model vertex is obtained by

$$m^{\omega\prime} = T m^{\omega}, \tag{11.14}$$

where m^{ω} is the vertex motion of the source model and $m^{\omega\prime}$ is the vertex motion of the deformed model. Finally, a vertex in the target model v^{ω}_t is displaced by the following equation:

$$m^{\omega}_t = b_1 m^{\omega\prime}_1 + b_2 m^{\omega\prime}_2 + b_3 m^{\omega\prime}_3, \tag{11.15}$$

where $b_{1,2,3}$ denotes the barycentric coordinates, m^{ω}_t the target vertex motion vector, and $m^{\omega\prime}_{1,2,3}$ the enclosing source triangle motion vectors.

11.5 Lip Contact Line

Our models have lips that touch at a contact line. This contact line between the upper and lower lips requires special attention. Although they are closely positioned, motion directions are usually opposite for upper and lower lip vertices. Severe visual artifacts occur when a vertex belonging to the lower lip happens to be controlled by an upper lip triangle, or vice versa. Therefore, careful alignment of the lip contact lines between the two models is very important. Misalignment results in misidentification of the enclosing triangles and subsequent lip vertex motions in the wrong direction.

Specific processes are followed to produce artifact-free mouth animations. First, include all the source model lip contact line vertices in the initial correspondence set for the RBF morphing step. Since source vertices do not usually coincide with target vertices [Fig. 11.8(a)], it is necessary to compute corresponding points in the target model. Compute the sum of the piecewise distances between the left and right corners of the lip contact line and normalize each length to the range [0, 1] for both models. Corresponding locations on the target lip line are found at normalized parameters matching those of the source lip line vertices. Label each vertex parameter in the lip contact line as $S_{1,2,3\,...}$ and $t_{1,2,3\,...}$ for the source and target model, respectively (Fig. 11.8). If parameter S_m falls between t_n and t_{n+1}, the corresponding 3D coordinate c on the target lip is interpolated by

$$c = 3D(t_{n+1}) * \frac{S_m - t_n}{t_{n+1} - t_n} + 3D(t_n) * \frac{t_{n+1} - S_m}{t_{n+1} - t_n}. \qquad (11.16)$$

With the above correspondences, the RBF morphing in Section 11.3 brings the source lip vertices into the target model's surface as shown in Fig. 11.8(a). Note that there are duplicate vertices at each point—one for the upper lip and one for the lower lip. If we perform the cylindrical projection in Section 11.3, the duplicate points represented by t_2, t_3, or t_4 in Fig. 11.8(a) will be controlled by upper-lip source model triangles since these points are located above the source model lip contact line. Therefore, another step is necessary to completely align the lip contact lines of the two models. Temporarily move the vertices of the target model lip contact

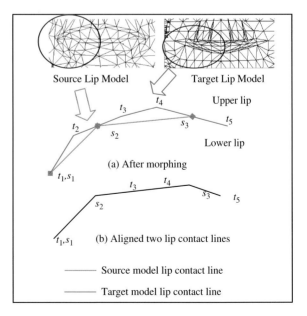

Fig. 11.8 Lip contact line alignment.

line onto the corresponding source model lip contact points. These corresponding positions are computed with normalized parameters and Eq. (11.16), as before, but this time the target vertices are moved onto the source lip contact line as opposed to the source vertices moving onto the target lip contact line. Figure 11.8(b) shows final aligned lip lines.

Two issues are noteworthy. First, there is no actual degradation of the fidelity of the target model from aligning its lip line vertices with the source model. Lip line alignment is only temporary to facilitate determining the enclosing source model triangles. The original target model lip vertex coordinates are used for animation. Second, by manipulating the contact line vertices for alignment, there may be cases where triangles flip if only the vertices on the lip contact line move. We recursively propagate the same displacements in the contact line neighborhood until no more triangle flipping is detected.

The next step determines which vertex at the lip contact points belongs to the upper and lower lip so that each can be assigned to the appropriate enclosing triangle. A naïve barycentric coordinate test may indicate both the upper and lower lip triangles as the enclosing triangles for both points on a lip contact line. We check the neighborhood of each vertex to see if neighbor vertices are located above or below the vertex.

Motion vector transformations also require special attention at the lip contact line. The matrices could easily be different for each of the duplicate vertices at a lip contact point due to their different local neighborhoods. This would cause the two vertices to move to different positions when driven with the same source motion vector. To ensure the same transformation matrices for both vertices on a lip contact point, consider the upper and lower lips connected. Specifically, the normal computations and local BB comparisons include neighbors from the upper and lower lips.

11.6 Automated Correspondence Selection

A small set of correspondences is needed for the RBF morphing. Since all other EC steps are fully automated, automatic initial correspondence selection would completely automate expression cloning. Automatic correspondences not only reduce tedious manual selection, but also remove the errors and variations produced by mouse clicking and judgment. We present 15 heuristic rules that identify more than 20 correspondences when applied to most human faces. In some cases, we find that up to 10 additional manual correspondences may be added to improve the animation quality. In all cases, an animator can simply edit erroneous automatic correspondences, substituting or adding their own selections.

Orient the face model to look in the positive z-direction. The y-axis points through the top of the head, and the x-axis points through the right ear. The model is assumed to have a neutral expression initially with the lips together and the contact line defined by duplicate vertices. For robust behavior during the heuristic correspondence searches, we skip (ignore) degenerate triangles that have one very short edge compared to the other two edges.

Heuristic rules

1. Tip of the nose: find the vertex with the highest z-value.
2. Top of the head: find the vertex with the highest y-value.
3. Right side of the face (right ear): find the vertex with the highest x-value.
4. Left side of the face (left ear): find the vertex with the lowest x-value.
5. Top of the nose (between two eyes): from the tip of the nose, search upward along the ridge of the nose for the vertex with the local minimum z-value.
6. Left eye socket (near nose): from the top of the nose, search down to the left side of the nose for the vertex with the local minimum z-value.
7. Right eye socket (near nose): from the top of the nose, search down to the right side of the nose for the vertex with the local minimum z-value.
8. Bottom of the nose (top of the furrow): from the tip of the nose, search downward to the center of the lips until reaching the vertex with the local minimum z-value. The vertex with the biggest angle formed by two neighbors is the bottom of the nose.
9. Bottom left of the nose: from the tip of the nose, search downward to the left side of the nose until reaching the vertex with the local minimum z-value. The vertex with the biggest angle formed by two neighbors is the bottom left of the nose.
10. Bottom right of the nose: from the tip of the nose, search downward to the right side of the nose until reaching the vertex with the local minimum z-value. The vertex with the biggest angle formed by two neighbors is the bottom right of the nose.
11. Lip contact line: find the set of duplicated vertices.
12. Top of the lip: from the center of the upper lip contact line, search upward along the centerline for the vertex with the local maximum z-value.
13. Bottom of the lip: from the center of the lower lip, search downward along the centerline for the vertex with the local minimum z-value after passing the vertex with the local maximum z-value.
14. Chin: from the bottom of the lip, search downward along the centerline for the vertex with the local maximum z-value.
15. Throat: from the chin, search downward along the centerline until reaching the vertex with the local minimum z-value. Along the search, find two vertices with two maximum angles. The one with smaller z-value is the throat (the other one should be near the chin point).

The labels given to these points may not be precise and are not important. We only seek to locate corresponding geometric points in both models. Figure 11.9 shows the correspondences automatically found with the above rules.

11.7 Results and Discussion

The specifications of the test models are summarized in Table 11.1. The "source man" model is used as the animation source for all the expressions that are cloned onto the other models. Source animations are created by (1) an interactive design

Fig. 11.9 Automated search results.

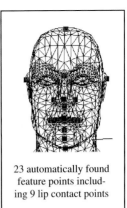

23 automatically found
feature points includ-
ing 9 lip contact points

Table 11.1 Models used for the experiments.

Model	Polygons	Vertices
Source man	1954	988
Woman	5416	2859
Man	4314	2227
Rick	927	476
Yoda	3740	1945
Cat	5405	2801
Monkey	2334	1227
Dog	927	476
Baby	1253	2300

system for creating facial animations and (2) motion capture data embedded into the source man model (Fig. 11.10). An algorithm similar to [15] is implemented to animate the source model with the motion capture data.

For expression cloning onto the woman and man models, only the 23 correspondences from the automated search are used. This means that the whole EC process is fully automated for these models. The Yoda model has large eyes and ears. We manually add three additional points on each eye socket and two points on each side of the face. The monkey model is handled similarly. The dog and

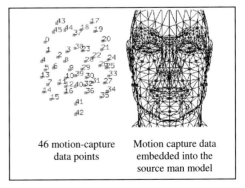

46 motion-capture
data points

Motion capture data
embedded into the
source man model

Fig. 11.10 Motion capture data and their association with the source model.

cat models do not have anything close to human face geometry. Twelve and 18 points are manually selected for the dog and cat, respectively, to replace erroneous automatic search results. Figure 11.11 shows the deformed source models produced to determine dense surface correspondences from these initial sets of points. The deformations closely approximate each target model. For example, the bumps on the Yoda eyebrows are faithfully reproduced on the deformed source model. The source model cheek is also smoothly bulged for the monkey model. The eyes are properly positioned for the man and woman model. Motion vector adjustments are depicted in Fig. 11.12. The monkey model has different local geometry from the source model. Motions are widely distributed (column 5) and more horizontal (column 2) in the mouth region. The finer geometry of the forehead produces denser but smaller motions (column 3).

Figures 11.13 and 11.14 show sample expressions from cloned animation sequences. Although the models have different geometric proportions and mesh structures, the expressions are well scaled to fit each model. For instance, the smile and nervous expressions are effectively transferred to the woman model (columns 3 and 4 in Fig. 11.13). Frown and surprise expressions are shown on the cat model (columns 5 and 6). Moderate-intensity expressions cause mostly small motions, and these are sometimes hardly distinguishable from neutral expressions in static images. Exaggerated expressions are tested in Fig. 11.14. A big round open mouth source expression creates a rectangular mouth shape for the monkey due to its much longer lip line. An asymmetric mouth shape is reproduced on the target models, and variations arise from differences in the initial target mesh expressions (column 4). The use of human source animations creates many human-like mouth shapes for the dog model rather than expressions more typical of a real dog (last row).

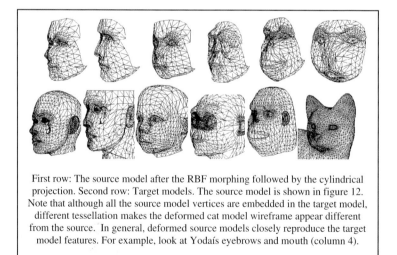

First row: The source model after the RBF morphing followed by the cylindrical projection. Second row: Target models. The source model is shown in figure 12. Note that although all the source model vertices are embedded in the target model, different tessellation makes the deformed cat model wireframe appear different from the source. In general, deformed source models closely reproduce the target model features. For example, look at Yoda's eyebrows and mouth (column 4).

Fig. 11.11 Deformed models produce dense surface correspondences.

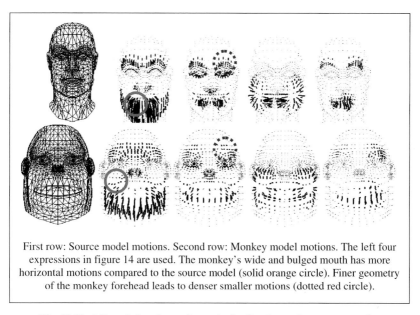

First row: Source model motions. Second row: Monkey model motions. The left four
expressions in figure 14 are used. The monkey's wide and bulged mouth has more
horizontal motions compared to the source model (solid orange circle). Finer geometry
of the monkey forehead leads to denser smaller motions (dotted red circle).

Fig. 11.12 Adjusted direction and magnitude after the motion vector transfer.

Assessing the emotional quality of the expressions produced by EC is clearly
subjective, but we can validate the quantitative accuracy of the algorithm by using
the "source man" model as both the source and target models. The EC algorithm
is applied to find the surface correspondences and adjust the motion vectors to any
local geometry variation. Ideally, the target vertex displacement should be identical
to that of the source model. Table 11.2 and Fig. 11.15 show error measures for
sample expressions. Staring with the automatically found 23 points, an additional
10 points are included for this test, 3 on each eye socket and 2 on each side of the
face. These points produce a more accurate surface match that reduces quantitative
errors. The error measure is defined as the size ratio between the position error and
the size of the motion vector:

$$\% Error = 100 \frac{size(PositionError)}{size(MotionVector)}. \tag{11.17}$$

Figure 11.15 depicts displacement errors such that a vertex with zero error is
yellow and a vertex position error one tenth of its motion vector length (10%) is red.
Errors between 0 and 10% are colored by interpolation. Vertices with no motion
are colored blue. Figure 11.15 shows that central face areas where most expression
motions occur have small errors and boundary regions generally have higher errors.
The larger boundary-area error percentage occurs because motions are relatively
small at the boundary, making the denominator in Eq. 11.17 small. With very small
motions, even numerical errors can adversely affect this error measure. Table 11.2
shows the average errors of all the vertices with motions. To better quantify the

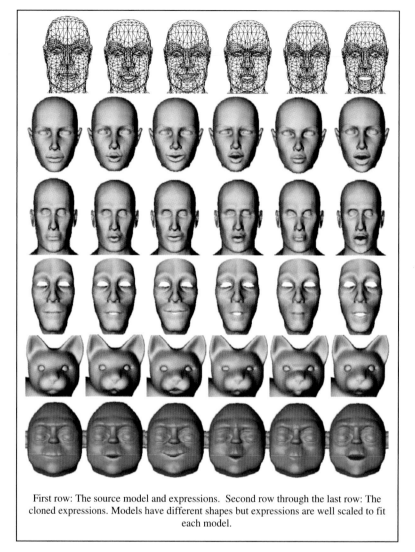

First row: The source model and expressions. Second row through the last row: The cloned expressions. Models have different shapes but expressions are well scaled to fit each model.

Fig. 11.13 Cloned expressions onto various models.

visual significance of the errors, the position error is also measured relative to an absolute reference, in this case the size of the model:

$$\%Error_{x,y,z} = 100 \frac{size_{x,y,z}(Position\,Error)}{size_{x,y,z}(Face\,Region\,Bounding\,Box)}. \qquad (11.18)$$

Note that in this case the error is computed separately along the x-, y-, and z-directions. Table 11.3 indicates that the average errors relative to the size of the model are negligible. Since the motion vectors are dense over the whole face, and

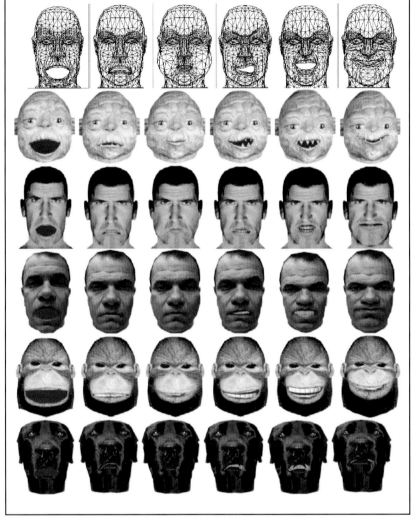

Fig. 11.14 Exaggerated expressions cloned on a wide variety of texture-mapped target models. The Yoda model is provided courtesy of Harry Change, http://Avalon.viewpoint.com.

Table 11.2 Average errors relative to the motion vector size.

Angry	Talking	Smiling	Nervous	Surprised
5.28%	8.56%	4.77%	4.07%	4.56%

their errors are small, visual artifacts are very difficult to perceive, even at high resolutions.

The experiments are performed on a 550-MHz Pentium-III PC. Except for the actual animations, all other processes are performed offline. The automated search takes $O(n)$ to find the tip of the nose, the top of the head, and other extreme points.

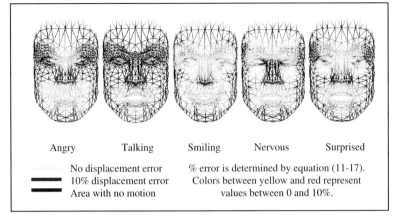

| | Angry | Talking | Smiling | Nervous | Surprised |

No displacement error   % error is determined by equation (11-17).
10% displacement error   Colors between yellow and red represent
Area with no motion   values between 0 and 10%.

Fig. 11.15 Visually depicted displacement errors.

Table 11.3 Average errors relative to the model size.

	Angry	Talking	Smiling	Nervous	Surprised
x	0.22%	0.14%	0.13%	0.14%	0.16%
y	0.18%	0.26%	0.16%	0.11%	0.12%
z	0.09%	0.23%	0.06%	0.05%	0.05%

Once those initial points are found, the search for other points (i.e., the chin) only requires a local search of neighborhood vertices. Therefore, the feature search is fast, taking only a few seconds in our experience. RBF morphing involves solving for eigensystems needed for the regularization parameter and the matrix inversion needed for the weight vectors. The size of the matrix is typically less than 30×30, so the morphing is also fast. A naïve cylindrical projection to find the correspondence between n source vertices and m target triangles takes $O(nm)$. Even with this brute-force approach, projection takes less than a minute for our models. This time could be reduced, by using a smarter search exploiting, for instance, spatial coherence. Unnecessary tests in the back of the head could be prevented by limiting the search to the frontal face. The transformation matrix to adjust the motion vector magnitude and direction is constructed per vertex, $O(n)$. Finally, the actual animation using already-computed barycentric coordinates is performed in real time ($> 30\,\text{Hz}$) including rendering time.

The manual intervention required for expression cloning is minimal, involving at most the selection of a small set of correspondences. We show that correspondence search can be at least partially automated by a heuristic analysis of the geometry. There are some regions, however, for which geometric descriptions are not practical. For example, locating the boundary of the face and finding detailed eye features appear difficult using only geometry. As an extension, automatic search may be expanded to use textures. Additional rules or methods would help identify a greater set of correspondences [23,33]. This could further automate facial animation cloning and reduce quantitative errors. The EC method currently transfers only motion vectors, but it seems possible to include color or texture changes as well [11].

Our goal is to easily create quality animations, and we assume that dense surface motion vectors are available. However, we also observe that stick figures and cartoons can convey rich expressions from a sparse representation. Future research could explore how sparse source data can become without loss of expressive animation quality. The issue may be addressed by locating the points with the most salient information for conveying the animation while the dense data field is algorithmically decimated. This knowledge may be useful for collecting motion capture data, and at that point EC may also be suitable for applications in compression.

Currently, our efforts are focused on transferring exactly the same expressions from a source to targets. It would be useful to put control knobs that amplify or reduce a certain expression on all or part of a face. The control knobs would directly modulate the sizes of the motion vectors. The expression motions could also be transformed to Fourier space where its coefficients could be manipulated [5]. It may also be possible to mix the motions of a set of expressions to produce a variety of speech and emotion combinations for any target model.

Clearly, the flexibility provided by control knobs could provide varied target animations from just a few source animations. The idea is actually implemented and discussed in more detail in Section 11.8.

Tongue and teeth model manipulations are not handled by EC at this point. If the source model includes tongue animation, we believe that the EC technique can generate animations for target tongue models [6, 34]. Similarly, teeth models can be rotated from source animations providing jaw rotation angles or just motion vectors for the teeth. Finally, assuming an eyeball as a separate model, an eyelid could be treated similar to the lip contact line, or eyelids could be rotated if the rotation angle is provided.

11.8 Extension 1: Motion Volume Control and Motion Equalizer

In Section 11.4, we show how to adjust motion vector sizes while transferred from the source model to target. As suggested, one way is to use local bounding boxes coupled with a global threshold. By considering the model shape variation locally, the mechanism reduces the adverse effects on motion vector scaling caused by global shape variation between the two models. Applying a global threshold enforces smooth scaling change across the whole face. Although the mechanism produces well-proportioned expression animation on various target models, it may be desirable to provide animators with a means to change resulting animations for their end animation goal. For example, the EC system equipped with control knobs would allow an animation sequence to be manipulated when cloned onto the target model. This way, diverse target animations can be possible from a source animation. This section delves into the issue of the animator controlled motion vector size manipulation.

A quick and intuitive way of varying motion vector size is to directly influence the vertex displacements determined by the EC system. This direct manipulation could be operated on each vertex, a group of vertices, or whole face vertices. Figure 11.16 shows various effects on the resulting animation when each vertex displacement is multiplied by constant scaling values. Varied scaling values amplify or reduce the expressiveness of original expressions at various degrees. This simple operation can be a powerful editing tool especially when applied to a group of vertices locally instead of to the whole face.

An interesting way to look at the direct multiplication of scaling values to the vertex displacement is to consider it as a volume control for music. A scaling value is then analogous to a volume gain. Exaggerated expressions correspond to high volumes while reduced expressions correspond to low volumes. This volume control influences the vertex displacements at each frame or spatially. In contrast, an audio equalizer modulates music in frequency domain. Depending on various settings of

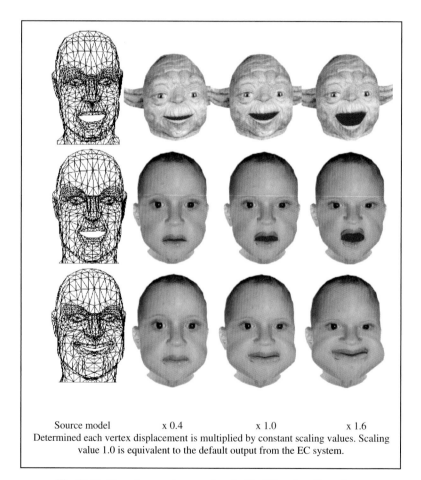

| Source model | x 0.4 | x 1.0 | x 1.6 |

Determined each vertex displacement is multiplied by constant scaling values. Scaling value 1.0 is equivalent to the default output from the EC system.

Fig. 11.16 Cloned expressions produced with different scaling values.

the low-frequency (bass) and high-frequency (treble) components, the overall feeling that music conveys varies. Analogously, we attempt to modulate the frequency of the vertex displacements in an animation sequence just like the audio counterpart. Motion signal processing [5] motivated this work where signals from an articulated body are decomposed into the frequency domain and manipulated. Our basic algorithm is same as that of [5]. Only the applied signals are different. Instead of joint angles, vertex positions in the face mesh are treated as input signals. Here is the reproduced motion signal filtering algorithm.

The number of frames m determines how many frequency bands fb are used. Let $2^n \leq m \leq 2^{n+1}$; then $fb = n$. The B-spline filter kernel of width 5 is $w_1 = cbabc$, where $a = 3/8, b = 1/4, c = 1/16$. The filter kernel is expanded by inserting zeros, $w_2 = c0b0a0b0c, w_3 = c000b000a000b000c$, etc. Now, steps 1 to 4 are performed simultaneously for each vertex motion signal.

1. Convolve the signal with the kernels to calculate lowpass sequence of all fb signals. G_0 is the original motion signal and G_{fb} is the DC or the average intensity. $G_{k+1} = w_{k+1} \times G_k$ or equivalently,

$$G_{k+1}(i) = \sum_{m=-2}^{2} w_1(m)G_k(i + 2^k m). \tag{11.19}$$

2. Compute the bandpass filter bands,

$$L_k = G_k - G_{k+1}. \tag{11.20}$$

3. Multiply the L_k by each gain value.
4. Reconstruct the motion signal:

$$G_0 = G_{fb} + \sum_{k=0}^{fb-1} L_k. \tag{11.21}$$

Our sample animation consists of 1201 frames, yielding $fb = 10$. The sample animation decomposes into 11 lowpass sequences, $G_0 - G_{10}$, and 10 bandpass sequences, $L_0 - L_9$. Multiplying an arbitrary gain value to any of L_k before reconstructing the motion signal back to G_0 alters the original animation. Suppose a gain value g is multiplied to band L_0. Equation (11.21) becomes $G_{0new} = G_{fb} + gL_0 + L_1 + L_2 + \cdots + L_{fb-1}$. Using (11.20), expanding and rearranging the equation yields $G_{0new} = G_0 + (g - 1)(G_0 - G_1)$. More generally, for a gain value g applied to band L_k,

$$G_{0new} = G_0 + (g - 1)(G_k - G_{k+1}). \tag{11.22}$$

This equation indicates that the new signal is sum of the original signal and difference of the lowpass sequence at level k multiplied by the gain factor minus one. The more the lowpass signals G are different between the two consecutive levels G_k and G_{k+1}, the more G_{0new} gets affected.

Next, suppose a gain value g is multiplied to bands L_0, L_1, and L_2. Equation (11.21) then becomes $G_{0new} = G_{fb} + gL_0 + gL_1 + gL_2 \ldots \ldots + L_{fb-1}$. Using (11.20), expanding and rearranging the equation yields $G_{0new} = G_0 + (g - 1)(G_0 - G_3)$. More generally, for a gain value g applied to m consecutive bands from L_k,

$$G_{0new} = G_0 + (g - 1)(G_k - G_{k+m}). \tag{11.23}$$

The interpretation of this equation is similar to above, but this time the more the lowpass signals G differ between the discrete levels G_k and G_{k+m}, the more G_{0new} is affected.

From Eqs. (11.22) and (11.23), we can see that $G_{0new} = G_0$ when the gain value equals 1. When the gain value is greater than 1, the difference between the lowpass bands are added to the original signal G_0. This operation somewhat amplifies the motion vector in its original direction. When the gain value is less than 1, the difference between the lowpass bands is subtracted from the original signal G_0. This operation also amplifies the motion vector to some degree but this time in the opposite direction.

Figure 11.17 shows the source model at two different frames when the gain value is 1, meaning that no motion signal processing happened. Since 10 bandpass sequences are used, $L_0 - L_9$, bands 10 through 13 are disabled as shown in the picture. In contrast, Fig. 11.18 shows various effects on the original facial animation depending on the different gain values applied to different frequency bands. The first row shows that the gain value 3 is applied to the bandpass frequency bands 0, 1, and 2. From Eq. (11.23), it can be seen that the difference between G_0 and G_3 is multiplied by $3 - 1 = 2$ and added to the original expression G_0. G_3, which is the 3-times smoothed version of G_0 by the B-spline filter along the temporal domain, is similar to G_0 so that the effect is small, and not much difference is observed from the original expressions in Fig. 11.17. The fourth row shows that the gain value -2 is applied to the frequency bands 0, 1, and 2. This time, the difference between G_0 and G_3 is multiplied by $2 + 1 = 3$ and subtracted from the original expression G_0. The effect is also small due to the small difference between G_0 and G_3.

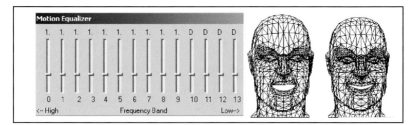

Fig. 11.17 Original source expressions at two different frames with all the gain values set to one.

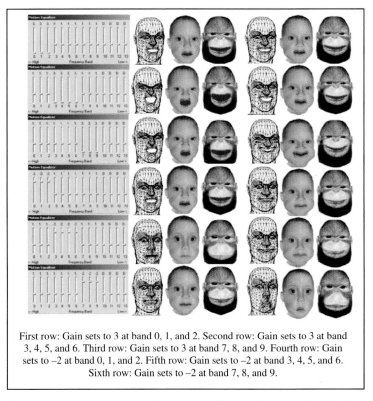

First row: Gain sets to 3 at band 0, 1, and 2. Second row: Gain sets to 3 at band 3, 4, 5, and 6. Third row: Gain sets to 3 at band 7, 8, and 9. Fourth row: Gain sets to –2 at band 0, 1, and 2. Fifth row: Gain sets to –2 at band 3, 4, 5, and 6. Sixth row: Gain sets to –2 at band 7, 8, and 9.

Fig. 11.18 Various expressions generated by applying different gain values. See Fig. 11.17 for the original expressions.

The second row shows, more salient effect. Compared to the original expressions in Fig. 11.17, the mouth is much more open due to the relatively big difference between G_3 and G_7. Similarly, the fifth row shows an interesting effect. The difference between G_3 and G_7 is subtracted from the original signal, resulting in reversal of the motion vector direction. The mouth is firmly closed. The third and sixth rows can be similarly explained. Especially, the comparison of second expressions shows that the mouth is wide and lip corners up in the third row while narrow and lip corners down in the sixth row.

Although not shown here, much more diverse effects can be obtained by manipulating gain values in different ways. For example, setting the gain value to 0 for the band L_0 yields $G_{onew} = G_1$. Since the high-frequency G_0 is removed from the original signal and replaced by the smoothed version G_1, this operation can be employed for the coarticulation effect for speech animation. For a smoother effect, the gain value for L_1 can be also set to 0, yielding $G_{onew} = G_2$. In fact, setting the gain value to 0 is equivalent to fitting a spline curve to each mouth vertex along the temporal axis.

Obviously, greater variations can be observed by individualizing gain values for each bandpass frequency band. In this case, analytic explanation may not be possible due to its complexity. However, random non-intuitive facial expressions are possible by setting the gain value for each band arbitrarily.

11.9 Extension 2: Direct Animation with Motion Capture Data

One of the well-known approaches to producing facial animation with motion capture data is to use the Guenter's algorithm [15]. In fact, the technique is utilized to create a source animation in Section 11.7. However, it entails tedious manual preprocessing of specifying feature correspondences between the motion capture data and the 3D model. In addition, the way to propagate feature point displacements to neighborhood heavily depends on the feature point distribution and the model's shape. If the actor and model do not conform in shape, the method will suffer.

Commercial software by Famous3D takes a different approach to generating facial animations with motion capture data. After the initial feature correspondence specification, a region of influence around each motion capture data is determined at the animator's discretion. This added manual intervention eliminates the problem of shape conformation between the actor and 3D model and provides flexibility for the resulting animation. Different animation can result with the same motion capture data depending on the animator's intention.

This section illustrates a mechanism to animate a 3D face model given motion capture data utilizing the expression cloning technique. The idea is to triangulate the motion capture data to produce a 3D face mesh and to apply the same technique treating the triangulated motion capture data as a source model. Once the triangulation is done and a source mesh is prepared, animation transfer between the source and target model is straightforward using expression cloning. So the focus in this section is placed on mesh generation from the provided motion capture data.

The steps to generate a plausible mesh are as follows:

1. Adjust the marker locations so that the left and right markers along the face centerline become symmetric.
2. Approximate the lip contact line with a Bezier curve.
3. Specify constraints (if any) to consider in the triangulation step.
4. Project 3D markers onto a 2D plane and triangulate.
5. Split upper and lower lips from the triangulated mesh.

11.9.1 Step 1: Symmetry of the Face

When facial motion data are captured, the makers are manually attached on the actor's face. In general, the initial marker positions are approximately symmetric with respect to the face centerline but not precisely. This asymmetry of the markers results in an asymmetric mesh if the triangulation is performed on the initial

Fig. 11.19 Asymmetric mesh vs. symmetric mesh.

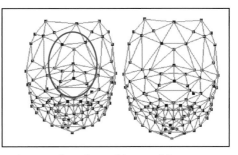

Asymmetric marker positions result in an asymmetric mesh as shown in the blue circle.

marker positions (Fig. 11.19). To produce a nice symmetric mesh, the initial marker positions needs to be adjusted.

The markers are divided into two groups. Assuming the orientation of the motion capture data is looking in the positive z-direction, the y-axis points through the top of the head, and the x-axis points through the right ear, the marker on the tip of the nose is the one with the highest z-value. The markers on the centerline are then determined as the ones with a similar x-coordinate to the nose marker. A tiny value ε defines the similar x-coordinate. The markers on the left side of the centerline points are one group and the rest is the other group (Fig. 11.20).

Individual marker correspondence between the two marker groups needs to be found to properly adjust the maker positions. This problem can be cast as an energy minimization problem. After the flipping of one marker group with respect to the centerline through the nose, the correspondence configuration generating minimum distance energy among all the possible correspondence configurations is the correct individual marker correspondence. More formally, we are looking for a correspondence configuration c such that E_c is minimum, where $E = ||M_L - M_R||$. M_L denotes the left-hand marker set, M_R the right-hand marker set, and $||.||$ the sum of the pairwise Euclidean distance for each correspondence configuration. The number of such configuration is $k!$, where k is the number of markers in each set.

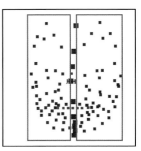

The left hand group, right hand group and centerline The point in the middle is the nose.

Fig. 11.20 Marker grouping.

Obviously, with the increase in the number of markers used, the search space becomes easily intractable. Since the two marker groups are roughly symmetric, however, sorting the markers based on the *y*-coordinate values first and considering a subset of markers one at a time can dramatically reduce the search space. In our case, three points from the left and five points from the right are considered each time starting from the top of the sorted markers, and the window is shifted down with the two unselected points from the right side carried over. Once the desired individual correspondence is found, the initial positions are pairwise-averaged. Finally, points in the centerline are also aligned with the nose point. The second picture in Fig. 11.19 shows the adjusted marker positions for symmetry.

11.9.2 Step 2: Lip Contact Line Construction

Most of the motion capture data do not contain the lip contact line points. Since the expression cloning technique assumes a mesh with the upper and lower lips fully defined, the lip contact points need to be artificially created. A way to approximate the arc-shaped lip contact line is to construct a Bezier curve with four control points [1,4].

The user specifies two lip corners and the number of points to be added along the lip line. Then a nice lip contour is generated (Fig. 11.21). The added points are displaced every frame for animation as the average of the neighbor points displacements.

11.9.3 Step 3: Constraint Specification (Optional)

The triangulation at step 4 is performed to maximize the minimum angle. It achieves the best triangulation in terms of the resulting triangle shapes. However, the user may want to have a specific edge connecting specific points. For example, an edge

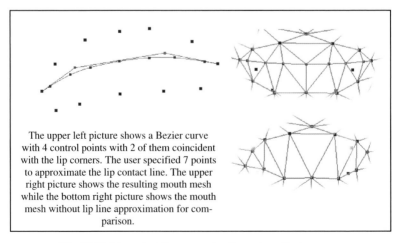

The upper left picture shows a Bezier curve with 4 control points with 2 of them coincident with the lip corners. The user specified 7 points to approximate the lip contact line. The upper right picture shows the resulting mouth mesh while the bottom right picture shows the mouth mesh without lip line approximation for comparison.

Fig. 11.21 Lip contact line approximation using a Bezier curve.

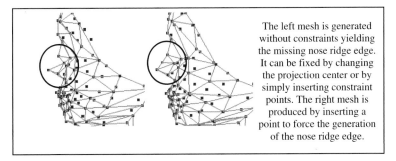

The left mesh is generated without constraints yielding the missing nose ridge edge. It can be fixed by changing the projection center or by simply inserting constraint points. The right mesh is produced by inserting a point to force the generation of the nose ridge edge.

Fig. 11.22 Side view of the meshes generated with and without a constraint.

separating the forehead from the lower part of the face might be desirable. Similarly, an edge representing the nose ridge might also be necessary. Although these edges are automatically produced most of the time by the adopted triangulation method, it can be forced to generate the edges if necessary, by simply inserting a small number of new points between the two endpoints where the edge is desired. With the inserted points, the inter-distance between points becomes smaller forcing an edge between them (Fig. 11.22). The inserted points can be stationary or displaced for animation as the average of the neighbor point displacements.

11.9.4 Step 4: Projection and Triangulation

Usually, a motion capture data is three-dimensional. Performing a triangulation in 3D space is a difficult task [9]. Therefore, 3D marker positions are spherically projected onto a 2D plane prior to the triangulation for a simpler 2D triangulation. The projection center can be interactively adjusted.

In general, skinny triangles cause trouble for animation, so a triangulation containing small angles should be avoided. The Delaunay triangulation [3] maximizes the minimum angle, avoiding sharp triangles in the resulting mesh. Triangulations are compared by their smallest angle and the one with the bigger angle is selected. If the minimum angles of two triangulations are identical, the comparison is performed with the second smallest angle, and so on. The connectivity among the points in the 2D plane is maintained while transferred to the 3D points for 3D mesh construction (Fig. 11.23).

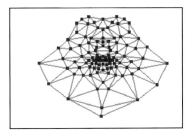

Fig. 11.23 Delaunay triangulation performed in 2D space.

Fig. 11.24 Open mouth after lip contact line split.

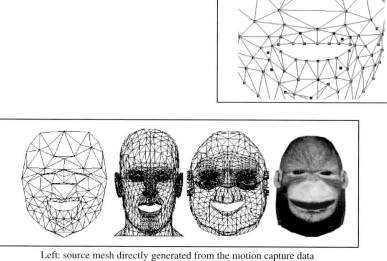

Left: source mesh directly generated from the motion capture data
Middle and Right: target models

Fig. 11.25 Expression cloning using the mesh directly generated from the motion capture data.

Since the triangulation is performed without consideration for the orientation of each triangle, normal variation might be inconsistent over the surface. For example, some triangles' normal would point outward while others would point inward. For correct rendering, a triangle is flipped if the angle between the triangle normal and ray from projection center through triangle center is greater than 90 degrees.

11.9.5 Step 5: Lip Split

The mouth should be split open for correct facial animation. To open the mouth, the artificially added lip contact line vertices in step 2 are duplicated and one is assigned to the upper triangle while the other is to the lower triangle (Fig. 11.24). This step completes the mesh generation from the initial 3D markers. The mesh now can serve as a source mesh containing the source animation. Expression cloning algorithm can be applied to various target meshes for animation transfer (Fig. 11.25).

11.10 Conclusion

The concept of expression cloning provides an alternative to creating animations from scratch. We take advantage of the dense 3D data in (possibly painstakingly created) source model animations to produce animations of different models with similar expressions. Cloning can be completely automatic, or animators can easily alter or add correspondences. Cloning effectively hides unintuitive low-level parameters from animators while allowing high-level control through correspondence selection. To naïve users, selecting a small number of correspondences is likely to be much more intuitive and easier than dealing with muscles or sculpting. Since EC starts with ground-truth data spatially (each frame) and temporally (a sequence of frames), the quality of output animation is very predictable. Because animations use precomputed barycentric weights and transformations to determine the motion vector of each vertex, the method is fast and produces real-time animations.

References

1. Bartels R, Beatty J, Barsky B (1987) *An Introduction to Splines for Computer Graphics and Geometric Modeling.* Morgan Kaufmann, New York.
2. Basu S, Oliver N, Pentland A (1998) 3D modeling and tracking of human lip motions. *ICCV*, pp 337–343.
3. Berg MD, Kreveld MV, Overmars M, Schwarzkopf O (1997) *Computational Geometry.* Springer-Verlag, New York.
4. Blanc C, Schlick C (1995) X-splines: A spline model designed for the end-user. *SIGGRAPH Proceedings*, pp 377–386.
5. Bruderlin A, Williams L (1995) Motion signal processing. *SIGGRAPH Proceedings*, pp 97–104.
6. Cohen MM, Massaro DW (1993) Modeling coarticulation in synthetic visual speech. In: *Models and Techniques in Computer Animation*. M. Magnenat-Thalmann and D. Thalmann (eds), Springer-Verlag, Tokyo.
7. Eck M (1991) Interpolation methods for reconstruction of 3D surfaces from sequences of planar Slices. *CAD und Computergraphik*, 13(5), February, pp 109–120.
8. Eck M, DeRose T, Duchamp T (1995) Multiresolution analysis of arbitrary meshes. *SIGGRAPH Proceedings*, pp 173–182.
9. Edelsbrunner H, Mucke E (1992) Three-dimensional alpha shapes. *Proceedings of the Workshop on Volume Visualization*, pp 75–82.
10. Eisert P, Girod B (1998) Analyzing facial expressions for virtual conferencing. *IEEE, Computer Graphics and Applications*, 18(5):70–78.
11. Fidaleo D, Noh J, Kim T, Enciso R, Neumann U (2000) Classification and volume morphing for performance-driven facial animation. *Digital and Computational Video* (DCV).
12. Franke R (1982) Scattered data interpolation: Tests of some method. *Math. Comp.*, 38(5): 181–200.
13. Gleicher M (1998) Retargeting motion to new characters. *SIGGRAPH Proceedings*, pp 33–42.
14. Golub GH, Heath M, Wahba G (1979) Generalized cross-validation as a method for choosing a good ridge parameter. *Technometrics*, 21(2):215–223.
15. Guenter B, Grimm C, Wood D, Malvar H, Pighin F (1998) Making faces. *SIGGRAPH Proceedings*, pp 55–66.
16. Hardy RL (1971) Multiquadric equations of topography and other irregular surfaces. *J. Geophys*, 76:1905–1915.
17. Kalra P, Mangili A, Thalmann NM, Thalmann D (1992) Simulation of facial muscle actions based on rational free from deformations. *Eurographics*, 11(3):59–69.
18. Kanai T, Suzuki H, Kimura F (2000) Metamorphosis of arbitrary triangular meshes. *Computer Graphics and Applications*, March, pp 62–75.
19. Kent JR, Carlson WE, Parent RE (1992) Shape transformation for polyhedral objects. *SIGGRAPH Proceedings*, pp 47–54.
20. Lee AWF, Dobkin D, Sweldens W, Schroder P (1999) Multiresolution mesh morphing. *SIGGRAPH Proceedings*, pp 343–350.

21. Lee, YC, Terzopoulos D, Waters K (1995) Realistic face modeling for animation. *SIGGRAPH Proceedings*, pp 55–62.
22. Lewis JP, Cordner M, Fong N (2000) Pose space deformation: A unified approach to shape interpolation and skeleton-drive deformation. *SIGGRAPH Proceedings*, pp 165–172.
23. Maurer T, Von der Malsburg C (1996) Tracking and learning graphs of image sequence of faces. In *Proceedings of International Conference on Artificial Neural Networks*, Bochum, Germany.
24. Moody JE (1992) The effective number of parameters: An analysis of generalization and regularization in nonlinear learning systems. *Neural Information Processing Systems* 4, 847–854, Morgan Kaufmann, San Mateo, CA.
25. Orr MJL (1998) Optimizing the widths of RBFs. *Fifth Brazilian Symposium on Neural Networks*, Brazil.
26. Ostermann J (1998) Animation of synthetic faces in MPEG-4. *IEEE Computer Animation*, pp 49–55.
27. Parke FI (1982) Parameterized models for facial animation. *IEEE Computer Graphics and Applications*, 2(9):61–68.
28. Penrose R (1955) A generalized inverse for matrices. *Proc. Cambridge Philos. Soc.*, 51: 406–413.
29. Pighin F, Hecker J, Lischinski D, Szeliski R, Salesin DH (1998) Synthesizing realistic facial expressions from photographs. *SIGGRAPH Proceedings*, pp 75–84.
30. Platt S, Badler N (1981) Animating facial expression. *Computer Graphics*, 15(3):245–252.
31. Poggio T, Girosi F (1989) A theory of networks for approximation and learning. Technical Report A.I. Memo No. 1140, Artificial Intelligence Lab, MIT, Cambridge, MA, July.
32. Pratt W (1991) *Digital Image Processing*, Second Edition. Wiley-Interscience, New York, ISBN 0-471-85766-1.
33. Shinagawa Y, Kunii TL (1998) Unconstrained automatic image matching using multiresolution critical-point filters. *IEEE Transactions on Pattern Analysis and Machine Intelligence*, 20(9):994–1010.
34. Stone MC (1991) Toward, a model of three-dimensional tongue movement. *Journal of Phonetics*, 19:309–320.
35. Tikhonov AN, Arsenin VY (1977) Solution of ill-posed problems and the regularization method. *Soviet Math. Dokl.*, 4:1035–1038.
36. Waters K (1987) A muscle model for animating three-dimensional facial expression. In M.C. Stone (ed), *Computer Graphics (SIGGRAPH Proceedings)* 21:17–24.
37. Waters K, Frisbie J (1995) A coordinated muscle model for speech animation. *Graphics Interface*, pp 163–170.
38. Williams L (1990) Performance driven facial animation. *SIGGRAPH Proceedings*, pp 235–242.

Chapter 12
Real-Time Adaptive Facial Animation

Stephane Garchery, Thomas Di Giacomo, and Nadia Magnenat-Thalmann

12.1 Introduction

Facial modeling and animation are important research topics in computer graphics. During the last 20 years, a lot of research has been done in these areas, but it still remains a challenging task. The impact of previous and ongoing research has been felt in many applications, like games, Web-based 3D animations, 3D animation movies, etc. Two directions are investigated: precalculating animation with very realistic results for animated films and real-time animation for interactive applications. Correspondingly, the animation techniques vary from key-frame animations, where animators set each frame, to algorithmic parameterized mesh deformation. Many of the proposed deformation models use a parameterization scheme, which helps control the animation. Computer graphics have evolved to a relatively mature state. In parallel to the evolution of 3D graphics technologies, user and application requirements have also dramatically increased from simple virtual worlds to highly complex, interactive, and detailed virtual environments. Additionally, the targeted display platforms have widely broadened from dedicated graphics workstations or clusters of machines to standard desktop PCs, laptops, and mobile devices such as personal digital assistants (PDAs) or even mobile phones. Facial animation can be one illustration of such closely related evolutions of graphics techniques and corresponding applications and user's requirements. Actually, despite much research and work on modeling, animation, and rendering techniques, it is still an important challenge to animate a highly realistic face with simulated hair and cloth, to display hundred of thousands of real-time animated humans on a standard computer, and it is still not possible to render animated characters on most mobile devices.

The focus of this chapter is to present dynamically adaptive real-time facial animation techniques. We discuss methods to automatically and dynamically control the processing and memory loads together with the visual realism of rendered motions for real-time facial animation. Such approaches would theoretically allow us to free additional resources for hair or cloth animation; for instance, it should also achieve real-time performance for facial animation on multiplatform and on lightweight devices, as well as enable improvements to virtual environments with the addition of more and more facially animated humans in a single scene.

Z. Deng and U. Neumann, *Data-Driven 3D Facial Animation.*
© Springer-Verlag London Limited 2008

12.2 State-of-the-Art

We present various facial deformation models and then level-of-detail and scal-abibility for animation, to conclude work related to media conversion.

12.2.1 On Facial Deformation

Generation of facial deformation is an issue that is particularly important for ani-mating faces. A face model without the capabilities of deforming is a passive object and has little role in virtual humans. The deformation model needs to consider that facial movements are naturalistic and realistic. This involves study and investiga-tion of the facial anatomy and of the motion and behavior of faces involving the generation of facial expressions, which are readily comprehensible.

The study of anatomy and physiology helped artists to create lively pictures and drawings. Similarly, this can give better insight for modeling and animating faces.

- **Skin** is significant both for the appearance and the movement of the face.

  - *Structure*: Human skin comprises several layers. This structure enables skin to move freely over the muscles and bones underneath.
  - *Motion*: The motion characteristics are due to the mechanical properties of skin, interaction of layers, and muscle activation. The main mechanical proper-ties are nonlinearity, anisotropy, viscoelasticity, incompressibility, and plastic-ity [80]. Aging changes properties of skin and causes emergence of wrinkles.

- **Muscles** are the principal motivators of facial actions and thus determine the facial movement.

  - *Structure*: Muscles lie between the bone and skin.
  - *Contraction and movement*: All facial actions occur as a consequence of mus-cular contraction. Muscles in general are of a large variety of size, shape, and complexity. Facial muscles are, in general, thin, voluntary, and subcutaneous. They also occur in pairs with one for each side of the face. Often muscles tend to be considered according to the region in which they occur. There are three types of facial muscles in terms of their actions: linear/parallel muscles, which pull in an angular direction; elliptical/circular sphincter muscles, which squeeze; and sheet muscles, which act as a series of linear muscles.

- **Bones** of the head, collectively termed as the skull, determine the proportion and shape of the face. The skull consists of two parts: the cranium and mandible.

In addition to the above, there are facial features with a distinct form and specific motion, e.g., eyes, tongue, and teeth. Eyes are a particular noticeable attribute and significant to the appearance and motion of the face.

The development of facial animation may be considered as dealing with defin-ing control parameterization and development of techniques and models for facial animation based on these parameterizations [62]. From animators' point of view, facial animation is a manipulation of the parameters and, therefore, parameterization is an important aspect to the animation model. There are three main schemes of parameterization, which have been used in the context of facial animation models:

- **FACS** (Facial Action Coding System) was developed by Ekman et al. [24] and was not intended for animation. Its primary goal was to develop a comprehensive system that could reliably describe all possible visually distinguishable facial movements. It defines fundamental basic actions, known as action units, which describe the contraction of one facial muscle or a group of related muscles. There are 46 action units. FACS seems complete for reliably distinguishing actions of the brows, forehead, and eyelids, but it does not include all the visible actions for the lower part of the face, particularly related to oral speech. In addition, it does not include the head movements. Still, the use of FACS in facial animation goes beyond what was intended. There have also been minor variants of FACS. For example, a basic facial motion parameter can be defined in terms of minimum perceptible action (MPA) [40]. Each MPA has a corresponding set of visible facial features such as movement of the eyebrows, the jaw, the mouth, or other motions that occur as a result of contracting muscles associated with the region. The MPAs also include nonfacial muscle actions such as nods and turns of the head and movement of the eyes. The MPAs for the mouth region are designed so that rendering of speech can be done reliably.
- MPEG-4 **facial animation** is an efficient coding method for geometry and efficient for the compressed transmission of corresponding animation parameters. Facial animation parameters (FAPs) are designed to encode animation of faces reproducing expressions, emotions and speech pronunciation. The 68 parameters are categorized into 10 different groups related to parts of the face. FAPs represent a complete set of basic facial actions and therefore allow the representation of most natural facial expressions. The parameter set contains two high-level parameters, the viseme and the expression. Since the FAPs are required to animate faces of different sizes and proportions, the FAP values are defined in face animation parameter units (FAPU). The FAPU are computed from spatial distances between major facial features on the model in its neutral state. It must be noted that the standard does not specify any particular way of achieving facial mesh deformation for a given FAP. The implementation details such as resolution of the mesh, deformation algorithm, rendering, etc., are left to the developer of the MPEG-4 facial animation system. The standard also specifies the facial animation table (FAT) to determine which vertices are affected by a particular FAP and how. Using the FAT is very appropriate, guaranteeing not only the precise shape of the face, but also the exact reproduction of animation.

Various models of deforming a face have been developed over the years [57]. Many of these models are adapted from general deformation models. We categorize them based on the mechanisms by which the geometry of the face is manipulated:

- **Shape interpolation**: One of the earliest approaches employed for animating faces, this is primarily based on running an interpolation function (linear or nonlinear) on the vertex positions of the extreme poses or expressions of faces. It has several limitations: the range of expressions obtained is restricted and the method is data-intensive, as it needs explicit geometrical data for each pose/expression.

- **Parametric model**: This model overcomes the restrictions of the interpolation technique [61]. Here, a collection of polygons is manipulated through a set of parameters. This allows a wide range of faces by specifying a small set of appropriate parameters associated with different regions of a face. However, the design of the parameters set is based on hardwiring the vertices for manipulating a part of the face, which makes the model dependent on the facial topology.

- **Muscle-based models**: The complete anatomical description of a face is rather complex; thus, it is not practical to design a model that entails the intricacies of the complete description of the face anatomy. However, efforts have been made to create models based on simplified structures of bones, muscles, skin, and connective tissues. These models provide the ability to manipulate facial geometry based on simulating the characteristics of the facial muscles. Most of these muscle-based models use the FACS parameterization scheme or its variant. The work by Platt and Badler [68] is one of the earliest attempts focused on muscle modeling and the structure of the human face, where the skin is considered as an elastic plane of surface nodes. Forces applied to elastic mesh through muscle arcs generate realistic facial expressions. Waters [78] propose a model based on a delineated deformation field for the action of muscles upon skin. Waters animates human emotions such as anger, fear, surprise, disgust, joy, and happiness, using vector-based muscles implementing FACS. Terzopoulos and Waters [73] propose a facial model with a more detailed anatomical structure and dynamics of the human face. A three-layered structure is considered, which correspond to skin, fatty tissue, and muscle, respectively. Muscle forces propagate through, the mesh systems to create animation. This model achieves great realism; however, simulating volumetric deformations with three-dimensional lattices requires extensive computation. A simplified mesh system reduces the computation time while still maintaining visual realism [82]. Here, the viscoelastic properties of skin are considered. Lee et al. [49] present models of physics-based synthetic skin and muscle layers based on earlier work [73]. The model accounts for volume preservation and skull penetration force. The model achieves a great degree of realism and fidelity; however, the model remains computationally expensive. In another method [39], a three-layer structure is used and a mass-spring system is employed for deformation. An editing tool is provided to design a coarse shape of muscles interactively, which is then used for automatic creation of a muscle fitting to the face geometry.

- **Pseudo-muscle modeling**: Simulated muscles offer an alternative approach by deforming the facial mesh in muscle-like fashion, but ignoring the complicated underlying anatomy and the physics. Deformation usually occurs only at the thin-shell facial mesh surface. Muscle forces can be simulated in the form of operators arising through splines [54, 55, 75, 76] or other geometric deformations [41].

- *Abstract muscle actions* (AMA) [51] refer to a procedure for driving a facial animation system. These AMA procedures are similar to the action units of FACS and work on specific regions of the face. Facial expressions are formed by a group of AMA procedures.

- *Free-form deformation* (FFD) is a common deformation technique. Rational free-form deformation (RFFD) incorporates weight factors for each control point, adding another degree of freedom in specifying deformations [41]. Kalra et al. [41] simulate the visual effects of the muscles using rational free-form deformation (RFFD) with a region-based approach. To simulate the muscle action on the facial skin, surface regions corresponding to the anatomical description of the muscle actions are defined. The skin deformations corresponding to stretching, squashing, expanding, and compressing inside the volume are simulated by interactively displacing the control points and by changing the weights associated with each control point. Displacing a control point is analogous to actuating a physically modeled muscle. Compared to Waters' vector muscle model [78], manipulating the positions or the weights of the control points is more intuitive and simpler than manipulating muscle vectors with a delineated zone of influence. However, RFFD (or FFD) does not provide a precise simulation of the actual muscle and the skin behavior, so that it fails to model furrows, bulges, and wrinkles in the skin. Furthermore, since RFFD is based upon surface deformation, volumetric changes occurring in the physical muscle are not accounted for.

- *Spline muscles*: Parametric surfaces or spline-based surfaces provide high-order continuities, usually up to C2. Furthermore, the affine transformations can be applied to a small set of control points instead of all the vertices of the mesh, hence reducing the computational complexity. Some models based on parametric surfaces have been used for defining the facial model [54, 55, 75, 76]. Wang et al. [76] show a system that integrated hierarchical spline models with simulated muscles based on local surface deformations. Muscles coupled with hierarchical spline surfaces are capable of creating bulging skin surfaces and a variety of facial expressions.

- **Finite element method** (FEM), in the context facial deformation, has been employed for biomechanical study and medical simulations, where accuracy is of importance. Larrabee [48] proposed the first skin deformation model using FEM. The skin is simplified to an elastic membrane with nodes spaced at regular intervals. The linear stress-strain relationship is employed for the skin membrane. This approach attempted modeling the effect of skin flap design for preoperative surgical simulation. Deng [17] proposed a more rigorous model comprising three-layered facial tissues. The model was used for simulating the closure of skin excision. Further work [67] extends Deng's model employed on facial data obtained from CT (computer tomography) for surgical simulations. One may notice that these methods have not really been used for facial animation; however, they do have potential. Guenter [30] proposes a simpler scheme of attaching muscles and wrinkle lines to any part of the face and using the global stiffness matrix for computing the deformation. The skin is modeled as a linear elastic rectangular mesh. Contraction of muscles is computed in 2D and then mapped onto 3D. FACS is used for control parameterization where muscles can be specified as one or more action units.

- **Others**: There are other deformation models that do not strictly fall in any of the above classes. Many of these models are based on local deformation of facial geometry. In some of the performance-driven animations [31, 64, 79], the deformation for the neighboring zone of the dot is computed through a distance function. A normalization or composition scheme is often desirable to overcome the unwanted effects when two regions overlap. In other approaches, a transformation method is used for modeling an individualized face from a canonical model [46]. The same method is also extended for animating a face. A set of control points is selected, and the transformation gives the displacement of these control points. The displacements of other points are computed using a linear combination of the displacements of the control points. The actual computation is done in 2D using cylindrical projection. FACS is used for control parameterization.

12.2.2 On Animation LoD and Adaptation

As for geometry, animation techniques can be adapted and simplified in certain cases, i.e., when motions are too fast, too far away, or too numerous for human sight as stated by Berka [6], or when motions are of low interest and therefore should not require complex calculations. Similarly to Level-of-Detail (LoD) for rendering and geometry, this approach can be applied for animation to manage expensive computations and memory costs of transformations and deformations, and provide a controlled trade-off between speed and realism. But unlike for geometry, in LoD for animation data that are out of the viewing-frustum still need to be processed. Actually, invisible objects are still animated and can enter the frustum at any time, so its motion updates need to be computed. Chenney et al. [14] propose to ensure a coherent treatment for this by setting the lowest level on objects out of the frustum. Most of the interest for animation LoD has been focused on deformation techniques, such as mass-spring networks and FEM: Hutchinson et al. [36] present a simple square mass-spring structure that is refined where and when the angle between springs increases and exceeds a user-defined threshold. Howlett et al. [35] extend this method by introducing non-active points, which play a role in the spatial subdivisions but none in the dynamics of the object. For FEM, adaptive techniques such as proposed by Wu et al. [81] using a progressive mesh, and by Debunne et al. [16] also using a progressive mesh with an adaptive timestep, fasten FEM computations to obtain real-time simulations. Capell et al. [12] use a multiresolution hierarchical volumetric subdivision to simulate dynamic deformations with finite elements and also use FEM to propose a framework for skeleton-driven deformations [11]. Animated natural phenomena have also taken advantage of LoD for animation, as proposed in [18, 65], as well as hair animation [7, 77] and character animation. The idea to control the skeleton complexity, by statically decreasing the sampling frequency of motions and degree of freedom of the hierarchy, has been proposed by Granieri et al. [29]. Cozot et al. [15] propose adapting the complexity of character animation by using different animation methods as different levels. They apply their method on walking humans, with standards criteria for level selection. O'Sullivan et al. [59] includes some LoD for motion in an integrated LoD system that also handles LoD for behavior. Ahn et al. [2] propose a simplification of motions based on a frame-based pre-processing stage to cluster joint motions. Recently, Redon et al. [70] presented adaptive forward dynamics with motion error metrics. Based on dynamic bodies, they simulate hybrid skeletons with active, (i.e., featuring acceleration, velocity, and position updates), passive (i.e., featuring bias acceleration and inverse inertia updates), and rigid joints (i.e., featuring only bias acceleration). Pettre et al. [66] also propose a framework for scalable rendering of crowds, with navigation graphs where individuals are spread, LoD for geometry including impostors, and basic LoD for motion with the use of pre-processed baked meshes rather than run-time animation.

Similarly to other media types, such as scalable video discussed by Kim et al. [43], audio presented for instance by Aggarwal et al. [1], or graphics as proposed by Boier-Martin [8], adaptation of content is also applicable to 3D graphics, as proposed by Van Raemdonck et al. [74] and Tack et al. [71] for instance, who propose a view-dependent quality metrics for decision-making based on Pareto plots, and also applicable to 3D animation as proposed by Joslin et al. [38].

12.2.3 On Media Conversion

Rendering and animating complex 3D scenes on very lightweight and mobile devices are still very important and challenging issues. Despite some methods on 3D graphics for mobiles, which use devices as display while the rendering is processed elsewhere [47], or which use existing optimization techniques [13, 22, 69], an important direction to investigate, especially when considering very lightweight devices, is the conversion of 3D graphics to other media, such as images or videos. Image-based techniques, when focusing on the simplification of 3D rather than on the improvement of the rendering realism, provide clues on the possible adaptation of 3D to other representations. Maciel et al. [50] propose replacing geometry with impostors that are roughly semi-transparent textured quads usually generated by pre-rendered images from predefined camera positions. Character animation has received particular attention from Tecchia et al. [72] and Aubel et al. [5]. These approaches animate impostors to reproduce the 3D animation of hierarchically articulated bodies with animated textures. Brosnan et al. [10] experiment the efficiency of impostors versus complete geometry on mobile devices. The results of their studies illustrate that impostors are suitable on such platforms. Although an impostor offers the advantage of preserving details with a small number of triangles, it cannot be easily applied to general detailed triangle meshes, especially those used for deformable surfaces. The *Geometry Video* is an innovative representation of animated meshes encoded as videos proposed by Briceno et al. [9]. Based on the geometry image representation, it is extended to videostreams compressible by common codecs, MPEG compression notably. The interest and work for 3D conversion to 2D vector graphics are very recent, and only a few investigations and experiments have tried to address them. One of the most significant works has been presented by Herman et al. [32]. It features a rotating 3D teapot in vector graphics, with wireless rendering and global rotations of the object. Other contributions are proposed in [60]. Unfortunately, none of the existing approaches handles complex shading, not even Gouraud, and particularly lack support for animation and deformation of high-resolution and articulated objects.

12.3 Example-based Real-Time Deformation Engine

A literature survey on different approaches to facial animation systems shows the most important characteristics to be featured in an ideal facial animation system. First, a facial animation system should be easy to use, multiplatform, and simple to implement. Thus, it should be suitable for any kind of geometry, require a minimum of time to set up face models for animation, and allow user input for animators to design specific deformations if necessary. It should also provide realistic results and provide a precise control on the animation.

To achieve a maximum of these goals, it is crucial to properly define which parameters are considered. In 1999, MPEG-4 defined a standard that proposed deforming the face model directly by manipulating feature points of the face and presented a novel animation structure. These parameters are completely model-independent, based on very few pieces of information, and leave open the adaptation of animations for each face model according to the facial engine that is used. A lot of research has been done in order to develop facial animation engines based on this parameterization system. Commonly, a piecewise linear interpolation function for each animation parameter [42, 58] is used to produce the desired result, and some research [56, 63] has been done to simplify the process, or to propose semiautomatic approaches. We now present an automatic way to simplify facial data construction.

12.3.1 MPEG-4 Overview

To understand facial animation based on MPEG-4 parameters, some keywords of the standard and the pipeline to animate compliant face models are described:

- **FAPU** (facial animation parameter units): all animation parameters are described in FAPU units. This unit is based on face model proportions and computed based on a few key points of the face (like eye distance or mouth size).
- **FDP** (facial definition parameters): this acronym describes a set of 88 feature points of the face model. FAPU and facial animation parameters are based on these feature points. These points could also be used in order to morph a face model according to specific characteristics.

- **FAP** (facial animation parameters): it is a set of values decomposed in high-level and low-level parameters that represent the displacement of some features points (FDP) according to a specific direction. Two special values (FAP 1 and 2) are used to represent visemes and expressions. All 66 low-level FAP values are used to represent the displacement of some FDPs according to a specific direction (see [26]). The combination of all deformations resulting from these displacements forms the final expression. A facial animation then is a variation of these expressions over time.

The FAP stream does not provide any information on the displacement of neighboring vertices; therefore, for each FAP, we use a method that defines each displacement, i.e., which vertices are influenced and in which weight and direction according to FAP intensities. MPEG-4 provides a referencing method called face definition tables (FDT) based on a piecewise linear interpolation in order to animate the face model [27]. These tables (also referred as FAT) provide information about which vertices should be translated or rotated for each FAP displacement. More information can be found in [53]. FDT is optional: the information it provides can be created by an animator by defining each influence on each FAP manually. However, areas such as the lips make this work very tedious due to the close proximity of 21 FAP values in a very small region.

12.3.2 Automatic Feature-based Geometrical Construction of Deformation Data

We present a generic approach to compute each region of influence. The main idea is to keep coherence and a maximum of simplicity in order to adapt this approach to different platforms or environments, but at the same time also to allow for realistic expressions.

12.3.2.1 Computation Description

The main problem is to find a correct definition of the influence area for each FAP according to its neighboring vertices. We propose an approach based on the following process:

- Compute the distribution of FDPs on the model and a relation of distance between them.
- For each vertex of the mesh, define which control point is able to influence it and define the ratio of influence of each control point.

A 3D face mesh is composed of different meshes for the eyes, teeth, tongue, and skin. The skin mesh is mainly defined by the holes for the eyes and the mouth. Also, often a face model has a vertex distribution that is not uniform over the mesh. In order to develop a model-independent approach, we have to take into account these specificities, and then we should define an appropriate distance measurement. A measurement based on Euclidean distance is efficient to manage the variations in mesh density, but it does not take into account problems like holes in the model. A measurement based on the topology like the number of edges between vertices takes the holes into account, but it is not efficient for the mesh density variations. We propose to use a metric based on both aspects: Euclidean distance and mesh topology. The metric is computed following this rule: "the distance is equal to the sum of the edge distances along the shortest path between two vertices." Using this metric, we are able to manage both holes and mesh density variation. Our approach is based on the definition of a list of influencing feature points for each vertex in the face mesh. Initially, all of the feature points are in the influence list. First, we find the closest feature point to the vertex with the previously defined metric. Then, we remove all the feature points from the list that are in the plane perpendicular to the vector between the vertex and the selected feature point (see Fig. 12.1). Then, we select the next closest feature point in the remaining list and we apply the same procedure until all feature points have been taken into account. When the list of influencing feature points is established, the influence of each of them on the current vertex is processed as a balanced sum d, where P is a vertex of the mesh:

$$d = \frac{\sum_{i=1}^{n} d_i * \cos \theta_i}{\sum_{i=1}^{n} \cos \theta_i},$$ (12.1)

where n equals the number of influencing feature points for P, θ_i is the angle between P and the feature point, and d_i is the distance between the feature point and the vertex. The weight associated to a specific feature point for P is computed as

$$W_{i,P} = \sin \left(\frac{\pi}{2} \left(1 - \frac{d_i}{d} \right) \right).$$ (12.2)

By computing $W_{i,P}$ for each vertex, we obtain for each feature point a list of the vertices that are influenced by it, with an associated weight. Some normalization process occur to keep skin deformation coherence.

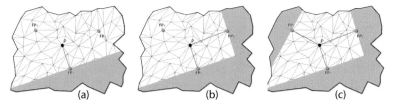

Fig. 12.1 Three steps to define a potential feature point [26].

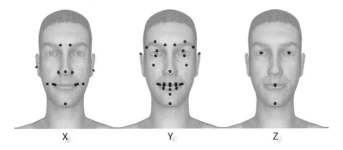

Fig. 12.2 Directional repartition of facial animation parameters [26].

12.3.2.2 Application to the Face by Defining Simple Constraints

Looking at the FAP repartition from a directional point of view, there are important differences in the feature points distribution (see Fig. 12.2). The method described above is applied to the 3D face model three times, one for each direction of deformation, to compute a different influence area according to each displacement direction. We obtain then three different lists of vertices influenced for each feature point for each region, used during the animation to deform the mesh. This information can easily be represented in the FaceDefMesh format and be used in an MPEG-4 compliant face system.

This initialization step of influence computation is done only once, can be stored, and only takes a few seconds for a model composed of more than 10 K polygons on a standard PC. The advantages of this approach are that it provides a quick way to simplify the number of influent points and it allows for the same computation on all vertices independently of their location on the face. Therefore, it is possible to add or remove feature points easily without changing the computation process.

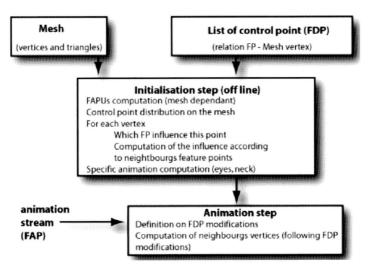

Fig. 12.3 Overview of global facial animation process.

This approach works not only with MPEG-4 but with any feature point-based deformation approach. Figure 12.3 shows a summary of the steps needed. First, starting from only a mesh (model topology) and FDP information, the system computes normalization values (FAPU), the distribution of FDP, and vertices. After this initialization step, during the animation process the system converts FAP information into new FDP positions and animates the mesh in order to follow the FDP spatial modifications.

After computing the influences, a designer can still edit this information and modify it if necessary or use it to control a specific deformation. Starting from already calculated influence areas is easier for the animator and saves a lot of manual work.

12.4 Scalability and Adaptation of Facial Animation

Traditionally, content has been tailored toward a specific device or a specific application. For instance, computer games have been developed with specific computers' capabilities in mind. In recent years, this trend of multiple contents for multiple devices has slowly shifted toward a single content for multiple devices approach. This has great advantage both for the content/service provider and for the end user. First, only a single content, of high quality, needs to be authored and provided for an entire suite of devices and conditions. Second, the user receives content that is optimized and that could fit not only the limitations of the device, mobile or not, but also the network capabilities, the user's own preferences, and the application performance.

12.4.1 Introduction to Bitstream Adaptation

This motivating goal is being explored in the framework of standardization, specifically by MPEG groups. Though early work in MPEG-7, e.g., proposed by Heuer et al. [33], adapts certain types of content, this concept is particularly being explored under the framework of MPEG-21 Digital Item Adaptation (DIA, see [37]). A digital item is the MPEG name given to any media type or content.

The adaptation of a bitstream is basically illustrated by Fig. 12.4, where parts of an original bitstream are dropped to generate an adapted bitstream. The principles are based on XML schemas called Bit Stream Description Language (BDSL), and its generic form is called generic Bit Stream Description Language (gBDSL). The idea is that compressed data are described using these schemas. BSDL uses a codec-specific language, meaning that the adaptation engine needs to understand the language and use a specific XML stylesheet, explained ahead, in order to adapt the bitstream.

The adaptation process is very flexible and decomposed in multiple levels. The components and elements working together to perform a complete adaptation are as follows:

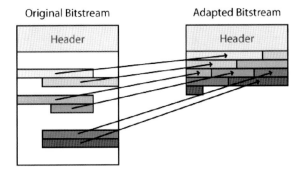

Fig. 12.4 Illustration of bitstream adaptation.

- The original bitstream, referred to as the Content Digital Item (CDI) in MPEG. This is the initial encoded format of the content. It should be the highest-quality version and should contain all elements and scalability mechanisms required for the adaptation.
- The bitstream description, being a gBSD for instance. The gBSD [3, 4] file is essentially localizing each of the important elements within the encoded file, marking lengths, offsets, and other information that enables the adaptation to occur. It can be generated in different ways, but the simplest is probably during the encoding of the original scalable bitstream. Another way is to generate a BSD with a binary to bitstream description engine (BintoBSD), as shown in Fig. 12.5. The BSD contains a description of the bitstream at a high level, i.e., not on a bit-by-bit basis, and can contain either the bitstream itself, represented as hexadecimal strings, or links to the bitstream.
- The context, refered as the Context Digital Item (XDI) in MPEG. The XDI contains the formatted information from the client and can also contain information from the server, on the target device, the user preferences, the network characteristics. It can be seen as a set of input control parameters for adaptation.
- The Adaptation Quality of Service (AQoS). According to the context, the AQoS is selecting specific parameters that will drive the XSLT (see ahead) and then the adaptation itself. For instance, the AQoS can relate an available bandwidth at a given time, provided by the context, to a desired layer of complexity for the XSLT to keep only bitstream parts belonging to this layer.

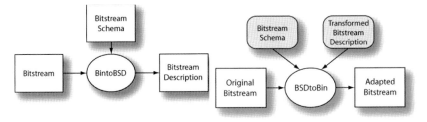

Fig. 12.5 On the left, generation of a bitstream description; on the right, adaptation of a bitstream processed by a transformed bitstream description.

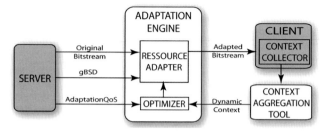

Fig. 12.6 Overall schematized architecture of the adaptation process.

- The transformation description, being an XML stylesheet (XSLT). The XSLT is the core for the adaptation. Actually, it relates the gBSD to the actual values or preferences given by the user or the terminal through the context and the AQoS. The XSLT contains processes for verification of a gBSD file against the required adaptation process, as well as the transformation process of bitstream descriptions itself with a set of rules. This is generally an execution routine and must be handcrafted for a particular task or set of tasks; for instance, for removing elements from the XML bitstream descriptions. During this stage, the bitstream's header might be changed in order to take into account the elements that were removed from the bitstream. For example, an initial mask might indicate the presence of all elements, but this would be modified to indicate which elements have remained after adaptation, to maintain consistency so that the decoder on the terminal does not become unstable. The XML document is then parsed via a BSDtoBin converter, which takes the XML document and converts it back into a bitstream, as shown in Fig. 12.5.

Figure 12.6 summarizes the whole adaptation process. The client requests a content to the server, which then sends it to the adaptation engine, together with the associated bitstream description. The AQoS and XSLT can be stored in the adaptation engine or also sent by the server. According to the AQoS and the aggregated context coming from the client and through the context aggregation tool, the optimizer outputs values for the XSLT to perform the transformation on the bitstream description. Once transformed, this description is used in the resource adapter to generate the adapted bitstream and send it to the client.

As mentioned in Section 12.2, adaptation of video, image, and audio has received a lot of attention by the research community, while graphics, and especially 3D graphics, has, until now, been less investigated. We present methods for 3D graphics data adaptation based on [20], with a focus first on the scalability of the geometry and then, on the scalability of facial animation data.

12.4.2 Scalable Representation

3D graphics data can be decomposed into geometrical parameters, such as vertices coordinates, normals, textures, etc., and animation data, such as the joints transformations, displacements of facial control points, etc. This part details an approach for the adaptation of geometry. It is based on previous work [44], which has been extended for supporting adaptation as introduced previously. The method is based on a clustered representation of the different resolution of the geometry. The idea of clustering is presented along with its extension to the compact representation of vertex properties and animation parameters for latter adaptation. The premise involves clustering all the data so that a specific complexity can be obtained by simply choosing a set of clusters. From the complex mesh $M_n(V_n, F_n)$, where V_n is a set of vertices and F_n is a set of faces, it is sequentially simplified to $M_{n-1}, \ldots, M_1, M_0$. A multiresolution model of this simplification sequence has, or at least is able to generate, a set of vertices V and faces M (see Fig. 12.7), where the union is denoted as $+$ and the intersection as $-$:

$$V = \sum_{i=0}^{n} V_i, \; M = \sum_{i=0}^{n} M_i.$$

There are many simplification operators, including decimation, region merging, and subdivision. Here we use half-edge-collapsing operators [34] and quadric error metrics (QEM) [28]. By an edge-collapsing operator, an edge (v_r, v_s) is collapsed to the vertex v_s. For instance, let say that faces f_1 and f_2 are removed by such a collapse and that faces f_3 and f_4 are modified into f_3' and f_4'. The clusters are therefore defined as $C(i) = \{f_1, f_2, f_3, f_4\}$ and $N(i) = \{f_3', f_4'\}$. The error metric is slightly modified to adopt the animation parameters. Each vertex has measurement of levels of animation. For example, a vertex that is close to the joint in body animation or a vertex that has large facial deformation parameters needs to be preserved during the simplification process (see Figs. 12.8 and 12.9). At one extreme, it is desired to preserve the control points of animation as much as possible. This level of deformation is the multiplied QEM of each vertex such that vertices with a high deformation parameter are well preserved through simplification.

V and M can be partitioned into a set of clusters. The first type is a set of vertices and faces removed from a mesh of the level i to a mesh of the level $i - 1$, denoted by $C(i)$. The other type is a set of vertices and faces that are newly generated by simplification, denoted by $N(i)$. A level i mesh is as follows:

$$M_i = M_0 + \left(\sum_{j=1}^{i} C(j) - \sum_{j=1}^{i} N(j)\right).$$

Fig. 12.7 Different mesh resolutions for upper body.

Fig. 12.8 The architecture for multiresolution generation using 3D modeling tools and appropriate modules for preserving animation parameters.

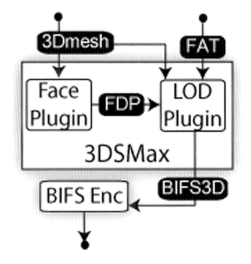

To evaluate this equation requires set, union and intersection, which are still complex. Using the properties of the simplification, it ensures $N(i)$ to be a subset of unions of $M_0, C(1), \ldots, C(i-1)$. Using this property, the cluster $C(i)$ is subclustered into a set of $C(i,j)$, which belongs to $N(j)$, where $j > i$, and $C(i,i)$, which does not belong to any $N(j)$. It is same for the M_0, where $M_0 = C(0)$. Thus, the level i mesh is represented as follows, which requires simple set selections:

$$M_i = \sum_{k=0}^{i}(C(k,k) + \sum_{j=i+1}^{n} C(k,j)).$$

The last process is the concatenation of clusters into a small number of blocks to reduce the number of selection or removal operations during the adaptation process. Processing vertices is rather straightforward, because the edge-collapsing operator (v_i, v_s) ensures that every $C(i)$ has a single vertex v_i as $C(i,i)$. By ordering vertices of $C(i,i)$ by the order of i, the adaptation process of vertex data for level i is a single selection of continuous block of data, $v_0, v_1, \ldots, v_i$. For the indexed face set, each

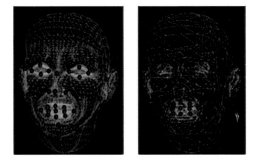

Fig. 12.9 Preservations of facial animation control points during the mesh simplification process.

$C(i)$ is ordered by $C(i,j)$ in the ascending order of j. Thus, an adaptation to level i consists of at most $3i + 1$ selections or at most $2n$ removals of concatenated blocks.

So far, we have described the process using only the vertex positions and face information. In the mesh, other properties have to be taken into account, such as normal, color, and texture coordinates. Because these properties inheritably belong to vertices, a similar process to vertex positions is applied. Exceptional cases are (1) two or more vertices use the same value for a property, and (2) a single vertex has more than two values. In both cases, there is a unique mapping from a pair of vertex and face to a value of properties. The cluster $C(i)$ has properties that have a mapping from (v_i, f_j), where $v_i \in C(i)$. If a property p belongs to more than one vertex such as $(v_i, f_1) \to p$ and $(v_j, f_2) \to p$, p is assigned to the cluster of $C(j)$, where $j < i$. By ordering this, p remains active as long as there is one vertex that has p as its property. Therefore, we have a valid set of clusters for each level i. Each cluster has a set of vertices and vertex properties such as vertex normal, color, and texture coordinates. Along with vertex information, the cluster has a set of indexed faces, normal faces, color faces, and texture faces. Also, each cluster can consist of subsegments with their own material and texture. Each level is selected by choosing blocks of clusters.

12.4.3 Adaptive 3D Facial Animation Technology

Now, we describe scalable mechanisms for facial animation parameters, with similar adaptation concepts. The scalability is based on the lowest-level facial animation parameters, i.e., the FAP. Two different methods for generating adaptive animation are presented: levels of complexity structures, referred to as levels of articulation (LoA), and face regions, see Table 12.1. Regions and LoA, which are levels of FAP complexity, are thus defined, although the LoA is also applied on each region. For scalability, the face is segmented into different regions. It is based on MPEG-4 FAP grouping, although we have grouped the tongue and the inner and outer lips in a

Table 12.1 Face regions definition and their associated number of FAPs per LoA. Note that the high level is for generic face expressions and that region 4 is the head rotation, which is controlled by the body animation and therefore omitted here.

Region	Definition	High	Medium	Low	Very Low
	High level	2	2	2	2
0	Jaw (chin, lips, tongue)	31	19	12	6
1	Eyeballs (eyelids)	12	8	4	1
2	Eyebrows	8	3	2	1
3	Cheeks	4	4	1	1
5	Nose	4	3	0	0
6	Ears	4	2	2	0
	Total	68	44	26	14
	Ratio	100%	65%	38%	21%

single region since these displacements are closely linked. This segmentation allows to group FAPs according to their influence regions with regards to deformation, and the LoA is therefore applied per region. A sample use of the face regions is an application based on speech, which would require detailed animation around the mouth region and less in other parts of the face. This would, for instance, result in a low LoA for the eyebrows, eyeballs, and nose and ears regions, a medium LoA for the cheek regions, and a high LoA for the jaw region.

Actually, we define four LoA based on the FAP influences with two different techniques. The first technique is to group FAP values together, with the following constraints:

- all grouped FAPs must be in the same area;
- all grouped FAPs must be under the influence of the same FAPU.

Additionally, when grouped by symmetry, the controlling FAP value is the one on the right part of the face. The second technique is reducing quality more rapidly, assuming some FAPs are insignificant at certain times, by introducing four LoA:

- *LoA high*: it uses all FAP values.
- *LoA medium*: certain FAPs are grouped together, resulting in a total of 44 FAPs instead of 68.
- *LoA low*: some FAPs are removed and other grouped, keeping only 26 FAPs.
- *LoA very low*: most FAPs are removed; only base values for minimal animation are maintained. It consists of merging FAPs from the low LoA by symmetry and removing other FAPs, resulting in a total of 14.

We also propose a scalability mechanism for the FAT. The generation of these tables is done with geometric deformation algorithms to compute FAP influences. It allows for an automatic computation of influenced vertices according to FDP only. Based on this technique, the animation engine is able to animate any face model with only the FDP. This method is also very practical for devising different resolutions, since only the influence information needs to be recomputed, using the same FDP, which is preserved by the adaptation of geometry. So from the highest-level model, we automatically construct the FAT, and since the vertices are ordered by FDP and influence, we can easily identify and extract the corresponding FAT information from the highest-level FAT for each resolution, as illustrated by Fig. 12.10.

12.4.4 Automatic Conversion of 3D to 2D Facial Animation

We present two methods for automatically converting 3D facial animation to 2D graphics and to 2D vector graphics. The goal is to provide an additional lowest animation resolution for devices that cannot render complex 3D graphics and for devices optimized to support natively vector graphics such as mobile phones. The difficulties in such conversion are to maintain intrinsic 3D properties in the 2D representation, such as depth and lighting, and to keep the size of the generated data small enough for light devices. Visually, the main criterion for a correct conversion

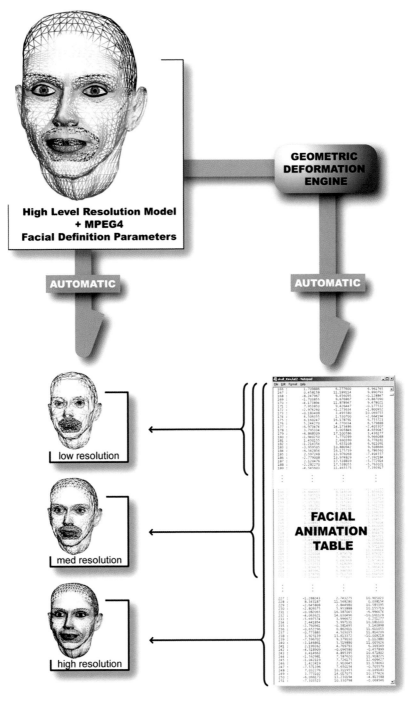

Fig. 12.10 Scalable FAT coupled with multiresolution geometry.

is the similarity between the generated copycat 2D animations and the original 3D ones. The first technique transforms MPEG-based 3D facial animation to 2D MPEG compliant facial animation, hence keeping advantages for interoperability, compacity, and delivery of content on any device featuring 2D graphics. It is also practical for integration with scalable 3D facial animation frameworks presented previously. Then we detail an approach that converts general 3D facial animation to 2D Vector Graphics (VG), including optimizations for the resulting VG animations and the simulation of Gouraud shading, which is not natively supported by 2D VG.

12.4.4.1 2D Adapted Facial Animation

Concerning the conversion of 3D to 2D facial animation with MPEG compliance [21], the goal is also to keep components as unchanged as possible and adapt only the necessary parts, i.e., with a two-, instead of three-, dimensional scene graph to represent the face. So basically, to obtain an animatable 2D face at the end of the conversion chain (see Fig. 12.11), 3D meshes are converted to 2D representations, including projected shaded images of the original model with the preservation of the topology, and the use of FAP and FAT in 2D as detailed ahead.

Conversion of Geometry for 2D

The concept used is based on warping-based facial image animation. It consists of two modifications in the facial representation data. The FDP contains, for 2D facial animation, a 2D warped indexed facet set instead of a 3D one, and the image texture portrait of the original face. The 2D mesh is consequently deformed using FAP. The 2D feature points are a subset of the 3D feature points, where 3D feature points, still visible on the frontal view after a projection from the 3D space into the 2D space, have been preserved. As this should happen in the neutral state, i.e., with a closed mouth, the teeth and tongue have no matching part in the image. Therefore, we are adding default teeth and tongue image patterns, placed behind the 2D warped mesh (see Fig. 12.12). They become visible when the mouth is opened. Actually, for good results, the face representation should consist of three 2D layers: the bottom one is the whole portrait image; the middle one provides the teeth and tongue image data; and the top one is the actual deformable face data.

Use of Animation for 2D

Each low-level FAP corresponds to a piecewise linear function that defines the function between vertex displacements and the corresponding FAP amplitude values. Thus, after the definition of the FATs, input FAPs can be recognized and handled reasonably to produce the intended face animation. This requires, that for each low-level FAP, the corresponding 2D vertex displacements for the 2D mesh have to be defined. The projection of the 3D vertex displacements can be used as a first guess

Fig. 12.11 Overview of the global architecture for facial animation adaptation, with the 2D conversion module.

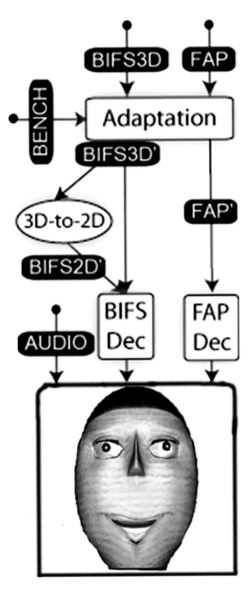

though further manual refinements are vital for good visual results. Based on the scalable FAT, an additional FAT layer is included to handle this 2D deformation. Facial animation parameters constituting changes in the z-direction are ignored as they have small impacts onto the 2D projection. In addition, rotations of the eyeball are substituted by 2D translations. Furthermore, animations of the tongue are currently neglected, as well as head rotations due to the reduction of one dimension. There are then some restrictions in animating the full set of FAP values. A possible solution to copy all 3D-based deformations of the face would be to generate 2D animations directly from the resulting updates of vertex positions. Additionally, some

Fig. 12.12 2D mesh warping on a face view prerendered image of the original 3D mesh. The eyes, tongues, and teeth are separate images.

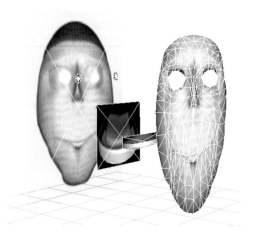

devices might not support 2D graphics with deformable meshes, so we present a method in the vector graphics domain to address those two issues.

12.4.4.2 Gouraud-Shaded Vectorial Animation

When vector graphics (VG) are supported, we propose to have a full VG animation instead of a 2D mesh deformed with FAP [19]. As an example, this conversion method for VG generates a scalable vector graphics (SVG) file, a widely adopted W3C standard format for VG.

Extraction of 2D Data

Basically, the conversion is processed into two main steps: the identification and extraction of appropriate 2D data and the generation of VG data accordingly (see Fig. 12.13). By decoupling the extracted 2D data from the generation, the method

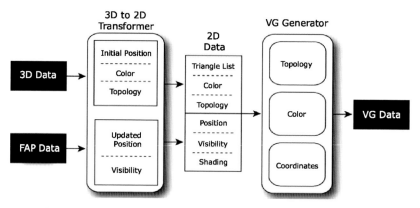

Fig. 12.13 This diagram illustrates the 3D-to-2D module for facial animation.

is immediately extensible with different formats, using additional file generator modules. Taking advantage of hardware processing, 2D data and extracted from 3D by prerendering 3D facial animation with a standard graphics library to compute projections. The 2D coordinates are then extracted with the projection matrix and the 3D coordinates. The 3D rendering is actually extended with a gathering of projected vertices data and faces visibility, according to the camera and vertices' positions. This process is conducted at each frame, and it is possible to select which one in the sequence serves as the neutral position of the face. View-frustum and backface cullings are performed on the 3D scene to create a per-frame visibility list for each polygon. Culling is performed on complete faces by setting a bit flag to true or false depending on the 3D face visibility and therefore provide information for visible or invisible states of 2D polygons.

Generation of VG Data

After the 2D data extraction process, VG data can be generated to mimic the original 3D animation. The SVG generator creates a file according to the 2D data present in the cache. To represent a 3D face, an SVG element capable of animation, deformation, and color filling is necessary. The *polygon* element supports 2D animation and color, but does not provide deformation mechanisms. Therefore, for a 3D polygon, a series of *nbF* SVG polygons, where *nbF* is the number of frames of the animation, would be required. Thus, inspired by the approach of Herman et al. [32], the internal SVG representation used in the presented method is based on *path*. It is the most appropriate SVG structure to represent a 3D polygon since it can specify a closed n-gon, on which each points are animatable independently and where visibility can be described for any frame. Positions of *path* points are directly related to the 2D projected vertices computed during the extraction. Filling a *path* can also be done with an image, a solid color, in the case of a simple flat shaded object, or a linear or radial gradient. Linear gradient is used for Gouraud shading simulation, as described ahead. At initialization, the 3D triangles are z-sorted to create an ordered list of *paths*, and then the visibility of each *path* is adjusted by the sequence of bit flags from the extraction module.

Post-Optimizations of VG

Depending on the number of polygons and the number of frames of the animation, generated SVG files might be several megabytes big. To reduce the output SVG file's size, we define and apply some post-process optimizations. The first optimization is to delete the animated coordinates data of a *path* when it is not visible. It is done by determining the range of frames where a face is hidden, thus specifying the data to be deleted. To further optimize the size of the output file, we also determine sequences of frames when the *path* is visible but does not move. All these optimizations basically merge animation data when possible, by adding *animate* tags. The *keyTime* attribute is another SVG feature one can exploit to perform such optimizations. Unlike *animate*, it does not add key frames but parameterizes the timing of each frame and, thus, *keyTime* is especially relevant in the case of many static frames while less efficient than *animate* in the case of dynamic long sequences.

Gouraud-Shaded VG

When generating an SVG file, instead of producing an animation with poor shading effect, it is possible to create an SVG file representing the current frame with Gouraud shading, in order to have a more realistic rendering. Gouraud shading is an intensity-interpolation method based on the illumination of vertices. First these values are calculated, and then interpolation is done among the three vertices to obtain a gradient. Our method implements it with the tools and specifications available with a vectorial language such as SVG. We therefore propose to apply three gradients per triangle, i.e., one per vertex, each one filling its respective part. To merge these gradients, we have to modify spatially the transparency, and then the closer a gradient is to the opposite edge of the triangle, the smaller is its alpha value. Because SVG does not allow several gradients per triangle, we have to superpose three triangles, one for each gradient, with the same coordinates. These triangles are then combined by applying a filter *fe Composite*. The result is again filtered with a filter *fe Colormatrix* in order to correct the opacity of the three previous layers. Afterwards, an additional triangle is set under this composition to ensure faces are hidden when required, by avoiding the coverage of triangles. Indeed, this background triangle's color is the average of the three vertices' colors and the first gradient.

12.5 Conclusion

Methods to control the processing and memory requirements of animating and rendering facial animation with respect to visual quality are important. Such a control should allow for rendering on light devices, for delivery of animation data over heterogeneous networks, as well as for optimizations on a standard PC. Additionally, a solution should be devised to provide facial animation even on non-3D-capable architectures. The same real-time facial animation engine has been used on different platforms such as the PC, Web, or mobile. Figure 12.14 presents the results of different models. We have applied for each model the same set of FAP values to generate the same expression. Each model presented in this example could be animated on a standard PC in real time.

The performance of this approach on a PDA is a rendering of 25 to 30 fps for a model with 750 polygons. For Web-based applications, based on MPEG-4 FAT and using Shout3D for rendering, which provides a Java API, good-quality models can be animated with low computation, and interactive speeds can be easily achieved. The details of the system can be found in [27], and this applet can be accessed on the

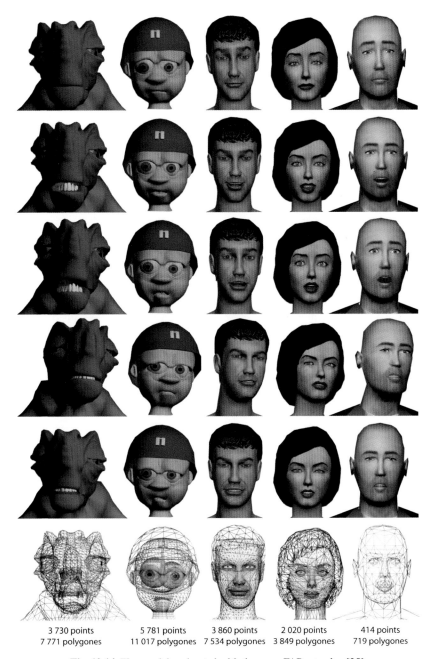

| 3 730 points | 5 781 points | 3 860 points | 2 020 points | 414 points |
| 7 771 polygones | 11 017 polygones | 7 534 polygones | 3 849 polygones | 719 polygones |

Fig. 12.14 Five models animated with the same FAP set value [25].

Table 12.2 Comparison of facial animation data sizes using different LoA.

Size	wow	baf	face23	macro	lips
High	21255	32942	137355	18792	44983
Medium	16493	24654	104273	14445	36532
Low	13416	20377	78388	11681	30948

MIRALab Website (http://www.miralab.unige.ch) in the *facial animation* section under the *research* topic.

To validate the efficiency of the discussed method that adapts facial animation, we have performed comparisons using several sample sequences covering a wide range of possible facial animations. Using the same animation frequency and the same compression scheme, we have encoded different FAP files to evaluate the influence of the LoA for the whole duration of animations. Sizes are compared in Table 12.2. Overall, with respect to the original file size, the results show a mean value of 77.4% for LoA medium, of 62.6% for LoA low, and of 54.4% for LoA very low. All the sample sequences, except the Lips one, consist of animation of all parts of the face. For each of them, the obtained reduction is quite similar, while the size reduction is smaller for the last sequence due to the lack of FAP suppressions.

Using the same sequences, we have also tested performance with processing times required for the rendering of animation. Results are given in Table 12.3, where the processing time gain for LoA medium is on average 86.6%, 75.2% for LoA low, and 68.2% for LoA very low. Once again, the gain is a little bit smaller for the last sequence compared to the other ones. This is due to the smaller amount of FAP used in the Lips animation.

For the conversion to 2D, some results on a PDA (Dell Axim series) are presented on Table 12.4, illustrating the needs and benefits of 2D rather than 3D facial animation on light devices. Figures 12.15 and 12.16 show the visual results obtained on such platforms.

To validate the conversion of 3D facial animation to animated and shaded vector graphics, three experiments have been set up. The first one evaluates the core elements of the method with an animated pyramid, namely the generation of vec-

Table 12.3 Comparison of facial animation processing times using different LoA.

Size	wow	baf	face23	macro	lips
High	4.17	6.10	25.04	4.08	10.90
Medium	3.56	5.23	21.23	3.54	9.81
Low	3.09	4.56	17.58	3.10	8.81

Table 12.4 Performance of facial animation on a PDA with various 3D resolutions and the 2D resolution. Sizes are indicated uncompressed.

	Nb of polygons	FPS	Size (kb)
3D high	17788	N.A.	2045
3D medium	8882	3	1013
3D low	1790	10	197
2D	600	25	0.8

Fig. 12.15 2D facial animation on a PDA, with audio and a background slide-show.

Fig. 12.16 Rotation of the plane where is mapped the 2D face textures.

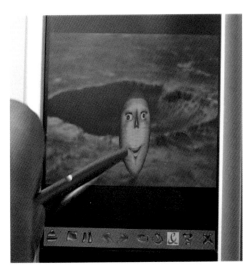

Table 12.5 Duration and generation are expressed in seconds, while sizes in kilobytes. The pyramid and face test sequences feature animation, while Gouraud is a single Gouraud-shaded face image.

	# polys	Duration	Raw size	Optim size	Generation
Pyramid	8	12.08	529	91	0
Face	484	8.28	5684	4798	8
Gouraud	484	N.A.	610	N.A.	3

tor graphics data, the visibility of faces, and the optimization techniques to reduce the size of the output file. The second test is conducted to compare SVG copies of 3D facial animation. Finally, we test the Gouraud shading simulation in SVG with images captured during the animation. The obtained sizes and generation time are given in Table 12.5. The 2D data extraction is done in real time; only the SVG data generation might take some additional time at the end of 3D animations to be converted.

References

1. Aggarwal, A., Rose, K., Regunathan, S.: Compander domain approach to scalable AAC. In *110th Audio Engineering Society Convention*, 2001.
2. Ahn, J., Wohn, K.: Motion level-of-detail: A simplification method on crowd scene. In *Computer Animation and Social Agent, CASA'04*, pages 129–137. Computer Graphics Society, 2004.
3. Amielh, M., Devillers, S.: Bitstream syntax description language: Application of XML-schema to multimedia content adaptation. In *International WWW Conference'02*. International World Wide Web Conference Committee, 2002.
4. Amielh, M., Devillers, S.: Multimedia content adaptation with XML. In *MultiMedia Modeling, MMM'01*, pages 127–145. Springer Verlag, 2001.
5. Aubel, A., Boulic, R., Thalmann, D.: Real-time display of virtual humans: Levels of detail and impostors. *IEEE Transactions on Circuits and Systems for Video Technology, Special Issue on Video Technology*, 2:207–217, 2000.
6. Berka, B.: Reduction of computations in physic-based animation using level of detail. In *Spring Conference of Computer Graphics*, pages 69–76. ACM Press, 1997.
7. Bertails, F., Kim, T.Y., Cani, M.P., Neumann, U.: Adaptive wisp tree: A multiresolution control structure for simulating dynamic clustering in hair motion. In *Symposium on Computer Animation*, pages 207–213, Eurographics Association, 2003.
8. Boier-Martin, I.: Adaptive graphics. *IEEE Computer Graphics & Applications*, 2(1): 6–10, 2003.
9. Briceno, H., Sander, P., McMillan, L., Gortler, S., Hoppe, H.: Geometry videos: A new representation for 3D animations. In *Symposium on Computer Animation, SCA'03*, pages 136–146. Eurographics Association, 2003.
10. Brosnan, A., Dobbyn, S., Hamill, J., O'Sullivan, C.: Animating humans on handheld devices for interactive gaming. In *Computer Animation and Social Agents, CASA'05*. Computer Graphics Society, 2005.
11. Capell, S., Green, S., Curless, B., Duchamp, T., Popovic, Z.: Interactive skeleton-driven dynamic deformations. In *ACM SIGGRAPH'02*, pages 586–593, 2002.
12. Capell, S., Green, S., Curless, B., Duchamp, T., Popovic, Z.: A multiresolution framework for dynamic deformations. In *Symposium on Computer Animation, SCA'02*, pages 41–47. Eurographics Association, 2002.
13. Chang C., Ger, S.: Enhancing 3D graphics on mobile devices by image-based rendering. In *IEEE Pacific-Rim Conference on Multimedia*, 2002.
14. Chenney, S., Forsyth, D.: View-dependent culling of dynamics systems in virtual environments. In *Symposium on Interactive 3D Graphics*, pages 55–58. ACM Press, 1997.
15. Cozot, B., Multon, F., Valton, B., Arnaldi, B.: Animation levels of detail design for real-time virtual human. In *Eurographics Workshop on Computer Animation and Simulation, EGCAS'99*, pages 35–44. Springer Verlag, 1999.
16. Debunne, G., Desbrun, M., Cani, M.P., Barr, A.: Dynamic real-time deformations using space & time adaptive sampling. In *ACM SIGGRAPH'01*, pages 31–36, 2001.

17. Deng, X.Q.: A finite element analysis of surgery of the human facial tissue. Ph.D. thesis, Columbia University, New York, 1988.
18. Di Giacomo, T., Capo, S., Faure, F.: An interactive forest. In *Eurographics Workshop on Computer Animation and Simulation*, pages 65–74. Springer Verlag, 2001.
19. Di Giacomo, T., Gaudry, M., Magnenat-Thalmann, N.: Converting 3D facial animation with Gouraud shaded SVG. *4th Annual Conference on Scalable Vector Graphics (SVG OPEN'05)*, August 2005.
20. Di Giacomo, T., Joslin, C., Garchery, S., Kim, H., Magnenat-Thalmann, N.: Adaptation of virtual human animation and representation for MPEG. *Elsevier Computer & Graphics*, 28(4):65–74, August 2004.
21. Di Giacomo, T., Kim, H., Garchery, S., Magnenat-Thalmann, N., Cailliere, D., Belay, G., Cotarmanac'h, A., Riegel, T.: Benchmark-driven automatic transmoding of 3D to 2D talking heads. *Modelling and Motion Capture Techniques for Virtual Environments (CAPTECH'04)*, December 2004.
22. Duguet, F., Drettakis, G.: Flexible point-based rendering on mobile devices. *IEEE Computer Graphics and Applications*, 24(4):57–63, 2004.
23. Ekman, P.: *Emotion in the Human Face*. Cambridge University Press, New York, 1982.
24. Ekman, P., Frisen, W.V.: Facial action coding system. In *Investigator's Guide Part II*, Consulting Psychologists Press Inc., 1978.
25. Garchery, S.: Real time facial animation multiplatform. Ph.D. Thesis, University of Geneva, n 569, 2004.
26. Garchery, S., Egges, A., Magnenat-Thalmann, N.: Fast facial animation design for emotional virtual humans. In *Measuring Behaviour*, Wageningen, NL, 2005.
27. Garchery, S., Magnenat-Thalmann, N: Designing MPEG-4 facial animation tables for web applications. In *Multimedia Modeling 2001, Amsterdam*, pages 39–59, 2001.
28. Garland, M., Heckbert, P.: Simplifying surfaces with color and texture using quadric error metrics. *IEEE Visualization'98*, pages 263–269, 1998.
29. Granieri, J., Crabtree, J., Badler, N.: Production and playback of human figure motion for visual simulation. *ACM Transactions on Modeling and Computer Simulation*, 5(3): 222–241, 1995.
30. Guenter, B.: A system for simulating human facial expression In *State of the Art in Computer Animation*, pages 191–202, 1992.
31. Guenter, B., Grimm, C., Wood, D., Malvar, H., Pighin, F.: Making faces, In *SIGGRPAH'98*, pages 55–67, 1998.
32. Herman, I., Hopgood, B., Duce, D.: SVG: Scalable vector graphics, tutorial notes. In *WWW Conference'02*, International World Wide Web Conference Committee, 2002.
33. Heuer, J., Casas, J., Kaup, A.: Adaptive multimedia messaging based on MPEG-7—the M3-box. In *Symposium on Mobile Multimedia Systems and Applications*, pages 6–13, 2000.
34. Hoppe, H.: Progressive meshes. In *ACM SIGGRAPH'96*, pages 99–108, 1996.
35. Howlett, P., Hewitt, W.: Mass-spring simulation using adaptive non-active points. *Blackwell Ltd., Computer Graphics Forum*, 17(3):345–354, 1998.
36. Hutchinson, D., Preston, M., Hewitt, T.: Adaptive refinement for mass/spring simulations. In *Eurographics Workshop on Computer Animation and Simulation, EGCAS'96*, pages 31–45. Springer Verlag, 1996.
37. ISO/IEC JTC1/SC29/WG11/N5845: *MPEG-21 Digital Item Adaptation DIA*. ISO/IEC 21000-7 Final Committee Draft, 2003.
38. Joslin, C., Magnenat-Thalmann, N.: MPEG-4 animation clustering for networked virtual environments. In *IEEE International Conference on Multimedia & Expo, ICME'02*, pages 365–368, 2002.
39. Khler, K., Haber, J., Seidel, H.-P.: Geometry-based muscle modeling for facial animation. In *Proceedings Graphics Interface*, pages 37–46, 2001.
40. Kalra, P., Mangili, A., Magnenat-Thalmann, N., Thalmann, D.: SMILE: A mult-layered facial animation system. In *IFIP WG 5.10*, pages 189–198, 1991.
41. Kalra, P., Mangili, A., Magnenat-Thalmann, N., Thalmann, D.: Simulation of facial muscle actions based on rational free form deformations. In *Eurographics*, 11(3):59–69, 1992.

42. Kim, J.W., Song, M., Kim, I.J., Kwon, Y.M., Kim, H.G., Ahn, S.C.: Automatic fdp/fap generation from an image sequence. In *ISCAS 2000—IEEE International Symposium on Circuits and Systems*, 2000.

43. Kim, J., Wang, Y., Chang, S.: Content-adaptive utility based video adaptation. In *IEEE International Conference on Multimedia & Expo, ICME'03*, volume 3, pages 281–284, 2003.

44. Kim, H., Wohn, K.: Multiresolution model generation with geometry and texture. In *Virtual Systems and Multimedia*, pages 780–789. IEEE Computer Society, 2001.

45. Kshirsagar, S., Garchery, S., Sannier, G., Magnenat-Thalmann, N.: Synthetic faces: Analysis and applications. In *International Journal of Imaging Systems and Technology*, 13(1): 65–73, 2003.

46. Kurihara, T., Arai, K.: A transformation method for modeling and animation of the human face from photographs. In *Proc. Computer Animation '91, Geneva, Switzerland*, pages 45–57, 1991.

47. Lamberti, F., Zunino, C., Sanna, A., Fiume, A., Maniezzo, M.: An accelerated remote graphics architecture for PDAs. In *Symposium of Web3D'03*, pages 55–63. ACM Press, 2003.

48. Larrabee, W. F.: A finite element method of skin deformation: I, biomechanics of skin and soft tissues. In *Laryngoscope*, 96:399–419, 1986.

49. Lee, Y.C., Terzopoulos, D., Waters, K.: Realistic face modeling for animation. In *SIGGRAPH Proceedings*, pages 55–62, 1995.

50. Maciel, P., Shirley, P.: Visual navigation of large environments using textured clusters. In *Symposium on Interactive 3D Graphics*, pages 95–102. ACM Press, 1995.

51. Magnenat-Thalmann, N., Primeau, N.E., Thalmann, D.: Abstract muscle actions procedures for human face animation. In *Visual Computer*, 3(5):290–297, 1988.

52. Magnenat-Thalmann, N., Thalmann, D. (Eds.): *Interactive Computer Animation*, Prentice Hall, 1996, ISBN 0-13-518309-X.

53. Magnenat-Thalmann, N., Thalmann D.: *Handbook of Virtual Human*, Wiley & Sons, Ltd., 2004, ISBN: 0-470-02316-3.

54. Nahas, M., Hutric, H., Rioux, M., Domey, J.: Facial image synthesis using skin texture recording. In *Visual Computer*, 6(6):337–343, 1990.

55. Nahas, M., Huitric, H., Saintourens, M.: Animation of a B-spline figure. In *The Visual Computer*, 3(5):272–276, 1988.

56. Noh, J.Y., Fidaleo, D., Neumann, U.: Animated deformations with radial basis functions. In *VRST*, pages 166–174, 2000.

57. Noh, J., Neumann, U.: A survey of facial modeling and animation techniques. In *USC Technical Report*, 1998.

58. Ostermann, J.: Animation of synthetic faces in MPEG-4. In *Computer Animation*, 1998.

59. O'Sullivan, C., Cassell, J., Vilhjálmsson, H., Dingliana, J., Dobbyn, S., McNamee, B., Peters, C., Giang, T.: Levels of detail for crowds and groups. In *Computer Graphics Forum*, 21(4):733–742, 2002.

60. Otkunc, C., Mansfield, P.: Interactive 3D viewer written in SVG. In *SVG Open Conference, SVG'03*, 2003.

61. Parke, F.I.: A parametric model for human faces. Ph.D. Thesis, University of Utah, Salt Lake City, Utah, UTEC-CSc-75-047, 1974.

62. Parke, F.I., Waters, K.: *Computer facial Animation*. A. K. Peters Ltd., 1996.

63. Pasquariello, S., Pelachaud, C., Greta: A simple facial animation engine. In *6th Online World Conference on Soft Computing in Industrial Appications, Session on Soft Computing for Intelligent 3D Agents*, 2001.

64. Patterson, E.C., Litwinowicz, P.C., Greene, N.: Facial animation by spatial mapping. In *Proc. Computer Animation '91, Geneva, Switzerland*, pages 31–44, 1991.

65. Perbet, F., Cani, M.P.: Animating prairies in real-time. In *Symposium on Interactive 3D Graphics, I3D'97*, pages 103–110. ACM Press, 2001.

66. Pettre, J., de Heras, P., Maim, J., Yersin, B., Laumond, J.-P., Thalmann, D.: Real-time navigating crowds: Scalable simulation and rendering. *Computer Animation and Virtual Worlds*, 17(3–4):445–455, 2006.

67. Pieper, S., Rosen, J., Zeltzer, D.: Interactive graphics for plastic surgery: A task level analysis and implementation In *Computer Graphics, Special Issue: ACM SIGGRAPH*, pages 127–134, 1992.
68. Platt, S., Badler, N.: Animating facial expression. In *Computer Graphics*, 15(3): 245–252, 1981.
69. Pouderoux, J., Marvie, J.-E.: Adaptive streaming and rendering of large terrains using strip masks. In *ACM GRAPHITE'05*, pages 299–306, 2005.
70. Redon, S., Galoppo, N., Lin, M.: Adaptive dynamics of articulated bodies. *ACM Transactions on Graphics*, 24(3):936–945, 2005.
71. Tack, N., Lafruit, G., Catthoor, F., Lauwereins, R.: Pareto based optimization of multiresolution geometry for real time rendering. In *ACM Press, International Conference on 3D Web Technologies*, pages 19–27, 2005.
72. Tecchia, F., Loscos, C., Chrysanthou, Y.: Image-based crowd rendering. *IEEE Computer Graphics & Applications*, 22(2):36–43, 2002.
73. Terzopoulos, D., Waters, K.: Physically-based facial modeling, analysis, and animation. In *Journal of Visualization and Computer Animation*, 1(4): 73–80, 1990.
74. Van Raemdonck, W., Lafruit, G., Steffens, E., Otero-Perez, C., Bril, R.: Scalable 3D graphics processing in consumer terminals. In *IEEE International Conference on Multimedia & Expo, ICME'02*, pages 369–372, 2002.
75. Waite, C.T.: The facial action control editor, FACE: A parametric facial expression editor for computer generated animation. Master's thesis, MIT, 1989.
76. Wang, C.L.Y., Forsey, D.R.: Langwidere: A new facial animation system. In *Proceedings of Computer Animation*, pages 59–68, 1994.
77. Ward, K., Lin, M., Lee, J., Fisher, S., Macri, D.: Modeling hair using level-of-detail representations. In *Computer Animation and Social Agents, CASA'03*, pages 41–48. Computer Graphics Society, 2003.
78. Waters K.: A muscle model for animating three-dimensional facial expression. In *Computer Graphics (SIGGRAPH Proceedings)*, 21:17–24, 1987.
79. Williams, L.: Performance-driven facial animation. In *Proc. SIGGRAPH '90, Computer Graphics*, 24(3):235–242, 1990.
80. Wu, Y.: Skin deformation and aging with wrinkles. In Ph.D. Thesis, University of Geneva, 1998.
81. Wu, X., Downes, M.S., Goktekin, T., Tendick, F.: Adaptive nonlinear finite elements for deformable body simulation using dynamic progressive meshes. *Computer Graphics Forum*, 20(3):349–358, 2001.
82. Wu, Y., Magnenat-Thalmann, N., Thalmann, D.: A plastic-visco-elastic model for wrinkles in facial animation and skin aging. In *Proc. 2nd Pacific Conference on Computer Graphics and Applications, Pacific Graphics*, 1994.

Chapter 13
Spacetime Faces: High-Resolution Capture for Modeling and Animation

Li Zhang, Noah Snavely, Brian Curless, and Steven M. Seitz

13.1 Introduction

Creating face models that look and move realistically is an important problem in computer graphics.[1] It is also one of the most difficult, as even the most minute changes in facial expression can reveal complex moods and emotions. Yet, the presence of very convincing synthetic characters in recent films makes a strong case that these difficulties can be overcome with the aid of highly skilled animators. Because of the sheer amount of work required to create such models, however, there is a clear need for more automated techniques.

Our objective is to create models that accurately reflect the shape and time-varying behavior of a real person's face from videos. For those models, we seek real-time, intuitive controls to edit expressions and create animations. For instance, dragging the corner of the mouth up should result in a realistic expression, such as a smiling face. Rather than programming these controls manually, we wish to extract them from correlations present in the input video. Furthermore, we wish to use these controls to generate desired animations that preserve the captured dynamics of a real face. (By "dynamics," we mean the time-varying behavior, not the physics per se.)

Creating human face models from images is by now a proven approach, with stunning results (e.g., [1]). However, the problem of accurately modeling *facial expressions* and other dynamic behavior is still in its infancy. Modeling facial dynamics is essential for creating animations, but it is more difficult to achieve due in part to limitations in current shape capture technology. In particular, laser scanners and most other high-resolution shape capture techniques do not operate effectively on fast-moving scenes (a transition to a smile can occur in a fraction of a second). Furthermore, the problem of creating animation tools that exploit captured models of 3D facial dynamics has yet to be explored.

In this paper, we present a novel, end-to-end system for producing a sequence of high-resolution, time-varying face models using off-the-shelf hardware, and we describe tools that use these models for editing and animation. This paper makes several specific technical contributions. First, we introduce a novel, globally

---

[1] ©ACM, 2004. This is a minor revision of the work published in *ACM Transactions on Graphics*, Volume 23, Issue 3, August 2004. http://doi.acm.org/10.1145/1015706.1015759.

Z. Deng and U. Neumann, *Data-Driven 3D Facial Animation.*
© Springer-Verlag London Limited 2008

consistent spacetime stereo technique to derive high-quality depth maps from structured light video sequences. Next, we propose a new surface fitting and tracking procedure in which the depth maps are combined with optical flow to create face models with vertex correspondence. Once acquired, this sequence of models can be interactively manipulated to create expressions using a data-driven inverse kinematics technique we call *faceIK*. FaceIK blends the models in a way that is automatically adaptive to the number of user-specified controls. We also describe a representation called a *face graph*, which encodes the dynamics of the face sequence. The graph can be traversed to create desired animations. While our animation results do not match the artistry of what an expert animator can produce, our approach makes it simple for untrained users to produce face animations.

13.1.1 Related Work

Modeling and synthesizing faces is an active research field in computer graphics and computer vision. Here we review three topics most related to our work: reconstructing moving faces from images, constraint-based face editing, and data-driven face animation. Other related work is discussed throughout the paper, as appropriate.

13.1.1.1 Reconstructing Moving Faces from Images

Very few shape capture techniques work effectively for rapidly moving scenes. Among the few exceptions are depth-from-defocus [2] and stereo [3]. Structured light stereo methods have shown particularly promising results for capturing depth maps of moving faces [4,5]. Using projected light patterns to provide dense surface texture, these techniques compute pixel correspondences to derive depth maps for each time instant independently. Products based on these techniques are commercially available.[2] Recent spacetime stereo methods [6,7] additionally integrate information over time to achieve better results. In particular, Zhang et al. [6] demonstrate how temporal information can be exploited for dynamic scenes. Compared to these previous structured light stereo methods, the shape capture technique presented in this paper produces higher-resolution shape models with lower noise.

While the aforementioned shape capture techniques yield spatially and temporally dense depth maps, a key limitation is that they do not capture *motion*, i.e., point correspondence over time, making it difficult to repose or reanimate the captured faces. 3D face tracking techniques address this problem by computing the deformation of a deformable 3D face model to fit a sequence of images [8–12] or 3D marker positions [13]. Blanz and Vetter [1] construct particularly high-quality models, represented as linear subspaces of laser-scanned head shapes. Although subspace models are flexible, they fail to reconstruct shapes that are outside the subspace. In order to handle expression variation, Blanz and Vetter [12] laser-scanned

---

[2] For example, www.3q.com and www.eyetronics.com.

faces under different expressions, a time-consuming process that requires the subject to hold each expression for tens of seconds. A problem with existing face tracking methods in general is that the templates have relatively few degrees of freedom, making it difficult to capture fine-scale dimples and folds, which vary from one individual to another and are important characteristic features. We instead work with a generic high-resolution template with thousands of degrees of freedom to capture such fine-grain features. This approach is related to the work of Allen et al. [14] for fitting templates to human body data, except that they rely on markers to provide partial correspondence for each range scan, whereas we derive correspondence information almost entirely from images.

An interesting alternative to traditional template-based tracking is to compute the deformable template and the motion directly from the image sequence. Torresani et al. [15] and Brand [16] recover nonrigid structure from a single video assuming the shape lies within a linear subspace. Although these methods are promising and work from regular video streams, they produce relatively low-resolution results, compared to, e.g., structured light stereo.

13.1.1.2 Direct 3D Face Editing

Following Parke's pioneering work [17] on blendable face models, most face editing systems are based on specifying blending weights to linearly combine a set of template faces. These weights can be computed indirectly from user-specified constraints [9, 18] or fit directly to images [1].

Our *faceIK* tool, as a general expression editing interface, is similar to the one in [18]. However, Joshi et al. [18] segment a face into a region hierarchy a priori, which decouples the natural correlation between different parts of the face. Zhang et al. [19] address this problem with a hierarchical PCA technique in which user edits may propagate between regions. Our faceIK method instead maintains the correlation across the whole face and only decouples it — automatically and adaptively — as the user introduces more constraints.

13.1.1.3 Data-Driven 3D Face Animation

A focus of our work is to use captured models of human face dynamics to drive animatable face models. Several previous authors explored performance-based methods for animating faces, using either video of an actor [12, 20], or speech [21–23] to drive the animation. These techniques can be considered *data-driven* in that they are based on a sequence of example faces.

Other researchers have explored data-driven animation techniques in the domains of human figure motion [24–27] and video sprites [28]. We adapt ideas from these other domains to devise 3D face animation tools.

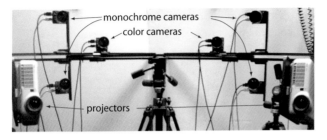

Fig. 13.1 Our face capture rig consists of six video cameras and two data projectors. The two monochrome cameras on the left constitute one stereo pair, and the two on the right constitute a second stereo pair. The projectors provide stripe pattern textures for high-quality shape estimation. The color cameras record video streams used for optical flow and surface texture. ©ACM, 2004. http://doi.acm.org/10.1145/1015706.1015759.

13.1.2 System Overview

Our system takes as input 6 synchronized video streams (4 monochrome and 2 color) running at 60 frames per second (fps) and outputs a 20-fps sequence of high-resolution 3D meshes that capture face geometry, color, and motion, for our data-driven editing and animation techniques. The videos are recorded by a camera rig, as shown in Fig. 13.1. Three of the cameras capture the left side of the face, and the other three capture the right side.

To facilitate depth computation, we use two video projectors that project gray-scale random stripe patterns onto the face. The projectors send a "blank" pattern every three frames, which is used to compute both color texture maps and time correspondence information (optical flow). We will refer to these as "non-pattern" frames. All of the components are off-the-shelf.[3]

The following sections describe the stages in the pipeline from the input streams to high-resolution editable and animatable face models. Section 13.2 introduces the spacetime stereo method to recover time-varying depths maps from the left and right stereo pairs. Section 13.3 presents a procedure that fits a time-varying mesh to the depth maps while optimizing its vertex motion to be consistent with optical flow. Section 13.4 describes how this mesh sequence is used for expression editing using faceIK. Section 13.5 describes two animation tools that use a face graph to model the dynamics present in the captured face sequence.

13.2 From Videos to Depth Maps

In this section, we present a novel method to recover time-varying depth maps from two synchronized video streams. The method exploits time-varying structured light patterns that are projected onto the face using a standard video projector. We first

---

[3] We use Basler A301f/fc IEEE1394 cameras, synchronized and running at 60 fps, and NEC LT260K projectors.

provide a brief review of traditional stereo matching and prior work in spacetime stereo, to motivate our new approach.

13.2.1 Binocular Stereo Matching

There exists an extensive literature on stereo matching algorithms that take as input two images and compute a depth map as output (for a good overview, see [29]). The key problem is to compute correspondences between points in the left and right images, by searching for pixels of similar intensity or color. Once the correspondence is known, depth values (i.e., distance from the camera) are readily computed [3]. Generally, the images are assumed to be rectified after calibration,[4] so that the motion is purely horizontal and can be expressed by a 1D disparity function.

More precisely, given two rectified images $I_l(x, y)$ and $I_r(x, y)$, we wish to compute a disparity function given by $d(x, y)$. For a pixel $I_l(x_0, y_0)$ in the left image, there is often more than one pixel with similar color in the right image. To resolve this ambiguity, most stereo algorithms match small windows W_0 around (x_0, y_0), assuming that the disparity function is locally nearly constant. Mathematically, this matching process involves minimizing the following error function:

$$E(d_0) = \sum_{(x,y) \in W_0} e(I_l(x, y), I_r(x - d_0, y)), \qquad (13.1)$$

where d_0 is shorthand notation for $d(x_0, y_0)$ and $e(p, q)$ is a similarity metric between pixels from two cameras. The size and shape of the window W_0 give a free parameter, with larger windows resulting in smooth depth maps and smaller windows yielding more detailed but also noisier reconstructions.[5] $e(a,b)$ can simply be the squared difference of color differences. We use the "gain-bias" metric [32] to compensate for radiometric difference between cameras.

13.2.2 Spacetime Stereo

Given two sequences of images, $I_l(x, y, t)$ and $I_r(x, y, t)$, a time-varying disparity map $d(x, y, t)$ may be computed by applying the above stereo matching procedure to each pair of frames independently. However, the results tend to be noisy, be low-resolution ([Figs. 13.3, (c), (d), (g), (h)], and contain temporal flicker as the shape changes discontinuously from one frame to the next (see the accompanying video). More accurate and stable results are possible by generalizing stereo matching into the temporal domain.

The basic idea, as originally proposed by Zhang et al. [6] and Davis et al. [7], is to assume that disparity is nearly constant over a 3D *spacetime* window $W_0 \times T_0$

---

[4] We calibrate our stereo pairs using Bouguet's software [30].
[5] Some methods allow the window size to vary, and compute sizes automatically [31].

around (x_0, y_0, t_0), and solve for $d(x_0, y_0, t_0)$ by minimizing the following error function:

$$E(d_0) = \sum_{t \in T_0} \sum_{(x,y) \in W_0} e(I_l(x, y, t), I_r(x - d_0, y, t)), \qquad (13.2)$$

where T_0 may be chosen to be anywhere from a few frames to the whole sequence, depending on how fast the scene is moving. As shown in [6], assuming locally constant disparity introduces reconstruction artifacts for oblique or moving surfaces. To model such surfaces more accurately, Zhang et al. [6] instead approximate the disparity variation linearly within the spacetime window as

$$d(x, y, t) \approx \tilde{d}_0(x, y, t) \stackrel{\text{def}}{=} d_0 + d_{x_0} \cdot (x - x_0) + d_{y_0} \cdot (y - y_0) + d_{t_0} \cdot (t - t_0), \quad (13.3)$$

where $d_{x_0}, d_{y_0}, d_{t_0}{}^{\text{T}}$ is the gradient of the disparity function at (x_0, y_0, t_0). They solve for d_0 together with $d_{x_0}, d_{y_0}, d_{t_0}{}^{\text{T}}$ by minimizing the following error function:

$$E(d_0, d_{x_0}, d_{y_0}, d_{t_0}) = \sum_{t \in T_0} \sum_{(x,y) \in W_0} e(I_l(x, y, t), I_r(x - \tilde{d}_0, y, t)). \qquad (13.4)$$

Under this linearity assumption, a 3D window $W_0 \times T_0$ in I_l maps to a sheared window in I_r, as shown in Fig. 13.2. Consequently, [6] developed an approach to minimize Eq. 13.4 by searching for the best matching sheared window at each pixel independently. The resulting depth maps are both higher-resolution and more stable than those produced using standard stereo matching as shown in Figs. 13.3(e) and (i) and the companion video.

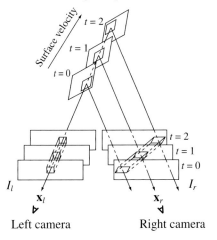

Fig. 13.2 Illustration of spacetime stereo. Two stereo image streams are captured from fixed cameras. The images are shown spatially offset at three different times, for illustration purposes. For a moving surface, a rectangular window in the left view maps to a warped window in the right view. The best affine warp of each spacetime window along epipolar lines is computed for stereo correspondence. ©ACM, 2004. http://doi.acm.org/10.1145/1015706.1015759.

A moving oblique surface

Left camera   Right camera

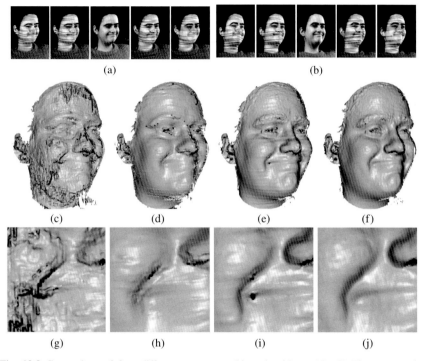

Fig. 13.3 Comparison of four different stereo matching algorithms. (a), (b) Five consecutive frames from a pair of stereo videos. The third frames are non-pattern frames. (c) Reconstructed face at the third frame using traditional stereo matching with a [15 × 15] window. The result is noisy due to the lack of color variation on the face. (d) Reconstructed face at the second frame using stereo matching with a [15 × 15] window. The result is much better because the projected stripes provide texture. However, certain face details are smoothed out due to the need for a large spatial window. (e) Reconstructed face at the third frame using local spacetime stereo matching with a [9 × 5 × 5] window. Even though the third frame has little intensity variation, spacetime stereo recovers more detailed shapes by considering neighboring frames together. However, it also yields noticeable striping artifacts due to the overparameterization of the depth map. (f) Reconstructed face at the third frame using our new global spacetime stereo matching with a [9 × 5 × 5] window. The new method removes most of the striping artifacts while preserving the shape details. (g)–(j) Closeup comparison of the four algorithms around the nose and the corner of the mouth. © ACM, 2004. http://doi.acm.org/10.1145/1015706.1015759.

13.2.3 Globally Consistent Spacetime Stereo

In practice, a spacetime stereo produces significantly improved depth maps for moderately fast moving human shapes. However, it also produces significant ridging artifacts, both evident in the original work [6] and clearly visible in Fig. 13.3(e). Our analysis indicates that these artifacts are due primarily to the fact that Eq. 13.4 is minimized for each pixel independently, without taking into account constraints between neighboring pixels. Specifically, computing a disparity map with N pixels introduces $4N$ unknowns: N disparities and $3N$ disparity gradients. While this formulation results in a system that is convenient computationally, it is clearly overparameterized, since the $3N$ disparity gradients are a function of the N disparities. Indeed, the estimated disparity gradients may not agree with the estimated disparities. For example, $d_x(x, y, t)$ may be quite different from $\frac{1}{2}(d(x + 1, y, t) - d(x - 1, y, t))$, because $d_x(x, y, t), d(x + 1, y, t), d(x - 1, y, t)$ are independently estimated for each pixel. This inconsistency between disparities and disparity gradients results in inaccurate depth maps, as shown in Figs. 13.3(e) and (i).

To overcome this inconsistency problem, we reformulate spacetime stereo as a global optimization problem that computes the disparity function, while taking into account gradient constraints between pixels that are adjacent in space and time. Given image sequences $I_l(x, y, t)$ and $I_r(x, y, t)$, the desired disparity function $d(x, y, t)$ minimizes

$$\Gamma(\{d(x, y, t)\}) = \sum_{x,y,t} E(d, d_x, d_y, d_t) \tag{13.5}$$

subject to the following constraints:[6]

$$\begin{aligned} d_x(x, y, t) &= \tfrac{1}{2}(d(x + 1, y, t) - d(x - 1, y, t)), \\ d_y(x, y, t) &= \tfrac{1}{2}(d(x, y + 1, t) - d(x, y - 1, t)), \\ d_t(x, y, t) &= \tfrac{1}{2}(d(x, y, t + 1) - d(x, y, t - 1)). \end{aligned} \tag{13.6}$$

Equation 13.5 defines a nonlinear least-squares problem with linear constraints. We solve this problem using the Gauss–Newton method [33] with a change of variables. To explain our approach, we use $\mathbf{D}$ to denote the concatenation of $d(x, y, t)$ for every (x, y, t) into a column vector. $\mathbf{D}_x$, $\mathbf{D}_y$, and $\mathbf{D}_t$ are defined similarly, by concatenating values of $d_x(x, y, t), d_y(x, y, t)$, and $d_t(x, y, t)$, respectively. Given an initial value of $\mathbf{D}, \mathbf{D}_x, \mathbf{D}_y$, and $\mathbf{D}_t$, we compute the gradient $\mathbf{b}$ and local Hessian $\mathbf{J}$ of Eq. 13.5 using Gauss–Newton approximation. Then, the optimal updates $\delta\mathbf{D}$, $\delta\mathbf{D}_x, \delta\mathbf{D}_y$, and $\delta\mathbf{D}_t$ are given by

$$\mathbf{J} \begin{bmatrix} \delta\mathbf{D} \\ \delta\mathbf{D}_x \\ \delta\mathbf{D}_y \\ \delta\mathbf{D}_t \end{bmatrix} = -\mathbf{b}. \tag{13.7}$$

Since Eqs. 13.6 are linear constraints, we represent them by matrix multiplication:

$$\mathbf{D}_x = \mathbf{G}_x\mathbf{D}\mathbf{D}_y = \mathbf{G}_y\mathbf{D}\mathbf{D}_t = \mathbf{G}_t\mathbf{D}, \tag{13.8}$$

where $\mathbf{G}_x$, $\mathbf{G}_y$, and $\mathbf{G}_t$ are sparse matrices encoding the finite difference operations. For example, suppose $d(x, y, t)$ is the ith component of $\mathbf{D}$, then the only nonzero columns in row i of $\mathbf{G}_x$ are j and j', which correspond to $d(x + 1,$

---

[6] At spacetime volume boundaries, we use forward or backward differences instead of central differences.

$y, t)$ and $d(x - 1, y, t)$ and take values of 0.5 and -0.5, respectively. Substituting Eq. 13.8 into Eq. 13.7, we obtain the optimal update $\delta \mathbf{D}$ by solving

$$
\begin{bmatrix} \mathbf{I} \\ \mathbf{G}_x \\ \mathbf{G}_y \\ \mathbf{G}_t \end{bmatrix}^{\mathrm{T}} \mathbf{J} \begin{bmatrix} \mathbf{I} \\ \mathbf{G}_x \\ \mathbf{G}_y \\ \mathbf{G}_t \end{bmatrix} \delta \mathbf{D} = - \begin{bmatrix} \mathbf{I} \\ \mathbf{G}_x \\ \mathbf{G}_y \\ \mathbf{G}_t \end{bmatrix}^{\mathrm{T}} \mathbf{b}, \tag{13.9}
$$

where $\mathbf{I}$ is an identity matrix of the same dimension as $\mathbf{D}$. We initialize $\mathbf{D}$ using dynamic programming with the spacetime window metric Eq. 13.2,[7] as described in [6], and set $\mathbf{D}_x$, $\mathbf{D}_y$, and $\mathbf{D}_t$ to be zero. Then we iteratively solve Eq. 13.9 and recompute $\mathbf{J}$ and $\mathbf{b}$ until convergence. Figures 13.3(f) and (j) show the resulting improvement when employing this new spacetime stereo method.

13.2.3.1 Scalable Implementation

Although $\mathbf{D}_x$, $\mathbf{D}_y$, $\mathbf{D}_t$, and J are very sparse, solving Eq. (13.9) using the conjugate gradient method [34] over the whole video is not practical; a 10-second video of 640×480 resolution at 60 Hz comprises nearly 180 million depth variables! To apply global spacetime stereo matching over a long video, we divide the video into a 3D (X, Y, T) array of 80×80×90 blocks that are optimized in sequence. When optimizing a particular block, we treat as boundary conditions the disparity values in its adjacent blocks that have already been optimized. To speed up the procedure, we distribute the computation over multiple machines while ensuring that adjacent blocks are not optimized simultaneously. While many traversal orders are possible, we found that the following simple strategy suffices: We first optimize blocks with odd T values, and distribute blocks with different T values to different CPUs. On each CPU, we traverse the blocks from left to right and top to bottom. We then repreat the same procedure for blocks with even T values. Our prototype implementation takes 2 to 3 minutes to compute a depth map on a 2.8, GHz CPU, and each depth map contains approximately 120K depth points.

13.3 Shape Registration

In this section, we present a novel method for computing a single time-varying mesh that closely approximates the depth map sequences while optimizing the vertex motion to be consistent with optical flow between color frames. We start by fitting a template mesh to the pair of depth maps captured in the first non-pattern frame, initialized with a small amount of user guidance. We then track the template

---

[7] When using dynamic programming for initialization, we use a [1 × 3] image window for frame-by-frame matching and a [1 × 3 × 3] window for spacetime matching.

mesh through other non-pattern frames in the sequence automatically and without the need for putting markers on the subject's face.

13.3.1 Template Fitting

Let $M = (\mathbf{V}, E)$ be an N-vertex triangle mesh representing a template face, with vertex set $\mathbf{V} = \{\mathbf{s}_n\}_{n=1}^{N}$ and edge set $\mathbf{E} = \{(n_1, n_2)|\mathbf{s}_{n_1} \text{ and } \mathbf{s}_{n_2} \text{ are connected}\}$. Let $h_j(x, y)$, $j \in \{1, 2\}$, be the two depth maps at frame 1, as shown in Figs. 13.4(a) and (b). Given the relative pose between these depth maps,[8] we wish to solve for a displacement $\mathbf{d}_n$ for each vertex such that the displaced mesh M_1, with vertex set $\{\mathbf{s}_n + \mathbf{d}_n\}_{n=1}^{N}$, optimally fits the depth maps. Our fitting metric has two terms: a depth matching term, E_s, and a regularization term E_r.

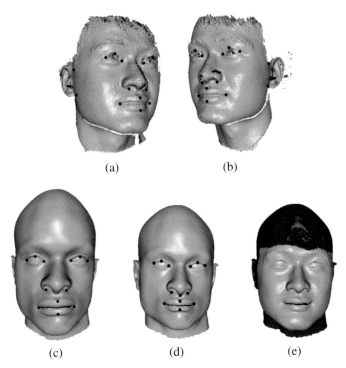

(a)   (b)

(c)   (d)   (e)

Fig. 13.4 Illustration of the template fitting process. (a), (b) Depth maps from two viewpoints at the first frame. (c) A face template. A few corresponding shape feature positions are manually identified on both the face template and the first two depth maps. (d) The template after initial global warp using the feature correspondence. (e) Initial mesh after fitting the warped template to the first two depth maps. The initial mesh is colored red for regions with unreliable depth or optical flow estimation. © ACM, 2004. http://doi.acm.org/10.1145/1015706.1015759.

---

[8] We obtain the relative pose between depth maps using the rigid registration tool provided in Scanalyze [35].

The depth matching term E_s measures the difference between the depths of vertices of M_1 as seen from each camera's viewpoint and the corresponding values recorded in each depth map. Specifically,

$$E_s(\{\mathbf{d}_n\}) = \sum_{j=1}^{2} \sum_{n=1}^{N} w_{n,j} \rho(\mathbf{s}_n + \mathbf{d}_n - \mathbf{h}_{n,j}{}_{z_j}, \sigma_s), \qquad (13.10)$$

where N is the number of mesh vertices, $\mathbf{h}_{n,j} \in \mathbf{R}^3$ is the intersection of the depth map $h_j(x, y)$ and the line from the jth camera's optical center to $\mathbf{s}_n + \mathbf{d}_n$, as shown in Fig. 13.5(a); $\cdot_{z_j}$ is the z-component of a 3D point in the jth camera's coordinate system; $\rho(\cdot, \sigma_s)$ is Tukey's biweight robust estimator, shown in Fig. 13.6; and $w_{n,j}$ is a weight factor governing the influence of the jth depth map on the template mesh. In experiments, we set $\sigma_s = 20$, which rejects potential depth map correspondences that are over 20 mm away from the template mesh. For $w_{n,j}$, we use the product of the depth map confidence, computed as in [36], and the dot product of the normals[9] at $\mathbf{h}_{n,j}$ and $\mathbf{s}_n + \mathbf{d}_n$; we set $w_{n,j}$ to 0 if the dot product is negative. Note that, in practice, we do not need to intersect a line of sight with a surface to compute each $\mathbf{h}_{n,j}$. Instead, we project each displaced template point into the depth map $h_j(x, y)$ and perform bilinear interpolation of depth map values to measure depth differences.

In general, the shape matching objective function, Eq. 13.10, is underconstrained. For instance, template surface points after being displaced could bunch together in regions while still matching the depth maps closely, as shown in

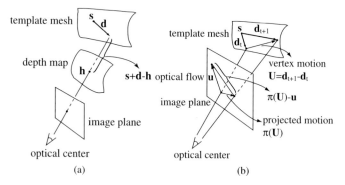

Fig. 13.5 Illustration of the error metric of a vertex used in template fitting. (a) $\mathbf{s}$ is a vertex on the template mesh and $\mathbf{d}$ is its displacement vector. Let $\mathbf{h}$ be the intersection of the depth map, shown as a surface, and the line from optical center to $\mathbf{s} + \mathbf{d}$. $\mathbf{s} + \mathbf{d} - \mathbf{h}$ is the difference vector between $\mathbf{s} + \mathbf{d}$ and the depth map. (b) $\mathbf{d}_{t+1}$ and $\mathbf{d}_t$ are the displacements for a vertex $\mathbf{s}$ on the template mesh at frame t and $t + 1$, respectively. $\mathbf{U} = \mathbf{d}_{t+1} - \mathbf{d}_t$ is the vertex motion from frame t to $t + 1$. The projection of $\mathbf{U}$ in the image plane, $\pi(\mathbf{U})$, should be the same as the optical flow $\mathbf{u}$. $\|\pi(\mathbf{U}) - \mathbf{u}\|$ is used as a metric for consistency between vertex motion and optical flow. © ACM, 2004. http://doi.acm.org/10.1145/1015706.1015759.

---

[9] We compute the normal of a vertex as the area-weighted average of the normals of its neighboring triangles.

Fig. 13.6 A plot of Tukey's biweight robust estimator. © ACM, 2004. http://doi.acm.org/10.1145/
1015706.1015759.

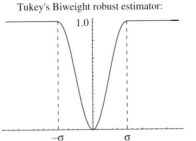

Tukey's Biweight robust estimator:

Fig. 13.7. Furthermore, the depth maps do not completely cover the face, and so the template can deform without penalty where there is no data. Thus, we add a regularization term E_r that penalizes large displacement differences between neighboring vertices on the template mesh. Specifically,

$$E_r(\{\mathbf{d}_n\}) = \sum_{(n_1,n_2)\in\mathbf{E}} ||\mathbf{d}_{n_1} - \mathbf{d}_{n_2}||^2 / ||\mathbf{s}_{n_1} - \mathbf{s}_{n_2}||^2, \qquad (13.11)$$

where the denominator $||\mathbf{s}_{n_1} - \mathbf{s}_{n_2}||^2$ helps to penalizes neighboring displacement differences according to the neighboring vertex distance. Notice that preferring a smooth displacement field is different from preferring a smooth displaced template mesh; the former preserves the shape details in the template mesh while the latter often smooths out the details [14].

To fit the template mesh M to the depth maps at frame 1, we minimize a weighted sum of Eqs. 13.10 and 13.11:

$$\Phi = E_s + \alpha E_r, \qquad (13.12)$$

with $\alpha = 2.0$ in our experiments.

We minimize Eq. 13.12 using the Gauss–Newton method. We initialize the optimization by manually aligning the template with the depth maps. Specifically, we select several corresponding feature positions on both the template mesh and the

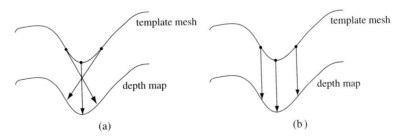

Fig. 13.7 The need of regularization in template fitting. (a) Without additional constraints, template surface points could bunch together while still matching the depth map closely. (b) A smooth vertex displacement field can be obtained by adding a regularization that penalizes large displacement differences between neighboring vertices on the template mesh.

depth maps [Figs. 13.4(a), (b) ,(c)]. Next, from these feature correspondences, we solve for an overconstrained global affine transformation to deform the mesh. To determine an affine transformation, at least 4 correspondences are needed; in practice, we specify about 15 feature correspondences. Finally, we interpolate the residual displacements at the feature positions over the whole surface using a normalized radial basis function [37] similar to the method of Pighin et al. [38]. After the initial warp, the selected feature correspondences are no longer used for template fitting. As shown in Fig. 13.4(d), the initial alignment does not have to be precise in order to lead to an accurate final fitting result, as illustrated in Fig. 13.4(e).

13.3.2 Template Tracking

Given the mesh M_1 at the first frame, we would now like to deform it smoothly through the rest of the sequence such that the shape matches the depth maps and the vertex motions match the optical flow computed for the non-pattern frames of the color image streams. Specifically, we seek to compute $\{\mathbf{d}_{n,t}\}$, which gives the time-varying shape $\{\mathbf{s}_{n,t} = \mathbf{s}_n + \mathbf{d}_{n,t}\}$. Let $I_k(x, y, t), k \in \{1, 2\}$, be color image sequences from two viewpoints with pattern frames removed. We first compute optical flow $\mathbf{u}_k(x, y, t)$ for each sequence using Black and Anandan's method [39]. The flow $\mathbf{u}_k(x, y, t)$ represents the motion from frame t to $t + 1$ in the kth image plane. We measure the consistency of the optical flow and the vertex interframe motion $\mathbf{U}_{n,t} = \mathbf{d}_{n,t+1} - \mathbf{d}_{n,t}$, called *scene flow* in [40], by the following metric:

$$E_m(\{\mathbf{d}_{n,t+1}\}) = \sum_{k=1}^{2} \sum_{n=1}^{N} \rho(\|\pi_k(\mathbf{U}_{n,t}) - \mathbf{u}_{n,t,k}\|, \sigma_m), \qquad (13.13)$$

where $\pi_k(\mathbf{U}_{n,t})$ is the image projection of $\mathbf{U}_{n,t}$ in the kth image plane and $\mathbf{u}_{n,t,k}$ is the value of optical flow $\mathbf{u}_k(x, y, t)$ at the corresponding location, $\pi_k(\mathbf{s}_n + \mathbf{d}_{n,t})$, shown in Fig. 13.5(c); $\rho(\cdot, \sigma_m)$ is the same Tukey's biweight robust estimator as in Eq. 13.10, with $\sigma_m = 20$ pixels.

Starting from M_1, we recursively compute M_{t+1} given M_t by optimizing a weighted sum of Eqs. 13.12 and Eq. 13.13 where $\mathbf{d}_n$ is replaced with $\mathbf{d}_{n,t}$:

$$\Psi = E_s + \alpha E_r + \beta E_m, \qquad (13.14)$$

with $\alpha = 2.0$ and $\beta = 0.5$ in our experiments.

We tried our mesh fitting and tracking methods on images sequences for several subjects and show results for three subjects here. In Figs. 13.8(a)–(d), sample results of mesh tracking for the first subject are shown in gray shaded rendering. The video on our Website `grail.cs.washington.edu/projects/ stfaces` shows the full sequence both as gray-shaded and color-textured rendering. The sequence has 332 face meshes, and each mesh has 14,883 vertices. Template tracking takes less than 1 minute per frame.

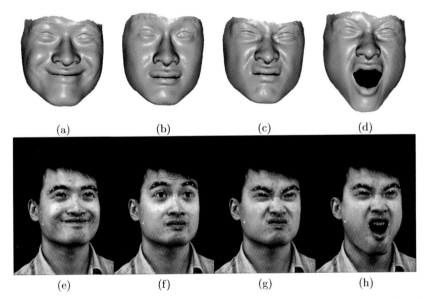

(a)   (b)   (c)   (d)

(e)   (f)   (g)   (h)

Fig. 13.8 Illustration of the template tracking result. (a)–(d) Selected meshes after tracking the initial mesh through the whole sequence, using both depth maps and optical flows. The process is marker-less and automatic. (e)–(h) The projection of a set of vertices from the selected meshes on the image plane, shown as green dots, to verify that the vertex motion is consistent with visual motion. Note that the subject had no markers on his face during capture; the green dots are overlaid on the original images purely for visualization purposes. © ACM, 2004. http://doi.acm.org/10.1145/1015706.1015759.

Notice that in Fig. 13.8, the forehead data are missing. This is because the hair hanging over the forehead and the forehead itself form two layers of motion, which confuses the optical flow algorithm. Therefore, the forehead motion is not correctly recovered, and we manually specify a mask and cut it out. In Fig. 13.9, we record sequences of the same subject when he wears a hair wrapper. In this case, the full facial shape and motion are recovered. This sequence has 384 mesh models, and each mesh has about 23,728 vertices.

In Fig. 13.10, we show four examples of template tracking results for the second subject. This sequence consists of 580 meshes, and each mesh has 23,728 vertices.

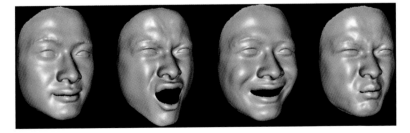

Fig. 13.9 Four examples of the template tracking results for another sequence. In this sequence, the subject wears a hair wrapper, and his forehead region is correctly recovered.

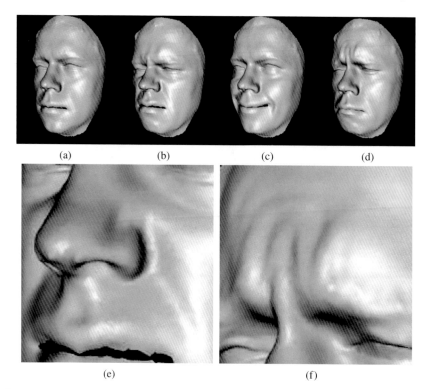

Fig. 13.10 (a)–(d) Four examples of the template tracking results for the second subject. (e) A closeup view of the skin deformation near the nose in the "disgusted" expression shown in (b). (f) A closeup view of the wrinkles on the "frowning" forehead of (d).

In Fig. 13.11, we show eight examples of the template tracking results for the third subject. This sequence consists of 339 meshes, and each mesh has 23,728 vertices. Notice that, in Figs. 13.10(e) and (f), and Figs. 13.11(i) and (j), we show closeup views of some of the face meshes, demonstrating the ability to capture fine features such as the wrinkles on a frowning forehead and near a squinting eye. These subtle shape details are extremely important for conveying realistic expressions, because our visual system is well tuned to recognize human faces. The uniqueness of our system is its capability to capture not only these shape details, but also how these shape details change over time. In the end, our system is an automatic, dense, and marker-less facial motion capture system.

13.4 FaceIK

In this section, we describe a real-time technique for editing a face to produce new expressions. The key property of the technique is that it exploits correlations in a set of input meshes to propagate user edits to other parts of the face. So, for instance, pulling up on one corner of the mouth causes the entire face to smile. This problem

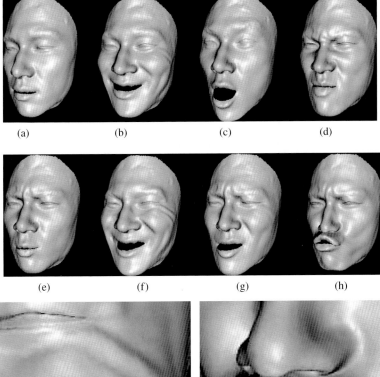

(a)   (b)   (c)   (d)

(e)   (f)   (g)   (h)

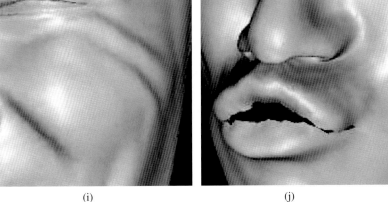

(i)   (j)

Fig. 13.11 (a)–(h) Eight examples of the template tracking results for the third subject. (i) A closeup view of the wrinkles near the left eye in (f). (j) A closeup view of the pouting lips in (h).

is analogous to the *inverse kinematics* (*IK*) problem in human figure animation in which the goal is to compute the pose of a figure that satisfies one or more user-specified constraints. We therefore call it *faceIK*.

Our approach is based on the idea of representing faces as a linear combination of basis shapes. While linear combinations have been widely used in face modeling [1, 38, 41], the problem of generating reasonable faces using only one constraint (e.g., the corner of the mouth), or just a few constraints, is more difficult, because the problem is severely underconstrained. One solution is to compute the coefficients that maximize their likelihood with respect to the data, using principle component analysis (PCA) [1, 14]. The maximum likelihood criterion works well for modeling face variations under similar expressions and human body variations under similar poses. However, applying PCA to facial expressions does not produce good results unless the face is segmented a priori into separate regions, e.g., eyes, nose, and mouth [1, 18, 19]. Unfortunately, segmenting faces into regions decouples the natural correlation between different parts of a face. Further, the appropriate segmentation is not obvious until run time, when the user decides what expressions to create. For example, to create an asymmetric expression, the left and right sides of the face must be decoupled. As discussed in Section 13.4.2, under- or oversegmenting the face can result in undesirable editing behavior. We instead describe a method that avoids these problems by adaptively segmenting the face into soft regions based on user edits. These regions are independently modeled using the captured face sequence, and then they are blended into a single expression. We could model these regions using PCA; however, because they are formed by user edits, we would then have to compute principal components, a costly operation, at run time for each region. To address this problem, we introduce a fast method, *proximity-based weighting* (PBW), to model the regions. We start by describing how to use PBW to model the entire face as a single region, and then extend it to handle multiple, adaptively defined regions.

13.4.1 Proximity-based Weighting

Suppose we are given as input F meshes, each with N vertices. We use $s_{n,f}$ to denote the nth vertex in mesh f. Let $\{p_l\}_{l=1}^{L}$ be user-specified 3D constraints, requiring that vertex l should be at position p_l; we call these constraints *control points*.[10] We seek a set of blend coefficients c_f such that for every l,

$$\sum_{f=1}^{F} c_f s_{l,f} = p_l \quad \text{and} \quad \sum_{f=1}^{F} c_f = 1. \tag{13.15}$$

The second equation poses an affine constraint on the blend coefficients. This constraint makes the blend coefficients invariant to global translation. Specifically, if we move all the meshes and control points by a same displacement, the same blend coefficients will still satisfy Eq. 13.15 for the displaced meshes under displaced constraints.

Because the number of constraints L is generally far fewer than the number of meshes F, we advocate weighting example faces based on *proximity to the desired expression*, i.e., nearby faces are weighted more heavily, a scheme we call proximity-based weighting. Specifically, we penalize meshes whose corresponding vertices are far from the control points by minimizing

---

[10] We assume the L constraints are for the first L mesh vertices, to simplify notation without loss of generality.

$$g(\mathbf{c}) = \sum_{f=1}^{F} \phi(\|\bar{\mathbf{s}}_f - \bar{\mathbf{p}}\|)c_f^2, \tag{13.16}$$

where $\mathbf{c} = c_1 c_2 \ldots c_F{}^{\mathrm{T}}, \bar{\mathbf{s}}_f = \mathbf{s}_{1,f}^{\mathrm{T}} \mathbf{s}_{2,f}^{\mathrm{T}} \ldots \mathbf{s}_{L,f}^{\mathrm{T}} 1^{\mathrm{T}}, \bar{\mathbf{p}} = \mathbf{p}_1^{\mathrm{T}} \mathbf{p}_2^{\mathrm{T}} \ldots \mathbf{p}_L^{\mathrm{T}} 1^{\mathrm{T}}, \|\bar{\mathbf{s}}_f - \bar{\mathbf{p}}\| = \sqrt{\sum_{l=1}^{L} |\mathbf{s}_{l,f} - \mathbf{p}_l|^2}$, and $\phi(\cdot)$ is a monotonically increasing function. In our experiments, we found that a simple function $\phi(r) = 1 + r$ worked well.

Minimizing Eq. 13.16 subject to Eq. 13.15 encourages small weights for faraway meshes and can be solved in closed form as

$$c_f = \frac{1}{\phi_f} \bar{\mathbf{s}}_f^{\mathrm{T}} \mathbf{a}, \tag{13.17}$$

where $\phi_f = \phi(\|\bar{\mathbf{s}}_f - \bar{\mathbf{p}}\|)$ and $\mathbf{a} = (\sum_{f=1}^{F} \frac{1}{\phi_f} \bar{\mathbf{s}}_f \bar{\mathbf{s}}_f^{\mathrm{T}})^{-1} \bar{\mathbf{p}}$. The derivation of this solution is given in Appendix 1.

13.4.1.1 Screen-Space Constraints

Rather than requiring that constraints be specified in 3D, it is often more natural to specify where the *projection* of a mesh vertex should move to. Given a set of user-specified 2D constraints $\{\mathbf{q}_l\}_{l=1}^{L}$, Eq. 13.16 is modified as follows:

$$g(\mathbf{c}) = \sum_{f=1}^{F} \phi(\|\pi(\bar{\mathbf{s}}_f) - \bar{\mathbf{q}}\|)c_f^2, \tag{13.18}$$

such that

$$\pi\left(\sum_{f=1}^{F} c_f \mathbf{s}_{l,f}\right) = \mathbf{q}_l \quad \text{and} \quad \sum_{f=1}^{F} c_f = 1, \tag{13.19}$$

where $\pi(\cdot)$ is the image projection operator, $\pi(\bar{\mathbf{s}}_f) \overset{def}{=} \pi(\mathbf{s}_{1,f})^{\mathrm{T}} \pi(\mathbf{s}_{2,f})^{\mathrm{T}} \ldots \pi(\mathbf{s}_{L,f})^{\mathrm{T}} 1^{\mathrm{T}}$, and $\bar{\mathbf{q}} = \mathbf{q}_1^{\mathrm{T}} \mathbf{q}_2^{\mathrm{T}} \ldots \mathbf{q}_L^{\mathrm{T}} 1^{\mathrm{T}}$. Since π is in general nonlinear, we approximate Eq. 13.19 by

$$\sum_{f=1}^{F} c_f \pi(\mathbf{s}_{l,f}) = \mathbf{q}_l \quad \text{and} \quad \sum_{f=1}^{F} c_f = 1. \tag{13.20}$$

This approximation works well in our experience, and minimizing Eq. 13.18 subject to Eq. 13.20 yields the closed-form solution

$$c_f = \frac{1}{\phi_f} \pi(\bar{\mathbf{s}}_f)^{\mathrm{T}} \mathbf{a}, \tag{13.21}$$

where $\phi_f = \phi(\|\pi(\bar{\mathbf{s}}_f) - \bar{\mathbf{q}}\|)$ and $\mathbf{a} = (\sum_{f=1}^{F} \frac{1}{\phi_f} \pi(\bar{\mathbf{s}}_f) \pi(\bar{\mathbf{s}}_f)^{\mathsf{T}})^{-1} \bar{\mathbf{q}}$. The derivation of this solution is the same as that for Eq. 13.17 with $\bar{\mathbf{s}}_f$ and $\bar{\mathbf{p}}$ replaced by $\pi(\bar{\mathbf{s}}_f)$ and $\bar{\mathbf{q}}$.

13.4.2 Local Influence Maps

The faceIK method presented so far assumes that the entire face is created by linear interpolation of input meshes with nearby meshes given larger weights. However, this assumption is too limiting, since, for example, an asymmetric smile cannot be generated from a data set that contains only symmetric smiles. We therefore propose a method to blend different face regions by defining an *influence map* for each control point. Specifically, we give each control point greater influence on nearby mesh points, and then blend the influences over the entire mesh to allow for a broader range of expressions that do not exist in the input data.

Accordingly, for each of the L control points, we compute a set of blending coefficients $\mathbf{c}_l$ by minimizing Eq. 13.16 or Eq. 13.18. This process is done independently for each control point. These L sets of coefficients will result in L meshes; each mesh satisfies one of the L constraints but not necessarily the others. The resulting L meshes are then blended together, using normalized radial basis functions [37] to define spatially varying weights. Specifically, we set the blending coefficient for vertex $\mathbf{s}_n$ as follows:

$$\mathbf{c}(\mathbf{s}_n) = \sum_{l=1}^{L} B(\mathbf{s}_n, \mathbf{s}_l) \hat{\mathbf{c}}_l, \tag{13.22}$$

where $B(\mathbf{s}_n, \mathbf{s}_l) = \frac{\exp(-\|\mathbf{s}_n - \mathbf{s}_l\|^2 / r_l^2)}{\sum_{l'=1}^{L} \exp(-\|\mathbf{s}_n - \mathbf{s}_{l'}\|^2 / r_{l'}^2)}$, with $r_l = \min_{l' \neq l} \|\mathbf{s}_l - \mathbf{s}_{l'}\|$, and $\hat{\mathbf{c}}_l$ is a F-dimensional vector defined at each control point l. In Appendix 1, we describe how to compute $\hat{\mathbf{c}}_l$ and prove that the components of $\mathbf{c}(\mathbf{s}_n)$ sum to 1 given that $\sum_{l=1}^{L} B(\mathbf{s}_n, \mathbf{s}_l) = 1$. For each vertex $\mathbf{s}_n$, we use $\mathbf{c}(\mathbf{s}_n)$ to blend corresponding vertices in the mesh data set.

Figure 13.12 shows the advantage of using local influence maps to adaptively segment the face based on user interaction, rather than specifying regions a priori. The main observation is that the optimal set of regions depends on the desired edit; for instance, generating an asymmetric smile from a set of roughly symmetric faces requires decoupling the left and right sides of the mouth. However, an edit that opens the mouth is more easily obtained *without* this decoupling. Our PBW scheme supports the adaptive segmentation in real time.

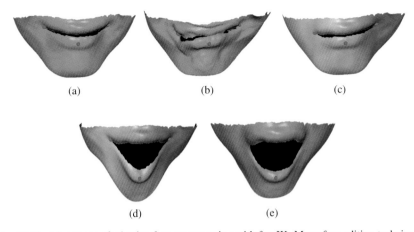

(a)   (b)   (c)

(d)   (e)

Fig. 13.12 Advantages of adaptive face segmentation with faceIK. Many face editing techniques presegment a face into regions (e.g., mouth, nose, eyes) and model each region separately with PCA. (a) Three symmetric control points are used to create a symmetric smile by applying PCA on the mouth region [14] to compute the maximum likelihood (ML) shape. (b) When the control points become asymmetric, ML behaves poorly, since all input mouth shapes are roughly symmetric. (c) For the same control point positions, faceIK creates an asymmetric smile by dividing the mouth into three soft regions (indicated by color variations) and blending the influence of each control point. Each control point influences its region using PBW in real time. By contrast, using PCA would require computing principal components, a costly operation, at run time for each new region. (d) With the same control vertices as in (c), if the point on the lower lip is moved by itself, the mouth opens unnaturally, because the two control points on the mouth corners decouple their correlation to the lower lip. (e) With only one control point on the lower lip, the mouth opens more naturally. These comparisons indicate that it is more desirable to adaptively segment a face into regions based on user edits, rather than a priori. ©ACM, 2004. http://doi.acm.org/10.1145/1015706.1015759.

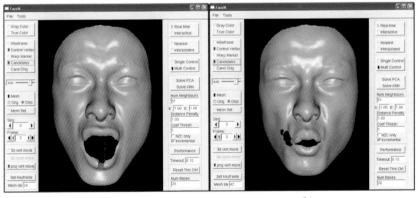

(a)   (b)

Fig. 13.13 FaceIK user interface. A user can click any point on the face to define a control point constraint, shown as the green ball. The positions of the control point in the input mesh sequence are then shown as a cloud of blue points. The user can move the control point within or slightly outside this point cloud to synthesize a new face that satisfies the constraint. For example, (a) when dragging the lower lip down, the user opens the mouth widely; (b) when dragging the left corner of the mouth to the right, the user pouts the lips.

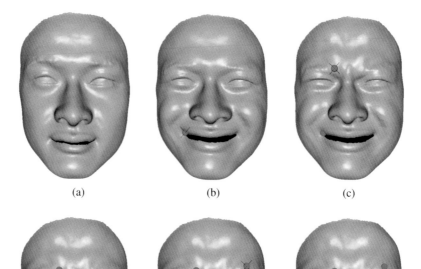

Fig. 13.14 A faceIK editing session. From (a) to (f), we show the creation of a complex expression by adding and moving control points one at a time, starting from neutral.

13.4.3 FaceIK User Interface

We implemented the proximity-based weighting and local influence map blending in real time, providing an interactive tool for expression synthesis by direct manipulation. Fig. 13.13 shows the interface of this tool. Fig 13.14 shows a sequence of edits that leads from a neutral face to a complex expression. A screen capture of a real-time FaceIK demo is available on our Website at http://grail.cs.washington.edu/projects/stfaces/capture2_fast2.avi.

13.5 Data-Driven Animation

Producing realistic animations of the human face is extremely challenging, as subtle differences in dynamics and timing can have a major perceptual effect. In this section, we exploit the facial dynamics captured in our reconstructed 3D face sequences to create tools for face animation. In particular, we describe two such tools, one for producing random infinite face sequences, and another for data-driven interpolation of user-specified key frames.

Before introducing these tools, we first describe our model of face dynamics using a graph representation. Our approach adapts related graph techniques used in video textures [42] and character animation [25–27] to the domain of face animation.

13.5.1 Face Graphs

Let $M_1, \ldots, M_F$ be a sequence of face meshes. We represent face dynamics using a fully connected graph with F nodes corresponding to the faces; we call this the *face graph*. The weight of the edge between nodes i and j specifies the cost of a transition from M_i to M_j in an animation sequence. This cost should respect the dynamics present in the input sequence, balanced with a desire for continuity. Given two frames M_i and M_j in the input sequence, we define the weight w of edge (i, j) as

$$w(i, j) = \mathrm{dist}(M_{i+1}, M_j) + \lambda \mathrm{dist}(M_i, M_j), \qquad (13.23)$$

where dist is a distance metric between meshes. (We use the L_2-norm, summed over all the vertices.) The first term prefers following the input sequence, while the second term penalizes large jumps.

13.5.2 Random Walks Through Face Space

Video textures [42] generate nonrepeating image sequences of arbitrary length. The same technique can be used to generate random, continuously varying face animations. To do so, we simply perform a random walk through the face graph. As in [42], we define the probability of a transition from mesh M_i to mesh M_j to be $P_{ij} = e^{-w(i,j)/\sigma}$, normalizing so that the sum of P_{ij} over all j is 1. The parameter σ is used to define the frequency of transitions between different parts of the input sequence; lower values create animations that closely follow the input sequence, whereas higher values promote more random behavior.

As in [42], we disguise transitions between two meshes that are not consecutive in the input sequence by a weighted blend of the two subsequences across the transition. Results are shown in the companion video.

13.5.2.1 Animation with Regions

A limitation of the method described so far is that the frames composing the animation are constrained to lie within the set of input meshes. We therefore generalize this approach by defining regions on the face, animating the regions separately using the above method, and then blending the results into a single animation.

Rather than grouping the vertices of the meshes into disjoint regions, we create "soft" regions using control points to define a set of weights for each vertex, as described in Section 13.4.2. The influence maps are taken into account in the computation of the cost graph by defining $d(M_i, M_j)$ to be weighted sum-of-squared distance, with per-vertex weights defined by the influence map.

The companion video shows an animation generated from this method using two control points. While a majority of the resulting sequence looks natural and compelling, it also contains some unnatural frames and transitions, due to the fact that different parts of the face are animated independently.

13.5.3 Data-Driven Key-Frame Animation

While the random walk technique produces animation very easily, it does not provide a mechanism for user control. However, the same concepts may be used to support traditional key-frame animations, in which in-between frames are automatically generated from user-specified constraint frames. The in-between frames are generated using a data-driven interpolation method, which seeks to follow minimum-cost paths through the graph [25–28].

Suppose that an animator has a sequence of meshes available and wants to animate a transition between two expressions that appear in the sequence. In the simplest case, the expressions comprise the endpoints of a subsequence of the input sequence. More generally, the interpolation must blend two or more noncontiguous subsequences.

To find a path between two key frames M_i and M_j, we construct the graph defined above, then search for the shortest path connecting M_i and M_j using Dijkstra's algorithm [43]. The result is a sequence of meshes. We then compute a per-vertex cubic-spline interpolation of the mesh sequence to generate a continuous animation, which is sampled using a user-specified parameterization to produce a desired set of in-between frames with desired timing.

13.5.3.1 Key-Frame Animation with Regions

The key-frame interpolation method is extended to work with multiple regions using the same technique as described for random walks. In particular, a separate graph is defined for each region. Optimal paths on each graph are computed independently, and the resulting animations are blended together using the influence functions to produce a composite key-frame animation. Fig. 13.15 shows an example key-frame animation, comparing our data-driven interpolation to traditional linear interpolation. We have also created a 43-second animation (shown in the companion video) using our data-driven technique. The animation uses 19 key frames, and each key frame has 3 control points.

13.6 Discussion and Future Work

We have presented an end-to-end system that takes several video sequences as input and generates high-resolution, editable, dynamically controllable face models. The capture system employs synchronized video cameras and structured light projectors to capture streams of images from multiple viewpoints. Specific technical contributions include first a novel spacetime stereo algorithm that overcomes overfitting deficiencies in prior work. Second, we described a new template fitting and tracking procedure that fills in missing data and brings the surfaces into correspondence across the entire sequence without the use of markers. Third, we demonstrated a data-driven, interactive method for face editing that draws on the large set of fitted templates and allows specification of expressions by dragging surface points directly. Finally, we described new tools that model the dynamics in the input sequence to enable new animations, created via key-framing or texture-synthesis techniques.

There are many important topics to explore in future work. First, the resolution of our template mesh is only about one eighth of the depth maps, and we only fit the template to one third of the depth maps (at non-pattern frames). A natural extension of our current work is to employ a hierarchical fitting approach to use templates whose resolutions are comparable with the depth maps, and also interpolate color along optical flow to obtain face models at 60 Hz.

Our capture technique requires illuminating the subject's face with two bright projectors and involves a relatively large rig with multiple mounted cameras. One

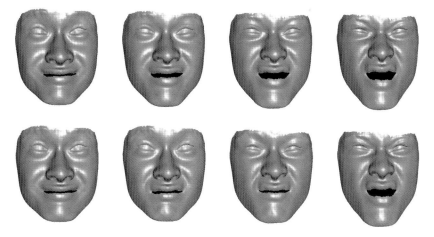

Fig. 13.15 Illustration of linear interpolation (top row) vs. data-driven interpolation (bottom row), with the first and last columns as key frames. Linear interpolation makes the mouth and the eyes move synchronously, which looks less realistic when played as an animation. Data-driven interpolation, instead, first purses the mouth, then squints the eyes, and finally opens the mouth. The sequential nature of the data-driven interpolation for this example arose naturally because that is the way the real subject behaved. © ACM, 2004. http://doi.acm.org/10.1145/1015706.1015759.

could imagine, however, embedding six small cameras on the sides of a monitor, and use imperceptible structured light [44] to make the capture process less objectionable.

Our registration technique depends on optical flow estimation, which can be unreliable for textureless regions. Although regularization helps to produce smooth meshes, we did observe some "vertex swimming" artifacts over the textureless regions. In the future, we hope to incorporate temporal coherence.

Our faceIK method generates natural results for control points that are relatively near the input faces, but can produce bizarre (and even disturbing) results for larger extrapolations. Although this behavior is not surprising, the user must explore the space of faces by trial and error. More useful would be if the tool could constrain the edits to the range of *reasonable* faces, by learning a set of good controls. Another limitation of faceIK is that, although it allows the user to segment the face adaptively, within an animation the segmentation cannot be changed. Therefore, before creating an animation, the user must specify enough control points so that any desired key frame can be created. This limitation did not pose a problem when we created the animation in the accompanying video; three controls (on both eyebrows and the lower lip) were enough to create the expressions we wanted. However, it would be desirable to allow the controls to vary across key frames.

The animation tools presented in this chapter are quite simple and could be extended and improved in several ways. One limitation is that we assume that the key frames are blends of the input frames. Although different regions can be controlled separately, the approach does not provide good support for extrapolated faces, since such faces may not be part of a motion sequence (i.e., there is no natural successor frame). Another limitation is that our data-driven interpolation technique requires a rich face sequence in order to produce natural-looking transitions between all the captured expressions. If our technique fails to find a desired transition in the face sequence, it may choose to use linear interpolation or an unnatural backwards transition instead. In addition, eye blinks may occur at inopportune moments, which complicates animation, and gaze direction is fixed by the input sequence; more careful modeling of the eyes, as well as insertion of teeth, would improve the quality of resulting animations. Finally, more intuitive control of timing would also help produce more realistic key-frame animations. All of these problems are important areas for future work.

While we have focused on animating a single face, it would be interesting to explore variations in dynamic behaviors among different human faces, similar in spirit to what has been done for static shape variations [1, 14].

Acknowledgment We would like to thank Kiera Henning, Terri Moore, and Ethel Evans for allowing us to use their face data. We also thank Jiwon Kim, Kiera Henning, Brett Allen, Yung-Yu Chuang, and Wilmot Li for their help in preparing the paper and companion video. This work was supported in part by National Science Foundation grants CCR-0098005, IIS-0049095, and EIA-0321235, an Office of Naval Research YIP award, the UW Animation Research Labs, and Microsoft Corporation.

13.7 Appendix 1: The Closed-Form Solution to PBW

In this appendix, we show that Eq. 13.17 minimizes Eq. 13.16 subject to Eq. 13.15. We first rewrite this constrained minimization problem using matrices as follows:

$$\text{Minimize } g(\mathbf{c}) = \mathbf{c}^{\mathsf{T}} \mathbf{Q} \mathbf{c}$$
$$\text{such that } \mathbf{B} c = \bar{\mathbf{p}} \tag{13.24}$$

where

$$\mathbf{Q} = \begin{bmatrix} \phi_1 & 0 & \cdots & 0 \\ 0 & \phi_2 & \cdots & 0 \\ 0 & 0 & \ddots & 0 \\ 0 & 0 & \cdots & \phi_F \end{bmatrix}, \quad \mathbf{B} = \begin{bmatrix} s_{1,1} & s_{1,2} & \cdots & s_{1,F} \\ s_{2,1} & s_{2,2} & \cdots & s_{2,F} \\ \vdots & \vdots & \vdots & \vdots \\ s_{L,1} & s_{L,2} & \cdots & s_{L,F} \\ 1 & 1 & \cdots & 1 \end{bmatrix}. \tag{13.25}$$

Using Lagrange multipliers, we know the minimizer of Eq. 13.24 should satisfy the following equation:

$$\mathbf{Q} c = \mathbf{B}^{\mathsf{T}} \mathbf{a}, \tag{13.26}$$

where $\mathbf{a}$ is the Lagrange multiplier. From Eq. 13.26, we obtain the following relation between $\mathbf{c}$ and $\mathbf{a}$:

$$\mathbf{c} = \mathbf{Q}^{-1} \mathbf{B}^{\mathsf{T}} \mathbf{a} = \begin{bmatrix} \frac{1}{\phi_1} \bar{\mathbf{s}}_1^{\mathsf{T}} \mathbf{a} \\ \frac{1}{\phi_2} \bar{\mathbf{s}}_2^{\mathsf{T}} \mathbf{a} \\ \vdots \\ \frac{1}{\phi_F} \bar{\mathbf{s}}_F^{\mathsf{T}} \mathbf{a} \end{bmatrix}. \tag{13.27}$$

Substituting Eq. 13.27 into the constraint equation in Eq. 13.24, we have

$$\mathbf{B} c = \mathbf{B} Q^{-1} \mathbf{B}^{\mathsf{T}} \mathbf{a} = \bar{\mathbf{p}}. \tag{13.28}$$

Solving Eq. 13.28, we have

$$\mathbf{a} = (\mathbf{B} Q^{-1} \mathbf{B}^{\mathsf{T}})^{-1} \bar{\mathbf{p}} = \left(\sum_{f=1}^{F} \frac{1}{\phi_f} \bar{\mathbf{s}}_f \bar{\mathbf{s}}_f^{\mathsf{T}} \right)^{-1} \bar{\mathbf{p}}. \tag{13.29}$$

Equations 13.29 and 13.27 together show that Eq. 13.17 indeed minimizes Eq. 13.16 subject to Eq. 13.15.

13.8 Appendix 2: The Normalized Property of Soft Region Weights

In this appendix, we prove that the blending coefficients for vertex $\mathbf{s}$, $\mathbf{c}(\mathbf{s})$, sum to 1 given that $\sum_{l=1}^{L} B(\mathbf{s}, \mathbf{s}_l) = 1$. Our proof is based on two facts. To state the facts succinctly, we first introduce two concepts. A vector is called *normalized* if its components sum to 1. A matrix is called *normalized* if all of its rows are normalized.

FACT1. If an invertible square matrix $\mathbf{A} = a_{i,j}$ is normalized, then $\mathbf{B} = \mathbf{A}^{-1}$ is also normalized.

PROOF. Let $\mathbf{B} = b_{i,j}$. $\mathbf{B} = \mathbf{A}^{-1} \Rightarrow \forall i, \forall j, \sum_k b_{i,k} a_{k,j} = \delta_{i,j} \Rightarrow \forall i, 1 = \sum_j \delta_{i,j} = \sum_j \sum_k b_{i,k} a_{k,j} = \sum_k \sum_j b_{i,k} a_{k,j} = \sum_k b_{i,k} \sum_j a_{k,j} = \sum_k b_{i,k}$.

FACT2. If a m by n matrix $\mathbf{A} = a_{i,j}$ is normalized and an m-dimensional vector $\mathbf{b} = b_i$ is normalized, then the n-dimensional vector $b^T \mathbf{A}$ is also normalized.

PROOF. $b^T \mathbf{A} = \sum_i b_i a_{i,j} \Rightarrow \sum_j \sum_i b_i a_{i,j} = \sum_i \sum_j b_i a_{i,j} = \sum_i b_i \sum_j a_{i,j} = \sum_i b_i = 1$.

Let $\mathbf{C} = \mathbf{c}_1 \mathbf{c}_2 \ldots \mathbf{c}_L{}^T$ and $\hat{\mathbf{C}} = \hat{\mathbf{c}}_1 \hat{\mathbf{c}}_2 \ldots \hat{\mathbf{c}}_L{}^T$. We know from the construction of RBF that $\mathbf{C} = B(\mathbf{s}_{l'}, \mathbf{s}_l) \hat{\mathbf{C}}$. Because both $\mathbf{C}$ and $B(\mathbf{s}_{l'}, \mathbf{s}_l)$ are normalized, the matrix $\hat{\mathbf{C}} = B(\mathbf{s}_{l'}, \mathbf{s}_l)^{-1} \mathbf{C}$ is also normalized, according to FACT1 and FACT2. Again, from the definition of RBF, we know that $\mathbf{c}(\mathbf{s})^T = B(\mathbf{s}, \mathbf{p}_l)^T \hat{\mathbf{C}}$. Because both vector $B(\mathbf{s}, \mathbf{p}_l)$ and matrix $\hat{\mathbf{C}}$ are normalized, $\mathbf{c}(\mathbf{s})$, the blending coefficient for vertex $\mathbf{s}$ is also normalized.

References

1. V. Blanz and T. Vetter. A morphable model for the synthesis of 3D faces. In *SIGGRAPH Conference Proceedings*, pages 187–194, 1999.
2. S.K. Nayar, M. Watanabe, and M. Noguchi. Real-time focus range sensor. *IEEE Trans. on Pattern Analysis and Machine Intelligence*, 18(12):1186–1198, 1996.
3. O. Faugeras. *Three-Dimensional Computer Vision*. MIT Press, 1993.
4. M. Proesmans, L. Van Gool, and A. Oosterlinck. One-shot active 3D shape acquization. In *Proc. Int. Conf. on Pattern Recognition*, pages 336–340, 1996.
5. P.S. Huang, C.P. Zhang, and F.P. Chiang. High speed 3-d shape measurement based on digital fringe projection. *Optical Engineering*, 42(1):163–168, 2003.
6. L. Zhang, B. Curless, and S.M. Seitz. Spacetime stereo: Shape recovery for dynamic scenes. In *Proc. IEEE Conf. on Computer Vision and Pattern Recognition*, pages 367–374, 2003.
7. J. Davis, R. Ramamoorthi, and S. Rusinkiewicz. Spacetime stereo: A unifying framework for depth from triangulation. In *Proc. IEEE Conf. on Computer Vision and Pattern Recognition*, pages 359–366, 2003.
8. I. Essa, S. Basu, T. Darrell, and A. Pentland. Modeling, tracking and interactive animation of faces and heads using input from video. In *Proc. Computer Animation*, pages 68–79. IEEE Computer Society, 1996.
9. F. Pighin, D.H. Salesin, and R. Szeliski. Resynthesizing facial animation through 3D model-based tracking. In *Proc. Int. Conf. on Computer Vision*, pages 143–150, 1999.
10. S. Basu, N. Oliver, and A. Pentland. 3D lip shapes from video: A combined physical-statistical model. *Speech Communication*, 26(1):131–148, 1998.

11. D. DeCarlo and D. Metaxas. Adjusting shape parameters using model-based optical flow residuals. *IEEE Trans. on Pattern Analysis and Machine Intelligence*, 24(6):814–823, 2002.
12. V. Blanz, C. Basso, T. Poggio, and T. Vetter. Reanimating faces in images and video. In *Proc. EUROGRAPHICS*, pages 641–650, 2003.
13. B. Guenter, C. Grimm, D. Wood, H. Malvar, and F. Pighin. Making faces. In *SIGGRAPH Conference Proceedings*, pages 55–66, 1998.
14. B. Allen, B. Curless, and Z. Popovic. The space of human body shapes: reconstruction and parameterization from range scans. In *SIGGRAPH Conf. Proc.*, pages 587–594, 2003.
15. L. Torresani, D.B. Yang, E.J. Alexander, and C. Bregler. Tracking and modeling non-rigid objects with rank constraints. In *Proc. IEEE Conf. on Computer Vision and Pattern Recognition*, pages 493–500, 2001.
16. M. Brand. Morphable 3D models from video. In *Proc. IEEE Conf. on Computer Vision and Pattern Recognition*, pages 456–463, 2001.
17. F.I. Parke. Computer generated animation of faces. In *Proc. ACM Annual Conference*, pages 451–457. ACM Press, 1972.
18. P. Joshi, W.C. Tien, M. Desbrun, and F. Pighin. Learning controls for blend shape based realistic facial animation. In *Proc. Eurographics/SIGGRAPH Symposium on Computer Animation*, pages 187–192, 2003.
19. Q. Zhang, Z. Liu, B. Guo, and H. Shum. Geometry-driven photorealistic facial expression synthesis. In *Proc. Eurographics/SIGGRAPH Symposium on Computer Animation*, pages 177–186, 2003.
20. J. Chai, X. Jin, and J. Hodgins. Vision-based control of 3D facial animation. In *Proc. Eurographics/SIGGRAPH Symposium on Computer Animation*, pages 193–206, 2003.
21. C. Bregler, M. Covell, and M. Slaney. Video rewrite: Visual speech synthesis from video. In *SIGGRAPH Conf. Proc.*, pages 353–360, 1997.
22. M. Brand. Voice puppetry. In *SIGGRAPH Conf. Proc.*, pages 21–28, 1999.
23. T. Ezzat, G. Geiger, and T. Poggio. Trainable videorealistic speech animation. In *SIGGRAPH Conf. Proc.*, pages 388–398, 2002.
24. Y. Li, T. Wang, and H.-Y. Shum. Motion texture: A two-level statistical model for character motion synthesis. In *SIGGRAPH Conf. Proc.*, pages 465–472, 2002.
25. O. Arikan and D.A. Forsyth. Synthesizing constrained motions from examples. In *SIGGRAPH Conf. Proc.*, pages 483–490, 2002.
26. L. Kovar, M. Gleicher, and F. Pighin. Motion graphs. In *SIGGRAPH Conf. Proc.*, pages 473–482, 2002.
27. J. Lee, J. Chai, P.S.S. Reitsma, J.K. Hodgins, and N.S. Pollard. Interactive control of avatars animated with human motion data. In *SIGGRAPH Conf. Proc.*, pages 491–500, 2002.
28. A. Schödl and I.A. Essa. Controlled animation of video sprites. In *Proc. Eurographics/SIGGRAPH Symposium on Computer Animation*, pages 121–127. ACM Press, 2002.
29. D. Scharstein and R. Szeliski. A taxonomy and evaluation of dense two-frame stereo correspondence algorithms. *Int. J. Computer Vision*, 47(1):7–42, 2002.
30. J. -Y. Bouguet. *Camera Calibration Toolbox for Matlab*. http://www.vision.caltech.edu/bouguetj/calib_doc/index.html, 2001.
31. T. Kanade and M. Okutomi. A stereo matching algorithm with an adaptive window: Theory and experiment. *IEEE Trans. Pattern Analysis and Machine Intelligence*, 16(9):920–932, 1994.
32. S. Baker, R. Gross, and I. Matthews. Lucas-kanade 20 years on: A unifying framework: Part 3. Technical Report CMU-RI-TR-03-35, Robotics Institute, Carnegie Mellon University, Pittsburgh, PA, November 2003.
33. J. Nocedal and S.J. Wright. *Numerical Optimization*. Springer, 1999.
34. W.H. Press, B.P. Flannery, S.A. Teukolsky, and W.T. Vetterling. *Numerical Recipes in C: The Art of Scientific Computing*, 2nd ed. Cambridge University Press, 1993.
35. K. Pulli and M. Ginzton. *Scanalyze*. http://graphics.stanford.edu/software/ scanalyze/, 2002.
36. B. Curless and M. Levoy. A volumetric method for building complex models from range images. In *SIGGRAPH Conf. Proc.*, pages 303–312, 1996.

37. D.S. Broomhead and D. Lowe. Multivariable functional interpolation and adptive networks. *Complex Systems*, 2:321–355, 1988.

38. F. Pighin, J. Hecker, D. Lischinski, D.H. Salesin, and R. Szeliski. Synthesizing realistic facial expressions from photographs. In *SIGGRAPH Conf. Proc.*, pages 75–84, 1998.

39. M.J. Black and P. Anandan. Robust dense optical flow. In *Proc. Int. Conf. on Computer Vision*, pages 231–236, 1993.

40. S. Vedula, S. Baker, P. Rander, R. Collins, and T. Kanade. Three-dimensional scene flow. In *Proc. Int. Conf. on Computer Vision*, pages 722–729, 1999.

41. T.F. Cootes, C.J. Taylor, D.H. Cooper, and J. Graham. Active shape models—their training and application. *Computer Vision and Image Understanding*, 61(1):38–59, 1995.

42. A. Schödl, S. Szeliski, D.H. Salesin, and I. Essa. Video textures. In *SIGGRAPH Conf. Proc.*, pages 489–498, 2000.

43. D.C. Kozen. *The Design and Analysis of Algorithms*. Springer-Verlag, 1992.

44. R. Raskar, G. Welch, M. Cutts, A. Lake, L. Stesin, and H. Fuchs. The office of the future: A unified approach to image-based modeling and spatially immersive displays. In *SIGGRAPH Conf. Proc.*, pages 179–188, 1998.

Chapter 14
Practical Considerations for Facial Motion Capture

Thomas W. Tolles

14.1 Introduction

Before we begin our discussion, I would like to point out the differences between what is considered classic R&D and production R&D. In the f/x production world, Blue Sky results are clearly desired, as the techniques that are novel and groundbreaking this year are passé the next. The motion capture industry operates in much the same way, leading to the expression "mochismo," which combines motion capture with machismo.

However, the real truth is that production R&D tends to be evolutionary, not revolutionary, since the 80% solution today is far superior to the supposed 100% next month. Production R&D benefits from the time-induced deadlines driven by production, as well as the chance to iterate and perfect the approach taken. With longer R&D times, the chances to iterate are reduced, giving such solutions less time in the crucible of production.

Given a production backdrop, it would be unreasonable to expect groundbreaking R&D coming out of the production world; however, the sharp focus of production and inherent time frames are an excellent proving ground for any relevant technologies.

14.2 Facial Capture Production Background

From my personal experience, the very first use of a Vicon optical motion capture system for real production occurred during the spring and summer 1996 for the remake *The Real Adventures of Johnny Quest*. While *Johnny Quest* remained a largely 2D animated cartoon, the remake included segments of a virtual *Quest World* based on 3D techniques. Each 22-minute episode included one to six minutes of CG in each show where the realistic movements of full-body and facial capture were used to animate the characters. The rest of the show used classic 2D animation techniques, which, of course, did not include motion capture.

The production schedule included shooting several days of motion capture across several episodes. For example, we might have shot three days of full-body capture

Z. Deng and U. Neumann, *Data-Driven 3D Facial Animation.* 277
© Springer-Verlag London Limited 2008

for four different episodes, followed by a single day of facial capture for those same four shows.

In terms of the actual facial capture, there were two significant notables: despite having only seven cameras to work with, we captured two performers at the same time, sitting side by side. The benefit of this approach is that each performer was able to key off the other, giving the facial captured performances more life and better timing. In addition, the facial performances were always captured after the full-body capture had been recorded. By playing back the reference video of the full-body captures and using SMPTE time-code to trigger the actual facial capture system, we not only gave the performers the ability to see what they were supposed to be doing but also let us maintain proper temporal alignment among the soundtrack, full-body data, and facial data.

Another significant facial capture project occurred during 1997 and included one of Hollywood's "A" list actors, Bruce Willis for the videogame "Apocalypse," which was published by Activision Studios. During a single day, Mr. Willis was facially scanned, facially captured, and body-captured. Unlike *Johnny Quest* and its use of 3D cartoon characters, Apocalypse contained a lifelike representation of Mr. Willis. As a result, the facial scanning was done both with and without the facial markers in order to help spatially align the facial capture markers with the model produced from the scan data.

Separately, the recreation of Marlene Dietrich was also an attempt at recreating reality, only this time the target performer was obviously deceased. In this case, a female performer who visually seemed to compare favourably to Ms. Dietrich was chosen as the facial capture performer, but clearly there was no need to scan or play back video of full-body capture.

The James Brown facial capture project had a different goal—although Mr. Brown was alive at the time, the goal of the Experience Music Project was to show a young Mr. Brown. Multiple methods were used to facially capture Mr. Brown, including film, HD video, and optical motion capture. Live action footage of Mr. Brown's younger dance double was combined with a digital equivalent of the real Mr. Brown's face, albeit younger than he was at the time, but driven by the motion capture data.

As a last example, House of Moves provided facial capture services for *Spider-man II*, capturing both Tobey Maguire and Alfred Molina. As before, the performers were scanned with and without facial markers on in order to maintain spatial integrity between the scan data and the motion capture data. However, unlike before, both the scanning and the motion capture data focused more on capturing specific facial poses, and less on capturing explicit performances.

14.3 Four Methods of Facial Capture

There seem to be roughly four types of facial capture methods that are available to professional production. I am excluding any of the facial animation techniques that are driven from phonemes or other methods of speech analysis but am including only methods that attempt to record or capture actual facial movements. In no particular order, these methods include

- optical capture for high-accuracy explicit marker data such as systems sold by Vicon Motion Systems and Motion Analysis,
- video capture intended to generate low-resolution MPEG-4 FAP files, a lightweight data stream relying on parameters such as "mouth width,"
- video capture combined with an intelligent contextual model of the face such as that provided by Imagemetrics,
- entire surface and/or texture capture such as recent efforts by Mova (Contour) and earlier tests by 3Q Systems.

While all of these methods have shortcomings, the most commonly used method of facial capture for professional production has historically been optical capture. However, while the general technique of optical motion capture remains fundamentally the same, there have been some significant advances that have helped push its use along.

14.4 2007 — So What Has Changed?

First, let me review the general configuration for the "old" approach for optical facial motion capture:

- dedicated facial setup,
- 8–12 cameras,
- 30–180 markers,
- 1.3-(or less) megapixel cameras,
- limited movement of the performer due to volume size,
- poor to decent data quality.

However, in the last two to three years, dedicated and small facial capture volumes have given way to larger "full-performance capture" setups that allow for facial capture along with hands and body. This new setups might consist of

- hybrid volume or full 360-degree volumes for performance capture setup,
- 32 or more cameras (even upwards to 200!),
- combined facial and body at same time,
- 360 degrees of coverage,
- very nice data quality.

So, while dedicated facial capture has tailed off, there has been an upswing in full-performance capture to take its place. The reasons for this change are not surprisingly related to advances in technology:

- camera resolution—Vicon's MX40 4-megapixel cameras provided a huge increase in the quality of data captured and size of a capture volume that would be created,

- continued efforts (and incremental success) in the high-end f/x world to solve CG facial animation increased the need to capture the body and face simultaneously,
- next-generation game platforms were looking to take digital characters to the next level, and facial capture was a natural place to look for improvements,
- commoditization of body-only motion capture meant the game developers and motion capture service and hardware providers were motivated to improve upon body-only capture.

While these advances are all well and good, there certainly are plenty of challenges of using discrete-point optical capture for capturing facial expressions. Before I highlight all of the cons, I would like to first to review the pros.

14.5 Optical Motion Capture Production Challenges—Pros and Cons

High-quality optical motion capture has the following strong suits:

- accuracy and repeatable capture points,
- ability to differentiate small and big markers through 3D marker modeling,
- unlimited length capture,
- does not require wearable technology,
- large volume capture.

In short, the ability to accurately and repeatedly capture known points on a performer without requiring the performer to wear any technology is a key driver to optical capture's success in the production field.

For example, in the scanning world, the Cyberware laser scanner is recognized as an industry leader. However, despite the accuracy with which the Cyberware scanner generates 250,000 points, users are always faced with figuring out how to reduce so much data to a much smaller and more workable amount. With discrete optical capture, that comes for free.

In addition, the fact that the performer does not have to wear head-mounted gear, or have wires or battery packs and can move freely about the capture volume, is another tremendous advantage. If the performance is no good, then capturing it is like kissing your sister—who cares?

Nonetheless, optical capture suffers from plenty of warts. In fact, after looking at the list below, it is almost hard to believe that optical capture seems to occupy the top perch in the world of production facial capture:

1. no good way to capture eyes,
2. not capable of detecting or capturing skin wrinkles,
3. no way of recording textures,
4. no way of capturing tongue movements,
5. applying (and maintaining) markers can be difficult,

6. head stabilization, though not necessarily unique to discrete optical capture, remains a challenge.

The first four items have no known solutions directly from optical capture. However, I would like to address some of the potential solutions for items five and six.

14.6 Effect of Differing Marker Locations Across Multiple Shoot Days

While applying discrete optical markers requires a steady hand, the right adhesives, and clean breath so as not to offend talent (or vice versa), there is no magic to actually applying the markers to someone's face.

In addition, while markers might fall off during a shoot day, the right methods for detecting missing markers, relocating fallen markers, and having the right food and drink items for talent can reduce the impact of these events.

For instance, premarking the face with small ink dots for each marker makes it easy to both spot a missing marker and relocate it. Giving the talent a drink with a straw may cut down on him or her "drinking" a lip marker by accident. Video cameras with weak lights help illuminate the facial markers and make it easier to spot missing ones.

A bigger challenge comes from requiring day-to-day repeatability. In other words, if you want to capture a given actor across multiple days, how do you ensure that markers are placed on this performer in an identical fashion?

Here are three tools that have been used to aid in this issue:

- great photos of ink dots on the performer's face,
- head casts and plastic masks,
- placement delta technology.

The first is the poor man's version—on the first day, apply ink dots (washable!) on the performer's face in the desired marker location. Take clear photos of these dots before applying any facial markers, and use these photos as a guide on subsequent days to replace ink dots in the same place. This approach is cheap, but not great.

A second version and far more robust approach is to make a head cast of the performer from which you make a clear plastic mask. Then, predrill the mask with holes in the desired locations of the markers. You can then use the mask across multiple shoot days to help ensure consistent marker placement.

A third technique involve the use of delta technology to help compensate for day-to-day differences (or even intra-day differences in the case marker are replaced). This approach makes two assumptions:

- that the delta between a given marker's placement is small enough such that the motion of the marker is the same,
- that the performer is capable of repeating a consistent "neutral" facial expression.

Given the preceding constraints, the basic approach to delta technology involves the following steps:

- from the first day of your shoot, declare a "Master Neutral" frame for your performer that is based on the neutral expression that he/she can most repeatedly make,
- start each capture from this same neutral expression,
- for each shot, process the marker data by removing the delta between any given frame of data and the defined first or neutral frame so you get a delta file that represents the motion of the markers for the shots from that day,
- for shots across multiple days, you can add the delta to the Master Neutral in order to remove any day-to-day variations that might have existed in the marker placement.

Combining delta technology with clear photos of the day 1 marker locations is probably the most cost-effective method, as opposed to going through the process of making a live cast and subsequent clear masks.

14.7 Head Stabilization

Head stabilization is one of the most underappreciated and seemingly contradictory challenges in the facial and full-performance capture worlds. Upon initial inspection, you might conclude that it is trivial—one must merely grab three or more markers that are attached to nonmoving parts of the face and make all of the other markers' motion relative to a coordinate system defined by those three or more markers.

The truth is that head stabilization is trivial to do—up to a point. After that point, it can be incredibly difficult to do. Here is one what one HOM employee said about head stabilization:

> To properly Gross Stabilize face data you will need four or more markers, placed as rigidly as possibly to each other and the performers face. These markers will vary depending on camera set up. Ideally you would drill into the performer's skull. If the performer agrees, drill into their skull. Without these markers, or if they are placed poorly, you will shoot yourself in the face. I am not kidding. **Your life will be void of joy**. You will welcome death. You will add 123,232,677,833 hrs to **every** day on the project.

The reasons why head stabilization ends up being so hard are as follows:

- It is very difficult, if not impossible, to attach a few markers to someone's head and expect that they are completely rigid with respect to each other.
- It can be very hard to differentiate between what a person's head is doing and what the facial expression is. In other words, by looking at a pose, it is hard to tell if the stabilization is correct and facial expression is driving the face, or if the stabilization is not correct.
- As we move from dedicated facial capture volumes to full-performance capture volumes, there is a natural tendency to larger and more violent head motions.

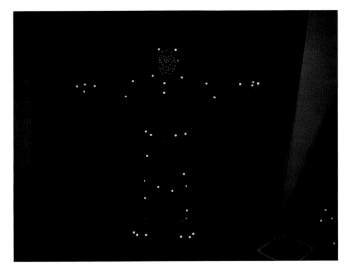

Fig. 14.1 Snapshot of human face and body motion capture.

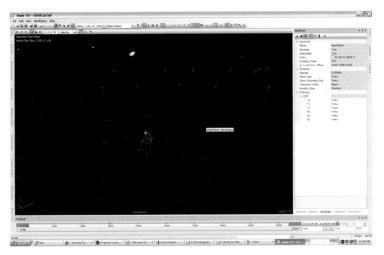

Fig. 14.2 Wide view of motion capture setting.

For a more complete review of how to capture and process facial motion capture data, please refer to the Facial Animation Survival Guide at the end of this chapter. Figures 14.1–14.3 show some snapshots of motion capture settings.

14.8 Conclusion

While it is a little hard to believe that sticking dots on people's faces is a good idea, optical capture is a proven technique and has demonstrated ability to operate even in fairly harsh settings. Movies like *Polar Express* and *Monster House* have shown

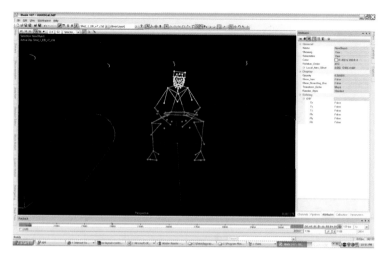

Fig. 14.3 Closeup view of motion capture setting.

that facial capture does work. One of the equipment manufacturers, Vicon Motion Systems, has a client using a real-time integrated capture zone (face and body) for a current production.

However, capturing the data is only the beginning, and several big challenges remain even with successful capture data. While I hope that discrete physical marker capture is replace by other techniques, I suspect that this will take longer than we currently imagine.

14.9 Appendix 1: Facial Capture Survival Guide

To capture facial movement, you generally place between 50 and 150 markers on a performer's face. Because there are so many markers in such a tight space, and because the movement of the face is so subtle, correct placement of the markers is absolutely critical. Once data capture is complete, you must be very careful during the editing process not to destroy the subtle motion that has been captured. The following tips and tricks are designed to help you capture and edit facial animation efficiently.

14.9.1 Marker Placement

Make sure you place four or more stabilization markers on a performer's face. All movement of other markers on a performer's face are measured from these markers so they must be completely rigid, or as close to rigid as humanly possible.

Make sure you define a completely straight centerline down the forehead, nose, lips, and chin. You need to define a straight line along the ears, sideburns, eyes, and nose. You must be able to clearly see these perfectly horizontal and vertical marker lines in order to stabilize, clean, and filter the data you capture.

Make sure you place markers on the inner corner of the eye, the bridge of the nose, and the sideburn areas of a performer's face. Place these markers so that they will move as little as possible during facial movement. These are key markers for facial motion capture.

In dense marker sets of 80 or more markers, make sure you "zipper" the eyelid markers such that no two markers on an upper lid or a lower lids are in line. Markers must "zig-zag" from upper to lower lid.

Symmetry is important. Place markers as symmetrically as possible on both sides of the face. Make sure that the lines of markers on a performer's face are as straight as humanly possible. Straight lines of markers make editing marker data easier.

14.9.2 Gross Stabilization

The process of gross stabilization is required to define the markers from which the movement of all other markers will be determined. Ideally, these markers on the performer's face will not move at all as the performer speaks.

If these markers are not completely rigid, then you will see "slide" in the position of other markers. This means that their positions will seem to change as a group over the course of an animation. Some slide is normal in a facial animation capture because there are no completely rigid points on a human face. But minimizing slide is absolutely critical because it is very time-consuming to eliminate once it is captured.

Choosing gross stabilization markers is a matter of trial and error. Every performer will have some stabilization markers that work and others that don't. Feel free to remove stabilization markers that do not work for a given performer in future captures.

Evaluate and clean stabilization markers first. For best results, try never to filter stabilization markers. Even very, very light filtering will cause slide over much of the animation.

Select the stabilization markers and create a rigid body. We recommend that you call your stabilization rigid body, STAB. After you create the rigid body, parent the face markers to this rigid body. Cut all of the keys on the STAB rigid body. This will plop the face down the world origin. The face is now "gross-stabilized," though it may not be in a good place for you to work on.

Hot tip: you must select the stabilization markers in the same way each and every time you create a rigid body for a given capture. The order in which the markers are selected determines how the rigid body is created, and this will affect processes down the line. So make sure you select the stabilization markers in the same order each and every time you create the rigid body.

14.9.3 Adjusting the Gross Stabilized Face for Easy Editing

Now that you have gross-stabilized the face using the STAB rigid body you created, you can adjust the position of the face to make editing the markers easier.

To do this, select the STAB marker. Rotate and move it into a good position for editing. We recommend that you place the horizontal eye line (as described previously) along the floor plane. The world origin should be precisely between the two sideburn markers. This will give you X-, Y-, and Z- axes you can use as additional references during the editing process.

If your animators specify a specific "neutral frame" display a specific "neutral pose," find a frame with the neutral pose, clean it, then extract the marker positions.

This is now your Master Neutral Reference Frame. You will place a copy of this frame at the front of every edited shot you deliver to animators. The Master Neutral Reference Frame should be a persistent dummy hierarchy of the Master Neutral Reference frame. All of your shots will be judged against this hierarchy for slide and general orientation. This Master Neutral Reference Frame will also be used by the animators to align their 3D geometry to all the markers you have captured.

In general, a good Master Neutral Reference Frame will show the character with eyes open, mouth closed, and jaw relaxed. You will need to maintain that orientation for all future shots, so use that Master Neutral Reference Frame for any tests you do as well as for full production.

14.9.4 Range Stabilization

There are two types of errors that you commonly encounter and fix during range stabilization: slides and hiccups.

Slides occur for several reasons. In a perfect world, the face remains stable relative to the gross stabilization markers. Markers only move up from eyes or down from the eyes and a solid eye line is maintained. This almost never happens. If you over alter the stabilization markers, you will cause slides. If the stabilization markers themselves are attached to a loose cap, there will be slides. If a performer mangles and stretches his/her face to the limit, there will be slides. If the scalp causes the cap to slide back and forth, you will get slides.

The best way to remove slides is to get absolutely fixed stabilization markers, clean them up very carefully, and never ever apply a filter to them if possible.

There are six types of slides you will frequently have to correct:

1. Up-down translation. Here the entire group of face markers translates up or down.
2. Left-right translation. The entire group of face markers translates left or right.
3. Front-back translation. The entire group of face markers moves forward or back.
4. Up-down rotation. The face rotates up and/or down as if the performers is shaking his/her head "yes." The motion may not be as drastic as a head shaking yes or no, but the markers will shift up and down uniformly. The face may only rotate 6 mm and stay up for 100 frames and then come down. These rotations are not as obvious as the less frequent translations.
5. Left-right rotation. The face rotates left and/or right as if the performers is shaking his/her head "no".
6. Twist rotation. The face rotates as if a pole is jammed through the front of the face. That's the best description I can come up with.

The goal of range stabilizing is to keep the face stable according to the eye line.

Markers should only move allowable distances from the eye line. Think of the skull underlying the face. The markers you are using to gauge the stability of the face are lying over fat and muscle. As you play an animation, you have to decide if markers are sliding or are moving correctly relative to the eye line, nose line, and stabilization markers.

If markers are appearing to move unnaturally, you must decide if gross stabilization has caused the errors. If that's the case, you may want to go back and gross-stabilize with different markers. Alternatively, you may want to select and edit groups of markers to fix small problems with gross stabilization.

Sometimes individual markers may be captured incorrectly. You will have to repair these errors by selecting and editing groups of markers. This can be a time-consuming process.

Hiccups are pops or sudden jumps in the facial animation. In some cases, a hiccup may exist for every marker in a scene, and when this is the case, there's a problem caused by stabilization markers that are not, in fact, stable.

To fix this error, you must either choose new stabilization markers, or edit markers to repair the damage. You will be able to identify most hiccups in the graph view. You will see significant changes in the trajectory of markers over just a few frames. We recommend that you cut out or fill as required to repair all the bad data you can identify.

At some point, you will probably have to repair bad data marker by marker. For particularly dense facial markers, 150+ markers, you may find this quite difficult. You must play any portion of the animation you need to edit over and over again to determine exactly what needs to change. Once you know exactly which marker needs to be modified and exactly how its movement has to be adjusted, you can make the edit. Failure to understand exactly what the minimum necessary edit is can result in smoothing out correct motion, which can be very difficult to fix later. After you have cleaned up the data significantly, you should take the data into the 3D animation application of your choice and have another look at it. You will discover additional movement that needs to be modified.

Once you have eliminated or repaired as much bad data as you can, you may apply a very, very light filter. This will give you a basically smooth curve without throwing off your data. You will still probably have a lot of small wobbles in the data, but by this point the data will not be dramatically jumpy.

14.10 Appendix 2: Case Study: Anatomy of an Integrated Performance Shoot—AND1 Streetball

One of the first productions to use the current generation of 4meg optical capture cameras in order to create a full-performance capture zone was for *AND1 StreetBall* published by Ubisoft and produced by Black Ops Entertainment.

Black Ops approached Vicon House of Moves in October 2004, corresponding to the period of time in which *Polar Express* was just finishing up and *Monster House* was going into production. The Vicon MX40 4-megapixel cameras had just started shipping. Previous attempts to do integrated capture in 1999 using 18 1-megapixel cameras had failed to be commercially and technically viable.

It is also worth noting the difference in the number of cameras and total megapixels of camera resolution that had been applied to full-performance capture volumes during this time frame:

- *Polar Express*—72 1.3-megapixel Vicon M2 cameras (total of 94 meg),
- *Monster House*—220 1.3-megapixel Vicon M2 cameras (total of 286 meg),
- *House of Moves*—32 4-megapixel Vicon MX40 cameras (total of 128 meg),
- *1999 HOM*—18 1.0-megapixel Vicon M1 cameras (total of 18 meg),

Vicon House of Moves ended up setting up a hybrid capture volume consisting of part full-body only and part full-body and facial capture. The volume was approximately 25 feet long with a 15-foot-long section for facial with 180 degrees of coverage. There were a total of 32 cameras, low by some standards. While audio was recorded, it was only for reference for separate ADR sessions.

The results of the capture session were delivered as marker data, with the full-body data delivered into Motion-Builder and the facial data delivered as stabilized marker data into Maya. Using MEL scripts, the 40 facial markers were assigned as clusters on the head rig via weighted vertices and exported for use in the game engine. Motion-Builder processed all of the full-body data, and the all data streams were combined and played back in the game engine.

Several lessons were learned or confirmed by this project, confirming the assertions made earlier in this chapter:

- Head stabilization is one of difficult parts of the process and remains equal parts art and science.
- Audio recorded on the set was not shippable, i.e., it was not clean audio. This required going back to the VO studio and doing an ADR session on the reference audio recorded.
- It would best to record final audio at the same time we are doing the facial capture. This will require a sound-proof stage for the full-body and facial capture.
- Eyes and tongue were not tracked, so they had to be programmatically created or animated. The eye tracking was resolved by putting target points in the game. The tongue was not animated, so sometimes there was less mouth fidelity movement and/or holes in the mouth geometry.

StreetBall credits are as follows:

- Director: Jose Villeta,
- Developed by: Black Ops Entertainment,
- Published by: Ubisoft,
- Platforms: PS2 and XBOX,
- Ship date: June 2006.

14.11 Author's Background

The author has been working with high-end 3D computer graphics since 1985, getting his start at Failure Analysis Associates (FAA), where he was one of the early adopters of Silicon Graphics workstations and Wavefront Software. In 1986, Tolles was the co-founder of an animation production company specializing in litigation and commercial productions.

Around 1995, while overseeing sales and marketing at Viewpoint Datalabs, he chanced across motion capture, which at the time was similar to the state of 3D in 1985. Realizing that the motion capture market had room to grow and acknowledging that the software tools of the days were quite crude, Tolles founded House of Moves Motion Capture Studios in 1996.

House of Moves went to become one the world's most successful independent motion capture service studios, working on projects like *Titanic, Spiderman*, as well as over 250 video games such as "Madden NFL" and "Guitar Hero." House of Moves simultaneously developed and release Diva, a high-end motion captured editing tool that has a very strong following in the industry.

In 2004, Tolles sold House of Moves to Vicon Motions Systems. Subsequent to the sale, Tolles assumed worldwide responsibility for Vicon's entertainment product marketing, ultimately developing and rolling out Vicon's next-generation animation production tool, Blade.

Tolles's educational background includes a masters and bachelors in mechanical engineering from Stanford University in 1981/82, where he specialized in microprocessor-controlled electromechanical devices. Tolles also received an MBA from the Anderson School at UCLA in 1991.

Index

Printed in Singapore